SOUTH ASIA'S WEAK STATES

SOUTH ASIA'S WEAK STATES

Understanding the Regional Insecurity Predicament

Edited by T. V. Paul

STANFORD SECURITY STUDIES
An Imprint of Stanford University Press
Stanford, California

Stanford University Press
Stanford, California

1096322877

Special discounts for bulk quantities of Stanford Security Studies are available to cor-
porations, professional associations, and other organizations. For details and discount
information, contact the special sales department of Stanford University Press. Tel:
(650) 736-1782, Fax: (650) 736-1784

Printed in the United States of America on acid-free, archival-quality paper

Library of Congress Cataloging-in-Publication Data

South Asia's weak states : understanding the regional insecurity predicament / edited
by T. V. Paul.
    p. cm.
 Includes bibliographical references and index.
 ISBN 978-0-8047-6220-5 (cloth : alk. paper) — ISBN 978-0-8047-6221-2 (pbk. : alk.
paper)
 1. South Asia—Politics and government. 2. National security—South Asia. 3. Internal security—South Asia. 4. South Asia—Foreign relations. I. Paul, T. V.
 DS341.S687 2010
 355'.033054—dc22
                            2010011547

Typeset by Bruce Lundquist in 10/14 Minion

In Memory of Professor T. T. Poulose
of Jawaharlal Nehru University, New Delhi (1922–2008)
—Teacher, mentor, and a pioneer of disarmament studies in India

Contents

Tables and Figures

Tables

Figures

Acknowledgments

This volume was motivated by a desire to understand the causes of the perennial insecurity challenges that South Asia has been facing ever since independent states emerged in the region. With that in mind, I assembled a group of scholars and practitioners at McGill University in Montreal for a conference in October 2008, where the first versions of these chapters were presented. The main sponsor of the conference was the Research Group in International Security (REGIS). A number of participants, beyond the paper presenters, made very useful observations at the conference that helped the contributors to subsequently revise their arguments. They include Siddharth Banerjee, Sujit Dutta, Christophe Jaffrelot, Saira Khan, Erik Kuhonta, David Malone, Sunil Mani, Daniel Markey, Philip Oxhorn, Vincent Pouliot, Norrin Ripsman, Manish Thapa, and Marie-Joelle Zahar. At the end of the conference, a policy roundtable on the topic *Transforming South Asia* was held, which was cosponsored by the Canadian International Council and the Center for Developing Area Studies at McGill University.

I would like to acknowledge the generous efforts of Stéfanie von Hlatky, who helped to organize the conference, and Theodore McLauchlin and Jessica Trisko, for the copyediting and formatting of the chapters. Theodore also offered many constructive suggestions to the contributors. Others who helped in organizing seminars or other forms of assistance include Amitav Acharya, Rajesh Basrur, Toby Gilsig, G. Gopakumar, Aaron Hywarren, Happymon Jacob, Christopher Manfredi, Amitabh Mattoo, Lawrence Prabhakar, C. Rajamohan,

Richard Schultz, and K. M. Seethi. Seminar presentations at the following institutions helped to sharpen the introduction and conclusions of the volume: Academic Staff College, Trivandrum; American University, Washington, D.C.; Bangladesh Institute of International and Strategic Studies, Dhaka; Bangladesh Institute of Peace and Security Studies, Dhaka; Calicut University; Center for Human Rights, Bhubaneswar; Cochin University; Fatima Mata National College, Kollam; Government College, Port Blair; Institute for Peace and Conflict Studies, New Delhi; Jammu University; Kannur University; Kashmir University, Srinagar; Maharaja's College, Ernakulum; Mahatma Gandhi University, Kottayam; Mangalore University; S. Rajaratnam School of International Studies, Singapore; Tribhuvan University, Kathmandu; and Utkal University, Bhubaneswar. Financial assistance came from REGIS, the Dean's Development Fund, James McGill Chair, Security and Defence Forum (SDF), as well as Fonds québécois de recherche sur la société et la culture (FQRSC) and Social Science and Humanities Research Council of Canada (SSHRC) research grants. Stanford University Press editor Geoffrey Burn showed much enthusiasm in the project, and the contributors benefited from the comments of the two anonymous reviewers. The aim of this volume is to generate further thinking on South Asian security and to diversify scholarship beyond the prevailing traditional security approaches within and outside the region. Efforts to explore security challenges comprehensively might lead to more effective policy prescriptions that may require recognition of the multifaceted nature of the South Asian insecurity dilemmas arising from both structural and domestic dynamics.

—*T. V. Paul*
Montreal, October 2009

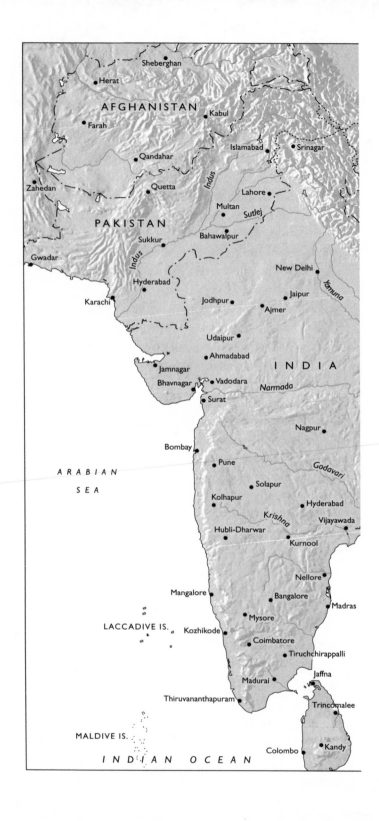

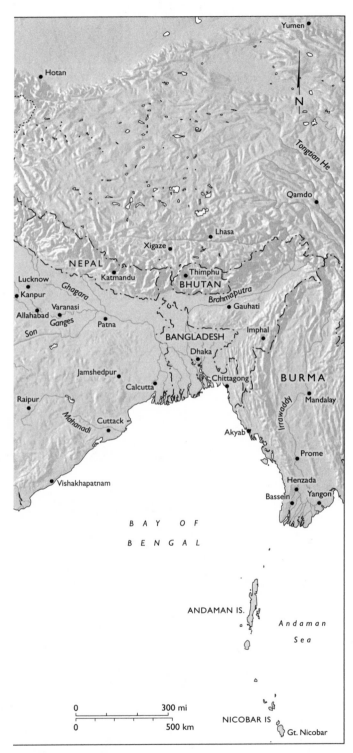

Yumen

Hotan

N

Tongtian He

Qamdo

Lhasa

Xigaze

NEPAL

Lucknow   Katmandu   Thimphu
Kanpur   Ghagara   BHUTAN
        Varanasi   Brahmaputra
Allahabad   Ganges   Gauhati
Son   Patna   Imphal

                        BANGLADESH

                                Dhaka

Jamshedpur   Chittagong   BURMA
        Calcutta   Mandalay

Raipur   Irrawaddy
        Cuttack   Akyab
Mahanadi
                                            Prome

Vishakhapatnam   Henzada
                                    Bassein   Yangon

        B A Y   O F
        B E N G A L

        ANDAMAN IS.   A n d a m a n
                                    S e a

0   300 mi
0   500 km   NICOBAR IS
                                        Gt. Nicobar

South Asia

SOUTH ASIA'S WEAK STATES

PART I
INTRODUCTION

1 State Capacity and South Asia's Perennial Insecurity Problems

T. V. Paul

South Asia, which consists of eight states of different sizes and capabilities, is characterized by high levels of insecurity in interstate, intrastate, and human dimensions. Although most emerged as independent nations in the 1940s, the states in the region have not yet been able to settle their several conflicts—internal and external—while some have become the epicenters of both traditional and non-traditional security problems, especially transnational terrorism fueled by militant religious ideologies. The region also has not developed adequate institutional mechanisms and normative frameworks for solving its myriad security challenges collectively and nonviolently. One result of this is that even when some conflicts are resolved, others emerge in their place, often leading to the continuation of the cycle of violence in other parts of the region.

What explains the chronic insecurity of South Asia? A large set of variables have been presented in the literature for this multifaceted insecurity problem. They include: 1. irreconcilable national identities; 2. lack of political development (i.e., the absence of proper democratic institutions and procedures); 3. weak economies; 4. unsettled territorial disputes; and 5. lack of regional institutions.[1] While these factors can explain a great amount of the chronic insecurity of the region, especially at the interstate level, we still lack a compelling explanation that can cover substantial ground for the perpetual multidimensional insecurity of South Asia. Most of the literature on South Asian security deals with interstate dimensions; there has been a somewhat excessive focus on the India-Pakistan rivalry and, in recent years, the nuclear relationship that has emerged between the two states.[2] As a result, scholarly and policy studies of the region's security problem do not treat it in a way that captures its multidimensionality or the relationship between internal, interstate, and human security dimensions.

I argue that South Asia's multidimensional insecurity can be explained largely by two critical factors: *the presence of weak states* and *weak cooperative interstate norms*. Both state capacity and weak cooperative norms act largely as intervening variables in causing regional insecurity, as they themselves may be caused by other underlying factors, which I do not cover in this chapter. Other chapters in this volume treat more closely the underlying factors for the weak state syndrome, such as difficulties with state formation and state consolidation in South Asia. It should be noted that state strength alone need not alleviate interstate insecurities, but in some instances it may exacerbate them.[3] Hence, the need for states that observe norms of cooperation, nonintervention and territorial integrity is all the more important for regional security. Moreover, state capacity becomes very crucial in dealing with internal security challenges, which tend to generate interstate conflicts, especially in South Asia.

Various estimates of state capacity place South Asian states among the weakest states globally. For instance, five of the South Asian states have entered the twenty-five weakest states in an annual index of 120 countries published by *Foreign Policy* magazine since 2006. These states—Afghanistan, Pakistan, Nepal, Bangladesh, and Sri Lanka—carry considerable conflicts internally and spillover effects externally.

The region also has weak norms of cooperative behavior. These norms or standards of behavior—often developed through institutional arrangements, as in the case of states in the Association of Southeast Asian Nations (ASEAN)—could provide a compensatory mechanism for preventing violent conflicts even among weak states. In South Asia, what is noticeable is a paucity of nonintervention norms. In other words, the states in the region are not often willing to live by the imperatives of the territorial status quo, as they exhibit characteristics of revisionism to varying degrees. Moreover, internally, states tend not to have highly effective mechanisms for the peaceful settlement of conflicts through democratic means, generating opportunities for disgruntled groups to engage in violent conflicts that are also tempting targets for external intervention. Nevertheless, states in South Asia are exceptionally

Second, secessionist and irredentist groups tend to operate from weak states and threaten the security and integrity of neighboring states. In such contexts, irredentism, which may combine with secessionism, is especially a problem, given that the same ethnic group may inhabit two neighboring states, and their allegiance to one or both states is often questionable.[14] Insurgents and terrorist groups could be tacitly or openly promoted by state elites or leaders of ethnic groups sympathetic to the cause of their co-nationals.

Third, regimes in weak states sometimes externalize internal conflicts to strengthen their domestic positions. The expectation is that diversionary wars or crises would distract popular attention from internal economic, social, and political problems while bringing legitimacy to the regime that engages in such activities. This would be supported by military, bureaucratic, and political institutions that thrive on such conflicts.[15] Engaging in external conflict can also allow a state to successfully pander to key interest groups. The actions they undertake would create negative security externalities or spillover effects for others, causing intensified security dilemmas not only in the traditional area of military security but in nontraditional domains such as human security.[16]

Finally, weak states offer fertile grounds for external powers, especially major powers, to meddle in their regions either as coalition partners or as sympathizers to antagonistic internal groups. The pathologies and behavioral attributes of weak states thus generate regional insecurity at the interstate, intrastate, and human dimensions.

How does South Asia fit into this characterization of weak states' insecurity dilemma? Before addressing this issue, I examine the chief characteristics of the South Asian region.

Asian Subsystem Characteristics

A region is a geographical cluster of states that are proximate to each other and are interconnected in spatial and cultural terms. This interconnectedness may manifest itself in strong security and, in some instances, economically. William R. Thompson defines a region as "a set of countries that perceive themselves to be politically interdependent," or as "patterns of interactions within a geographic area that exhibit a particular regularity and intensity to the extent that a change at one point in the region affects another point."[17] The states in a system thus interact regularly in many ways, creating patterns of intricate relationships. David Lake

sensitive to the norms of sovereignty and sovereign equality, even when they do not fully believe in respecting the sovereignty of their neighbors.

What Is a Weak State?

Before discussing weak states, it is important to examine state capacity, a topic that has received considerable attention in the sociology and comparative politics literatures. I define state capacity as "the ability of a state to develop and implement policies in order to provide collective goods such as security, order, and welfare to its citizens in a legitimate and effective manner untrammeled by internal or external actors." This definition modifies a view of a coercive state as a strong state by adding welfare and legitimacy factors into the mix of attributes for determining capacity. In the contemporary world, a proper democratic system may be essential for a state to have legitimacy. This definition draws from the existing scholarship on the subject.[4]

At the most general level, a weak state is a state low in capacity, defined in terms of its ability to carry out its objectives with adequate societal support.[5] Since this definition draws together characteristics of the state apparatus itself and its relationship to societal actors, scholars have identified many different phenomena that indicate the general concept of capacity. According to Robert Rotberg, a weak state suffers from deficiencies in the areas of (a) security (i.e., the state security forces, both military and police, are unable to provide basic security to all citizens in a legitimate and effective manner); (b) participation (open participation is limited as elections, if they take place at all, may not be fair and impartial); and (c) infrastructure (the physical infrastructure of the state is in very poor condition while health and literacy are accorded low levels of national priority).[6] A weak state, according to Kal Holsti, suffers from low levels or the absence of "vertical" and "horizontal" legitimacy. The former implies that "substantial segments of the population do not accord the state or its rulers loyalty." The result is that the decisions and decrees of state rulers do not elicit "habitual compliance." An absence of horizontal legitimacy refers to the definition and political role of the community; that is, there is "no single community whose members, metaphorically speaking, have signed a social contract among themselves. Instead, there are numerous communities and categories that shape the nature of politics and authority structures."[7]

A weak state by its very nature is unable to provide sufficient levels of protection to all its citizens. Sometimes political or military elites have the wherewithal to acquire wealth and develop capacity in some kinds of coercive instruments. But the ruling elite often lacks legitimate authority and control in much of the country and frequently will have to engage in brute force to suppress dissidence among disenchanted ethnic or political groups. Possessing some capacity distinguishes this kind of situation from one in which the central government has no coercive resources at all. But this suppression neither creates peace nor increases the support base of the regime. The absence of legitimacy and the full allegiance of population are major chronic challenges that a weak state would face.[8]

The characterization of weakness has to be seen in relative terms, as most states have some elements of strength. A state may be weak in some areas while in others it may show relative strength. That is why not all weak states are "failed states."[9] For instance, Pakistan has a fairly strong army for waging external wars, and to that extent it is able to provide a measure of security to its citizens against external threats, particularly vis-à-vis India, but it is weak in almost all other aspects of state strength. Moreover, we frequently find the pattern that a state has a modicum of coercive resources but lacks the ability to provide welfare and the legitimacy required for long-run stability—a kind of "strength" that "is ultimately based on fear, force, and coercion rather than on consent or voluntary compliance. It therefore suffers from a legitimacy deficit."[10]

A Typology of Weak States

Based on the above discussion, four types of weak states can be identified for the South Asian region: failed states, very weak states, weak states, and strong-weak states.

Failed State:

This is a state that has failed in all crucial aspects of state strength: security, welfare, and legitimacy. Such a state may have limited control over the territory it contains. It depends heavily on foreign financial and military support for its daily existence. Afghanistan is the closest case in South Asia, as it survives largely through external support and has limited or no control over vast chunks of its territory.

Very Weak (Fragile) State:

Such a state has somewhat better control over its territory, but this control is tenuous, especially since it is coupled with a lack of legitimacy and an inability to provide welfare. In South Asia, Nepal comes closest to this category.

Weak State:

The weak state may be weak in legitimacy, welfare, and ultimately security, but it has substantial coercive power. Due to its lopsided coercive capacity, it would use force to suppress internal dissidence but in the end not become much stronger. Pakistan, Sri Lanka, and Bangladesh come under this category.

Strong-Weak State:

The state is strong in several aspects, especially in its legitimacy and control over most parts of the country. It is weak in terms of its ability to provide welfare and internal security. However, over time such a state exhibits the highest prospects for emerging as a strong state, given its advantages in legitimac[y]. India typifies such a state in South Asia.

• • •

These categories are only for analytical purposes, and they need no[t] all the nuances in assessing state strength. A state could move p[ ] from a very weak to a weak category and return to the former s[ ]. The crucial point here is that all states in South Asia are weak in sions of state strength and that the relationship between sta[te] security, broadly conceived, is complex and multidimensio[n]

How Weak States Affect Security: Causal Linka[ge]

Weak states contribute to insecurity in multiple w[ays] lar to define state weakness in terms of an inabili[ty] then see state weakness as a *cause* of insecurity. ness helps bring out some interesting dimensio[n] particular, weak states can face dilemmas in state weakness sets up complex, multidimer weak states cannot often face internal secu[ ] poorly developed police and internal sec[ ] dilemma," rulers of these states atten[ ] presence, which "generates resistanc[e] overcome resistance, governments power centers of various types, a[s] groups."[12] Moreover, weak state[s] to tackle security challenges e hoc approaches to security th[ ] defines a regional system as "a set of states affected by at least one transborder but local externality that emanates from a particular geographic area. If the local externality poses an actual or potential threat to the physical safety of individuals or governments in other states, it produces a regional security system or complex."[18] A regional subsystem has also been said to generate a set of "security complexes" which "rest, for the most part, on the interdependence of rivalry rather than on the interdependence of shared interests."[19]

The definitions of region and regional security complex that rely exclusively on states suffer from problems, as they tend to offer very traditional approaches to the understanding of a regional subsystem. The main focus in such analyses is the interactions among states in an anarchic system, where the assumption is that states are the pivotal actors and have the capacity to engage in intense competition or rivalry. However, a regional subsystem can include both state- and societal-level interactions and insecurities.[20] Employing the lens of the state to view all the security problems of a given region may fail to capture the independent role of nonstate actors as players in security affairs.

Despite this major problem, the scholarship on regional subsystems has relevance to South Asia. Conflict and cooperation patterns in the regional subsystem may be a reflection of the particular interdependencies and externalities of the interconnected states as well as societal groups. The South Asian region has some subsystemic characteristics as well as different clusters of relationships that cannot be placed neatly under a systemic framework. Most of the South Asian states emerged in the decolonization era, and the two principal actors—India and Pakistan—underwent a bloody partition during that process. Although variations can be seen in the levels of state capacity (India with the highest and Afghanistan the lowest), almost all of the eight countries of South Asia are weak states with strong societies. They all have experienced difficulties with state formation and consolidation. State and nation are incongruent in these countries.[21]

The region is geographically and demographically India-centric, given that nearly 70 percent of the land mass and population lie with India; hence it is also called the Indian sub-continent. The region is also characterized by multitudes of divisions, based on religious, ethnic, and other identities. Though India-centric, South Asia cannot be described as a hegemonic subsystem, although India can exert quite a bit of influence over the smaller states such as Bhutan, Maldives, and Nepal. Part of the reason for this lack of hegemony is the unwillingness of key states to accept Indian leadership, let alone dominance on many issues. The region is not economically interdependent, and as a result a potential source of power that India could exert is missing. Unlike the Americas, where most of the smaller states have implicitly accepted U.S. hegemony in return for economic benefits and implicit or explicit security guarantees, South Asian states (barring tiny Bhutan and Maldives) neither have developed such a relationship with India nor do they have potential to do so in the near future. The newly emerging states are hypersensitive about their sovereignty, a theme that I will address later in this chapter.[22] More than that, India has yet to become overwhelmingly preponderant in the security and economic arenas, a development that may take place in a few decades given the country's recent rapid economic growth. The normative dispositions of most of the states are not quite congruent with the Indian ethos of democracy or secularism, lessening its power over the smaller neighbors. In many respects, these small states want to create a national identity dissimilar to India's.

Weak States and Conflict Patterns in South Asia

The South Asian states generally exhibit weaknesses in terms of their ability to deal with security, including economic and human dimensions. However, they do carry considerable lopsided coercive power, as evidenced in the near impossibility of secession for disgruntled regions.[23] Secession might also have become difficult due to the unwillingness of outside powers to offer recognition and possibly due to the emergence of a territorial integrity norm in international politics.[24] This does not mean that secessionist movements will simply fade away, as states appear unable to completely quell or integrate the groups clamoring for independence.

The security problems in the region have three key dimensions: interstate, intrastate, and human security. These three types of conflicts are interrelated and are influenced by the way the people and governments of the region interact. The weak state problem affects security at these three levels. At the interstate level, the India-Pakistan rivalry is the largest conflict. It has escalated to three major wars (1947–48, 1965, and 1971), one minor war (1999), and nine interstate crises.[25] The acquisition of nuclear weapons by the two states, especially in the aftermath of their nuclear tests in May 1998, has created a sort of deterrent relationship, marred by a stability-instability paradox, that is, some stability at the strategic level but instability at the substrategic level. Since 2004, the nuclear-armed neighbors have engaged in peace negotiations, but chances look dim for a final termination of the rivalry or the settlement of the key issues dividing them in the near term. The Pakistan-Afghanistan conflict is yet another interstate conflict with strong internal dimensions. India and Bangladesh have a conflict over unsettled borders, although its intensity is not too strong. These interstate conflicts generate internal security challenges and in turn human security problems for a large number of people, especially ethnic minorities living on both sides of the border.

The intrastate conflicts are numerous and highly visible, and I discuss some of them below for each country. Here I want to highlight terrorism as one important kind of crossover between the intrastate and interstate security challenges. According to estimates, South-Central Asia registered one of the highest rates of terrorist attacks in 2007 and several previous years.[26] The Afghan conflict; the rise of the Taliban; Pakistan's past support for the Taliban and continued support for the Kashmir insurgency; and the active presence of terrorist cells in Pakistan, India, and Bangladesh all denote a mélange of groups engaging in violent terrorist activity in the region for more than two decades. Terrorist incidents are becoming more frequent, and states appear unable to quell them, partly due to weak police and intelligence capabilities. Some terrorist groups indeed are challenging any move toward full democratic rule and any semblance of secular policies.

Human security implies people's freedom from both violent and nonviolent threats. For human security advocates, people are the point of reference, in a departure from the national security state's focus on the security of territory or governments. Ensuring human security entails taking preventive measures to reduce vulnerability and minimize risk and taking remedial actions when violations take place.[27] Pervasive threats to human security constitute one of the region's most significant challenges. A low emphasis on human security in the region is tied to the historical underdevelopment of South Asia, its highly unequal social order, its multitudes of ethnic divisions as well as caste and class divisions, and the poor economic policies pursued by the governments of the region over the years. Although with increased economic growth rates some human security problems can be tackled, what is noticeable is that the reverse appears to be happening in a large segment of South Asia. Economic globalization and liberalization may indeed accentuate human security problems unless states become strong and are able to implement policies aimed at reducing the social dislocations that accompany these economic trends.

Let us look at each of the key states:

Afghanistan, situated in the periphery of the region, is an extreme case of long-standing external penetration and internal violence, largely bred by the absence or the nonestablishment of a strong state.[28] It has had the misfortune of falling in a geostrategic location that has attracted the intense interests of great powers in the modern era, Britain and Russia first and then the Soviet Union and the United States, while neighboring Pakistan's policies have contributed to its perennial insecurity. Afghanistan's weaknesses cause Pakistan insecurity in the form of refugees and transborder crimes such as drug trafficking. The major events of Afghanistan's past thirty years—the Soviet invasion in 1979, followed by the ten-year-long brutal war with the U.S- and Pakistani-supported *mujahidin*, the Soviet departure in 1989, the arrival of the Taliban in 1996 and their offer of safe haven for al-Qaeda, followed by the U.S.-led war that saw their deposition from power and the continued war since 2002 between the allies and a resurgent Taliban—all have made this very fragile state the epicenter for security challenges facing South Asia and to some extent the entire world, in the early twenty-first century.

Pakistan is very much a state without a fully developed nation and also shows the signs of a garrison state.[29] The incongruence between state and nation is very marked in this case. Islam, the original source of Pakistan's identity, in juxtaposition to India, is not a sufficient unifying force as multiple loyalties based on ethnicity, intra-Islamic divisions, and economic and class affiliations weaken cohesion. The absence of sustained democratic rule, a proper federal structure, and economic integration of the provinces have made Pakistan a weak state. Its own long-standing involvement in neighboring countries (Indian Kashmir and Afghanistan) and the elite's willingness to use multiple instruments, including terrorism, for obtaining tactical goals, have made the country a breeding ground for long-standing insecurity for both itself and its neighbors. Pakistan also has a very poorly developed educational system, with 70 percent of its primary education offered through religious seminaries or *madrasahs*. This absence of a liberal educational system has generated conditions whereby many Pakistani youth join radical religious movements that now have emerged as a major challenge not only to Pakistan's internal stability and South Asia's security but to global security as well.[30]

Pakistan has been facing several internal conflicts on religious and ethnic lines. The most prominent are the Sunni-Shia divide, the ethnic and secessionist conflicts in Baluchistan, Pashtun areas of the Northwest Frontier states, and the Sindh and, in recent times, conflicts between various Islamist groups and the military-led and current civilian regimes. The upsurge in conflict in the Northwest areas, especially in Waziristan, and the state's absence of effective control over this region pose considerable security problems for neighboring Afghanistan and the Western coalition forces battling the Taliban. While the internecine conflicts themselves weaken the Pakistani state, the lack of proper state capacity allows the conflicts to continue. This feedback loop is a fundamental source of perpetual violence in the region.[31] The weak state capacity has once again become very clear in the inability of the state to control the new wave of violence perpetrated by Taliban forces within Pakistan. In 2009, these forces had made steady inroads in several parts of the country, especially in the Swat valley. Pakistan has faced an intense barrage of terrorist attacks since 2007, and in 2008-09 alone it registered 1400 deaths due to terrorist strikes.[32]

Sri Lanka experienced one of the most violent internal conflicts in the region, a conflict that lasted nearly three decades. The violent phase of the conflict began in the early 1980s when the Tamil minority began to make stronger power-sharing demands in response to attempts by the Sinhalese political elite to marginalize them and deny equal citizenship rights. The hardening of positions on both sides led to the formation of the Liberation Tigers of Tamil Eelam (LTTE), which began a violent insurgency in the northeast in 1983, where it wanted to create a separate homeland. The Sinhalese government's response was military repression, which further alienated the Tamils. In response, Tamils have employed extremely violent methods, such as suicide bombings and other forms of terrorist activity. In 2002, a peace agreement under the sponsorship of Norway was signed, but after four years of relative calm it broke down in 2006, and violence resumed once again. In April 2009, the Sri Lankan army defeated the LTTE. The fundamental causes of this conflict lie in the inability of Sri Lanka to fulfill the political and economic aspirations of the Tamil minority.[33] In that sense, even after the Sri Lankan army's military victory, the island nation is unlikely to achieve peace without a proper reconciliation of the aspirations of the Tamil population.

Nepal also has had a violent internal conflict that has recently made a crucial turn toward a settlement. A landlocked country, Nepal had monarchic rule until it was abolished in May 2008. The monarchy had little concern for either offering security or prosperity to the Nepalese. The resulting abject poverty generated intense violence in the form of a Maoist insurgency that lasted from 1996 to 2006. The internal conflict is also accentuated by the inability of the politically dominant group, high-caste Hindus from the hill regions (especially the ruling monarchy), to offer political and economic opportunities to lower-caste groups that include Dalits (untouchables) and people from the Terai region, or Madhesis.[34] The Maoists exploited the deprived groups' grievances in gaining support for their militant struggle. In April 2008, the Maoists won national elections for a new Constituent Assembly, and one of the first decisions they took was to abolish the monarchy. Although subsequently the Nepali political parties succeeded in forming a Constituent Assembly with the aim of drafting a new constitution and the Maoists installed themselves as new leaders for a brief period, there are no guarantees of an amicable democratic political system emerging for all groups. A weak Nepal generates considerable internal security challenges for its neighbors, especially for India. The Maoists have links with fellow insurgents in several Indian states. Refugees from Nepal and trafficking in women are two other human security issues in the India-Nepal context. Part of Nepal's problems is the absence of a healthy relationship with India. The Nepalese do not often view India in a sympathetic light despite the massive economic aid that India has provided to the beleaguered country. India's support for the monarchy, its frequent meddling in Nepalese politics, and its inability to restrain border-area groups such as the Madhesis have caused divisions in this relationship.

Bangladesh exhibits several internal conflicts, with the army and political parties waging frequent battles for control of the state. After its emergence in 1971, following a bloody civil war that saw India's military intervention, Bangladesh has struggled to develop a democracy while restraining its military. Even when Bangladesh has had successful elections and representative governments, one of the peculiar aspects of its democracy has been the unwillingness of the opposition parties to give the winner a chance to govern. Agitations start the day after an election, causing military rule or anarchic order to re-emerge. As a partly low-lying country that is afflicted by the vagaries of the Bay of Bengal, with its storms and floods, Bangladesh's immense poverty pushes a large body of its population to migrate to India for economic reasons. This has produced intense opposition in Assam, Tripura, and West Bengal and considerable violence in Assam especially. In order to stem the tide, India has fenced the border with Bangladesh, but this has created much ill will among Bangladeshis, who seem to consider borders irrelevant in South Asia, especially vis-à-vis their cultural brethren-states of West Bengal and Tripura.

India, though perhaps the strongest of all the states in the region, has often been described as a "strong-weak" or "soft" state. Although it meets several criteria of a strong state—long-standing and fairly developed political and bureaucratic institutions, armed forces under civilian control, and a nationally integrated economy—it still seems to suffer from the strong-weak state syndrome: strong in some areas but weak in others. In recent years, India has registered an impressive economic growth rate of 7–8 percent, which has secured it a role as an emerging major economic and military power.[35] However, its institutions, especially political parties, parliament, bureaucracy, and judiciary, as well as domestic security forces, have often been blamed for subpar performance, including in the area of internal security.[36] India constantly faces internal conflicts, especially involving minority populations in Kashmir and the northeast states. Kashmir is the most visible and intense of the conflicts in the region and has both intrastate and interstate dimensions. The majority Muslim province has been a hotbed of violence since 1947, and conflict over its status has been punctuated by several crises and wars between India and Pakistan. It is often argued that India's inability to integrate Kashmir is partly because of its policies, but Pakistan's irredentist claim and Islamabad's active support for Kashmiri insurgent groups are also strong reasons. The inability of the myriad groups within Kashmir to come to a clear political position is another part of the reason for the absence of a solution.[37] The Kashmir imbroglio has also created a fertile ground for increasing terrorist activity within India. In 2007, India recorded the largest number of terrorist-related deaths—2300—for any single country, even higher than Afghanistan and Iraq.[38] Some of the terrorist activity is generated by foreign-trained individuals who, in concert with local sympathizers, engage in violent activities. India's security forces have serious difficulties in coping with this scourge.

India's other major internal security challenge occurs in the northeast of the country. The insurgency movements in Nagaland, Mizoram, Manipur, Tripura, and Assam have tied down India's security forces over a long period of time.[39] In these states, a variety of movements have been fighting for more political control or independence. Their demands spring from the continued lack of attention by India's power elite to developing these regions economically, as well as from porous borders that allow the groups to get training from outside, including from Nepal, Bangladesh, and Myanmar. India's response, resorting to coercive military means to quell the unrest, seems to have helped to increase alienation in the region.

Despite its impressive economic growth rates since the early 1990s, India has a highly lopsided economic development pattern. The upper strata of society have become wealthier, and although the middle class has increased, nearly 300 million still live on an income of less than $1 a day.[40] Among them are the poor peasants in tribal belts and the lower castes, who are increasingly demanding their rights and equal opportunities. These demands have taken many forms—in some cases, peaceful electoral politics, but in others, violent responses to the state and its institutions. Conflict over demands for economic quotas, especially in employment and education, forms a major part of the internal struggle in India today. In recent years, a corridor has formed in India's tribal belts from the north to the south, under the influence of Naxalites (ultraradical Maoists). In this corridor, Indian security forces are largely unable to assert their control because the latter use guerrilla tactics and have wide support among the deprived masses, especially in tribal areas.[41]

India also has difficulty with the full integration of minority groups, especially Muslims, although it has a better record on the issue of minority rights compared with its South Asian neighbors.[42] The large Muslim minority, comprising 14 percent of the national population, constitutes a huge underclass in terms of economic development and social opportunities, some of which offer fertile ground for Islamic radicalism.[43] In addition, during the Bharatiya Janata Party (BJP) rule in states like Gujarat, intense violent incidents occurred, shattering Muslim confidence in the ability of the Indian state to protect them. In recent years, Christians, especially in Orissa and Gujarat, have also been targeted by Hindu fundamentalist groups and sometimes by BJP-led governments in their effort to prevent alleged conversions to Christianity by lower-caste Hindus, repressed by their upper-caste brethren. To India's credit, the Hindu-Muslim conflict now seems confined to pockets and rarely spreads to the national level.

The internal conflicts in all key countries also pose considerable problems at the human security level for the inhabitants of the region, the majority of whom are living in abject poverty, illiteracy, poor health conditions, low calorie intake, and inadequate sanitary conditions, akin to sub-Saharan Africa.[44] A stark manifestation of the human security problem is exhibited by the high number of refugees and internally displaced persons that the region copes with. South Asia's cities are filled with shantytowns and slums populated by rural migrants seeking better opportunities. The region also has high levels of child labor, trafficking in women, drug trafficking, diseases such as HIV/AIDS and tuberculosis, and a host of other nontraditional and human security challenges that are assuming new and wider proportions in the globalization era.

The presence of weak states in the region has resulted in the active involvement of major powers, especially the United States and China.

External Actors and South Asia's Weak States

Major powers can intervene in a region through competition, cooperation, engagement, disengagement, hegemony, or a mixture of these ideal types. As Benjamin Miller contends, major powers can influence a region's conflict pattern, transforming it from cold war to hot war or cold peace to warm peace and vice versa. Major powers cannot resolve the problem of nation-to-state incongruence, but they can, through their support or the absence of support, generate conditions for conflict to persist or dissipate over time.[45] The major powers play an important role in South Asia, despite India's dominant power position in the region. The region's pivotal geostrategic location is part of the reason for this phenomenon, but the presence of weak states in conflict contributes to this activism by outside powers, as in the cases of Afghanistan and Pakistan.

Both India and Pakistan were targets as well as often willing partners in the cold war competition between the United States and the Soviet Union. Pakistan has been a willing partner in the U.S.-led alliance system, and it developed a strong military relationship with Washington that has experienced ups and downs since 1954. The Soviet invasion of Afghanistan in 1979 set in motion a powerful wave of superpower involvement in the region. The defeat and disorderly withdrawal of the Soviet forces in 1989 and the emergence of the Taliban in Afghanistan in 1996 brought considerable insecurity to the region and continued great power interest. The Taliban also brought al-Qaeda to the region by sheltering Osama bin Laden and his network of terrorists until they were deposed in 2002 through a military invasion led by the United States, following the September 11, 2001 attacks.

In the post–cold war era, major power involvement is largely focused on the Afghanistan/Pakistan area. The warming bilateral relations between India and the United States and China, and the decreasing interest of Russia in the subcontinent, have reduced opportunities for major power competition in the region. However, China's activism in some South Asian states and neighbors, especially in Pakistan and Myanmar and increasingly in Nepal, and India's efforts to counter such efforts, have generated competitive dynamics in the subsystem's security predicament. In recent years, the United States has shown some equidistance in India-Pakistan relations and has helped to conduct the peace process between the two states, but the military option is still its dominant approach to the war on the Taliban and al-Qaeda in Afghanistan and Pakistan. Major power activism in the region is likely to increase if the Sino-Indian relationship develops into a rivalry and the United States gets involved in the form of new balance-of-power coalitions. Moreover, as of 2009, the Afghan conflict shows no signs of resolution, and without radical transformation, this part of South Asia is likely to pose considerable challenges to major powers, especially the United States.

Cooperation Patterns in South Asia: Absence of Strong Norms

The conflict dynamics seem to have affected cooperation patterns in the region in a major way. The South Asian Association of Regional Cooperation (SAARC) has been struggling to make an impact for a long period of time. Although it was established in 1985, it has not been as effective as ASEAN in Southeast Asia or Mercosur in South America in fostering regional cooperation and the peaceful settlement of disputes. The intense rivalry between India and Pakistan may be part of the cause for this absence of sustained regional cooperation. Regional cooperation is hampered by a peculiar dynamic in South Asia. In particular, South Asian states are hypersensitive on sovereignty but are unwilling to fully accept the sovereignty norm vis-à-vis their neighbors. They are somewhat revisionist or anti–status quo on the issue of territorial borders.

South Asia's states thus willingly or inadvertently challenge the norm of nonintervention (especially in internal affairs) and respect for territorial borders, two of the cardinal principles of state sovereignty in the modern era. Part of the problem is that states are sometimes unable to control borders, but there is also a deliberate strategy on the part of elites to intervene in the affairs of others, generating considerable ill will toward each other as well as lingering mutual suspicions. Over the years, both India and Pakistan have engaged in internal interventions, with India helping the division of Pakistan in 1971 and Pakistan abetting insurgencies in Punjab and Kashmir. India intervened in Sri Lanka between 1987 and 1990 in the form of peacekeeping, only to withdraw after major losses to its forces in their battles with the Tamil liberation guerrillas. Bangladesh and Nepal, often due to their instabilities, allow their conflicts to spill over to India. While India has, in recent years, refrained considerably from external interventions, the small states of the region still view India as hegemonic, rightly or wrongly. The Pakistani elite strategy involves active intervention in the affairs of India and Afghanistan through asymmetric means. Terrorist incidents, with or without the connivance of Pakistani officials, have occurred with increasing frequency in India, especially since 1989, when the Kashmiri insurgency began. While these interventions serve the limited tactical calculations of particular elites, in terms of regional order they have produced chronic insecurity and lingering mutual antagonisms.

Comparing with Other Regions

How have other regions with weak states fared in the security arena? South Asia's immediate neighboring region to the east, Southeast Asia, has been much more successful in creating a regional institutional mechanism that has helped prevent conflict at the interstate level. Although they have high levels of intrastate insecurity, the original ASEAN states (Brunei, Indonesia, Malaysia, the Philippines, Singapore, Thailand) have abstained from interstate war since the 1960s, and the new members (Cambodia, Laos, Vietnam, and Myanmar) also currently refrain from interstate violence. The ASEAN states have also settled most of their border disputes, even those involving China, though in 2009 the Cambodia-Thailand border dispute was flaring up. Southeast Asia has developed a limited security community with two norms of behavior—nonintervention in internal affairs and defensive military postures—in spite of the fact that there have been no common policies on defense or security and despite the states' use of alignments, bandwagoning, and limited balancing, especially of the soft balancing variety. Informal norms are most often prevalent in regional interaction. The relative stability in the region has encouraged some scholars to call it a "nascent security community" characterized by the absence of war and the expectation of no military attacks among member states.[46] The "ASEAN way" of cooperation, based on limited institutional engagement, is believed to help change state behavior through consultation, "socialization inside international institutions," and "persuasion" as well as "modes of behavior," through "habits of cooperation."[47] The nonintervention principles include refraining from criticizing the actions of governments toward their own people and denying recognition and sanctuary to groups that seek to overthrow a neighboring state's government. ASEAN governments are encouraged to support member state policies against subversive groups.[48] These nonintervention principles may be one of the reasons why the Southeast Asian states (unlike their South Asian counterparts) have avoided interstate conflicts but persist with high levels of internal violence. The ASEAN states also have been fairly successful in limiting great power intervention and conflict initiations through institutional mechanisms. The ASEAN Regional Forum (ARF) has been a crucial forum for great powers to engage and thereby adopt norms of cooperation as far as the region is concerned.

Africa is another region that has attempted to develop limited institutional mechanisms for security management, but with less success than Southeast Asia. Almost all the forty-two states in sub-Saharan Africa are weak states, while a few are called "failed" or "failing" states.[49] Although the African states are not often in a position to engage in intense military challenges (somewhat similar to the small states of South Asia), they created interstate norms—such as the adherence to the territorial integrity norm—that entrench colonially created borders. With the changing capacity of African states, this norm has been watered down, and the continent is witnessing more internal conflicts spilling over to different states, but interstate wars are still rare.[50] However, the presence of several civil conflicts has also prevented African states from emerging as strong entities.[51]

Latin America, especially the Southern Cone of Mercosur member states (Brazil, Argentina, Paraguay, and Uruguay, and to an extent associate member Chile), has also developed much higher levels of cooperation than South Asia, despite the presence of internal violence and undemocratic states. An implicit acceptance of U.S. hegemony also means that, barring a few occasional renegades like Cuba, Nicaragua (under the Sandinistas), and Venezuela (under Hugo Chavez), most of the regional states simply do not engage in activities directly hostile to the United States. Here, almost all states have come to agree to the existing territorial divisions and rarely challenge the territorial order militarily. The most notable sign of progress is the near absence of war among the region's states.[52] Despite the regional economic organization and Mercosur's efforts to widen cooperation, the region's absence of proper democratic order and perpetual internal instability have caused it to remain less integrated than Western Europe and Southeast Asia.[53] Despite all these problems, it still seems better off than South Asia in the areas of regional cooperation and peaceful order, especially at the interstate level.

These three regions offer some insights into how regional cooperation may develop among weak states, even when they have different security environments and historical trajectories. The key to the reduction of security challenges in Southeast Asia and the Mercosur region arises from the focus on economic cooperation. Further, the absence of a major territorial dispute similar to Kashmir has helped these states to form limited security communities.

Why is South Asia different, with its high levels of interstate and internal conflicts? In some sense, South Asia contains some of the conflict patterns of the Middle East and Africa. The Middle East is defined in terms of the Arab-Israeli conflict, although the great power penetration is much more intense there than in South Asia. A low level of state capacity also is a reason for the continued problems that the Middle East is facing today. However, differences between these regions, such as the vital importance of oil in the Middle East, the presence there of different, separated security theatres (the Gulf, Israel and its neighbors, and the western end of North Africa), and the absence of a single leading Middle Eastern state make accurate comparisons difficult. The spillover of conflict across borders that characterizes much of contemporary Africa's insecurity situation is replicated in South Asia; however, it is not matched by a comparable degree of traditional interstate conflict.

Research Questions
Some pertinent research questions that guide this volume are:
- What explains the chronic insecurity of the South Asian region?
- How does state capacity affect security at interstate, intrastate, and human dimensions in the region?
- How does the relative paucity of strong cooperative norms determine or contribute to the regional insecurity problem?
- What are the causes of the persisting weak state syndrome in South Asia?
  —Are these causes due to historical/structural factors or the way states were formed in the region, the disjunction between state and nations that constitute them, and the interjection of external actors within the region? How do economic factors affect state capacity and security?
  —What role does civil society play in the persistence or amelioration of the weak state syndrome in the region?
- What solutions can be proposed for making states strong while engendering cooperative norms of behavior?

This volume aims at exploring these and related questions and thereby understanding the myriad ways in which low levels of state capacity in conjunction with the absence of cooperative and noninterventionist interstate norms have affected the region and prevented it from developing a peaceful security order. It engages scholars of international relations and comparative politics in order to explore the underlying and proximate factors that cause and contribute to the perpetual insecurity and human suffering in South Asia.

The first set of chapters (Part II) discusses the different theoretical and conceptual dynamics of weak states and links that to the South Asian insecurity problem. The chapters deal with state capacity in general and its implications for security, broadly defined. In Part III, each of the key countries—India, Pakistan, Afghanistan, Bangladesh, Nepal, and Sri Lanka—is analyzed in order to see how state capacity impinges on their security (interstate, intrastate, and human) and how it has affected their security policies toward their neighbors. Due to space limitations and their tiny size, the region's two other states, Maldives and Bhutan, are not discussed. Part IV contains the concluding chapter, which draws out the implications of the previous chapters, examines why strong, cooperative interstate norms are not developing, and inquiries into what can be done to transform the region. The insights each chapter provides will be useful to any scholar or policymaker interested in understanding South Asia's persistent conflict patterns and insecurity dilemmas and in offering possible solutions.

Notes to Chapter 1

1. For some of these causes, see chapters in T. V. Paul, ed., *The India-Pakistan Conflict: An Enduring Rivalry* (Cambridge: Cambridge University Press, 2005).

2. Key works include: Paul, *India-Pakistan Conflict*; Raju Thomas, ed., *Perspectives on Kashmir: The Roots of Conflict in South Asia* (Boulder, CO: Westview, 1992); Sumit Ganguly and Devin Hagerty, *Fearful Symmetry: India-Pakistan Crises in the Shadow of Nuclear Weapons* (New Delhi: Oxford University Press, 2005); S. Paul Kapur, *Dangerous Deterrent: Nuclear Weapons Proliferation and Conflict in South Asia* (Stanford, CA: Stanford University Press, 2007); Rajesh Basrur, *Minimum Deterrence and India's Nuclear Security* (Stanford, CA: Stanford University Press, 2006); Amitabh Mattoo, Kapil Kak, and Happymon Jacob, eds., *India & Pakistan: Pathways Ahead* (New Delhi: KW Publishers, 2007); E. Sridharan, ed., *The India-Pakistan Nuclear Relationship: Theories of Deterrence and International Relations* (Delhi: Routledge, 2007).

3. Maya Chadda, in her chapter in this volume, argues that France and Germany were strong states prior to 1945 but had intense rivalry, and that the emergence of a

strong Nepal or Pakistan need not result in peace between them and India. For her, the structural causes that generate these conflicts are not addressed by state capacity alone. I concur that state capacity is a necessary and not a sufficient variable for a peaceful regional order. However, in conjunction with robust norms of cooperation, strong states, especially democracies, generate peace, as contemporary France and Germany show.

4. See, Joel S. Migdal, *Strong Societies and Weak States: State-Society Relations and State Capabilities in the Third World* (Princeton: Princeton University Press, 1988), pp. 4–5; Peter Evans, *Embedded Autonomy* (Princeton: Princeton University Press, 1995).

5. Eric A. Nordlinger, "Taking the State Seriously," in *Understanding Political Development: An Analytical Framework*, ed. Myron Weiner and Samuel P. Huntington (Boston: Little Brown, 1987), p. 369.

6. Robert I. Rotberg, ed., *State Failure and State Weakness in a Time of Terror* (Washington, DC: Brookings Institution Press, 2003).

7. Kalevi J. Holsti, *The State, War, and the State of War* (Cambridge: Cambridge University Press, 1996), pp. 104, 106.

8. Regime security could thus be intermingled with state security for such a state. See Mohammed Ayoob, *The Third World Security Predicament* (Boulder, CO: Lynne Rienner, 1995).

9. Peter Dauvergne, "Weak States, Strong States: A State-in-Society Perspective," in *Weak and Strong States in Asia-Pacific Societies*, ed. Peter Dauvergne (St. Leonards, NSW: Allen & Unwin, 1998), p. 8. *Foreign Policy* uses twelve social, economic, and political indicators in determining the status of a state in its "failed state index." These are mounting demographic pressures, massive movement of refugees, a legacy of vengeance-seeking group grievance, chronic and sustained human flight, uneven economic development along group lines, sharp economic decline, criminalization/ delegitimization of the state, progressive deterioration of public services, suspension or arbitrary application of the rule of law and widespread violation of human rights, nonstate security apparatuses operating within a state, and the rise of factionalized elites and intervention of other states or external actors.

10. Holsti, *State, War*, p. 84

11. On these see, Holsti, *State, War*, p. 40; Francis Fukuyama, *State Building: Governance and World Order in the 21st Century* (Ithaca: Cornell University Press, 2004), chapter 3.

12. Holsti, *State, War*, p. 117.

13. On the role of effective institutions to overcome dislocations engendered by economic and social change, see Samuel P. Huntington, *Political Order in Changing Societies* (New Haven: Yale University Press, 1968).

14. On this, see David D. Laitin, *Nations, States and Violence* (Oxford: Oxford University Press, 2007), pp. 3–6, and Stephen M. Saideman and R. William Ayres, *For Kin or Country: Xenophobia, Nationalism and War* (New York: Columbia University Press, 2008).

15. On diversionary wars, see Jack S. Levy, "The Diversionary Theory of War: A Critique," in *Handbook of War Studies*, ed. Manus I. Midlarsky (Ann Arbor: University of Michigan Press, 1993), pp. 259–288.

16. For negative security externalities, see David A. Lake, "Regional Security Complexes: A Systems Approach," in *Regional Orders*, ed. David A. Lake and Patrick M. Morgan (University Park, PA: Pennsylvania State University Press, 1997), p. 49. On the security dilemma in internal conflicts, see Jack Snyder and Robert Jervis, "Civil War and the Security Dilemma," in *Civil Wars, Insecurity, and Intervention*, ed. Barbara F. Walter and Jack Snyder (New York: Columbia University Press, 1999), pp. 15–37.

17. These definitions are drawn from William R. Thompson, "The Regional Subsystem: A Conceptual Explication and a Propositional Inventory," *International Studies Quarterly* 17, no. 1 (March 1973), p. 101.

18. Lake, "Regional Security Complexes," in David A. Lake and Patrick M. Morgan, *Regional Orders: Building Security in a New World* (University Park, PA: Penn State Press, 1997), pp. 48–49. Peter Katzenstein considers regions as having "both material and symbolic dimensions, and we can trace them in patterns of behavioral interdependence and political practice." Katzenstein, *A World of Regions* (Ithaca: Cornell University Press, 2005), p. 2. See also Douglas Lemke, *Regions of War and Peace* (Cambridge: Cambridge University Press, 2002).

19. Barry Buzan, "A Framework for Regional Security Analysis," in *South Asian Insecurity and the Great Powers*, ed. Barry Buzan and Gowher Rizvi (Houndmills, UK: Macmillan, 1986), p. 8.

20. One exception to the focus on states to the exclusion of nonstate actors is Barry Buzan and Ole Wæver, *Regions and Powers: The Structure of International Security* (Cambridge: Cambridge University Press, 2004).

21. For Miller, "a state-to-nation imbalance" is present when "the regional states (entities or institutions administering a certain territory) and the national sentiments of the peoples in the region (that is, their political aspirations of living as national communities in their own states)" do not match. Benjamin Miller, *States, Nations and the Great Powers: The Sources of Regional War and Peace* (Cambridge: Cambridge University Press, 2007), p. 18.

22. The microstate of Maldives recognizes the need for smaller countries in South Asia to be sensitive to India's security concerns. Maldives's foreign minister, in an interview with the author, contended that his country views India as an opportunity with its huge market, and believes that a form of benign *finlandization* (similar to Finland's relationship with the Soviet Union/Russia) of smaller states is perhaps necessary for regional peace and order in South Asia. To him, the small states should try to work with India and not against the larger neighbor's security interests. He warns against the temptation among some small states in the region to form balance-of-power coalitions with outside powers, which could be disastrous for these states themselves. For the South Asian states, barring Pakistan, have little structural reasons for intense conflict with India, and much of the differences of opinion are perceptual, deriving from notions of sovereign equality desired by new states and the legacy

of nonalignment and Third World solidarism propounded by Nehru, Suharto, and Nasser. Author's interview with Ahmed Shaheed, Foreign Minister of Maldives, Male, February 3, 2009.

23. Rizvi argues that the separation of Bangladesh was a very rare event due to geographical distances and the repressive policies of the military government of Pakistan; but without Indian intervention, it would not have happened. Even Pakistan, while "politically a weak state . . . has considerable coercive power to prevent further secession." Gowher Rizvi, "Pakistan: the Domestic Dimensions of Security," in Buzan and Rizvi, *South Asian Insecurity*, p. 83. See also M. P. Singh and Veena Kukreja, eds., *Pakistan: Democracy, Development and Security Issues* (New Delhi: Sage Publications, 2005), p. 13.

24. On this, see Robert H. Jackson, *Quasi-States: Sovereignty, International Relations and the Third World* (Cambridge: Cambridge University Press, 1990); Mark Zacher, "The Territorial Integrity Norm: International Boundaries and the Use of Force," *International Organization* 55, no. 2 (2001), pp. 215–250.

25. The latter figure is as of 1997. See Michael Brecher and Jonathan Wilkenfeld, *A Study of Crisis* (Ann Arbor: University of Michigan Press, 1997), p. 821.

26. U.S. Department of State, *Country Reports on Terrorism 2007*, chapter 2, http://www.state.gov/s/ct/rls/crt/2007/103709.htm.

27. United Nations Development Programme, *Human Development Report 1994*, http://hdr.undp.org/en/reports/global/hdr1994/. See also Giorgio Shani, Makoto Sato, and Mustapha Kamal Pasha, eds., *Protecting Human Security in a Post–9/11 World: Critical and Global Insights* (New York: Palgrave Macmillan, 2007).

28. On Afghanistan, see Rasul Bakhsh Rais, *Recovering the Frontier State: War, Ethnicity, and the State in Afghanistan* (Lexington, KY: Lexington Books, 2008).

29. See Christophe Jaffrelot, ed., *Pakistan: Nationalism without a Nation* (London: Zed Books, 2002); Ayesha Siddiqa, *Military Inc.: Inside Pakistan's Military Economy* (London: Pluto Press, 2007). According to Lasswell, a "garrison state" is one that has a "preoccupation...with danger," where "the specialists on violence are the most powerful group in society," and principal preoccupations of ruling elite are "skillfully guiding the minds of men . . . [through] symbolic manipulation," and "prevent[ing] full utilization of modern productive capacity for non-military consumption purposes." Harold Lasswell, "The Garrison State and Specialists on Violence," in Lasswell, ed., *The Analysis of Political Behavior* (London: Routledge and Kegan Paul, 1948), pp. 146, 149, 153, 154.

30. On the educational system, see C. Christine Fair, *The Madrassah Challenge: Militancy and Religious Education in Pakistan* (Washington, DC: United States Institute of Peace Press, 2008).

31. On Pakistan's weaknesses, see Stephen Philip Cohen, *The Idea of Pakistan* (Washington, DC: Brookings Institution Press, 2004), pp. 3–4; Husain Haqqani, *Pakistan: Between Mosque and Military* (Washington, DC: Carnegie Endowment for International Peace, 2005).

32. Aijaz Maher, "Pakistan Lists 1400 Terror Dead," *BBC News*, April 18, 2009, http://news.bbc.co.uk/2/hi/south_asia/8004731.stm.

33. On this conflict, see Jayadeva Uyangoda, "Ethnic Conflict in Sri Lanka: Changing Dynamics," *Policy Studies* no. 32 (Washington, DC: East-West Center, 2007); Sankaran Krishna, *Post-Colonial Insecurities: India, Sri Lanka and the Question of Nationhood* (Minneapolis: The University of Minnesota Press, 1999).

34. On this see, Susan Hangen, "Creating a 'New Nepal': The Ethnic Dimension," *Policy Studies* no. 34 (Washington, DC: East-West Center, 2007).

35. On this, see Baldev Raj Nayar and T. V. Paul, *India in the World Order: Searching for Major Power Status* (Cambridge: Cambridge University Press, 2003); C. Raja Mohan, *Crossing the Rubicon: The Shaping of India's New Foreign Policy* (New York: Palgrave-Macmillan, 2003).

36. On this, see Devesh Kapur and Pratap Bhanu Mehta, eds., *Public Institutions in India: Performance and Design* (New York: Oxford University Press, 2007).

37. For a comprehensive treatment, see Paul, *India-Pakistan Conflict.*

38. U.S. Department of State, *Country Reports on Terrorism 2007.*

39. It is estimated that over 109 movements operate in the region, some pushing for outright independence, others for more indigenous rights or autonomy. Sanjib Baruah, "Postfrontier Blues: Toward a New Policy Framework for Northeast India," *Policy Studies* no. 33 (Washington, DC: East-West Center, 2007); Monirul Hussain, *Interrogating Development: State, Displacement and Popular Resistance in Northeast India* (New Delhi: Sage Publications, 2008).

40. On whether India's liberalization has helped the poor or not, see Baldev Raj Nayar, *The Myth of the Shrinking State: Globalization and the State in India* (New Delhi: Oxford University Press, 2009).

41. On the Naxalite problem, see Pratul Ahuja and Rajat Ganguly, "The Fire Within: Naxalite Insurgency Violence in India," *Small Wars and Insurgencies* 18, no. 2 (June 2007), pp. 249–274.

42. On ethnic conflicts in India see Maya Chadda, *Ethnicity, Security and Separatism in India* (New York: Columbia University Press, 1997); Ashutosh Varshney, *Ethnic Conflict and Civic Life: Hindus and Muslims in India* (New Haven: Yale University Press, 2002).

43. Soutik Biswas, "Why Do Indian Muslims Lag Behind?" *BBC News Online*, August 9, 2007, http://news.bbc.co.uk/2/hi/south_asia/6938090.stm.

44. On this, see Amartya Sen, *Development as Freedom* (New York: Anchor Books, 2000), pp. 99–103.

45. Miller, *States, Nations*, pp. 62–81.

46. On security communities, see Emanuel Adler and Michael Barnett, eds., *Security Communities* (Cambridge: Cambridge University Press, 1998). On Southeast Asia, see Amitav Acharaya, *Constructing a Security Community in Southeast Asia: ASEAN and the Problem of Regional Order* (London: Routledge, 2001).

47. Alastair Iain Johnston, "Socialization in International Institutions: The ASEAN Way and International Relations Theory," in *International Relations Theory*

and the Asia-Pacific, ed. G. John Ikenberry and Michael Mastanduno (New York: Columbia University Press, 2003), p. 108.

48. Herman Craft, "The Principle of Non-Intervention: Evolution and Challenges for the Asia-Pacific Region," in *Non-Intervention and State Sovereignty in the Asia-Pacific*, eds. David Dickens and Guy Wilson-Roberts (Wellington, New Zealand: Center for Strategic Studies, 2000).

49. Foreign Policy and the Fund for Peace, "Failed States Index 2008," *Foreign Policy*, July-August 2008.

50. Robert H. Jackson and Carl G. Rosberg, "Why Africa's Weak States Persist: The Empirical and the Juridical in Statehood," *World Politics* 35, no. 1 (1982), pp. 1–24; Jeffrey Herbst, *States and Power in Africa: Comparative Lessons in Authority and Control* (Princeton: Princeton University Press, 2000).

51. Jeffrey Herbst, "States and War in Africa," in *The Nation-State in Question*, ed. T. V. Paul, G. John Ikenberry, and John A. Hall (Princeton: Princeton University Press, 2003), p. 166.

52. See Arie M. Kacowicz, *Zones of Peace in the Third World: South America and West Africa in Comparative Perspective* (Albany: SUNY Press, 1998); Jorge I. Dominguez, ed., *International Security and Democracy: Latin America and the Caribbean in the Post-Cold War Era* (Pittsburgh: University of Pittsburgh Press, 1998).

53. According to Andrew Hurrell, although the region does not yet constitute a security community, it may be in the process of developing into one. See Hurrell, "An Emerging Security Community in South America?" in Adler and Barnett, *Security Communities*, pp. 228–264.

PART II
STATE CAPACITY

2 State Failure and States Poised to Fail

South Asia and Developing Nations

Robert I. Rotberg

Is Burma (Myanmar) a failed state?, inquired a very knowledgeable colleague. "Yes and no," I replied. By so many criteria, Burma must be considered an abject failure, irrespective of its junta's atrocious behavior after the devastating 2008 cyclone. But no simple answer is possible. On the one hand, Burma provides very few political goods to its citizens, being backward in terms of education, health, rule of law, economic opportunity, and political freedom. On the other hand, Burma is very secure; its military rulers are powerful and controlling. Thus, I told my colleague, Burma is failed in every respect but the last. So it can be called a weak state with a hollow center. In other words, Burma, like North Korea and Turkmenistan, two other Asian despotisms, escapes the label "failed" only because it as a nation-state fully monopolizes all legitimate uses of violence. Its tyrannical security saves it from failure, as did Saddam Hussein's Iraq until after the flawed United States intervention in 2003.

Burma, in common with all failed and near-failed states, has been taken to the precipice of failure by human agency. No structural deficits or institutional deficiencies doomed Burma. Nor have natural disasters or geographical constraints contributed to Burma's descent from strength to the pit of weakness and the edge of failure. We cannot ascribe Burma's current condition to the policies of British colonial rule or to the crimes and highly placed collaborators of the Japanese occupation.

My inquiring colleague and I both knew that Burma was once a rich and well-educated nation-state that had fallen on hard times. After a very brief period of largely participatory rule and good governance (1948 to 1958), it was run first by General Ne Win, an idiosyncratic autocrat and previous collaborator with the Japanese occupiers, who, from 1962 to 1988, isolated and systematically de-developed his previously proud nation-state. For reasons of ideology, numerology, paranoia, and power, he pursued a policy of rigorous autarky, ending much of Burma's historic participation in world trade and global intellectual capital. Autarky still prevails, along with strong considerations of paranoia and power preservation.

Ne Win was deposed by the State Law and Order Restoration Council (SLORC), a tightly disciplined military junta, in 1988. Earlier that year, students and Buddhist monks led a widespread uprising against Ne Win's capricious rule. About 1000 protesters were gunned down in Rangoon. Later in the same year, the SLORC slaughtered another 3000 activists in Rangoon, Mandalay, Sagaing, and other towns. About 10,000 students and monks fled. Subsequently, the SLORC ruled Burma under martial law until agreeing to a popular election in 1990. To the somehow overconfident or politically blinded SLORC's apparent surprise and consternation, Burmese voted overwhelmingly in favor of the cause championed by the students and monks, and thus for the new National League for Democracy (NLD), led by Daw Aung San Suu Kyi. However, her victorious coalition was not allowed to occupy the parliamentary seats that it had won; she and her closest political colleagues were soon jailed.

Since 1990, the SLORC, in 1997 renamed the State Peace and Development Council (SPDC), has continued to govern Burma, keeping Suu Kyi almost always under house arrest and real democracy (not the staged variety) dormant. However, the SPDC has improved relations with many of the dissident ethnic groups that occupy territory on the edges of the Burmese heartland; various long-running conflicts between the central government and minority-dominated provinces have ended. The country is stable, after Cyclone Nargis as before, even if or because its peoples are repressed and held hostage by corrupt soldiers who deny nearly all Burmese free expression, individual entrepreneurial opportunity, political participation, access to the wider world through travel or the Internet, advanced education of all kinds, more than rudimentary health care, and the pursuit of any goals that are not specifically sanctioned by General Than Shwe, head of the steely junta. Burma, in other words, is orderly and rigorously organized, but the 43 to 52 million citizens of the country (no one knows the exact number) receive almost no other political goods. If it were embroiled in an ongoing civil war it could be definitively classified as failed, but with enforced conformity more common than rebellion, it remains one of those Asian nations poised mightily to fail.[1]

The Theory

There are several ways to discuss nation-state failure, but if we want to be as specific and as conclusive as possible, it behooves us to substitute clear for muddy criteria, and empirical for impressionistic measures. Doing so then enables us to be diagnostic—to determine which nation-states are strong, which are weak, which are failing (approaching failure or poised on the cusp of failure), which are fully failed, and which have so thoroughly failed that they may be considered collapsed.

As I explained earlier in *When States Fail*, the test of failure is the extent to which nation-states (such as in the SPDC'S Burma or Sheikh Hasina's Bangladesh) perform or fail to perform for their peoples, that is, the extent to which they deliver high or low levels of political goods and thus satisfy the fundamental, expressed expectations and needs of their citizens.[2] A prime function of the nation-state, after all, is to provide political goods to persons living within its borders. I aggregate those political goods under five main categories—safety and security, rule of law and transparency, participation and human rights, sustainable economic opportunity, and human development. To examine weakness, failure, or collapse, I measure the provision of political goods, assigning quantitative values to the various components of the main categories. For example, the extent to which various measurements show that the educational or health political goods are being satisfied within a nation-state can be expressed numerically, especially in comparison with its neighbors or its peer cohort of nation-states. Crime rates differentiate easily along the safety continuum among countries. Battle deaths show how much violence there is within a nation-state, and so on.

Failed states are those states which fall below a threshold of political goods and always fail to satisfy the safety and security minimums. Those states close to the threshold might be at that near threshold point for decades, as Haiti was before violence consumed it in 2002, or Nepal before the monarchical implosion, or they might suddenly fall from strength to failure because of a sudden reversal of legitimacy, as was the case of Cote d'Ivoire in 2000. Pakistan, a failing entity, has teetered on the brink of outright failure for decades, but its governmental illegitimacy in the Musharraf and post-Musharraf eras encourages the breakdown of public order, cascading insecurity, the rise of nonstate actors such as the Taliban and al Qaeda, and deficits of political goods of staggering complexity. By assigning numbers to these many values (of subcategories of each political good), we can track precipitous declines from strength to weakness to the edge of failure. We can show precisely how close to failure a nation-state might be. Without the numbers, and without precise criteria, all assignments of weakness or failure are guesswork, subject to selection bias or prejudice.[3]

The hierarchy of political goods is topped by publicly provided security. The state's prime function is to prevent cross-border invasions, to eliminate attacks on the national order or social structure, to minimize crime, and "to enable citizens to resolve their differences with the state and their fellow inhabitants without recourse to arms or other forms of physical coercion."[4]

When there is security, indeed, only when security prevails, the delivery of the other desirable political goods becomes possible. Pakistan's 2009 dilemma illustrates the overriding imperative of Weberian security. So does Bangladesh in the aftermath of the 2009 mutiny. Now that Sri Lanka has militarily deprived the Liberation Tigers of Tamil Eelam (LTTE) of the last vestiges of internal territory and killed its leaders, it is finally possible that the government can "secure" the entire nation-state for the first time in three decades.

Second after security is the provision of "predictable, recognizable, systematized methods of adjudicating disputes . . ."—an enforceable rule of law and an effective judicial system.[5] Third is the political good that allows free and open participation in the national political arena. This good also encompasses the essential freedoms, including fundamental civil and human rights. The remaining political goods contribute to economic growth and human development: health and educational opportunities, well-developed arteries of commerce and communications networks, respect for the environmental commons, and a well-managed economy, as explained in *When States Fail* and in the introductions to the 2007, 2008, and 2009 editions of *Strengthening African Governance.*[6]

By these criteria, strong states deliver a broad range of high-quality political goods and score well on all of the standard indices of economic, political, and social performance. All strong states are secure and comparatively safe states. Weak states may be inherently weak for structural reasons or may be fundamentally strong but situationally or temporarily compromised. Weakness comes from performance or delivery inadequacies that are quantifiable and are not artifacts of exogenous variables. Often these weak nation-states display ethnic or other inter-communal tensions that have not yet been turned violent. They are poorly governed; that is, they have a diminished ability (not capacity) to supply some or many of the basic political goods, nearly always honoring the rule of law in the breach. They show declining economic and social attainments, and their physical infrastructure betrays neglect. Often this kind of nation-state is ruled by a tyrant, elected or not.

In failed nation-states there are insurgencies, civil unrest, and a heady mixture of discontent and dissent. These kinds of states are violent, but "it is not the absolute intensity of violence that identifies a failed state." Instead, it is the "enduring character of that violence"—a crescendo of antagonism that is directed at the regime in power. These (mostly) civil wars are rooted in ethnic, linguistic, or other intercommunal enmity, but are propelled by avarice enticed by pools of mineral or similar wealth. It is important to reiterate that all failed states exhibit communal competition, but state failure should not be ascribed predominantly to failures of nation building.[7]

Failure Described

Failed states victimize their own citizens. As in the Taliban's Afghanistan, rulers oppress, extort, and control their own compatriots while privileging a favored ethnic, linguistic, or religious cohort. Failed states cannot control their own hinterlands and sometimes one or more of their internal regions. They frequently cannot express real power beyond a capital city or an ethnically preferred area. In Sri Lanka, a weak state teetering for decades on the edge of failure, parts of the north and parts of the east were not subject to central government hegemony for the better part of thirty years.

In failed states, inflation grows, corruption flourishes, and economic growth shrinks. Officials loot the state. Goods grow scarce in the stores. Sometimes, as in North Korea, Cambodia, and Zimbabwe, segments of the population are deprived of food and go hungry or starve. Criminal violence is prevalent. As state authority lessens and becomes simultaneously more criminal, so lawlessness spreads. Criminal gangs proliferate. Arms and drug trafficking intensify. For protection, ordinary citizens naturally turn, as in Iraq, to incipient warlords or religious protectors, or as in Afghanistan, to warlords or the Taliban.

Many weak states have flawed communication and transportation infrastructures. In failed states, these blemishes become catastrophes, with roads returning to tracks and potholes swallowing highways. Fixed telephone lines become anachronistic. Effective educational and medical systems become dysfunctional, with once-prized institutions being deprived of budgetary cash or foreign exchange. Hospitals run short of medicines and bandages. Schools lack teachers and textbooks. Literacy rates slide, and infant mortality numbers soar. Life expectancies plummet from the sixties to the thirties. Gradually, citizens, especially rural dwellers, realize that the (distant) central government has abandoned them to the capricious and harsh forces of nature. Many Pakistanis, in their different provinces, presumably have sensed this abandonment.

Above all, a nation-state fails when it loses legitimacy—when it forfeits "the mandate of heaven."[8] When citizens finally perceive that the rulers are running the state as a criminal enterprise for themselves as sole beneficiaries—when citizens realize that the state no longer cares about most of its inhabitants—then nearly everyone understands that the social contract binding rulers to the ruled and vice versa has been irreparably breached and allegiances are transferred to nonstate actors.

The Classic Cases

Afghanistan, the Democratic Republic of Congo, Cote d'Ivoire, Haiti, and the Sudan, all enmeshed in one or more enduring conflict, are classic failed states. They are failed because of their intrinsic insecurities as well as because each is unable to supply more than a paucity of the other necessary political goods to their inhabitants. Each harbors at least one, if not several, ongoing insurgencies. Death rates as a result of civil warfare are high and comparatively easy to quantify. Human security (safety of persons and freedom from crime) is almost wholly absent. None of these nation-states boasts more than a rudimentary rule of law or protections for human rights. Human development attainments such as educational opportunity, health care, access to potable water, and so on are weak; life expectancy rates are low or falling. Growth rates and per capita GDP numbers are rising in the case of Afghanistan and the Sudan, largely because of poppy sales and foreign aid in the case of Afghanistan and oil and remittances in the case of the Sudan, but the other classical failed states are still mired in poverty.

It is easy to classify such typical failed states since all but the two special cases show declining outcomes and outputs (the preferred measurements) combined with massive internal combustion and confrontation. It is tougher to parse the borderline cases. In 2010, are Sri Lanka, Pakistan, and Nepal failed states or weak ones? Answering such a question illuminates the theory and the distinctions that should be made in attempting—for purposes of crafting better policies—to classify such cases.

Sri Lanka was engulfed in civil war from the early 1970s until 2009. For many years in recent decades the LTTE managed to create a de facto autonomous enclave in the north and part of the east of the country, to survive intervention by Indian troops, and to outmaneuver the Sri Lankan army and navy on numerous occasions. About 90,000 Sri Lankans died as a result of such internecine warfare. In terms of the security political good, Sri Lanka clearly could have been considered a failed state.

Through suicide and other bombings, the LTTE on occasion carried the war for autonomy or Tamil independence in the north and east to Colombo, the capital, and to Sinhalese-dominated areas in the west and south of the island country. Those areas, roughly 80 percent of the country, however, were largely free of all but such episodic involvement in the civil war. Nevertheless, in order to decide whether Sri Lanka was a failed or a weak state, it is important to focus first on the provision of political goods in the major portions of the nation-state that were spared all but infrequent engagement in the ongoing conflict. In 80 percent of the country, we found very high levels of the delivery of the other political goods—human development, sustainable economic opportunity, participation and human rights, and rule of law. Indeed, despite its civil war, the Sri Lankan government was, even before 2009, delivering to its citizens comparatively robust qualities and quantities of these essential political goods. GDP levels were high for South Asia. So were participation rates, educational accomplishments, medical care, life expectancy levels, judicial independence, and so on.

That these numbers fell off dramatically in the north and east, where less than 20 percent of the population, nearly all Tamil-speaking, lived, made Sri Lanka a special case of a weak state, almost a strong state, encapsulating a zone of earlier failure. Indonesia was classified in that same general way in 2004—as a near failure saved by high levels of political goods in 80 percent of the vast archipelago, before—under new leadership—it negotiated peace in Aceh, dampened the rumbling conflicts in the Maluku Islands, and reduced hostilities in Papua (Irian Jaya).[9] Then, as a result, it became a weak nation-state, gaining strength and not tending toward failing or failure. That is its categorization in 2010, after a successful election and after the dampening of conflict across much of the far-ranging archipelago.

Until 2008, Nepal had been a classical failure. After the monarchy's loss of legitimacy and the broad rise of the Maoist insurgency, in 2004, Nepal had shifted from being an endemically weak state, with few political goods for its citizens, to a failed one riven by civil war. But since the negotiated end of the war, and elections in 2007, Nepal once again returned to weakness. That is, so long as hostilities are suspended, the nation-state's abysmal provision of political goods keeps it on the edge of failure but not failed. Renewed fighting (possible in 2010) would once again tip it over the edge.

Pakistan is a very special case. Given that many critical sections of the country are not in 2010 completely under the control of the central government, and thus in breach of the control of the instruments of violence that is fundamental to the security good, failure is the best current designation. When one combines that categorization with the sheer casualty count from suicide and other bombings, or from clashes between the Pakistani-based Taliban and internal or external security forces, it is clear that a sustainable case can begin to be made that Pakistan, big and wealthy as it is, and with nuclear weapons, has finally failed. (In 2009, *Foreign Policy*, using a different methodology, described Pakistan as the tenth most failed state in the world, after Guinea and before Cote d'Ivoire.) But a large swathe of the country has Sri Lankan aspects. Educational and health services are being provided at more than minimal levels, participation levels since former President Pervez Musharraf's authoritarian rule was relaxed in 2007 are reasonable, the rule of law is at least discussable, and the economy is moving forward, albeit not thriving.

A careful quantitative assessment, and a comparison of that assessment with the countries in the rest of Asia and the rest of South Asia, would help clarify—for external and internal policy purposes—exactly where Pakistan lies along the strong-collapse continuum. That careful quantitative assessment cannot be offered here for lack of data. But were it to be obtained, we might be able to concentrate the minds of Pakistanis and outsiders on the consequences and the components of its failure. Either way, its governmental actions and the actions of its neighbors, and the West, would be influenced.

After all, it is not only in the sometime geographical expression of Somalia—a collapsed state—that nonstate actors proliferate and warlords prevail.

The inability of Islamabad to project power beyond the Punjabi heartland is at least reminiscent of the absence of a government in Somalia. Admittedly, Somalia is nothing more than a geographical expression. All the Somali state has is its internationally accepted territorial borders. Nothing else of the state apparatus exists, hence its characterization as a collapsed (not just a failed) polity. Warlords (nonstate actors) do provide some security in the cities and districts that they control. Mosques and clans have organized a modicum of schooling, and there are shari'a courts in parts of the territory controlled by al Shabab. Otherwise, however, there are no political goods, and those that do exist are not provided by a recognized nation-state (even in Somaliland, which is far from failed but unrecognized internationally). Pakistan, a much stronger state, exhibits extreme Somali-like tendencies in the Northwest Frontier provinces of South and North Waziristan, in Swat, and in large parts of Baluchistan.

As a policy tool, a careful, quantitatively based method of assessing the character of a nation-state should drive policy both internally and from the outside. If it is recognized why a state like Nepal, which delivers very few political goods to its people, stays weak, but can easily cross back into failure, and why and how much more effective nation-states like Sri Lanka and Indonesia might fail, but have not, it is possible to prescribe remedies, call for outside assistance in one or more areas, or focus the attention of the United Nations and developed, donor countries. Pakistan is another South Asian nation-state where failure was unthinkable until late 2008 or early 2009, with the global financial crisis and intensified insurgency making the unthinkable plausible, absent decisive presidential leadership or internal military intervention. Indeed, in devising ways to assist Nepal and Pakistan, and even Sri Lanka or Bangladesh, it is wise to learn why and how collapsed states like Lebanon in the 1970s, Tajikistan in the 1990s, and Sierra Leone and Liberia in the 1990s and in this century were able to un-collapse and un-fail themselves with significant security assistance (respectively from Syria, Russia, Britain, and the United Nations) and, once secure, to strengthen, thanks to massive outside governance assistance.[10] Their experiences hold many lessons for polities like Nepal and Timor Leste, as well as for countries in Central, South, and Southeast Asia (and elsewhere) now at risk of failure.

Because of their demonstrated weaknesses as providers of rule of law, human rights and participation, sustainable economic opportunity, and human development (in each case the numbers and rankings are low), nation-states such as Kyrgyzstan, Tajikistan, Laos, and Papua New Guinea are in 2010 each at risk of failure if and when civil wars resume or break out. The first two, with their fundamental regional and political antagonisms, are held together only by thin levels of comity and the possibility of Russian intervention. Laos has experienced interregional and interethnic violence before; if the grip of the communist rulers weaken, hostilities are likely again. Papua New Guinea has among the worst crime rates in the world, and nearly two hundred fractious ethnicities on the main island plus dissidents (who have warred against the main island) on outer islands. Wildly corrupt as well, it is held together mainly by the possibility of Australian intervention. Fortunately, for diagnostic and policy purposes, we can quantify the levels of governance of each of these places and thus approximately assess the risks to each.

Actions of Leaders

It is important to classify nation-states in this way: strong, weak, failing, failed, and collapsed. Doing so helps to distinguish the quality of nation-states in the developing world in order to respond to their needs, to prevent them from descending from strength to weakness and failure, and to rebuild the ones that are eventually overwhelmed by outright failure. Good policy decisions flow from an appreciation of the differences among these kinds of nation-states and especially of how certain kinds of weak nation-states in the developing world are driven by their leaders into the full embrace of failure.

Nation-states do not become failed. Instead, they are failed by the purposeful actions of a leader or leaders. Presidents Mobutu Sese Seko in Zaire/Congo, Siaka Stevens in Sierra Leone, Samuel Doe and Charles Taylor in Liberia, Gaafar Nimeiri in the Sudan, and Idi Amin in Uganda (to mention only a few of those personally culpable, like Ne Win, for nation-state decline and decay), plus Mullah Muhammad Omar in Afghanistan, are all examples of depraved leaders who systematically deprived their constituents of fundamental political goods, ultimately even the overriding political good of security. They each provoked or demanded civil strife in order to profit from the resulting insecurity or otherwise drove their loyal and long-suffering citizens into rebellion by acts of commission and omission.[11]

Likewise, democratic or quasi-democratic leadership—at a minimum, nondespotic leadership—helps to explain why nation-states avoid outright failure. Pakistan under the politicians, corrupt as they are, might therefore with better leadership have been able to avoid tumbling into failure. Nepal has emerged from failure because of compromises negotiated by leaders at the supposed end of a civil war; whether the country can avoid lurching back into failure depends entirely on leadership decisions, not on structure. The antagonistic and heavy-handed leadership of the Bandaranaikes, husband and widow, brought about the long Sri Lankan struggle between Tamil separatists and the state. Their successors, including a Bandaranaike daughter, sometimes worsened the conflict by their actions and sometimes moderated it, including establishing the long cease-fire of 2006–2008. But peace in Sri Lanka now demands new leadership qualities for peace by the Rajapaksa trio on the government side.

Effective, participatory, honest leadership, or the lack thereof, also was decisive throughout Bangladesh's short history, especially during the earlier reigns of Sheikh Hasina and Begum Khaleda Zia. The intervention of General Moeen U. Ahmad in 2007 brought a new kind of discipline and probity (without much participation) to the affairs of Bangladesh. Whether his relatively brief interregnum until 2009 was long enough or instructive enough to alter the course of modern Bangladeshi politics is still unclear. But, unlike Musharraf, he was determined not to overstay his welcome and to attempt bravely to usher in a new approach to political responsibility and behavior. He believed in stewardship and in doing what was right for Bangladesh, not for his kinsmen or families.

Preventing Failure

The distinctions made here between failure and near failure are more than arbitrary or academic. They differentiate situations that threaten world order from those that are deteriorating but remain mostly of serious local or regional concern. Without weapons of mass destruction, imploding states are usually threats only to themselves and their unfortunate inhabitants. In terms of the 2005 Responsibility to Protect United Nations document, each of these cases where presidents willfully destroy their own states and the livelihoods and social welfare of millions of their own constituents rightfully should compel a regionally or UN-supervised intervention, but usually will not. As the *Boston Globe* once editorialized: "Millions of people in the world need a UN that is willing and able to protect them from their rulers—instead of protecting those rulers from outside interference in their internal affairs."[12]

The UN and larger powers usually wait to become involved until intrastate hostilities become too hot, and too many people die, or until foreign nationals are threatened. By then, as in Burma or Darfur, or earlier in Liberia and Sierra Leone, it is far too late.

Governance, that is, how a nation-state performs for its citizens—how it delivers high-quality political goods—is among the key responsibilities of the international system. International or regional organizations cannot govern individual nation-states. But they can set standards and find the means through Chapter VII of the UN Charter or through new understandings collectively arrived at to chastise those leaders and regimes who prey on their own citizens and govern so corruptly and cravenly that they create failure. What is important is that the United Nations and its key leaders refuse to tolerate tyranny and instead speak out strongly against infractions and miscreants—that they demonstrate political will sufficient to decry lapses of standards, abuse of norms of governance, and mobilize public diplomacy, sanctions, and intervention actions to save innocent civilians in despotic countries from their despots. Thus far, however, neither the UN secretary-general nor leaders of the G8 have been willing systematically to mobilize world public opinion for such objectives, much less act directly against the Than Shwes of the world. From this perspective, even the unilateral attack on Saddam Hussein came decades too late. World order and the UN, its proxy, should have acted immediately after the gassing of thousands of innocent Kurds in Halabja in 1988.

This analysis of strong, weak, failed, and collapsed nation-states can be utilized to provide early indicators of crisis. Just as it has been possible month by month and year by year to chart a country's regression from strength to weakness and near failure, and to use a variety of simple statistics to plot the national slippage toward failure, so it is possible to use a set of proxy measures to watch all weak states for signs of impending trouble. Efforts at prevention by international bodies, or by neighboring coalitions, would then be possible in South Asia and beyond.

There are several kinds of preventive tools that are available, if employed before a crisis erupts into full-scale failure and outright conflict. Preventive diplomacy is always relevant: either (1) quiet, private discussions by senior figures in a region or globally, or (2) internationally arranged missions capable of counseling strong leaders or mediating between leaders and opponents. Sanctions of various kinds are available. So is the mobilization of a rapid reaction force capable of interposing itself between contenders. Overall, the responsibility to protect should arouse Security Council declarations and the dispatch of peacekeepers or peace enforcers.

The declaration of a full humanitarian emergency obviously motivates these kinds of actions. But, well before a state fails and conflict erupts, the available numbers report exactly what is happening to a state. Simultaneously, local observers understand the increasing seriousness of a state being plunged into the abyss of de-development and incipient failure and can confirm what the numbers suggest in a stark and recognizable form. The qualitative and quantitative assessments of impending failure (as in Cote d'Ivoire on the eve of its swift slide from strength to failure in 2001) in turn depend on an awareness of the utility of a new definition of governance.

The failure and collapse of nation-states is a dynamic process. Little is foreordained. No matter how impoverished a state may be, it need not fail. The origins of a state, whether arbitrary or absent-minded (as in much of colonialism), again do not predispose to, or fully account for, failure. States born weak and forlorn, such as Botswana, have emerged strong and high performing as a consequence of gifted leadership, and not primarily as a result of a subsequent resource bonanza. Wealth must be well managed and distributed genuinely if a nation-state, such as Pakistan, or Nigeria or Equatorial Guinea, is to emerge from failure or weakness and become stronger; otherwise, there is always the possibility of slippage (as in Nigeria in the 1980s) and failure. In other words, the road to failure is littered with serious mistakes of omission and commission. Where there is little accountability and no political culture of democracy, especially in fragile, isolated states in the developing world, these errors of commission are almost always made for personal gain by leaders. Human agency drives and accounts for failure, or near failure, as in the ongoing cases of Pakistan, Bangladesh, and Sri Lanka. Likewise, nation-states strengthen under positive leadership for good, as in Indonesia and India.

State failure and state success, in other words, is largely man-made, not accidental.[13] Cultural clues are relevant but are inadequate to explain persistent leadership attributes or flaws. Likewise, institutional fragilities and structural weaknesses accelerate failure, but such deficiencies stem from decisions or actions of men (sometimes women, too, as in South Asia). In the absence of implanted democratic political cultures, greed explains more about malign leadership action than do structural or institutional insufficiencies.

Thus it is leadership error that destroyed or fractured nation-states for personal and political gain. Just think of what the Bandaranaikes did in Sri

Lanka or the Bhuttos in Pakistan. Solomon and Sirimavo Bandaranaike, one after the other, drove the LTTE into reactive combat by abrogating minority rights and vitiating the implicit social contract on which the country had been established. The preexisting constitutional and institutional barriers to such behavior proved too fragile to constrain determined executive action, as similarly in Sri Lanka. In Afghanistan, one of the continuing failed states, Gulbuddin Hakmatyar and Burrhan ul-Din Rabani attempted to prevent Afghans other than their own Pashtun and Tajik kin from sharing the perquisites of governance. Their own narrowly focused, self-enriching decisions enabled the Taliban to follow them in triumph in the 1990s; Afghanistan then descended into all-out terror and collapse.

Wherever there has been state failure or collapse, human agency has engineered the slide from strength or from weakness, and rulers have willfully presided over destabilizing resource shifts from the state to the ruling few. As those resource transfers grew more potent, and human rights abuses mounted, countervailing violence signified the extent to which the states in question had sundered underlying social contracts and become hollow receptacles of personalist privilege, private rule, and national immiseration. Inhabitants of failed states hence came to appreciate what it meant for their lives to be poor, nasty, brutish, and short (as national numbers demonstrate).

The Downward Spiral

Failure, it should be said, does not creep stealthily into the domain of a body politic. Its pending arrival is there for all to see—if they would but notice. Three kinds of signals—economic, political, and military—provide clear, timely, and actionable warnings. On the economic front, for example, Lebanon in 1972–1979, Nigeria in 1993–1999, Indonesia in 1997–1999, Pakistan in 2008–2009, and Zimbabwe in 1998–2008 each provided ample early warning signals. In each case, rapid reductions in income and living standards presaged the possibility of failure early enough to have been noted and for preventive measures to have been encouraged from outside or explored from within.

Once the downward spiral starts in earnest, only a concerted, determined effort can slow its momentum. Corrupt autocrats and their equally corrupt associates usually have few incentives to arrest their state's slide. They themselves find clever ways to benefit from impoverishment and misery; they are not the ones to suffer. As foreign and domestic investment dries up, jobs vanish, and per capita incomes fall, the mass of citizens in an imperiled state see their health, educational, and infrastructural entitlements erode. Food and fuel shortages occur. Privation and hunger follow. Typically, as the poor get poorer, ruling cadres get richer. State treasuries are skimmed, currency perquisites are employed for private gain, illicit gun- and narco-trafficking increases in scale, and secret funds flow out of the country into private structures and nonpublic bank accounts.

In the political realm, too, available indicators are abundant. Maximum leaders and their associates subvert democratic norms, restrict participatory processes of all kinds, coerce civil society, and override institutional checks and balances supposedly secure in legislatures and bureaucracies. They curtail judicial independence, harass the media, and suborn security forces. In other words, rulers show more and more contempt for their own nationals, surround themselves with family, lineage, or ethnic allies, and greatly narrow the focus of their concern and responsibility. Many of these arrogant leaders grandly drive down national boulevards in massive motorcades, commandeer national commercial aircraft for foreign excursions, put their faces prominently on national currencies and in private as well as public places, and are seemingly convinced—as was Louis XIV—that the state and the riches of the state are theirs personally to dispose.

A third indicator is derived directly from levels of violence. If they rise precipitously because of conflicts or outright civil war, the state clearly is crumbling. As national human security levels decline, the probability of failure increases. Not every civil conflict precipitates failure, but each offers a warning sign. Indeed, absolute or relative crime rates and civilian combat death counts cannot prescribe failure conclusively. But they do indicate that a society is deteriorating and that the glue that binds a new or an old state is becoming dangerously thin.

There are implicit tipping points. Yet, even as a weak state is becoming a failing state and seemingly plunging rapidly toward failure, desperate descents can be arrested by timely external diplomatic or military intervention. Usually, however, those interventions are too timid and tepid, or much too late. Hundreds of thousands thus die, as in Cambodia, Pakistan, Sri Lanka, East Timor, Rwanda, the Sudan (and Darfur), the Congo, Sierra Leone, Liberia, and Lebanon. Many thousands of others flee their homes for sanctuaries or refugee camps. In 2010, Afghanistan and Pakistan were experiencing some of this flight, and killings, if on a reduced scale.

There is a better way, and Responsibility to Protect in theory offers a firm guide to what is needed and should be done. Under the two governing paragraphs in the 2005 UN General Assembly document, a responsibility to protect would be triggered by a secretary-general's request to the UN Security Council. That would condition a strengthened UN security apparatus, and an enlarged Department of Peacekeeping Operations, to intervene diplomatically and militarily if and when nation-states should slip toward failure. There would thus be a proactive accelerator for action. Doing so now depends more on individual national initiative than on the UN, as witnessed after the Burmese cyclone, the 2007 Kenyan election, or the 2008 second Zimbabwean election. If Responsibility to Protect is developed, the importance of sovereignty will be balanced judiciously against the need to protect innocent lives in nation-states that are failing.

If nation-states do continue to stumble and fail, as they will, then world order has a responsibility to resuscitate and reconstruct them. In post-conflict situations there is an urgent humanitarian as well as an explicit security need for conscientious, well-crafted nation building, for a systematic refurbishing of the political, economic, and social fabric of countries that have crumbled, that have failed to perform and to provide political goods of quality and in quantity, and that have become threats to themselves and to others. Good governance needs to be reintroduced into polities that have failed. Legal systems need to be recreated. Economies need to be restored.

The examples of Tajikistan and Lebanon, two failed states that have recovered to the point of weakness and strength, respectively, demonstrate that it can be done.[14] Furthermore, the accomplishments of the UN transitional administrations in Cambodia and East Timor, and of the NATO/EU/UN interim administration in Kosovo, suggest that effective postconflict nation building is possible if there is sufficient political will and targeted and well-funded external aid.

Reconstruction

Too often, the reconstruction process is half-hearted or rushed, or both. Interim administrations are understandably anxious to complete their ostensible missions and leave. So they prefer short-term fixes to sustainable, long-term efforts of real nation-building. Effective, enduring resuscitation (as in today's southern Sudan) requires creating or restoring capacities for security, for governance, and for institution building. Doing so often takes a generation or more. In Sri Lanka, this is now a task for the government as it moves Tamils out of holding camps and prepares to return democratic rule, or something like democratic rule, to the Sri Lankan north.

The hierarchy of reconstruction is based on experience and on an understanding of the components of good governance. A lasting cease-fire must be achieved first, before any other improvements can be introduced. An interposing force, or some other buffering method, must be found to sustain the cease-fire, avoid skirmishes, and remove fear. Then it becomes imperative to disarm, demobilize, and reintegrate combatants, a critical endeavor that, if imperfectly accomplished, hinders if not overwhelms other rebuilding initiatives. Mozambique's resuscitation was measurably assisted in the early 1990s by a particularly effective process of demobilization and disarmament; a skillful effort at reintegration was essential to success in Mozambique and to Mozambique's subsequent peaceful political and economic evolution. There, and elsewhere, effective removal of leftover land mines, a thorough collection of weapons caches, and other fear-reduction efforts are critical components of a nation-state's recovery from war; often economic recovery depends on such comprehensive, transparent activities. Reducing the daily availability of small arms—a much tougher and more intractable task—is also critical. Thus effective disarmament—an opportunity missed in Somalia and Cambodia—is fundamental to this stage of recovery. So is a method of reintroducing ex-combatants into civil society and productive agricultural or urban employment—an endeavor of years, not days. In Pakistan these are tasks which are being honored in the breach in 2010.

Before a peace process can be transformed into a rebuilding endeavor, any transitional governing body must be able to deliver the key political good of security. Roads must be made safe for commerce and travelers. In Sierra Leone, only the arrival of British paratroopers and UN peacekeepers restored that failed state's sense of internal security (in 2002). In Tajikistan, Russian soldiers provided the necessary glue in the aftermath of its long civil war. Who will do so in Pakistan?

Without fundamental law and order, nation building is hopeless. But once stability and confidence have been at least partially restored, and citizens begin to have a measure of hope that their lives will improve, transitional agencies and international administrations can together focus on three primary and parallel goals: reintroducing the rule of law, jump-starting battered economies, and rejuvenating civil society. In the economic arena, it is imperative to re-implant fiscal and macroeconomic stability, manage the money supply, pay civil servants and security officers, and put people to work. East Timor, for example, would not have begun to recover if, in the very first weeks after Australian troops restored order in 1999, U.S. officials had not devised a means to employ thousands of Timorese on road, school, and other physical reconstruction projects.

Without such accomplishments, a new probity, and a coming sense of prosperity, the local economy will languish and continue to rely on dubious exports like opium, blood diamonds, and the trafficking of women and children.[15] Equally necessary for economic recovery and societal rebuilding is an enforceable code of laws. Doing so can come in stages, as human and physical capacities are rebuilt, but war-ravaged citizens will tentatively support reconstruction efforts only once they are certain that legal safeguards are in place and that legal redress will be available.

A functioning court system should be among the first political institutions to be reborn. Renewed police efforts are essential. So are refurbished roads and communications networks. Building or repairing radio transmitters, as in East Timor and Congo, is but one example of how the restoration of the provision of reliable information assists the rebuilding and accountability processes. A central bank must be reorganized. Teachers and health workers must be hired and schools and hospitals rebuilt. Together, these and many other critical initiatives will reestablish a sense that a new government exists and has begun to work for, rather than against, a nation's people.

Another critical area of the rebuilding effort involves the training or retraining of personnel: police, judges, bureaucrats, and parliamentarians. The security forces have to be reconfigured. Once, but not before, these advances start to succeed, it will then become important to convene a constituent assembly to write a new constitution (Burma still has no legitimated constitution) and to anoint an indigenous government through well-prepared and well-supervised elections. Rushing forward into such national political contests is inadvisable before peace, law and order, economic recovery, and a capable administration are in place. Restoring the people's trust in the state is an essential platform for successful reconstruction.

When states fail and collapse, the process of disintegration mutilates institutions and destroys the underlying social contract between a government and its citizens. That is precisely why sustained nation building requires time, massive capacity for uplifting and reconfiguring, large sums from outside, debt relief, and serious measures of tutelage. Rich nations must not abandon state rebuilding efforts before the tough work is concluded—before a failed or collapsed state has functioned well for several years and has had its political, economic, and social health restored. The worst enemy of the reconstruction of failed states is a premature exit by international organizations and donors, as in East Timor, Haiti in the 1990s, and Somalia.

South Asia in World Order

Numbers of nation-states will continue in this and succeeding decades to fail, that is, to provide insufficient political goods to their citizens. They will do so by failing to ensure security for the state and for individuals, by abrogating the rule of law, by denying political freedoms and economic opportunities, by crippling infrastructures, and by making the lives and futures of their people physically and socially poorer.

When regimes create civil wars or otherwise prey in this manner on their citizens, world order is seriously compromised. For the sake of world order broadly, and for the general safety and well-being of other inhabitants of the world, it is therefore imperative that the United Nations and regional organizations develop a capacity that none now exercises—to intervene to protect the innocent and otherwise weak inhabitants of such threatened countries. How to generate the international political will sufficient to crack down sharply on regimes that cross a line of good governance is a task for the architects and enforcers of world order. So is defining in broad, acceptable terms where that line should be drawn and how and when its breaches should be condemned.

South Asia is particularly at risk, given the prowess and power of non-state actors in Afghanistan and Pakistan and the failure of both governments effectively to provide qualitatively or quantitatively adequate levels of good governance to their citizens. That failure caps decades of regime failure in Afghanistan and at least one decade of weakness verging on failure in Pakistan. In both cases, as in Bangladesh, governance deficits stem originally from leadership misdirections, not from structural flaws or postcolonial inheritances. Winning the war against insurgents in Sri Lanka should give President Rajapaksa's administration an opportunity to move that nation-state from a position of continued weakness to strength, providing that his administration can build on a newly established security to deliver good governance to all, and not just the major part, of the country. India is a special outlier in the region, with several of its constituent states delivering high orders of political good, others less so, but all within an encompassing framework of security, law, participation, human development, and, finally, sustainable economic opportunity.

Notes to Chapter 2

1. *Foreign Policy* and the Fund for Peace use a perception-based method of assessing state failure. According to their method (critiqued by me in the same issue), in 2009 Burma was the thirteenth most failed state in the world, just after Haiti and immediately before Kenya. See *Foreign Policy* (July-August 2009), 83.

2. Robert I. Rotberg, "The Failure and Collapse of Nation-States: Breakdown, Prevention, and Repair," in *When States Fail: Causes and Consequences*, ed. Robert I. Rotberg (Princeton: Princeton University Press, 2004), pp. 1–45. Originally there were nine categories. Now I use five, encompassing the nine.

3. See Robert I. Rotberg, "Disorder in the Ranks," *Foreign Policy* (July-August, 2009), 91.

4. Rotberg, "Failure and Collapse," p. 3.

5. Ibid, p. 3.

6. Robert I. Rotberg and Rachel Gisselquist, *Strengthening African Governance: the 2009 Index of African Governance* (Cambridge, MA: Kennedy School of Government, Harvard University, 2009).

7. Rotberg, "Failure and Collapse," p. 5.

8. See also Michael D. Barr, *Lee Kuan Yew: The Beliefs Behind the Man* (Richmond, Surrey, UK, 2000), p. 218.

9. Michael Malley, "Indonesia: The Erosion of State Capacity," in *State Failure and Weakness in a Time of Terror*, ed. Robert I. Rotberg (Washington, DC: Brookings Institution Press, 2003), pp. 183–218.

10. Oren Barak, "Lebanon: Failure, Collapse, and Resuscitation," in Rotberg, *State Failure and State Weakness*, pp. 305–340.

11. For elaboration and detail, see the essays in Rotberg, *State Failure and State Weakness*.

12. "Annan's New Direction," *Boston Globe*, July 30, 2005.

13. This and several succeeding paragraphs draw on the argument originally advanced in Rotberg, "Failure and Collapse," pp. 25–27.

14. For these instructive cases, see Rotberg, *State Failure and State Weakness*, pp. 245–264, 305–339.

15. See Robert I. Rotberg, "Renewing the Afghan State," in Rotberg (ed.) *Building a New Afghanistan* (Washington, DC, 2007), pp.1–19.

3 State Formation, Consolidation, and the Security Challenge

Exploring the Causes of State Incapacity in South Asia

Matthew Lange

In this chapter, I investigate how South Asian states affect violence and unrest in the domestic arena. To begin, I describe how states have the potential to affect domestic security by either instigating violence, containing it, or both, and claim that the states in South Asia are implicated in the region's unrest both by instigating conflict and through their inability to contain it. Next, I discuss four general factors that shape the capacity of states to contain domestic conflict—geographic conditions, economic resources, ethno-national diversity, and histories of state building—and apply them to South Asia. While all four help to explain the limited organizational capacities of South Asian states, special attention is given to the historical impact of colonialism. I describe how colonialism affected both the structure of states as well as the ethno-national identities of their populations and suggest that these legacies—perpetuated since independence through path dependence—have posed long-term problems to domestic security. In this way, South Asian states have difficulty meeting security challenges because they were set up to meet particular and outdated challenges (the ones facing colonial rulers), and postcolonial leaders have generally been unable to either implement major state reforms or assuage ethno-national divisions.

States and Domestic Security

Along with capitalism, urbanization, educational expansion, and increased life expectancy, states provide an example of how many non-Western countries have followed the developmental trajectories of the West. First emerging in Western Europe in their modern forms over the past two to three hundred years, they have proliferated into all corners of the world to become the dominant form of political organization. Indeed, clans, tribes, chiefdoms, and empires have all declined, leaving a world divided among and dominated by states.

Different factors have helped to promote the spread of states. Most importantly, European and Japanese colonial powers built states throughout the world as part of their imperial efforts. And, when states were not forcibly imposed on populations, indigenous leaders sometimes purposively imported European models of the state in an effort to fend off colonial aggressors. Noting a famous example, Cumings describes how Japanese leaders made a concerted effort to replicate the German state.[1] They sent officials to Germany in order to study its structure, and these officials tried to reconstruct the German model in Japan. Finally, because states have become the dominant form of political organization, global institutions legitimize them and thereby promote their proliferation.[2] Indeed, the state model is so powerful that groups cannot be recognized internationally without them.

Despite their dramatic proliferation, the world's states are quite varied. Their differences, in turn, have enormous implications on diverse social phenomena. Of interest to this volume, scholars and policymakers increasingly recognize that states affect domestic security in two opposing ways. First, state power is based on force, and state coercion can be exercised in ways that instigate violence.[3] At its most extreme, state actors implement coercive policy that brutalizes the population. The Burmese state's vicious attacks on democratic demonstrators in 1988 and 2007 are two examples.

States can also spark resistance when large segments of the population oppose the implementation of unpopular state policy—be it coercive or noncoercive. Popular opposition to state expansion provides a notable example. Tilly finds that the construction of direct and territory-wide forms of rule sparked the Vendée Rebellion in post-revolutionary France.[4] In a broader study of state building in Europe, he claims that "[r]esistance and counter-revolutionary action followed directly from the process by which the new state established direct rule."[5] Hechter makes similar observations and proposes a general theory about the causes of nationalist rebellion.[6] He recognizes that nationalist movements are recent phenomena and argues that their emergence is linked to the expansion of states with the capacity to interfere in social relations across wide swaths of territory. Such states reduced local political autonomy and sparked resentment, opposition, and thereby violent rebellions throughout much of the world.

Finally, states can instigate violence in ways other than through the implementation of formal policy. Evans and Mamdani describe how official abuse of their positions for personal benefit commonly results in personalized and predatory rule.[7] Under these circumstances, state officials are able to prey on society for personal gain, actions that can be violent in their own right and can, in turn, spark antistate violence. Mamdani, for example, finds that severe violence has been a common outcome of despotic rule by chiefs in sub-Saharan Africa.

Despite obvious and copious examples of state-instigated violence, over the last decade many scholars have paid less attention to the ways in which states promote violence and focused increasingly on the opposite: the role states can play in containing violence in the domestic arena. These works analyze how a state's organizational capacity empowers leaders to contain civil wars, terrorism, revolutions, and other forms of domestic conflict. They recognize that bureaucracy and state infrastructural power are two extremely important determinants of state organizational capacity and help limit violence by empowering state officials to gather resources, coordinate actors, collect information, and penetrate society.[8] Goodwin's analysis of insurgencies in the developing world provides a notable example.[9] He shows that a large and well-equipped military, tax revenue, and bureaucratic organization provide resources that allow states to effectively combat insurgency groups. He also provides evidence that a strong and even state presence (i.e., state infrastructural power) allows the state to act throughout its territory. When combined, the state's institutional resources and territorial reach strongly deter mass revolts and violence by allowing the state to arrest insurgents and cut off resources to rebel groups.

Others also analyze state containment of violence but shift their focus to the rule of law. As Durkheim and Weber both recognize, an effective legal system promotes peaceful social relations by enforcing basic rules of social interaction—such as forbidding stealing and murder and enforcing contracts.[10] Drawing on the Weberian tradition, O'Donnell describes how the rule of law limits violence by placing power in the law, not the individual. As a consequence, an effective legal system helps free people from hierarchical relations of dependence based on overt and systematic coercion.[11]

Although seemingly oppositional, the instigation and containment views of states and violence are compatible, as state action can simultaneously do both.[12] Indeed, if state efforts to contain domestic conflict are extremely coercive and inflict considerable hardship on the population, such efforts might increase support for antistate violence. Moreover, as Tilly and Hechter note, efforts to construct states with high organizational capacities can themselves instigate antistate violence. In this way, a growing or intrusive state presence seems to promote violence in one way while simultaneously providing a means of limiting it in another. States can therefore find themselves with a delicate balancing act or even a catch-22.[13]

All six South Asian countries covered by this volume have been afflicted by different types of civil violence: ethnic conflict, terrorist attacks, separatist rebellions, interclass conflict, banditry, and civil wars. And, as the different case studies in this volume show, the region's states are implicated in the violence—both instigating it in some instances and failing to contain it in others. One must therefore consider factors that caused this common outcome in South Asia.

Factors Affecting State Containment of Violence

The American-led war on terror has caused growing concern about the weakness of states and their inability to contain violence, both domestically and internationally. As a consequence, state building has increasingly become a goal of policy experts. Yet, the construction of states capable of containing violence is a difficult process influenced by a number of factors. Efforts to build effective states are not bound to succeed, and successful cases require favorable circumstances and a long-term effort.[14] For one thing, the balancing act of containing but not instigating is delicate and risky—state officials' attempts at containing conflict through state expansion and increased regulation of social relations can provoke antistate violence. In addition, a review of the literature highlights diverse factors affecting whether state officials are able to build effective states. Among the factors mentioned most commonly are geography, economic resources, societal characteristics, and history.

Geography
One of the key features of modern states is their fixed territoriality, and the geological and environmental characteristics of the territories that states control undoubtedly affect whether states are able to contain violence. In a

well-known work, Herbst suggests that human geography affects state structures and capacities, as certain environments and population distributions make it difficult for states to control their lands and peoples.[15] In particular, he claims that arid and tropical environments have been a major detriment to state building throughout sub-Saharan Africa because they promote relatively small populations dispersed over vast territories. As a consequence, it is not cost-effective to build state infrastructure throughout the territory that is capable of regulating all peoples and providing public goods, leaving large pockets of people outside the realm of state power.

Other environmental arguments focus more explicitly on how the actual terrain affects state presence. Fearon and Laitin find that states with mountainous territories have a more difficult time regulating their populations because mountains are difficult to travel through and provide an advantaged environment to hide from the state and launch rebellions.[16] As a consequence, populations living in mountainous environments often have considerable autonomy from their respective states, and states with large mountainous regions have a higher risk of civil wars. Others with real-world experience noted the importance of mountains much earlier. General Grivas, who studied guerrilla movements and led a guerrilla war against British colonialism in Cyprus during the 1950s, lamented that the landscape of Cyprus was not rugged enough for a large-scale insurrection and therefore decided to organize a smaller movement focusing on the destruction of infrastructure.

Turning to South Asia, environmental factors appear to provide some insight into the region's security problems. Afghanistan and Pakistan have among the greatest security problems in the world, and both also have among the most problematic environments for the construction of powerful states—they have large and sparsely populated regions with rugged mountains. And mountainous regions with limited state infrastructure have created fecund environments for lawlessness and rebellion, as the present severe problems with terrorist groups and insurgencies in Pakistan's Northwest and Southern Afghanistan show. Similar environmental conditions also aided the Maoist insurgency in Nepal over the past two decades, as the mountains helped limit the state's presence and provided the insurgents with an environment that facilitated the avoidance of state control. Alternatively, Bangladesh has the most beneficial environment for state infrastructural power, and it has been the only country in the region to avoid large-scale insurgency movements since its separation from Pakistan in the mid-1970s. Although the war to separate Bangladesh from

Pakistan suggests that this environment did not prevent insurgency movements altogether, the large distance separating East and West Pakistan seems to be another geographical factor that facilitated antistate violence.

Notably, the environmental argument does not hold for Sri Lanka, as the interior mountains have been little used by insurgency movements, and the island's population density and size are quite favourable to the projection of state power despite the fact that the state has at different periods lost control over much of northern and eastern Sri Lanka. Other factors beyond the physical environment therefore appear to be at work.

Economic Resources

A second general factor that affects the construction of an effective state is economic resources, although the literature points to different ways in which resources affect the state's capacity to contain violence. Several recent works focus on the presence of lootable resources—that is, valuable resources that are quite compact and can be produced and traded outside of the state's regulatory reach. The most notable examples of such resources include diamonds and narcotics. These resources supposedly hinder state building because they create incentives for nonstate groups to control the production and trade of these resources and to use extreme force to do so. As a consequence, the state is not able to project its power, and powerful and coercive forces outside of the state are present and compete with the state for dominance.[17] The civil war in Sierra Leone during the 1990s, which saw the state and insurgents fighting over the country's diamond reserves, provides a notable example.

While the presence of lootable resources can be a curse, the lack of resources is also a severe impediment to state effectiveness. Large and infrastructurally powerful states are very expensive to organize and run, making the construction of an effective state a difficult job in a resource-scarce environment. While the scale of the state poses a financial impediment, bureaucracy requires large resources for additional reasons: disciplined state actors are necessary for effective bureaucratic organization, and high salaries help promote the latter. Most obviously, a liveable wage helps limit the need to abuse one's position to acquire life's basic necessities and thereby focuses state employees on state interests instead of personal needs. In addition, and likely more important, high salaries provide the material basis for high status. The latter, in turn, helps create strong occupational norms and an esprit de corps among state employees, both of which increase the likelihood that officials will monitor their own actions as well as those of their peers.[18]

For most of South Asia, lootable resources have not affected the prevalence of domestic conflict. Afghanistan is an exception, as opium production has helped finance insurgency groups, and the state's recent suppression of poppy production helps fuel antistate resentment. Alternatively, all South Asian countries—albeit to different extents—are presently afflicted by poverty, which has obstructed state expansion, promoted corrupt practices, and hindered state legitimacy, all of which limit the organizational capacity of the states. In addition, the Sri Lankan case highlights how the scarcity of jobs caused state employment to be used as a powerful means of patronage, thereby limiting meritocracy, creating incentives for haphazard state expansion, and causing officials to focus on issues other than the interests and needs of the state.

The Population and Ethno-nationalist Identities

Sociologists and political scientists increasingly recognize that the social characteristics of populations affect the capacity of the states that rule over them. Gorski, for example, describes how a disciplinary revolution within Dutch society in the seventeenth century aided state building and enhanced the state's ability to implement policy.[19] Specifically, the disciplined population willingly followed state directives, thereby allowing the state to implement policy without having to actively monitor and coerce the population. Similarly, Putnam finds that the level of civic-mindedness greatly affected the effectiveness of regional state institutions in Italy because it promoted both citizen participation in politics and positive-sum relations between state and society.[20]

Instead of focusing on norms or participation, Smith suggests that the national identities of the population affect state effectiveness.[21] He notes that the states in Western Europe and their settler offshoots have relatively homogeneous populations that share a common national identity. As a consequence, the populations are more likely to accept state authority and support state policy. Alternatively, where populations refuse to either submit to state control or participate in national politics, state officials can have an extremely difficult time projecting their power and regulating social relations. Very localized norms and identities, for example, can cause people to reject state authority and oppose its attempts at establishing a system of rule. Similarly, ethnic diversity can impede the construction of common national identities and lead to ethno-national separatist movements when subordinate communities are alienated from the state.

The states in South Asia generally face considerable social obstacles to state building. Sri Lanka is a notable case in which state building has been very negatively affected by competing national communities, as the Tamil separatist movement waged a war of independence for over 25 years. This movement was sparked by a Sinhalese-dominated state that actively pursued Sinhalese interests, thereby delegitimizing the state in the eyes of the Tamils. Similarly, competing ideas of nation split colonial India in two (eventually three). The remnants of this Hindu-Muslim divide are still felt across the subcontinent, but it is especially evident in India with the ongoing conflict in Kashmir and the recent string of terrorist attacks perpetrated by Islamic groups. Other antistate movements are also present in India. Sikh nationalism in Punjab and nationalist movements in Assam and among the northeastern hill tribes were also motivated, at least in part, by a rejection of Indian nationalism in favor of more localized ethnic nationalism.

While not afflicted by active separatist movements per se, both Pakistan and Afghanistan face their own severe problems. In both, tribal groups oppose state domination and assert their own autonomy, and this environment has promoted tribal competition and violence, attacks on the state, and a fecund environment for Taliban insurgents and al-Qaeda militants.

History and Path Dependence

While the previous three factors focus on general conditions that affect all countries throughout the world, comparative-historical works within both political science and sociology suggest that the particular historical processes through which states emerge have long-term effects on state organizational capacity. Their arguments focus on two things. First, the period of institutional formation is of critical importance, as small disparities in form or sequencing can eventually lead to large differences. The period of institutional origins is therefore profoundly influential.

Next, scholars of path dependence describe how institutions generally reproduce themselves over time with only minimal changes, causing initial conditions to have long-term consequences. Several mechanisms promote path-dependent institutional change.[22] As Mahoney and Pierson note, institutions frequently reproduce themselves because of increasing returns.[23] That is, because many institutions are so large and complex, the cost of major reforms is astronomical and the outcome uncertain, creating a cost-based incentive to maintain the preexisting structure as long as possible. Besides increasing returns, institutions empower some at the expense of others, and different segments of the economic, political, and cultural elites usually benefit from the present institutional order. They are therefore averse to major changes and exercise their power in order to obstruct institutional transformation. Finally, institutions are socializing agents and therefore shape the norms and cognitive frameworks of large numbers of people. As a consequence, actors frequently accept state structure as natural and proper and do not consider alternatives, thereby perpetuating state structures.

Both the critical importance of origins and the tendency of institutional re-production are extremely relevant for states. Their overwhelming size and the fact that they consist of hundreds of interconnected organizations make major state reforms extremely expensive and their ultimate success highly uncertain. Even more, states are the ultimate means of power, causing elites to oppose major state reforms that potentially weaken their positions. Finally, states shape the values and outlooks of both societal members and state officials, thereby creating cognitive blinders that help perpetuate state organizational structures. Along these lines, numerous scholars suggest that state institutional change usually occurs in a path-dependent fashion and that the history of state formation therefore creates obstacles to radical institutional change.[24]

Because of the path-dependent tendencies of states, two historical factors strongly influence the ability of many states to contain violence. First, colonial states frequently had very limited organizational capacities.[25] Second, colonial state-building efforts preceded nation-building efforts. Moreover, colonial officials did not attempt to build a common political community and in fact frequently heightened ethno-nationalist divisions among the colonized. Both features of colonialism have left legacies after independence and underlie much of the violence presently afflicting South Asia.

History of State and Nation Building

As Max Weber notes in his work on the political and economic rise of Europe, parts of Western Europe had particular environments with a number of characteristics that—when combined—instigated a long-term trajectory leading to states with impressive organizational capacities.[26] Indeed, a major contribution of Weber is his recognition that the rise of states in Europe resulted from a unique cocktail of conditions that led to a unique political organization. For one thing, early capitalist development provided resources and personnel that facilitated the construction of large state organizations run by salaried officials. In addition, a very strong and rational legal tradition made possible the rise of rule-based state organizations. Indeed, bureaucracy simply applies laws to organizations, which helps to explain why state officials in early modern Europe were usually well-versed in law. Of equal or greater importance, Weber notes that state formation in Europe occurred in an extremely competitive international environment in which political elites needed to build effective states to conquer or be conquered. The end result was a system of relatively effective states able to organize a modern military, limit internal rebellions, and extract resources. In Charles Tilly's famous words, "war made the state, and the state made war."[27]

Outside Western Europe, state formation occurred in very different environments and in diverse ways. As a consequence, the states that were initially constructed—even if built by Europeans or inspired by the Weberian model—were usually very different, and these variations persisted to different extents due to institutional path dependence. In regions that avoided being conquered or colonized by Western European states, state building was often a reaction to pressure exerted by Western Europe. In Japan and Thailand, for example, major state reforms were implemented in an attempt to stave off foreign conquest, and these reforms were based—to different extents—on the nation-state model that emerged in Western Europe. Elsewhere, state rebuilding occurred when Western European interference helped destroy empires, as illustrated by the Austro-Hungarian, Chinese, and Ottoman Empires.

The most common cause of modern state formation outside of Western Europe was European imperialism. Within the set of former colonies, however, colonially instigated state building took diverse forms, and one of the most important differences concerns the extent of European settlement. In Argentina, Canada, and other settler colonies, the settlers shared ideas with the colonizers about the structure and legitimacy of states and knowingly and unknowingly helped colonial officials to build state institutions similar to those in Europe. In colonies with only limited European settlement and large indigenous populations, on the other hand, states were imposed on the indigenous population by colonial officials, and the goal was rarely the transfer of a state based on the European model (although this did occur in some colonies) but the coercive imposition of their authority over large populations in an attempt to extract wealth while using as few resources as possible. The end result was frequently a minimal state consisting of a hodgepodge of agents of colonial control—state officials, missionaries, indigenous intermediaries, plantation owners, capitalists, and so on. In this way, the infrastructural power of the colonial state was usually quite limited, state officials depended on nonstate or quasi-state actors, and state power was diffuse and took different forms. Moreover, the use of numerous actors within a minimal state

resulted in the state's dependence on diverse principles of organization—
coercion, capitalism, faith, patrimonialism—that were frequently at odds
with bureaucratization. Under these circumstances, the states emerging from
nonsettler colonialism were commonly characterized by divided authority
and a fissiparous and incoherent organizational structure.

Along with their basic structures, the states that emerged in Western Europe were also quite unique in that state building and nation building generally occurred either simultaneously or in close proximity to one another.[28]
Specifically, state officials proved relatively successful at shaping the identities of their subjects, thereby helping to construct common ideas of political
community. To do so, they used different techniques: state-sponsored education emphasizing the national community and a common culture and history; the state imposition of a national language; state-sponsored rituals that
emphasized common national identity; the construction of national infrastructure and markets that facilitated transportation, communication, and
exchange; and the exclusion, expulsion, and murder of the "other." These
state-sponsored efforts were rarely, if ever, completely successful, and state
and nation building proved long and violent processes. Even today, competing
ideas of the nation persist in nearly all Western European countries (i.e., Cor-
sican nationalism in France, Scottish nationalism in Great Britain, and Basque
nationalism in Spain). Despite such difficulties, state-led nation building was
relatively successful in Western Europe because of an advantageous situation:
the idea of a nation was only emerging at the time that state-building nationalism was being implemented, causing the relative weakness of competing national identities within the populations. Moreover, state building in Western
Europe generally occurred over such a long period of time that local identities
had time to break down and merge into a larger national identity.

In former settler colonies, state building and nation building also occurred either simultaneously or in close proximity to one another, and their
populations today generally share common ideas of nation. In nonsettler
colonies, however, state building was rapid and almost always occurred long
before any attempt at nation building. Indeed, colonial officials rarely tried
to create a common political identity among the inhabitants and constantly
emphasized that the colonizers and the colonized were inherently different
and members of different races, let alone nations. Because of this political
exclusion and separation, colonialism frequently alienated the colonized from
the emerging state structure.

Even more detrimental to the construction of national identities than the division between the colonized and the colonizers was that the colonizers frequently heightened ethnic and racial differences among the colonized. Most notably, the colonizers sometimes pitted different groups against one another in a strategy of divide and rule. For example, Belgian colonial officials helped construct Hutu and Tutsi identities and collaborated with the minority Tutsis in order to limit local opposition to colonial rule. As a consequence, very strong and oppositional ethno-nationalist identities were formed during colonialism, and these opposing identities helped fuel ethnic conflict and genocide.[29] Along these same lines, Carroll claims that divide and rule "was the story of the British Empire's success, and its legacy of nurtured local hatreds can be seen wherever the Union Flag flew, from Muslim-Hindu hatred in Pakistan and India, to Catholic-Protestant hatred in Ireland, to . . . Jew-Arab hatred in Modern Israel."[30]

Even when divide-and-rule policies were not employed, colonialism still had the potential to be much more of a disintegrating than an integrating force because of a common policy of recognizing cultural difference and institutionalizing community-based institutions. According to some, colonial officials institutionalized communal identities because they saw them as natural; the colonial mindset focused on racial difference and hierarchy, and colonial officials and anthropologists therefore attempted to categorize their subjects accordingly.[31] Along these lines, Abernethy claims that British colonialism "formally acknowledged differences of religion, language, continental origin, culture, and political tradition among its non-European subjects," a general policy that "reinforced diversity, as groups became more conscious of their separate identities and interests."[32]

Thus, weak states and states with borders that do not coincide with any popular idea of nation are common legacies of colonialism. Both, in turn, appear to promote violence, as states with limited organizational capacity have difficulty containing ethnic conflict and insurgency, and a mismatch between state and nation frequently promotes state coercion and ethnic rebellion. As described below, this dual legacy helps explain South Asia's domestic security problems.

State and Nation Building in South Asia

In South Asia, the particular histories of state and nation building appear to have had powerful and long-term effects on domestic security. Although

Afghanistan and Nepal avoided formal overseas colonialism, the remaining countries of South Asia were part of the British Empire, and the colonial roots of both state and nation continue to hinder the capacity of the region's post-colonial states to contain domestic unrest.

The Indian colonial state—which ruled over Bangladesh, Burma (until 1937), India, and Pakistan—attracted the best administrators from Great Britain, a supposedly incorruptible group of Cambridge and Oxford graduates who shared a common esprit de corps and formed the apex of the state bureaucratic machine. As a consequence, colonial India is often described as having had a very effective state. While relatively large in absolute terms, the central state was minuscule in relation to the size of the population—on a per capita basis, colonial India had five times fewer colonial officials than colonial Nigeria, which had the smallest number of administrators per capita in all of British Africa.[33] The central state's tiny size, in turn, prevented it from reaching down to the local level and necessitated additional tiers of colonial control that depended on local intermediaries. Some of these collaborative forms of rule were formally recognized as indirect rule, while others were categorized as direct despite sharing some telltale signs of indirect rule (i.e., administrative dependence on patrimonial collaborators). Whether classified by colonial officials as direct or indirect, all forms of local collaboration severely limited the state's infrastructural power and level of bureaucratization and empowered local intermediaries.

In the areas that were formally categorized as indirect rule, the colonial administration recognized some 600 princely states that comprised approximately two-fifths of the area of colonial India and possessed one-quarter of the population.[34] The princely states had British residents who assisted and influenced the princes, yet the princes were given considerable autonomy, especially during the 20th century as a result of princely opposition to Indian nationalists.[35] As a consequence, the colonial state's presence was often very limited and based more on patrimonial relations than on bureaucratic organization. Although several scholars view the princes as effective traditional rulers, others claim that such a position is overly romantic and nationalistic and overlooks a reality of exploitative relations. Along these lines, Kulkarni describes the Indian princely states as a "wilderness of oppression and misrule": "By guaranteeing protection to its feudatories from internal rebellion and external attack, British paramountcy made it impossible for the ninety-three million people of the states to launch any such struggle for emancipating themselves from capricious and oppressive rule."[36]

In the tribal areas in the northeast and northwest regions of colonial India, different forms of indirect rule were also used. They differed, however, in that the tribes generally maintained greater autonomy, being at times little more than a buffer between colony and noncolony. In addition, they were generally much less centralized than the princely states, as the British collaborated with a number of tribal leaders instead of one princely authority.

The small size and infrastructural weakness of the colonial state forced the British to employ local intermediaries in much of the supposedly directly ruled territories as well. *Zamindars, taluqdars*, and other tax-collecting land-lords are the most notable examples. These colonial agents were supposedly carried over from precolonial times and were employed in approximately 20 percent of colonial India, including most of Bihar, Rajasthan, and present-day Bangladesh. In order to exploit their services, the colonial state gave them personal possession of large tracts of land, the power to collect taxes from the peasants living on the land, and the right to keep the majority of the revenue for personal use. In order to perform their duties, the landlords managed their own patrimonial administrations with multiple layers of assistants and possessed formal and informal power. While this personal system of admin-istration severely limited state bureaucratization and infrastructural power, several scholars agree that the formal and informal powers of the landholders in combination with colonial backing institutionalized their control of hier-archical relations of dependence at the local level.[37]

Major changes have occurred in the subcontinent since 1947, yet the colo-nial origins of the states in Bangladesh, India, and Pakistan are still evident. Although the formal powers of princes, *zamindars*, and other local interme-diaries have been removed, formal state agents remain largely absent at the grassroots level in many areas, leaving large parts of the subcontinent under only limited state control and under the disproportionate influence of local elites and petty officials.[38] The limited ability of the state to project its power, in turn, creates a fecund environment for caste, class, nationalist, and reli-gious violence. In fact, limited state capacity has created a security dilemma: it promotes a nourishing environment for domestic unrest, and state attempts to contain such violence through overt coercion (given the lack of legal-administrative means) only strengthen popular resentment against the state and thereby foment further unrest.

Northeast India provides an example. There, limited state presence made possible prolonged ethnic violence that eventually turned into Bodo and

Assamese nationalist movements. When the Indian state finally stepped in, it did so militarily, given the general ineffectiveness of its legal-administrative institutions in the region. A growing military presence, in turn, has heightened tension between the region's peoples and the Indian state, providing a potential base for continued nationalist violence.[39] A similar yet much more severe situation exists in Northwest Pakistan. Historically, the colonial and postcolonial state had a very limited presence in the tribal areas and an even more limited ability to regulate social relations.[40] This limited presence created an opening for al-Qaeda and Taliban forces in the mid-1990s. Since the September 11, 2001 attacks, U.S. pressure has pushed the Pakistan Government to try to dislodge both groups. Its efforts, based on brute military force, have been unsuccessful and have only intensified local resentment against the government.

Along with the colonial impact on state organizational capacity, deep ethno-nationalist divisions were also a common legacy of colonialism in South Asia. While the hodgepodge of a colonial state was being assembled on the subcontinent, little if any effort was made to integrate the inhabitants of colonial India into a common nation. Indeed, colonial India was divided in so many ways that the colonizers themselves did not view the region in a singular manner, something that helps explain why they decided to separate Burma from India in 1937 and Pakistan from India a decade later.[41] The one major unifying force with the potential to bind the colonized was the nationalist movement against the British. Given the strength and long history of this movement, one cannot deny that some degree of national unity occurred.[42] Yet, as the ultimate dismantling of colonial India shows, centrifugal forces were dominant.

Three historical factors appear to have hindered national integration in colonial India. First, and most basically, the British made no effort to construct a common Indian nationality. In fact, because of the British fear of the nationalists, they actually attempted to limit the construction of a common nationality by encouraging India's princes and Muslims to oppose the nationalist movement led by the Congress Party.

Second, the hodgepodge system of rule created a very divided political structure in which there was considerable local and regional autonomy. Thus, other than an elite administration dominated by British citizens and a legislative assembly during the final decades of colonialism, the colonial state lacked powerful unifying elements. Even more, the colonial use of indirect intermediaries with "traditional" authority—like princes, tribal chiefs, and *zamindars*—helped to reinforce regionalism. The princes of four princely states (Junagadh, Hyderabad, Jammu and Kashmir, and Tripura), for example, strongly opposed union with the rest of India at independence.

Finally, British colonial policy helped to divide the population by promoting distinct and oppositional identities. For example, the line system in Northeast India helped institutionalize economic and political divisions between tribal and nontribal populations. Of considerably greater significance, British colonialism heightened divisions between Hindus and Muslims. Many recognize that there was not a singular Hindu religion prior to British colonialism, as it consisted of a number of related but separate local religions. Through their own misperceptions, colonial officials and orientalist scholars assembled written texts and constructed a single Hindu religion, a task for which they were assisted by Brahmin intellectuals.[43] Thus, by helping to construct a unified Hindu identity, colonialism created the most basic element needed for oppositional Hindu-Muslim identities.

In turn, British policy helped intensify these religious divisions once they were present. After the 1857 conflict between Indians and British, the British dismantled the Mughal Empire and thereby systematically removed Muslims from power. In their place, Hindus were able to usurp many of their positions, creating a religious reversal of fortune that heightened one's awareness of religious identity.[44] Years later, the British switched sides and attempted to weaken the independence movement by collaborating with the Muslim community.[45] First, they helped organize politics along communal lines by instituting communal electorates for local boards in the 1880s, the provincial Legislative Councils in 1909, and the colony-wide Legislative Council in 1919. Once politics became communalized, British officials supported the Muslim League as a counterweight to Congress. Through both, British colonial officials successfully placed religion as a central element of political identity and heightened religious-based political competition.[46] As Breuilly writes, "Muslim nationalism was shaped—indeed, produced—by the structure of the collaborator system established by the colonial state."[47] Similar arguments have been made to explain the rise and politicization of powerful Sikh identities.[48]

Since independence, fractured nationalism has continued and contributed to several episodes of ethno-nationalist violence in India. Both Assam and Punjab, for example, have experienced secessionist violence. Similarly, the Bodo, Naga, and other tribes began violent movements to increase their political autonomy. Finally, violence in Kashmir and the terrorist attacks by Indian Muslims over the past decade highlight the continued impact of Hindu-Muslim divisions in postcolonial India.

In sum, colonialism in South Asia generally constructed states with low organizational capacities, did not attempt to construct unified national identities among the colonized, and actually promoted the rise of oppositional ethno-nationalist identities. Despite the end of colonialism, both have persisted into the postcolonial period. As a consequence, the states have frequently proved incapable of containing violence, and different sorts of conflict have erupted frequently, given the fecund social environments for ethno-nationalist competition. Because of the limited organizational capacities of the states combined with fractured nationalism, efforts by the states to contain nationalist movements have frequently depended on military force, which poses a severe risk of intensifying resentment against state interference.

Conclusion

In this chapter, I recognize the diversity among the world's states and describe how states affect domestic insecurity and violence in two primary ways. First, states frequently instigate violence by either implementing coercive or discriminatory policy or allowing state officials to abuse their positions to prey on society. Next, I describe how states can help to contain violence by providing a rule of law and quelling violence before it gets out of control.

In the second section of the chapter, I explore factors that limit the construction of states that are capable of containing violence and apply these findings to South Asia. I describe three general factors that affect the impact of states on violence: the environment, economic resources, and ethno-nationalist divisions. In addition, I review path-dependent claims that history matters and describe particular aspects of state and nation building that appear to affect long-term trajectories of violence.

While exploratory, the analysis provides initial evidence that the states in South Asia have been important causes of domestic insecurity and that the region faces considerable obstacles to the construction of states that are capable of containing unrest. Moreover, since the factors that affect a state's capacity to contain violence cannot be easily changed, one cannot expect the region's states to rapidly improve their abilities to quell violence. As a result, states will likely continue to promote South Asia's insecurity dilemmas in the near future, if not longer.

Despite such a gloomy conclusion, one must recognize that improvements in state capacity are not unthinkable and can occur without sparking severe social opposition—even in former colonies facing difficult conditions. In both Botswana and Malaysia, for example, rapid and dramatic state expansion improved the organizational capacities of the states despite ominous conditions and did not spark violent opposition.[49] In Malaysia, in fact, the growing organizational capacity of the state proved vital in the defeat of communist insurgents. Three factors promoted rapid and effective state expansion in both cases: growing incentives to transform the state structures, consensus among past rivals about the need to reform the state, and the empowerment of groups in favor of reform and the weakening of traditional elites opposed to it. All three, in turn, promoted a concerted and long-term effort to expand the state.

Considering South Asia, the Indian state has also improved its organizational capacity since independence despite continued weakness throughout large pockets of the country. Such improvements were more gradual than in Botswana and Malaysia and differed in their content. While the reforms in Botswana and Malaysia primarily involved the expansion of the central state, in India such expansion has been more moderate and has been combined with the decentralization of power to the regional state governments. This balancing act between central and regional power, in turn, has helped limit ethno-regional rebellions and thereby keep India intact—a rather impressive feat, given the enormous size and diversity of the population.

Besides India, potential openings might favor rapid state building elsewhere in South Asia in the near future. The cessation of the Maoist insurgency in Nepal and their present participation in formal politics might offer the consensus needed to implement state-building reforms should there be the will for such reforms. In Sri Lanka, despite decades of civil war, the government's recent defeat of the LTTE might create an opportunity for peace and state reform. Thus, although the construction of states with greater capacities to limit domestic unrest is bound to be a difficult process in South Asia, it is not impossible, and there are reasons to believe that rapid improvements can be made, given the right circumstances and astute leadership.

Notes to Chapter 3

1. Bruce Cumings, "State Building in Korea: Continuity and Crisis," in *States and Development: Historical Antecedents of Stagnation and Advance*, ed. Matthew Lange and Dietrich Rueschemeyer (New York: Palgrave Macmillan, 2005), pp. 211–235.

See also, John A. Hall, "Nation-States in History," in *The Nation-State in Question*, eds., T. V. Paul, G. John Ikenberry, and John A. Hall (Princeton: Princeton University Press, 2003), pp. 1–26.

2. John Meyer, et al., "World-Society and the Nation-State," *American Journal of Sociology*, 103 (1997), pp. 144–181.

3. See Mahmood Mamdani, *Citizen and Subject* (Princeton: Princeton University Press, 1996); William Reno, *Corruption and State Politics in Sierra Leone* (New York: Cambridge University Press, 1995); James Scott, *Seeing Like a State: How Certain Schemes to Improve the Human Condition Have Failed* (New Haven: Yale University Press, 1998).

4. Charles Tilly, *The Vendée* (Cambridge, MA: Harvard University Press, 1964).

5. Charles Tilly, *Coercion, Capital, and European States, AD 990–1992* (Cambridge, MA: Blackwell, 1992), p. 110.

6. Michael Hechter, *Containing Nationalism* (New York: Oxford University Press, 2000).

7. Peter Evans, *Embedded Autonomy: States and Industrial Transformation* (Princeton: Princeton University Press); Mamdani, *Citizen and Subject*.

8. James Fearon and David Laitin, "Ethnicity, Insurgency, and Civil War," *American Political Science Review* 97, no. 1 (2003), pp. 75–90; Jack Goldstone, et al, "State Failure Task Force Report: Phase III Findings" (McLean, VA: Science Applications International Corporation, 2000), http://globalpolicy.gmu.edu/pitf/SFTF%20 Phase%20III%20Report%20Final.pdf ; Theda Skocpol, *States and Social Revolutions* (New York: Cambridge University Press, 1979).

9. Jeff Goodwin, *No Other Way Out: States and Revolutionary Movements, 1945– 1991* (New York: Cambridge University Press, 2001).

10. Emile Durkheim, *The Division of Labor in Society* (New York: Free Press, 1984); Max Weber, *Economy and Society* (New York: Bedminster Press), p. 668.

11. Guillermo O'Donnell, "On the State, Democratization and Some Conceptual Problems," *World Development* 21, no. 8 (1993), pp. 1355–1369.

12. Matthew Lange and Hrag Balian, "Containing Conflict or Instigating Unrest? A Test of the Effects of State Infrastructural Power on Civil Violence," *Studies in Comparative International Development* 43, nos. 3–4 (2008), pp. 314–333.

13. For example, efforts to increase the state's capacity to contain violence through military expansion might do more harm than good. If military force is the only option, however, recognition that coercive state action frequently sparks anti-state sentiments and violence suggests that military action must be combined with some sort of "hearts and minds" campaign and must make a concerted effort to limit civilian hardship and casualties. The failure to do just this appears to be at the heart of American difficulties in Afghanistan and Iraq. See Lange and Balian, "Containing Conflict."

14. Matthew Lange and Dietrich Rueschemeyer, *Historical Antecedents of Stagnation and Advance* (New York: Palgrave Macmillan), 2005.

15. Jeffrey Herbst, *States and Power in Africa: Comparative Lessons in Authority and Control* (Princeton: Princeton University Press, 2000).

16. Fearon and Laitin, "Ethnicity."

17. Paul Collier, "Economic Causes of Civil War and Their Implications for Policy," in *Managing Global Chaos*, ed. Chester A. Crocker, Fen Osler Hampson, and Pamela Aall (Washington, DC: United States Institute of Peace Press, 2000); Fearon and Laitin, "Ethnicity"; Reno, *Warlord Politics*; Richard Snyder and Ravi Bhavnani, "Diamonds, Blood, and Taxes: A Revenue-Centered Framework for Explaining Political Order," *Journal of Conflict Resolution* 49, no. 4 (2005), pp. 563–597.

18. Dietrich Rueschemeyer, *Power and the Division of Labor* (Stanford, CA: Stanford University Press, 1986), p. 60; Philip Gorski, "The Protestant Ethic Revisited: Disciplinary Revolution and State Formation in Holland and Prussia," *American Journal of Sociology* 99, no. 2 (1993), pp. 265–316.

19. Philip Gorski, "Protestant Ethic."

20. Robert Putnam, *Making Democracy Work* (Princeton, NJ: Princeton University Press, 1993).

21. Anthony Smith, "State-Making and Nation-Building," in *States in History*, ed. John A. Hall (New York: Basil Blackwell, 1986), pp. 228–263.

22. For a general discussion of mechanisms promoting path dependence, see James Mahoney, "Path Dependence in Historical Sociology," *Theory and Society* 29, no. 4 (August 2000), 507–548.

23. Mahoney, "Path Dependence"; Paul Pierson, *Politics in Time: History, Institutions, and Social Analysis* (Princeton: Princeton University Press, 2004).

24. Daron Acemoglu, Simon Johnson, and James Robinson, "Colonial Origins of Comparative Development: An Empirical Investigation," *American Economic Review* 91, no. 5 (2001), pp. 1369–1401; Daron Acemoglu, Simon Johnson, and James Robinson, "Reversal of Fortune: Geography and Institutions in the Making of the Modern World Income Distribution," *Quarterly Journal of Economics* 117, no. 4 (2002), pp. 1231–1294; Matthew Lange, *Lineages of Despotism and Development: British Colonialism and State Power* (Chicago: University of Chicago Press, 2009); Lange and Rueschemeyer, *States and Development*; Douglass North, *Institutions, Institutional Change, and Economic Performance* (New York: Cambridge University Press, 1990).

25. Notably, several colonial states had considerable organization capacities. For an analysis of the diverse organizational capacities of the colonial states within the British Empire, see Lange, *Lineages of Despotism*.

26. Weber, *Economy and Society*.

27. Charles Tilly, "Reflections on the History of European State-Making," in *The Formation of National States in Western Europe*, ed. Charles Tilly (Princeton: Princeton University Press, 1975), p. 42. As Tilly recognizes elsewhere, however, the link between warfare and state building in Europe depended on the specific historic context, as modern weaponry and readily available international aid and finance presently diminish the need to create a large state able to regulate social relations, raise a large army, and buy of its citizens through public goods, creating incentives for a militarily coercive state instead. See Tilly, *Coercion*.

28. John Breuilly, *Nationalism and the State*, 2nd ed. (Chicago: University of Chicago Press, 1993); Smith, "State-Making"; Eugen Weber, *Peasants into Frenchmen: The*

Modernization of Rural France, 1870–1914 (Stanford, CA: Stanford University Press, 1976).

29. Mahmood Mamdani, *When Victims Become Killers* (Princeton: Princeton University Press, 2001).

30. James Carroll, *Constantine's Sword: The Church and the Jews* (Boston: Houghton Mifflin, 2001), 81–82.

31. Zaheer Baber, "'Race,' Religion, and Riot: The 'Racialization' of Communal Conflict in India," *Sociology* 38, no. 4 (2004), pp. 701–718; Richard King, "Orientalism and the Modern Myth of 'Hinduism,'" *Numen* 46, no. 2 (1999), pp. 146–185.

32. David Abernethy, *The Dynamics of Global Dominance: European Overseas Empires, 1415–1980* (New Haven: Yale University Press, 2000), p. 160.

33. Michael Fisher, *Indirect Rule in India: Residents and the Residency System, 1764–1858* (Delhi: Oxford University Press, 1991), p. 8.

34. B. B. Misra, *The Unification and Division of India* (Delhi: Oxford University Press, 1990), p. 15.

35. Simon Smith, *British Relations with the Malay Rulers from Decentralization to Malayan Independence, 1930–1957* (Singapore: Oxford University Press, 1995), p. 20.

36. V.B. Kulkarni, *British Dominion in India and After* (Bombay: Bharatiya Vidya Bhavan, 1964), pp. 153–154.

37. Ram Gopal, *British Rule in India: An Assessment* (New York: Asia Publishing House, 1963); Atul Kohli, *The State and Poverty in India: The Politics of Reform* (New York: Cambridge University Press, 1987); Anand Kumar, *State and Society in India: A Study of the State's Agenda-Making, 1917–1977* (New Delhi: Radiant Publishers, 1989); Barrington Moore, *Social Origins of Dictatorship and Democracy: Lord and Peasant in the Making of the Modern World* (Boston: Beacon Press, 1966).

38. Stuart Corbridge, Glyn Williams, Manoj Srivastava, and Rene Veron, *Seeing the State: Governance and Governmentality in India* (New York: Cambridge University Press, 2005).

39. Sanjib Baruah, *Durable Disorder: Understanding the Politics of Northeast India* (New York: Oxford University Press, 2005).

40. Hugh Beatie, *Imperial Frontier: Tribe and State in Waziristan* (Richmond, UK: Curzon Press, 2002).

41. Moreover, there was discussion among officials of separating the tribal areas of Northeast India and potentially merging them with northern Burma, thereby creating a separate colony.

42. Some suggest there is more national unity in India than commonly assumed. See Alfred Stepan, "Comparative Theory and Political Practice: Do We Need a 'State-Nation' Model as Well as a 'Nation-State' Model?" *Government and Opposition* 43, no.1 (2008), 1–25.

43. King, "Orientalism"; Ashis Nandy, *The Intimate Enemy: Loss and Recovery of Self Under Colonialism* (Oxford: Oxford University Press, 1983).

44. R. Coupland, "Hindu-Moslem Antagonism," in *The British in India: Imperialism or Trusteeship?* ed. M. D. Lewis (Boston: D.C. Heath, 1962), pp. 77–80.

45. Stephen Koss, "John Morley and the Communal Question," *Journal of Asian Studies* 26, no. 3 (1967), pp. 381–387.

46. Breuilly, *Nationalism*; G. R. Thursby, *Hindu-Muslim Relations in British India* (Leiden, Netherlands: E. J. Brill, 1975).

47. Breuilly, *Nationalism*, p. 214.

48. Tony Ballantyne, *Between Colonialism and Diaspora: Sikh Cultural Formations in an Imperial World* (Durham, NC: Duke University Press, 2006).

49. Matthew Lange, "Developmental Crises: A Comparative-Historical Analysis of State Building in Colonial Botswana and Malaysia," *Commonwealth and Comparative Politics* 47, no. 1 (2009), pp. 1–27.

4 State, Nations, and the Regional Security Order of South Asia

Benjamin Miller

Questions of regional war and peace have assumed crucial importance in the post–cold war era due to the growing salience of regional conflicts, with the end of the superpower rivalry, and their potential implications for international stability. The events of September 11, 2001 show, moreover, that the relationship between global security, U.S. national security, and regional conflicts (e.g., neighbors' intervention in the domestic affairs of Afghanistan or the India-Pakistan rivalry over Kashmir) is as tight as it was during the cold war, if not more so. The result is that the sources of regional conflicts, and regional peacemaking and resolution of such conflicts, must be addressed not only because of their intrinsic importance but also because they bear directly on key issues of international security. Indeed, South Asia might serve as a prominent example where domestic and transborder issues—such as ethnic cleavages in Pakistan and Afghanistan and their spillover to neighboring states, the control by the Pakistani and Afghan governments of their respective border areas, the domestic situation in India's Kashmir, or the question of the internal stability of a nuclear state like Pakistan—affect the regional and international realms.[1]

Thus, two key questions are addressed here both theoretically and empirically: (a) what are the substantive causes of regional war and peace? and, (b) could these causes help us better explain the war-proneness of South Asia since decolonization?

A number of recent books have made important contributions to our understanding of the great variety of regional orders emerging in the post–cold war era.[2] These works serve as a useful antidote to purely systemic analyses and especially to the widely assumed increasing globalization of world affairs.[3] However, they fail to develop a coherent theory of regional orders that would make sense of regional war and peace. The related useful literatures on territorial conflicts,[4] enduring rivalries,[5] and civil and ethnic conflicts[6] focus mostly on the dyadic level rather than on the regional one. Developing a coherent theory of regional security, therefore, is the key objective of this paper.[7] South Asia is used in order to illustrate this chapter's key theses.

I argue in this chapter that the most powerful explanation of regional war and peace is based on the introduction of *the state-to-nation imbalance* in a certain region as the key underlying cause of regional war propensity. I use the state-to-nation balance in two novel ways; both in conceptualizing it as a regional cause and in using it to account for regional outcomes.[8] The state-to-nation balance incorporates two key factors: state strength and national congruence, or the extent to which a given state has a monopoly over the means of organized violence, and whether the borders of a given state coincide with the national identification of its inhabitants, respectively. Thus, the key issues that explain states' and regions' war and peace propensity are related to state-to-nation elements, whereas other possible causes (such as the balance of power, economic decline/prosperity, democratization) are proximate causes.

To illustrate the theory, I look at South Asia and show that regional and domestic elements of the state-to-nation model best account for South Asia's war propensity. I focus mainly on the India-Pakistan rivalry over Jammu and Kashmir and the case of Afghanistan to show that a severe regional state-to-nation imbalance-which mostly includes ethno-national, tribal, and ideological issues-coupled with either strong states or weak states, better accounts for the war-proneness of South Asia. The analysis of South Asia also demonstrates why and how state-to-nation challenges are interrelated and hence affect all the actors in the region.

The chapter continues as follows: The first section introduces the state-to-nation balance and operationalizes the two components that constitute it—state strength and national congruence. The second section presents the key propositions—the causal linkages between state-to-nation challenges and regional violence. The third part discusses the effects of the extent of state-to-nation congruence and of state strength on states' war-proneness. The fourth presents a brief overview of South Asia's security dynamics according to the propositions about state-to-nation balance. Finally, I sum up some of the key findings.

The Explanation—The State-to-Nation Balance as an Underlying Cause of Regional War

The State-to-Nation Balance

The regional state-to-nation balance has two distinctive dimensions. The first dimension refers to the prevalence in the region of strong or weak states. This is the "hardware" of state-building. The second refers to the extent of congruence or compatibility between political boundaries and national identifications in a certain region. This is the "software" of nation-building.

The Extent of State Strength (or the Success of State Building)[9]

This variable refers to the institutions and resources available to states for governing the polity.[10] Weak states lack effective institutions and resources to implement their policies and to fulfill key functions. Most notably, they lack effective control over the means of violence in their sovereign territory and an effective law enforcement system. Thus, weak states face great difficulties in maintaining law and order and providing security in their territory. This, in turn, severely handicaps the economic activity in these states. They are unable to raise sufficient revenues and to collect enough taxes to be able to maintain an effective bureaucracy and provide even elementary socioeconomic and other vital services to the population (including mail delivery, regular water supply, road network, electricity, education, health care, and so on). Strong states control the means of violence in their sovereign territory and possess an effective set of institutions. Tilly focused on the ability of the state to coerce, control, and extract resources as the key to state-making.[11] Thus state strength or capacity can be measured by the ability of the state to mobilize manpower for military service and to extract financial resources from its society.[12] Per capita income is also a useful proxy for state strength.[13]

The Degree of Congruence (or the Extent of the Success of Nation Building)

This refers to the extent of congruence between the existing division of a given region into territorial states and the national aspirations and identities of the people in the region. It deals specifically with the extent to which the current political boundaries in a certain region reflect the national affiliations of the main groups in the region and their aspirations to establish states or to revise existing boundaries.[14] High congruence means that the regional states (as entities or sets of institutions administering certain territories) reflect the national sentiments of the people in the region (that is, their aspirations to live as national communities in their own states).[15] In other words, there is a strong acceptance and identification of the people in the region with the existing states and their territorial boundaries. Such an acceptance must not be based only on ethnic homogeneity of the regional states; it can also be based on civic nationalism.[16] Civic nations share cultural features but are generally multiethnic in their makeup, most notably in the immigrant societies of the New World (the Americas and Australia) and also in many cases of the state-initiated nationalism of Western Europe. In other "Old World" societies, however, nationalism and ethnicity are more closely related.

A state-to-nation incongruence leads to a nationalist dissatisfaction with the regional status quo. Before I present these challenges, however, two issues must be addressed: the independent measurement of incongruence and under what conditions incongruence results in revisionist challenges.

Avoiding Tautology:
Measuring State-to-Nation Incongruence as an Independent Variable

There are two primary senses in which a region's geopolitical and national boundaries may be *incongruent* in relation to the ethno-national criterion of one state per one nation:

1. "Too few states": A single geopolitical entity may contain numerous national groups. This is the internal dimension of incongruence.
2. "Too many states": A single national group may reside in more than one geopolitical entity. This is the external dimension of incongruence.

Thus, one potential way to measure the regional state-to-nation balance is by combining the effects of the following two measures:

1. The proportion of states in the region which contains more than one national group.
2. The proportion of states in the region in which the *majority* ethnic group lives in substantial numbers; also in neighboring and other regional states, either as a majority or a minority.

The higher the combined effect of the two measures, the higher the state-to-nation incongruence in the region.[17]

A closer look at South Asia reveals that the state-to-nation balance and the two factors that constitute it—state strength and national congruence—have been affecting the region's war-proneness. Whereas India holds many attributes of state capacity, and Pakistan, perhaps, in a limited sense, also can be considered a partially strong state due to its capacity to mobilize its armed forces and its ability to extract revenues from its respective population, states like Afghanistan or Sri Lanka can be considered as very weak. Pakistan might be considered a partially strong state due to its capacity to project power and to engage in external wars, as discussed below, but there are great limitations to Pakistan's state capacity due to its considerable internal incongruence and its related failure in nation building, and the limited control of the central government in large areas such as the Tribal Areas, North West Frontier, North Waziristan, South Waziristan, and also Baluchistan.[18] The extent of the region's national incongruence is also acute since both the "too few states" and "too many states" dimensions exist. There are both elements within national groups, like the Sikhs (who were supporters of the Khalistan movement) in India or the Baluchis in Pakistan who demand some form of national self-determination, and other groups, like the Pashtuns in Afghanistan and the northern areas of Pakistan, that reside in more than one state and aspire to be unified at the expense of the states in which they are currently located, or secede from one state and be annexed to what they consider as their legitimate home, like Muslims in Jammu and Kashmir.[19]

Explaining Variance: Demography and History

There might be, however, variations in the translation of the state-to-nation incongruence to nationalist challenges to the regional status quo. Two key factors—demography and history—affect the likelihood that this incongruence will be translated to nationalist challenges to the existing states system. The first factor is demography, or more precisely, the geographical spread of the national groups in the region. The second factor is the history of the state and the nation in the region; which preceded which, and especially if some ethno-national groups lost the dominance they once held of the territories they now settle, or in adjacent areas.

Demography

The first sense of incongruence—one state with a number of nations—is more likely to lead to secessionist challenges under the following two conditions:

1. Concentrated majorities of ethnic groups (i.e., the members of the group reside almost exclusively in a single region of the state) are more likely to risk violence to gain independence than other kinds of settlement patterns such as urbanites, dispersed minorities, or even concentrated minorities. Thus, the more concentrated the ethnic majorities are in the region, the higher the number of attempts at secession.[20]

2. The state is more likely to oppose violently such endeavors if it is a multinational state which fears precedent setting by the secession of one ethnic group, which would trigger secessionist attempts by other ethno-national groups in its territory.[21]

Thus, the combination of conditions 1 and 2, that is, the presence of multinational states with concentrated ethno-national majorities in a number of regions, is likely to lead to violence as in Chechnya, whereas the binational nature of Czechoslovakia eliminated the fears that following the secession of Slovakia there would be other such attempts. The case of India shows the pattern described above: the state forwards a civic national identity and fears that secession by ethno-national groups, especially if they reside in substantial numbers in a specific geographical location like the Sikhs in Punjab or Muslims in the Indian-controlled areas of Jammu and Kashmir, would create a domino effect and undermine India's strength and control or even dismember the Indian state.[22]

The second sense of incongruence—of a single ethnic nation residing in a number of regional states—poses revisionist challenges if in at least one of these states there is an ethnic majority of this group. It is more likely that such a majority, rather than minority groups, can mobilize the state's resources for its nationalist agenda. External incongruence is also magnified in proportion to the extent of the transborder spread of the national groups in the region; the greater the spread, the greater the imbalance. That is, the spread of a single ethnic nation into five neighboring states creates a greater imbalance in the whole region than the spread into two states, which might create conflict only between those two states.

History
More specifically, this refers to the history of state formation and of national independence.

If the state preceded the nation, it is more likely that there will be state-to-nation congruence; if ethnic nationalism preceded the state, incongruence is more likely. The state has often preceded the nation, notably in the case of Western Europe, where nationalism was initiated by the state,[23] and in the case of the immigrant societies of the New World.[24] In Eastern Europe, the Balkans, and the Middle East, however, ethnic nationalism had emerged before the states system was created following the collapse of the multinational Ottoman and Habsburg empires. Because at least some of the new states' boundaries did not coincide with the preexisting ethnic nations, this led to a mismatch between states and nations in these regions.

The Causal Linkages between State-to-Nation Challenges and Regional War

Figure 4.1 presents the causal relations between incongruence and violence. It especially underlines the role of demography and history as antecedent conditions that affect the impact that the independent variable is likely to have on producing nationalist challenges to the status quo and thus on the likelihood of violence. The leaders of these challenges (state leaders or non-state leaders of nationalist groups) might truly believe in these nationalist causes or manipulate them for their own power purposes because of the popular appeal of these ideas. They will not be able, however, to manipulate these forces unless there are some popular forces and movements in the region who subscribe to these beliefs and are committed to act to advance them. Such forces are going to be stronger, the greater the mismatch between the state boundaries and the nations in the region on the grounds of the preexisting ethno-national affiliation of the population or national-historic rights to the territory.

Antecedent conditions >	*Independent variables* >	*Manifestations* >	*Outcomes*
Demography and history >	The state-to-nation congruence >	Nationalist challenges >	Hot war

FIGURE 4.1 The causal chain between incongruence and violence

Key manifestations of the state-to-nation imbalance include the intensity and level of the presence of each of the following five nationalist challenges in the region: "illegitimate states"; pan-national movements; irredentist-revisionist states; incoherent or "failed" states; and "illegitimate nations." Knowing the figures for each of these components in a certain region does not allow us to predict the precise likelihood of war. Yet, this knowledge enables us to compare the level of war-proneness of different regions. In addition, changes in such figures in a certain region over time allow us to assess the rising or declining likelihood of armed conflict in the region. External incongruence and strong states lead to the first three elements of nationalist revisionism in the region,[25] while internal incongruence and weak states lead to failed states and secession.

The Combination of External Incongruence and State Strength Is Conducive to Revisionism

The presence of relatively strong states that are externally incongruent may lead to the following phenomena.

1. When there is a shared ethnic majority in two or more states, one can expect attempts at *national unification* led by a revisionist state. Such attempts will be supported by pan-national movements which challenge the legitimacy of existing states in the region and call for their unification because, allegedly, they all belong to the same nation and were divided by imperial powers. Examples include movements such as Pan-Germanic, Pan-Arab, and Pan-Islamic, which see the Muslims as belonging to a single *Umma* or "nation" that should unify in a single Muslim caliphate or empire like in earlier "golden" ages of the Muslims, preceding European colonialism. There are Pan-Islamic movements in South Asia in both Pakistan and Afghanistan. The most extreme and violent version is al-Qaeda, whose leadership was located, pre-2001, in Afghanistan under the Taliban and in recent years in the border area between Pakistan and Afghanistan. In this area, the state-to-nation imbalance is especially high. It is nationally incongruent, as the Pashtun tribes there, with their own distinct identities and loyalties, straddle the international border and are not loyal to their respective central governments in Kabul and Islamabad, while the control of the respective governments is very weak.

2. A related phenomenon is the *illegitimate state*—a state whose right to exist is challenged by its revisionist neighbors either because in their eyes the state's population does not constitute a nation that deserves a state of its own or because its territory should belong to a neighboring nation on historical

grounds. Historical examples include the illegitimacy of Bangladesh in the eyes of Pakistan, and to some extent also Pakistan in the eyes of Afghanistan, due to their hold over the Pashtun areas.[26]

3. The *irredentist-revisionist state* claims territories held by other states on the grounds of national affiliation of the population or national-historic rights to the territory. This type culminates in "the Greater State" (such as "Greater Germany," "Greater Syria," "Greater Israel," "Greater Serbia"). The likelihood of this category depends on the presence of political boundaries in the region that cross ethnic nations so that a sizable portion of the ethnic nation is beyond the boundaries of the state which claims to represent this group or is dominated by it. Examples include Pakistan's revisionist aspirations vis-à-vis East Pakistan (i.e., Bangladesh) and vis-à-vis Indian-controlled Jammu and Kashmir.

The Presence of Internally Incongruent and Weak States Is Conducive to Incoherence and Attempts at Secession

1. *Incoherent or "failed" states* are weak states which are also without nations, namely, those states which have failed to build political communities that identify with their states as their national homeland and that accept their territorial identity. These states tend to be both multinational and very poor and thus lack the resources necessary to control the means of violence in their territory and to build effective institutions and coherent nations. Numerous African states belong to this category. Afghanistan and Sri Lanka are key examples in South Asia.

2. *Secession* -is an attempt by dissatisfied stateless nations in the region to fulfill their aspirations for self-determination by seceding from existing state(s). Examples in South Asia include the Tamils in Sri Lanka and the Kashmiris in India (in addition to the irredentist claim of Pakistan vis-à-vis Muslim Kashmir).[27] These attempts at secession might be supported by regional states due to strategic or economic motivations but will especially attract support from states dominated by ethnic kin of the secessionist group.[28]

• • •

Based on these indicators we can distinguish between different regions, both on whether they suffer from a state-to-nation imbalance in general and on the two dimensions of the balance. Thus, South America and Western Europe have lower state-to-nation imbalances than most other regions. Phenomena like "illegitimate states," strong pan-national movements, and the "Greater

State" are almost nonexistent, although some weak states are present in South America and a few illegitimate nations exist in Western Europe.[29] Among the regions with a high state-to-nation imbalance, Africa is notable for its low state coherence due to the combination of internal incongruence and state weakness. South Asia has a high degree of nationalist revisionism and incoherent or failed states due to the combination of both internal and external incongruence, coupled with states with some coercive capacity such as Pakistan and Sri Lanka, and full-blown failed states like Afghanistan.

Regional Effects of the State-to-Nation Imbalance

The two dimensions of state-to-nation incongruence are interrelated and mutually reinforcing. To the extent that a revisionist state calls for the subordination of the regional states to a larger movement or authority, or advocates irredentist claims to the territories of neighboring states, it also undermines the internal coherence and the domestic legitimacy of the other regional states. This is especially so if domestic groups within these states respond to the revisionist calls out of ideological/nationalist conviction or due to economic/political bribes and military assistance offered by the revisionist states. Both settlers and refugees undermine state coherence and encourage nationalist revisionism. Kashmir, for instance, is a good example as most of its population is Muslim but the territory is partly under India's control (the cease-fire of the first India-Pakistan war resulted in nearly two-thirds of Kashmir under Indian's control and one-third under Pakistan's). The irredentist aspirations of Pakistan to annex these territories and people due to majority-majority relations between Muslims in Pakistan and Muslims in Jammu and Kashmir have constantly driven Islamabad toward revisionist ventures like the wars in 1947, 1948, and in 1965. Yet, it also affected India's war-propensity vis-à-vis Pakistan and its unification attempts. Thus, when the Muslims of Azad Kashmir, supported by Pashtun tribesmen, entered the capital, Srinagar, and threatened the maharaja's rule in October 1947, he had no alternative but to adhere to India's demands and allow Indian troops to enter, restore order, and in effect control the area.[30]

Conversely, nationally incoherent and domestically unstable and illegitimate states invite aggression and intervention by strong revisionist neighbors and also "export instabilities"[31] to neighboring states. Thus, domestic attempts at secession and border changes are likely to spill over and involve a number of regional states. Such spillovers may occur through the migration of refugees who seek shelter in neighboring states, or by the incoherent state hosting armed groups with secessionist or irredentist claims which infiltrate into adjacent states. The influx of Muslim refugees from Hindu-dominated areas during the partition of the subcontinent and the consequent demographic and geostrategic changes created strong secessionist and irredentist sentiments all over the region, which constantly spill over to adjacent states. Since Muslims and the large Pashtun tribe[32] transcend Pakistan's border, Pakistan was the subject of irredentist aspirations on the part of the Afghans who desired to annex the Pashtun areas on the Pakistani side of the Mortimer-Durand line.[33] However, Pakistan also considered Afghanistan an illegitimate state, and due to fears of an Indian-Afghan-Soviet alliance during the cold war, it trained and assisted Pashtun *mujahidin* fighters in their campaign against the Soviets.[34]

Terrorist groups may also take advantage of such states. Hosting a terrorist organization may at times be involuntary and result from the incoherence and weakness of the host state. Revisionist states, on the other hand, may host such groups by choice, in order to undermine their neighbors' domestic order.[35] Moreover, irredentist sentiments concerning one national group can be "contagious," diffusing to other groups and states in the region.[36]

To sum up, the state-to-nation balance in a certain region exercises important effects on the balance of power between the status quo states on the one hand and revisionist states and nonstate political movements (irredentist, pan-national, or secessionist) on the other. The greater the state-to-nation imbalance, the more powerful the nationalist-revisionist forces are in relation to the status quo forces in the region and vice versa. Under a state-to-nation imbalance, the supply-demand ratio of states is imbalanced: either the demand considerably exceeds the supply, leading to wars of secession, or the supply exceeds the demand, resulting in wars of national unification.

The State-to-Nation Imbalance and the War Propensity of States

The state-to-nation imbalance affects both the motivation for the resort to violence and the opportunity to do so. National incongruence affects the level of motivation by incorporating substantive issues of war such as territory, boundaries, state creation, and state building. External incongruence, in particular, affects motivations for interstate war related to nationalist revisionist ideologies such as wars of national unification and irredentism. Thus, the state-to-nation imbalance provides an explanation for many of the territorial conflicts among states. The extent of domestic incongruence affects the motivation for civil wars and for wars of secession.

The degree of state strength, for its part, exercises major effects both on the capacity of states to wage international wars as well as on the opportunities to initiate civil wars and for external intervention in the territory of the state. Accordingly, we get four combinations of types of states and types of violent conflicts in which states tend to be involved, if at all.

Table 4.1 shows the combined effect of the two dimensions of the state-to-nation balance on state war-proneness. This combined effect produces four distinctive types of states with regard to their war-proneness. Each one of these types of states has, in turn, distinctive effects on the types of wars in the region. Thus, the question of war and peace in a given region depends on the relative prevalence of each of these types of states. At any rate, the production of four distinctive types of states by the two dimensions of the state-to-nation balance—state strength and national congruence—shows that these two dimensions are generally independent of each other even if there might be some

TABLE 4-1 The effects of the extent of the state-to-nation congruence and of state strength on state and regional war-proneness

	Congruence	*Incongruence*
Strong states	*4* *Status-quo states* Peaceful conflict resolution The Kingdom of Bhutan	*1* *Revisionist states* and nationalist unification; pan-national movements; wars of aggression and diversionary wars
		Pakistan vis-à-vis Jammu and Kashmir, and East Pakistan. (NB: Pakistan should only be considered strong in respect of its external force projection capability.)
Weak states	*3* *"The Frontier state"* Nepal(?)	*2* *Civil War & Intervention in Incoherent/"failed" states—* separatism; security dilemma
		Afghanistan; Sri-Lanka vis-a-vis Tamil secessionism; East Pakistan until 1971; Jammu and Kashmir since 1947.

relationship between them in certain cases. Thus, the production of the four types demonstrates the utility of the distinction between the two dimensions for explanatory purposes.

In cell 1, relatively strong states, which are nationally incongruent, pursue revisionist policies based on the "too many states" logic. There is a widespread national feeling, even if manipulated by leaders for their own political agenda, that the nation is artificially and arbitrarily divided into a number of states. In this nationalist view, the nation should unify into a single state, which would reflect the national aspirations and sentiments of the single unified nation. For this "noble" purpose of national unification, the strongest state of that nation should not hesitate to use force.

A related variant is the "Greater State", claiming territories beyond its boundaries based on the national identity of the people or historical rights. To the extent that the revisionist state has internal incongruence, in addition to external incongruence, its leadership has domestic incentives to behave aggressively and embark on diversionary wars according to the scapegoat theory. Leaders are likely to believe that wars with external enemies will strengthen their state and lead to national unity and solidarity, thus reducing challenges to their leadership and strengthen their hold over power. The policies of, for example, "Greater Serbia," "Greater Iraq," and "Greater Syria" illustrate this state category. This type of state will be able to pursue such irredentist policies only so long as it maintains the monopoly over the means of violence in its territory, is able to mobilize relatively large armies and to raise considerable revenues from taxing its populations, and is able to ensure that overall state institutions function effectively. If state institutions become much weaker and cease to function effectively, the state's internal incongruence might lead to large-scale violence among the rival ethno-national groups in the state, leading these states to move to cell 2—the failed states.[37]

In cell 2, *incoherent* or "failed states" are the combined product of weak states in which there is also a low level of identification of the citizens with the state and with its territorial identity—that is, there are strong aspirations for secession. At any rate, the transborder ties with members of the same ethnic group residing in neighboring states are stronger than the affiliation with the citizens of their own state that belong to a different ethnic group. The weakness of incoherent states is permissive for violent actions of revisionist groups and encourages other groups to defend themselves. Such moves trigger a cycle of escalation, which the weak state is unable to contain because it is unable to defeat or bribe the insurgents.[38] Incoherent states may also bring about challenges to the regional order, even though they are militarily and domestically weak vis-à-vis their own societies. In this case, the eruption of civil/ethnic wars should be expected within these states. This creates a temptation for their neighbors to intervene in these conflicts because of either security fears or a quest for profit. Afghanistan and Somalia are good examples of this type of state.

In cell 3, the combination of congruence and the weakness of the state brings about the "frontier state," which is not fragmented ethnically and nationally, but does not fully control its territory and does not have clearly demarcated boundaries. Regions populated by weak states with state-to-nation congruence, as in cell 3, are still prone to regional wars although they might have the potential for peaceful conflict resolution at a later stage if state building succeeds through the strengthening of the regional states. As long as these states are weak, there is a high likelihood of territorial and boundary wars because the states' control over their territory is incomplete and the boundaries are not fully fixed, agreed upon, or clearly drawn. As a result, there are numerous boundary disputes. This type of state was prevalent in nineteenth century South America until the relative strengthening of the regional states starting in the 1880s.

In contrast, as in cell 4, the combined effect of congruence and strong states results in a much lower likelihood of resorting to violence. As a result of the state-to-nation congruence, states have less motivation to resort to violence and have fewer quarrels with their neighbors. They tend to be status quo states without ambitions of territorial expansion. Thus, mutual fears and the security dilemma are likely to decline. As strong states, they are not only able to negotiate peaceful agreements with regional states but also to maintain their commitments and to guarantee stable peace. Thus, both wars of profit and of insecurity will be less likely, as will be diversionary wars. Twentieth century South America is a good example of the emergence of a dominant status quo orientation in strong and congruent states (mainly Argentina and Brazil).

The State-to-Nation Imbalance of South Asia

The antecedent conditions of history and demography are crucial to understanding the state-to-nation impediments in a region. While I will focus on postcolonial South Asia, it is important to appreciate the legacy and actions of the British Empire and the British East India Company in the region in the colonial era. The divide and rule policies of the Western colonizers as well their bureaucratic apparatus helped to create national identities, often in contention with each other. The division of the region into municipal and administrative units, together with the introduction of modern bureaucratic mechanisms, led to consolidating national identities, such as Hindus versus Muslims, and even affected the class divisions within British India. As British officials understood at the time, to grasp and effectively govern India, they sought to collect information about the caste and religious divisions. To this end censuses were conducted during the nineteenth and twentieth centuries, which further strengthened these divisions.[39]

The departure of the British in 1947 left an acute incongruence that would continue to hinder prospective peacemaking efforts. The *Two Nation Plan* that was conceived by the British and supported by the Muslim League under Mohammed Ali Jinnah (i.e., the Direct Action) also created not only two states based on rival national identities, but also gave rise to national groups with secessionist and irredentist aspirations. The partition of 1947 and the war that followed changed the demographic and geostrategic characteristics of the region. Dividing the subcontinent included the disintegration of the army and state institutions as they were rebuilt especially in the new Muslim state, Pakistan. Around 7 million individuals migrated to Pakistan and 5.5 million Hindus and Sikhs moved to India, whereas between 200,000 and 1 million died in the process.[40] The result was that the region became severely imbalanced both between the new states and within them, which in turn affected the region's subsequent war-proneness.

India endorsed a civic-based national identity, though its nation-building efforts[41] were never successfully completed due to its cross-border ties and its internal incongruence. Internally, India is 80.5% Hindu, 13.4% Muslim, and 1.9% Sikh.[42] Externally, although India's nation-building program intended to encompass all ethnic and religious groups, the cross-border ties of the Hindu majority in India with Hindus in East Pakistan (which became Bangladesh in 1971) and with Hindus in Jammu and Kashmir challenged India's identity. Thus, India had to face both international strife with its Muslim neighbor and separatist ethno-nationalist aspirations at home. A key example of ethno-nationalist threats to India's territorial integrity was the Sikh demand for independence (i.e., Khalistan).[43] Although the Sikh demand was not a serious threat in itself, such a vision would probably have affected Jammu and Kashmir's own secessionist aspirations and thus would have undermined the justification for an inclusive India that is the state of all of its citizens.[44] Of course, there is also a demographic and geostrategic calculation here on the part of India. Encouraging Jammu and Kashmir's quest for secession might result in the dismemberment of India from two key parts that are adjacent to Pakistan, India's antagonist.[45]

Pakistan was established as the home for India's Muslims and thus became committed to incorporate and even annex territories in the region considered to be Muslim. The key issue here was mostly related to demography, especially regarding Jammu and Kashmir, and East Pakistan: "There was a Hindu majority in Jammu in the south, but overall the Muslims of the kingdom [Jammu and Kashmir] outnumbered the Hindus by three to one. By all the logic of partition, therefore, Kashmir should have gone to Pakistan, a country created in the name of India's Muslims."[46] Indeed, the founding father of Pakistan, Mohammed Ali Jinnah, said in August 1947 that "Kashmir will fall into our lap like a ripe fruit."[47] Consequently, Pakistan has always meddled in Kashmir and has provoked the Muslims there to fight against the rulers, such as the maharaja in September 1947. In that case, the North West Frontier Provinces (NWFP) sent supplies and arms, and later in October also troops, to fight against the maharaja, with Pakistani officials collaborating or at least doing nothing to stop the invasion.[48]

Pakistan's external incongruence also affected its war-proneness against India, especially because of its irredentist aspiration toward the whole of Jammu and Kashmir. It is seen in Pakistan's reluctance to fully incorporate Gilgit and Baltistan (also known as the Northern Areas in Kashmir) since they believe such an act ". . . would undermine Islamabad's case that the whole issue of Kashmir should be resolved on the basis of UN resolutions."[49] Since Pakistan was once (though maybe less so nowadays) committed to a "Greater Pakistan" that encompassed all of India's Muslims and Muslim territories, the whole of Kashmir should be annexed to Pakistan as legitimized by the majority of Muslims that reside there.

Another issue refers to East Pakistan, where the population, despite its Muslim heritage, also held strong national sentiments and a sense of community, especially with respect to the Bangali language. Indeed, this issue, which was a problem in Pakistan as well, turned violent in March 1948 after the strict refusal of Pakistan's prime minister to accept the Bangali language, by his asserting that all Pakistanis should speak Urdu. Since East Pakistan was separated from West Pakistan by a huge stretch of Indian territory, Islamabad was anxious about nationalist sentiments there, especially because Hindus were still living there after the partition. In 1971 after a prolonged civil war in East Pakistan and a constant flow of refugees into India, India's Prime Minister Indira Gandhi decided to go to war, with the goal of destroying the Pakistani forces there and helping the Bengalis to establish an independent state.[50] In the Bengalis' fight for independence one can also see how state-to-nation impediments in the region, especially between India and Pakistan, affected the pattern of war even if not directly between the two powers. India did not invade East Pakistan merely because of the influx of refugees but also because of strategic calculations, according to which they could undercut Pakistan's influence in the region. Assisting the campaign for a free Bangladesh became an important Indian strategic interest.

Pakistan had, moreover, to tackle its internal state-to-nation incongruence and its external incongruence, which affected its external policies. Pakistan is dominated by the Punjabi majority and the Urdu language, yet there are several other ethno-linguistic groups in the country that are often dissatisfied with Islamabad's coercive approach. The Pakistani population is 44.68% Punjabi, 15.42% Pashtun, 14.1% Sindhi, 8.38% Sariaki, 7.57% Muhagir, 3.57% Balochi, and 6.28% is from other ethnic groups.[51] Pakistan, therefore, had to address strong tribal movements, which constantly demanded more autonomy, such as Baluchistan in the southwest and the North West Frontier provinces in which Pashtuns reside.[52] As Nawab Akbar Bugti Khan, a Baluch tribal chief, put it, "I have been a Baluch for several centuries . . . I have been a Pakistani for just over fifty [years]."[53] Thus, Pakistan's officials have always attempted to create a Pakistani identity that would suppress subnational aspirations. As a result, Pakistan's internal incongruence has pushed Islamabad to coerce its inhabitants both in Pakistan proper and in East Pakistan into a unified Pakistani national identity where all should speak Urdu and abandon their tribal and provincial affiliations. It might have also led Pakistani's leaders to engage in diversionary conflicts, mainly against India, with the hope of consolidating a Punjabi-Muslim national identity that would suppress all other subnational aspirations.

Today's Pakistan is experiencing strong state-to-nation challenges not only between Hindus and Muslims in the region but also between Sunni and Shiite communities in Pakistan, which have been affected by the Shiite revolutionary ideology spread by neighboring Iran. Major challenges are presented by the independent-minded tribal forces in the NWFP, which lie formally within the state but have strong transborder ties with the Pashtun tribes in Afghanistan.[54] Particularly destabilizing are Islamists and extremists that are allied mostly with the Taliban and al-Qaeda and reside in the border area with Afghanistan. Indeed, this area, which is populated by members of the Pashtun tribe, has been a stronghold of the Taliban and al-Qaeda since the U.S. invasion of Afghanistan in late 2001. Thus, what is becoming a major threat to regional stability is Pakistan's descent into state weakness, if not failure.[55] Islamabad is still a strong center with the ability to mobilize its security forces, yet it is unable to fully control and penetrate all of its territories. The fear is that strong Islamist groups like the JUI (Jamiat Ulema-e-Islam), with support from Taliban fighters and Pashtuns, will continue to undermine Islamabad's control and further weaken Pakistan—a country with nuclear capability.[56]

However, domestic Pakistani instability does not end at Pakistan's borders and has much to do with its external incongruence and rivalry with India. Due to these state-to-nation challenges, Pakistan has assisted many Islamist groups in their fights with India in Jammu and Kashmir and also in Afghanistan (notably, the Taliban), once again due to geostrategic calculations vis-à-vis India. Yet, these efforts have now backfired, as many of these groups are disappointed with Pakistan's alliance with the United States and are therefore willing to undermine Islamabad's control by means of violence. An example of this pattern is the Sipah-e-Sahaba, an organization that has perpetrated numerous attacks against the Shiite minority, of whom 3,600 have been killed during the last decade. Another is the Jaish-e-Muhammad, which has fought against Indian control in Kashmir and has been labeled as a terrorist organization by the United States.[57]

Afghanistan is an intriguing case of state-to-nation imbalance since its external incongruence pushed it toward irredentist aspirations during the late 1940s and 1950. But due to its weakness in comparison with Pakistan, it became the arena for interventions by Pakistan's security and intelligence services with U.S. support, and after the cold war became a hub of Islamic fundamentalism and terrorist campaigns. Once British India was partitioned, only one Muslim state, Pakistan, was established, which legitimized its existence based on a Muslim identity and on its role as *the* sole Muslim homeland in the region. Afghanistan, therefore, was not a legitimate state according to the "too many states" criterion. Afghanistan, in contrast, did not consider its neighbor as the legitimate successor of British India and desired to annex Pakistani territories where its Pashtun brethren lived (the NWFP and North Baluchistan).[58] However, due to the growing strength of Islam-abad, assisted by U.S. support during the cold war, "Pakistan developed a capacity for covert asymmetric jihadi warfare, which it eventually used in both Afghanistan and Kashmir."[59]

Today's Afghanistan displays one of the key state-to-nation challenges in the region—the failed state syndrome. The inability of Kabul to penetrate its society and territories outside the capital, not to mention the poor condition of its infrastructure and institutions, is the result of underlying internal and external incongruence coupled with a failed state. Although the resistance to U.S. and allied military presence contributes to the ongoing violence there, Af-ghanistan had suffered from national incongruence long before the invasion in 2001. Afghanistan has always been a difficult state to govern and control due to its topographical landscape and its ethnically diverse population, and thus was constantly a weak if not a failed state.[60] This in turn attracted outside intervention on behalf of both state and nonstate actors. During the cold war, Afghanistan's *mujahidin* fiercely fought the Soviets, and due to geostrategic cal-culations they were supported by the United States. Once the cold war ended, under the strict and fundamentalist Taliban regime, Afghanistan became the home for Osama bin Laden and al-Qaeda headquarters. Pakistan, for that mat-ter, assisted the Taliban until 2001 by providing them with supplies, arms, and intelligence due to their strategic goals in the region in relation to India.

Conclusions

This chapter argues that national groups that transcend the borders of the states in which they are situated, or states that consist of more than one na-tional group, provide the motivations for the violence of state and nonstate actors. Such geopolitical/demographic constellations are often used by a revisionist leadership to legitimize hot conflicts, wars of aggression, diver-sionary wars, and irredentist/secessionist ventures. Moreover, the ability of states in a given region to penetrate their societies and territories, and the ef-ficiency of their institutions, determine the capabilities and means for violent campaigns. Hence, the combined effect of national incongruence and either strong or weak states brings about rivalry and hot wars—inter-state in the case of strong states (even if only partially strong) and civil war and foreign intervention in the case of weak states.

Specifically, strong states and external incongruence result in revisionist campaigns and irredentist ventures, especially when people affiliated with the majority national group in the state in question also reside in substantial numbers in neighboring states. As noted, Pakistan has some mixed attributes with regard to state strength. On the one hand, it is a strong state due to its capacity to project force externally. On the other hand, it has some important elements of a weak state due to the absence of full control over its territory while facing domestic (and transborder) violent challenges.

The external incongruence of Pakistan, for instance, has driven its leaders to use the stronger attributes of its stateness to constantly meddle in Indian Kashmir, to engage in hot wars with India since independence, and also to interfere in Afghanistan to establish an ally against India or at least to prevent an Indian-Afghan alliance. However, states that still can project military power externally but suffer from internal incongruence are likely to initiate diversionary wars in order to divert attention from domestic unrest and also to solidify a national identity by expressing the common denominator of the society rather than its internal cleavages. Here again Pakistan is a good example since, as the weaker components of its stateness suggest, it had to face domestic unrest from ethno-linguistic groups that either demanded to secede from the Pakistani state, like East Pakistan before 1971 or the Baluchis, or to be unified with their brethren over the border like the Pashtuns. Weak states, conversely, that suffer from national incongruence, and thus become failed states, are likely to become arenas of external interventions by neighbors out of fear, because of ideological/nationalist aspirations, or because of the opportunities they can offer to states or to nonstate organizations such as drug traffickers or terrorist organizations. Afghanistan is a good example of many levels of foreign intervention in a failed state affecting regional and international security in some major ways. To a lesser extent Sri Lanka also displays a weak[61] and nationally incongruent state, where a Tamil minority that inhabits the northwest and northeast of the country has aspired, at least until recently, to secede and establish their own state.

In sum, the extent of the state-to-nation imbalance as measured by national (external and internal) incongruence and different levels of state capacity are the major factors which determine the regional (in)security order in South Asia by producing interstate conflicts, civil wars, and external interventions. Thus, the effectiveness of international cooperation norms is contingent upon an underlying balance between states and nations that is not, at present, favorable to norms of cooperation in South Asia.

Notes to Chapter 4

1. For a discussion of South Asia from the domestic, regional and global stances, see Barry Buzan and Ole Wæver, *Regions and Powers: The Structure of International Security* (Cambridge: Cambridge University Press, 2003), pp. 93–171.

2. See, most notably, Barry Buzan, *People, States and Fear: An Agenda for International Security Studies in the Post-Cold War Era*, 2nd ed. (Boulder, CO: Lynne Rienner, 1991); Brian Job, ed., *The Insecurity Dilemma: The National Security of Third World States* (Boulder, CO: Lynne Rienner, 1992); Mohammed Ayoob, *The Third World Security Predicament* (Boulder, CO: Lynne Rienner, 1995); K. J. Holsti, *The State, War, and the State of War* (Cambridge: Cambridge University Press, 1996); David A. Lake and Patrick M. Morgan, eds., *Regional Orders: Building Security in a New World* (University Park: Penn State University Press, 1997); Etel Solingen, *Regional Orders at Century's Dawn* (Princeton: Princeton University Press, 1998).

3. For an overview of the literature on globalization, see Ian Clark, *Globalization and Fragmentation: International Relations in the Twentieth Century* (Oxford: Oxford University Press, 1997).

4. K. J. Holsti, *Peace and War: Armed Conflicts and International Order 1648–1989* (Cambridge: Cambridge University Press, 1991); John A. Vasquez, *The War Puzzle* (Cambridge: Cambridge University Press, 1993); Paul K. Huth, *Standing Your Ground: Territorial Disputes and International Conflict* (Ann Arbor: University of Michigan Press, 1996).

5. Gary Goertz and Paul F. Diehl, *Territorial Changes and International Conflict* (London: Routledge, 1992); Paul K. Huth, "Enduring Rivalries and Territorial Disputes, 1950-1990," in *A Road Map to War*, ed. Paul F. Diehl (Nashville: Vanderbilt University Press, 1999), pp. 37-72.

6. For recent works, see Barbara F. Walter, *Committing to Peace: The Successful Settlement of Civil Wars* (Princeton: Princeton University Press, 2002), and Monica Duffy Toft, "Indivisible Territory, Geographic Concentration, and Ethnic War," *Security Studies* 12, no.2 (2002/3), pp. 82-119.

7. For an extended discussion and application to a number of regions, see Benjamin Miller, *States, Nations and the Great Powers: The Sources of Regional War and Peace* (Cambridge: Cambridge University Press, 2007).

8. The closest is Stephen Van Evera, "Hypotheses on Nationalism and War," *International Security* 18, no. 4 (1994), pp. 5-39, who uses the term "the state-to-nation ratio." I further develop the partly related concepts of the "state-to-nation balance" and "congruence" and use them, in conjunction with the effects of the great powers, to create a coherent account of variations in regional war and peace; see Miller, *States, Nations and the Great Powers*.

9. On state-building, see Joel S. Migdal, *Strong Societies and Weak States: State-Society Relations and State Capabilities in the Third World* (Princeton: Princeton University Press, 1988); Ayoob, *Third World*.

10. On institutionalization as a key to political development, see Samuel P. Huntington, *Political Order in Changing Societies* (New Haven: Yale University Press,

1968). See also J. P. Nettl, "The State as a Conceptual Variable," *World Politics* 20, no. 4 (July 1968), pp. 559-592, who developed the concept of "stateness"—the institutional centrality of the state; for a recent review of stateness, see Peter Evans, "The Eclipse of the State? Reflections on Stateness in an Era of Globalization," *World Politics* 50, no.1 (October 1997), pp. 68-82.

11. Charles Tilly, "Reflections on the History of European State-Making," and "Western State-Making," in *The Formation of National States in Western Europe*, ed. Charles Tilly (Princeton: Princeton University Press, 1975).

12. See Gregory F. Gause, "Sovereignty, Statecraft, and Stability in the Middle East," *Journal of International Affairs* 45 (1992), p. 457, and the references he cites.

13. James D. Fearon and David D. Laitin, "Ethnicity, Insurgency, and Civil War," *American Political Science Review* 97, no. 1 (2003), pp. 75-90, especially 80. See also the indicators in Robert I. Rotberg, ed., *State Failure and State Weakness in a Time of Terror* (Washington, DC: Brookings Institution Press, 2003), pp. 4–22.

14. This section draws especially on Van Evera, "Hypotheses." See also James Mayall, *Nationalism and International Society* (Cambridge: Cambridge University Press, 1990); Buzan, *People, States and Fear*; Michael Brown, ed., *Ethnic Conflict and International Security* (Princeton: Princeton University Press, 1993), and Brown, ed., *The International Dimensions of Internal Conflict* (Cambridge, MA: MIT Press, 1996).

15. On the definition of state and nation, see Ernest Gellner, *Nations and Nationalism* (Oxford: Blackwell, 1983), pp. 3–7; Walker Connor, *Ethnonationalism: The Quest for Understanding* (Princeton: Princeton University Press, 1994), pp. 90–117); Anthony D. Smith, *The Nation in History* (Hanover, NH: University Press of New England, 2000), p. 3; and especially Lowell W. Barrington, "'Nation' and 'Nationalism': The Misuse of Key Concepts in Political Science," *PS: Political Science & Politics* 30 no. 4 (1997), pp. 712–716, who emphasizes "the belief in the right to territorial self-determination for the group" as a central part of the definition of a "nation" which is crucial for distinguishing nations from other collectivities. While many groups hold common myths, values, and symbols (including ethnic groups), nations are unified by a sense of purpose: controlling the territory that the members of the group believe to be theirs. As Gellner suggests, "nationalism" is "a political principle, which holds that the political and the national unit should be congruent"; see Gellner, *Nations and Nationalism*, p. 1. Thus, nationalism is the active pursuit of control by a national group over the territory which it defines as its homeland. As a result, every nationalist movement involves the setting of territorial boundaries (Barrington, "'Nation' and 'Nationalism,'" p. 714), and national conflicts must involve disputes over territory to be truly "national."

16. Civic nationalism focuses on citizen identification with the nation-state at its current territorial boundaries as opposed to a loyalty based on subnational or transborder ethnic ties that may challenge the existing boundaries. In ethnic nationalism, based on lineage and common ancestry, the nation precedes the state (the "German model"), whereas in the civic version, the state precedes the nation (the "French model"). See Rogers Brubaker, *Nationalism Reframed: Nationhood and the National Question in the*

New Europe (Cambridge: Cambridge University Press, 1996). On the distinction between ethnic and civic nationalism, see Anthony Smith, "State-Making and Nation-Building," in *States in History*, ed. John Hall (Oxford: Basil Blackwell, 1986), and Liah Greenfeld, *Nationalism: Five Roads to Modernity* (Cambridge: Harvard University Press, 1992). For a useful overview, see Charles A. Kupchan, ed., *Nationalism and Nationalities in the New Europe* (Ithaca: Cornell University Press, 1995), chapter 1.

17. For example, in region A there are ten states. Seven of them are multinational, while in eight of them there is at least one majority ethno-national group that resides also in other regional states. In region B there are also ten states, of which six are multinational, and in only two of the regional states lives a majority national group that also inhabits other states in the region. The combined s/n measure for region A is 7+8/10 = 15/10; the combined s/n for region B is 6+2/10 = 8/10. Thus, the s/n imbalance is much higher in region A than in region B.

18. It should be noted that both India and Pakistan are far from the Western European model of stateness yet are able to operate as unitary actors in the international realm and thus carry some elements of state strength. For an alternative measurement of the region's stateness levels see Foreign Policy and the Fund for Peace, "The Failed States Index 2008," *Foreign Policy* (July/August 2008), 64–68.

19. On the Pashtuns' national aspirations and other groups in Pakistan, see Grare Frederic, *Pakistan: In the Face of the Afghan Conflict 1979–1985* (New Delhi: India Research Press, 2003), pp. 3–14. On the Sikh question, see Ian Talbot, *India and Pakistan* (Oxford: Oxford University Press, 2000), pp. 265–273.

20. On the effects of settlement patterns on the inclination, legitimacy, and capacity of ethnic groups to secede, see Toft, "Indivisible Territory." See also Ted Robert Gurr, *Peoples Versus States: Minorities at Risk in the New Century* (Washington, DC: United States Institute of Peace Press, 2000), pp. 75–6.

21. See Toft, "Indivisible Territory," pp. 95–96 on the importance of precedent-setting logic. See also Barbara F. Walter, "Explaining the Intractability of Territorial Conflict," *International Studies Review* 5, no. 4 (2003), pp. 137-153.

22. See Talbot, *India and Pakistan*, pp. 265–273, and M.J. Akbar, *India: The Siege Within*, rev. ed. (New Delhi: UBS Publishers, 1996), pp. 93–95.

23. L. E. Cederman, *Emergent Actors in World Politics: How States and Nations Develop and Dissolve* (Princeton: Princeton University Press, 1997), p. 142, and Charles Tilly, *Coercion, Capital, and European States, AD 990–1992* (Oxford: Blackwell, 1992).

24. Michael Walzer, *On Toleration* (New Haven: Yale University Press, 1997), 30–35.

25. On revisionist territorial demands among states, see Goertz and Diehl, *Territorial Changes*, pp. 23–25.

26. On Bangladesh see Talbot, *India and Pakistan*, pp. 251–259. On the 1971 war between India and Pakistan, due to the secessionist attempts of the Bengali movement, see Prakash Chander, *India and Pakistan: Unending Conflict* (New Delhi: A.P.H. Publishing Corporation, 2003), vol. I, pp. 217–256. For more on the Pashtuns see Grare Frederic, *Pakistan*, pp. 3–5.

27. For a comprehensive list, see Gurr, *Peoples Versus States.*

28. Stephen M. Saideman, *The Ties That Divide: Ethnic Politics, Foreign Policy, and International Conflict* (New York: Columbia University Press, 2001).

29. For an extended conceptual discussion of all these various types of states and nations, see Miller, *Nations and Great Powers* (2007, chapter 3). For empirical details on South America and Western Europe, see Miller (ibid., Chapters 7 and 8 and Appendix A, pp. 422–24) and also the CIA *World Factbook* (http://www.cia.gov/cia/publications/factbook/).

30. See Frederic, *Pakistan*, p. 15.

31. In Lake's terms, such effects constitute security externalities or transborder "spillovers." David A. Lake, "Regional Security Complexes: A Systems Approach," in Lake and Morgan, *Regional Orders*, pp. 45–67.

32. The Pashtun tribe is considered one of the "largest tribal societies" and consists of between 17 to 20 million people. See Bernt Glatzer, "Being Pashtun—Being Muslim: Concepts of Person and War in Afghanistan," in *Essays on South Asian Society: Culture and Politics II*, ed. Bernt Glatzer (Berlin: Das Arabische Buch, 1998), pp. 83–94.

33. See Frederic, *Pakistan*, 3; Lawrence Ziring, this volume.

34. See Barnett R. Rubin, "Saving Afghanistan," *Foreign Affairs* (January/February, 2007). For more on Pakistan's state/nation challenges and their regional effects see Mariam Abou Zahab, "The Regional Dimension of Sectarian Conflicts in Pakistan," in *Pakistan: Nationalism without a Nation?*, ed. Christophe Jaffrelot (London: Zed Books, 2002), pp. 115–128.

35. For a useful overview of both irredentism and the secession challenge, see Mayall, *Nationalism*, pp. 57–63.

36. With respect to war, a number of empirical studies have shown evidence of such "contagion" or "diffusion" at an intra-regional, rather than inter-regional level. See Daniel S. Geller and David J. Singer, *Nations at War: A Scientific Study of International Conflict* (Cambridge: Cambridge University Press, 1998), pp. 106–108, for an overview.

37. This is what happened, for example, to post-2003 Iraq.

38. Daniel Byman and Stephen Van Evera, "Why They Fight: Hypotheses on the Causes of Contemporary Deadly Conflict," *Security Studies* 7, no. 3 (1998), pp. 1–50.

39. See Bernard S. Cohn, "The Census, Social Structure and Objectification in South Asia," in *An Anthropologist Among the Historians and Other Essays* (New York: Oxford University Press, 1987), pp. 242–243. For another good survey of the effects of British rule on India's social structure see Talbot, *India and Pakistan*, pp. 9–31. See also Lange's chapter in this volume.

40. Talbot, *India and Pakistan*, p. 157.

41. For more on India's nation-building program from partition to the end of the twentieth century, see ibid., pp. 162–195.

42. See Central Intelligence Agency, *World Factbook,* https://www.cia.gov/library/publications/the-world-factbook/geos/in.html#People. This relies on the 2001 census.

43. For more on the Sikh ethno-national aspirations, especially their militant behavior during the 1980s, see Talbot, *India and Pakistan*, pp. 265–273.

44. See Akbar, *India*, pp. 93–95.

45. See ibid, 94, and the map in Selig S. Harrison, Paul H. Kreisberg, and Dennis Kux, "Introduction," in *India & Pakistan*, ed. Selig S. Harrison, Paul H. Kreisberg, and Dennis Kux (Cambridge: Cambridge University Press, 1999), p. 2.

46. Akbar, *India*, p. 210. The brackets were added by the author.

47. Owen Bennett Jones, *Pakistan: Eye of the Storm* (New Haven, CN: Yale University Press, 2002), p. 56.

48. See Jones, *Pakistan*, pp. 63–64.

49. Ibid., pp. 70–71.

50. Ibid., pp. 172–173. For more on the 1971 War, see Sumit Ganguly, "India: Policies, Past and Future," in Harrison, Kreisberg and Kux, *India & Pakistan*, pp. 161–163, and Talbot, *India and Pakistan*, pp. 256–259.

51. See Central Intelligence Agency, *World Factbook*, https://www.cia.gov/library/publications/the-world-factbook/geos/pk.html#People. For an earlier account that also specifies the linguistic groups and their development, see Christophe Jaffrelot, "Introduction," in Jaffrelot, *Pakistan*, p. 48. For more on the domination of the Punjab identity in Pakistan see Ian Talbot, "The Punjabization of Pakistan: Myth or Reality?," in Jaffrelot, *Pakistan*, pp. 51–62.

52. See Anatol Lieven, "The Pressures On Pakistan," *Foreign Affairs* (January/February, 2002).

53. See Jones, *Pakistan*, p. 109.

54. See Mariam Abou Zahab, "The Regional Dimension of Sectarian Conflicts in Pakistan," in Jaffrelot, *Pakistan*, pp. 115–128.

55. The Failed States Index defines Pakistan in 2008 as "critical." Foreign Policy and the Fund for Peace, "Failed States Index."

56. See Lieven, "Pressures."

57. Ibid.

58. Rubin, "Saving Afghanistan."

59. Ibid.

60. For a historic review of the attempts and failures to occupy Afghanistan, see Milton Bearden, "Afghanistan, Graveyard of Empires," *Foreign Affairs* (November/December 2001), pp. 17–30.

61. The Failed States Index ranks Sri Lanka twentieth of the sixty most at-risk states. Foreign Policy and the Fund for Peace, "Failed States Index."

5 Economic Globalization and State Capacity in South Asia

Baldev Raj Nayar

Both critics and supporters of economic globalization see the increasing expansion of markets under it to lead to the erosion—that is, the weakening—of state capacity, and perhaps eventually to dismantlement of the state. This, however, is a rather extravagant claim about globalization's potency. States and markets, while interrelated, are separate institutions, with different logics. No zero-sum game need be posited between them;[1] indeed, globalization may be "enabling" or "empowering" for the state.[2] Empirical studies demonstrate that there is little basis for fears about a reduced economic or welfare role for the state.[3]

Globalization holds both opportunities and risks. The challenge for decision-makers is to maximize net benefits. Globalization is not a panacea, however. It cannot compensate for the results of perverse institutions, imprudent policies, and kleptocratic leadership. Governance continues to matter. Nor can globalization entirely undo the consequences, externally, of geopolitical location and status or, internally, of ethnic heterogeneity—key themes informing the discussion below. Therefore, in examining the impact of globalization on state capacity, this chapter takes a more comprehensive view since multiple factors are involved, entailing both structure and agency.

The principal arguments of this chapter are that (1) state capacity among the South Asian states has long been weak as a result of the region's geopolitics, colonial inheritance, ethnic heterogeneity, and policy-driven slow economic growth; (2) globalization's impact has largely been positive, though not adequate, in strengthening state capacity (chiefly through elevating the importance of economic growth and actually accelerating economic growth and, consequently, endowing the state with greater resources); (3) the accelerated economic growth through quickening the pace of social mobilization and, resultantly, public expectations has also raised new pressures for the state to adequately discharge its function of supplying public goods, such as internal security and investment in the social sectors; and (4) institutional capacity is critical to performing the state's basic function of supplying public goods. Fundamentally, two distinct models are manifest among the South Asian states in respect of state capacity and managing ethnic heterogeneity.

How Globalized Is South Asia?

South Asian states vary in their integration with the world economy. On the basis of trade (exports plus imports) in goods and services, Sri Lanka as a small island has always been globalized; indeed, it was more globalized in 1960 (with trade as a share of GDP at over 90%) than in 2005 (around 80%).[4] In contrast, India was in 1970 the least integrated into the world economy of the South Asian states (a very low 8.10%), while the other states were far more integrated. Even as late as 1990, India remained the least globalized (15.71%); Pakistan and Nepal commanded a share that was at least twice as much as India's. By 2006, however, India's share in trade had advanced considerably (47.19%), exceeding that of Bangladesh (42.14%) and Pakistan (39.94%); Nepal's share (56.28%) was higher. Sri Lanka aside (75.65%), the other economies of South Asia are now about equally globalized in the area of trade.

As regards movement of capital (FDI), all of the economies of South Asia were rather tightly closed until the mid-1970s. Since then, they have to varying degrees opened up to FDI. By 2005, Pakistan was receiving the largest net FDI inflows as a share of GDP (1.96%), followed by Bangladesh (1.34%) and Sri Lanka (1.16%). India's net FDI inflows were less than 1% of GDP, while Nepal received almost nothing. In terms of movement of people, South Asia has benefited enormously from emigration. Pakistan was initially a spectacular beneficiary, with inward remittances averaging about 9 percent of its GDP over the five-year period 1980–1984. By 2006, India's receipts of remittances were the least as a share of GDP (2.84%); surprisingly, Nepal emerged as the country with the highest share (15.04%), followed by Bangladesh (8.85%), Sri Lanka (7.74%), and Pakistan (4.19%).

Taking all three indicators (trade, FDI, and emigration) together, Sri Lanka would seem to be the most integrated with the world economy and Nepal the least. The other three countries are now about equally globalized, with India's integration perhaps more broad based than that of the other two.

The Past as Prologue

As part of the developing world, the South Asian states were, not surprisingly, deficient in state capacity even before globalization. To varying degrees, all states suffered from severe problems, even crises and breakdowns, in respect of institutional structure, political order, national integration, and economic growth and welfare. The causes of this outcome lay not only in social structure and external shocks, but also in public policy.

The Primacy of Geopolitics and Its Costs

Although part of a single region, South Asia's states differ vastly. Consider size—India is a giant among the world's nation-states, towering over the region with more than three-quarters of its population in 2006. The next largest state in South Asia is Pakistan; larger than Germany and France combined, it has only about 10% of the region's population. Bangladesh has more than 7% and both Nepal and Sri Lanka have less than 2% each. Similar is the story with GDP, where India had close to 80% of the region's GDP in 2006 compared with Pakistan's 11%, Bangladesh's 7%, Sri Lanka's a little over 2% and Nepal's less than 1%. Likewise, India dominates the subcontinent's territorial space with 3 million square kilometers, about three-quarters of the region's total. South Asia thus constitutes a unipolar system, with India occupying its geographic core, spread physically across its middle expanse, with the other states situated along its periphery without adjoining each other. Size matters. In actuality, it forms the "deeper structure" of the subcontinent's geopolitics and the consequent debilitating conflicts.

Given its overwhelming size and its perception of itself as the inheritor of the distinctive Indic civilization, India from the very beginning of its independent history has seen itself as a rightful claimant to the role of a major power in the world. The world's major powers, not the region's states, are inherently its reference point in external behavior.

India's vaulting ambition in the 1950s to play a major power role in the world as a leader of the nonaligned movement, even while lacking the material capabilities for it, brought it into diplomatic conflict with the United States, which set about to "contain" India through a military alliance with Pakistan.[5] Meanwhile, India's assertive role also set up a tacit rivalry with neighboring China, which soon turned into hostility in 1959. Disputes over borders erupted, leading finally to a clash of arms in 1962, in which India suffered a humiliating defeat that has left behind deep scars in its worldview. Geopolitically, the enduring legacy of the war has been a determined Chinese strategy—despite intermittent bonhomie—of containment and encirclement of India through entente and alliances with India's neighbors.

The 1962 war proved to be extremely damaging for India's economic and political stability and institutions. It led to the breakdown of the national consensus on defense, foreign policy, and economic strategy. The doubling of military expenditures, the consequent increases in taxation, and rising inflation ground the economy to the "Hindu" rate of growth, unraveled the stable "Congress system," and led to protracted political turmoil after the mid-1960s.

Given India's size and major-power ambitions, the other South Asian states have seen India as an actual or looming hegemonic power and have been wary about its intentions. This wariness finds its extreme expression in the foreign policy behavior of Pakistan, but the other smaller powers have also sought comfort and insurance through drawing close to one or another extra-regional power to balance off India. However, in pursuing such a policy, none can match the energy and tenacity of Pakistan, whose posture is not reactive but proactive, with its sources going beyond the question of mere size. The consequences of this policy for state capacity have nonetheless been hugely consequential.

For reasons that have very much to do with the élan and fervor of its dominant religious ethos, and its self-image as a putative successor to the Mughal Empire and as the vanguard of Islam in the region, Pakistan as a self-proclaimed Islamic Republic has found the very idea of India as a major power abhorrent.[6] Therefore, from the very beginning, Pakistan has pursued a revisionist strategy to challenge India's major-power ambitions and to restructure the region's geopolitics. Indeed, many of Pakistan's subsequent problems have arisen precisely from the resulting fundamental imbalance between its ambitious revisionist goals and its relatively weaker capabilities. Military adventurism, through conventional and non-conventional violence, has been one consequence, against not only India but also Afghanistan, which in turn has had "blowback" effects for Pakistan.

Under the aegis of an alliance between the military and the mosque or *jihadi* extremists,[7] Pakistan has readily initiated conflict and war,[8] seeking to destabilize multiethnic India so as to generate its disintegration, which would not only preclude any threat from India but would instead facilitate "regional preeminence for Pakistan."[9] With such ends in view, Pakistan entered into a military alliance with the United States to enhance its capabilities with American military and economic aid.

The consequent strengthening of Pakistan (not state weakness) soon led to hubris, and Pakistan initiated a major attack against India in 1965. Failure in that war proved consequential for Pakistan. The military regime began to unravel amidst a cycle of high defense expenditures, inflation, and violent protests and agitations. The end result was not just the weakening but the breakup of the state in 1971, following the secession of Bangladesh. The regime has, however, continued to employ unconventional warfare against its neighbors, which at times has provoked the United States to threaten declaring Pakistan a terrorist or rogue state.[10]

Bangladesh, which emerged as an independent state out of the breakup of Pakistan, initially adopted the "Indian developmental model" as its own. But in the midst of economic and political turmoil and an orgy of political assassinations in the mid-1970s, it reverted to the institutional design that it was accustomed to within Pakistan. It also made Islam the state religion and manifested the same attitudes of hostility and antagonism toward India that Pakistan had. A particular consequence of these attitudes has been the infiltration into India, particularly its northeast, of some 10 to 15 million illegal Bangladeshi immigrants, whom many in India regard not as economic refugees but as part of a sinister Bangladeshi geopolitical design to establish an Islamic *Lebensraum* in northeast India.[11]

Sandwiched between India and China, landlocked Nepal has always been aggrieved by India's regional preeminent position, and the arrogance that goes with it, as also by its own extreme trade and economic dependence on India. It has, over the decades, skillfully played the two neighboring giants, India and China, off against each other. It has also attempted, but without much success, to diversify its economic and trade ties with India. Sri Lanka, too, has from time to time collaborated with Pakistan against India; interestingly, Pakistan cultivated "close ties with the governments of South Asian states" and, "in an effort to encircle India," established covert operations bases in them.[12]

Mistrust, conflict, and periodic wars have been characteristic of much of the subcontinent's postcolonial history. The consequence for the smaller powers—most visible in the case of Pakistan, but to some extent in Bangladesh as well—has been the bloating of the power of the military relative to the rest of society and, as a result, several episodes of military takeovers, long periods of military rule, and the suppression of different ethnic groups. The region's geopolitics has thus had an enormous impact on the institutional profile of some of the South Asian states.

Beyond generating institutional decay, the underlying strategic conflict in the subcontinent made for lack of economic integration and cooperation among the region's states. South Asia is notorious for being the least integrated region in the world; the share of intra-South Asian trade in the total world trade of South Asia is less than 5%.[13] There has been little direct trade between India and Pakistan. Economic cooperation between India and Bangladesh (over sharing of waters and natural gas, and over transit facilities) and between India and Nepal (over developing and sharing hydroelectric power) has been inhibited by suspicion and fears over deeper dependence on the larger neighbor. Strategic conflict in the region, rather than representing the externalization of state weakness, has been instrumental in weakening the economies, and therefore the states, of South Asia.

The Colonial Inheritance of Institutional Imbalance

The South Asian states were born weak in that their colonial inheritance was limited and imbalanced institutional development, with strong bureaucratic structures and feeble political infrastructure. Unsurprisingly, then, the powerful bureaucratic and security forces intervened to overthrow elected regimes after independence.

This process started early in the case of Pakistan, as early as 1951. A more dramatic rupture occurred in 1958 through a military coup d'état. Since then, the history of Pakistan has been that of a garrison state, broken by civilian rule intermittently (1972–1977, 1988–1999, 2008–). Even when there has been civilian rule, there has remained behind its veil the reality of the overpowering presence of the military, which sees itself as the guardian not just of the nation's territory but also of its ideological frontiers.

Pakistan's political parties have been weak because independence came too easily to Pakistan, without the sustained struggle and sacrifice necessary for the growth of strong political parties. Internecine political warfare followed independence, which brought on military intervention again and again. The military rulers, in turn, adopted a deliberate strategy to suppress, divide, and disorganize the political parties. State weakness was thus built into the very birth of Pakistan. That legacy was shared by Bangladesh, which also faced a similar pattern of frequent military intervention.

Interestingly, Sri Lanka did not develop a mass nationalist movement prior to independence. Mass mobilization developed only after independence, and it exposed the deep fault line between the Sinhalese Buddhist majority and the Tamil Hindu minority. The resulting civil war (terminated in 2009)—despite continued democratic rule—elevated the role of the military, transforming it into a mono-ethnic armed force and leading to "the militarization of society and the emergence of a war economy,"[14] with violence pervasive in society. Nepal, with a Hindu monarchy, witnessed a long-haul political conflict in which the king sought to consolidate power while political groups, inspired by mass movements elsewhere in the subcontinent, sought a democratic opening up of the system.[15] Eventually, the monarchy was overthrown, in 2008, following a long Maoist insurgency, but stable political institutions have yet to emerge.

The Indian case was exceptional in that its nationalist movement had a long run of over six decades, during which it saw several leadership and generational successions. Particularly critical was its transformation in the early 1920s into a mass movement led by a mass party organization, whose leaders and followers made tremendous sacrifices. At independence, India was unusually blessed with a large band of extraordinarily capable leaders, who worked collectively to establish strong electorally legitimated political institutions, thus subordinating the civilian and military bureaucracy to democratic control. No matter how tattered it would become subsequently, the Indian political trajectory was therefore very different from that of the other South Asian states.

Ethnic Heterogeneity and Institutional Deterioration

The ethnic heterogeneity of the subcontinent is proverbial. It has been a key element in the subsequent institutional deterioration and the consequent state weakness. After independence, ethnic competition resulted in political decay and breakup of the umbrella nationalist organizations. Demands for separation and movements for secession soon followed.

In postcolonial South Asia, essentially two different models have prevailed in managing ethnic heterogeneity and ensuring national integration. One is the pluralist and inclusive model followed by India, with a secular state unidentified with any particular religion, combined with democracy that provides voice to the population and with federalism that gives considerable autonomy to various ethnic groups, supplemented by special provisions in favor of minorities. The remaining states have largely followed another model, combining a de jure or de facto unitary state with basically authoritarian rule and identification with one religion and one language. Sri Lanka is an exception to authoritarian rule, but some refer to it as "control democracy."[16] This second model is, in essence, one of mono-ethnic majoritarian states amidst heterogeneous societies.

Pakistan exemplifies the second model par excellence. The state's institutional structure began to unravel when a divided political leadership failed to reach consensus over ethnic power sharing. With the state (military) elites holding to a vision of Punjabi domination, ethnic grievances escalated among the Bengali population after the 1965 India-Pakistan War and generated a massive autonomy movement. The end result was, with the secession of Bangladesh, the bifurcation of the state in 1971. Presided over at the time by an apparently strong state headed by the army, Pakistan witnessed not just the weakening of the state but its very collapse. The successor regimes have continued to be besieged by ethnic conflicts in its various regions. State weakness, resulting from ethnic conflict, has thus had structural roots in society.

Bangladesh is overwhelmingly a homogeneous state both in terms of religion (Islam) and language. Partly that is a result of its easing out to India— nowadays characterized as "ethnic cleansing"—much of a once substantial Hindu community. The state has also tended to ride roughshod over its small Buddhist minority among the Chakma tribes. It now increasingly faces a challenge from Islamic fundamentalists, however.[17]

Sri Lanka, by elevating the religion of Buddhism and the language of its majority Sinhalese people in the affairs of the state in the mid-1950s within a unitary polity, ended up alienating its Tamil Hindu minority, which boiled over into a major insurgency by the Tamil "tigers."[18] Sri Lanka was, however, unrelenting in its determination to crush the rebels militarily and refused to countenance federalism in resolving the problem. The rigidity of the Sinhalese community, backed by the Buddhist clergy, on federalism stemmed from the suspicion that the Tamil community is inherently secessionist and that federalism would be a stepping stone to secession.

India, too, has faced ethnic conflict between different communities, ethnic pressures of different kinds on its federal system, and even secessionist threats in various parts of the country. With its sturdier institutional structure and its bargaining political culture, it has had considerable success in coping with some of the assertive ethnic demands, as in Tamil Nadu and Punjab, through a combination of accommodation and firmness or coercion. However, this policy has failed to satisfy some of the more determined ethnic groups in northeast India, where insurgencies have persisted over a long time. India seems to have believed, perhaps mistakenly, that as a state of such enormous size and power it will prevail over any insurgency. Its strategy has been to wear out antagonist groups until they are ready to be accommodated by a state that is committed to pluralism and perceives itself to be generous in its treatment of ethnic groups. The large number of ongoing insurgencies, however, suggests that either the state's resources are stretched too thin or that it is constrained by its democratic sensibilities to not inflict undue damage on its citizens. Meanwhile, India continues to suffer from the terrible blight of intermittent intercommunity violence.

In summary, ethnic heterogeneity and the consequent ethnic conflicts have been, and are, a source of fundamental weakness for South Asian states.

The Costs of Poor Economic Performance

Poor economic performance by a majority of the South Asian states during the preglobalization period also served to constrain state capacity. Apart from reducing the legitimacy of the state, it placed limits on the state's ability to invest in programs for human development and poverty alleviation. Besides, with population growth galloping, demographic pressures generated an agrarian crisis, following the successive fragmentation of farms, and enormously degraded the urban infrastructure.

The experience of slow economic growth finally persuaded decision-makers to shift away from their inward-oriented economic strategies. The timing varied among South Asian states in turning to economic reform or liberalization and integrating with the world economy. Assigning a definite date for any particular country's shift to liberalization is difficult, since reform was often staggered over a considerable period of time. India started its economic liberalization hesitantly in 1975 and gradually increased its pace in the 1980s, and finally undertook more radical reform in 1991.[19] Other countries either preceded or followed the change in India's economic policy, sometimes with greater vigor while at other times less energetically.

India neatly illustrates the poor economic performance in the region prior to economic liberalization. Up to around 1980, its average rate of economic growth was 3.5% (Table 5.1) even as population was growing at around 2%.

Bangladesh's economic growth between 1971 and 1990 averaged less than 3%. Similarly, Nepal's growth averaged around 3% before 1990. These three countries were thus trapped in a low-growth equilibrium. It's little wonder that South Asia remained among the poorest regions of the world, with the world's largest concentration of the poor.

Pakistan and Sri Lanka, however, stood apart from the other South Asian countries in their economic growth history, with both demonstrating superior performance. Largely on the shoulders of American aid, Pakistan's economic performance was spectacular, with a growth rate of around 6% sustained over some three decades after 1960. But Pakistan squandered its economic advantages through heavy investment in defense, military adventurism, and institutional volatility. In comparison to Pakistan, Sri Lanka's performance before 1990 at over 4% seems modest, but better than that of the other South Asian economies.

To sum up, the states of South Asia have been weak for long. Although the different states varied in its manifestation, institutional poverty or deterioration was a key feature of the period before globalization. Some of the causes for it were structural while others were a function of leadership choices. Not all the South Asian states were alike, however. While sharing the region's general weaknesses, especially with the passage of time, India, with the fundamental continuity of its institutional structure, still stood out as an island of relative strength among fragile, at times failing, states on its periphery, whose condition often had spillover effects for it.

The Impact of Globalization

Three principal effects of globalization are discernible, and on balance they seem favorable to augmenting state capacity to a larger or smaller extent—the heightened elite perception of the importance of international economic integration; accelerated economic growth; and increased social mobilization. The last process is likely more ambiguous in its impact.

The Salience of International Economic Integration

Regardless of whether or not South Asian states were initially coerced into economic liberalization by the IMF or the World Bank, there grew among them subsequently an appreciation of the benefits of international integration after becoming aware of the great leap in economic growth made by the East Asian "tigers."

Undoubtedly, all states remain sensitive to geopolitical considerations, and geopolitics surely trumps all other considerations when national security is at stake. Still, the awareness of the benefits of globalization elsewhere also led to a reassessment among state elites of the damaging costs of geopolitical rivalry in South Asia and the accompanying lack of regional economic cooperation. That reassessment resulted in according higher importance to increased openness to the world economy and even to regional economic cooperation among the South Asian states.

The reassessment is evident in the move in SAARC (South Asian Association for Regional Cooperation), founded in 1985, to establish first a South Asian Preferential Trading Arrangement (1995) and then a South Asian Free Trade Area (SAFTA) in 2004. It is evident as well in the free trade agreement (FTA) between India and Sri Lanka and—beyond South Asia—in India's FTA with Thailand, its Comprehensive Economic Cooperation Agreement (CECA) with Singapore, and its FTA with ASEAN. In April 2007, India decided to allow free market access to imports from the least-developed countries of the region. True, Pakistan has been resistant to implementing SAFTA on the ground that trade cooperation with India must wait on a prior resolution of territorial disputes. But Pakistan has, in fact, moved to expanding incrementally its positive list of items for trade with India, and there have even been authoritative voices in Pakistan that favor engaging in economic cooperation even if territorial disputes remain unresolved for the present (the India-China model). Incidentally, the explosive expansion of China-India economic relations also reduces incentives for China to openly encourage hostility among other South Asian states against India. No doubt, some have seen portents of deglobalization in the world economic crisis of 2008, but interestingly, South Asian statesmen vigorously opposed protectionism amidst the crisis.

Consistent with the upgrading of the importance of economics, there has been some lowering of tensions and the adoption of confidence-building measures as manifest in the opening of some travel links between India and Pakistan and the softening of the borders ("line of control") in Jammu and Kashmir. But progress has been slow because of suspicions over Pakistan's "two-track policy" of overt peace overtures and covert nonconventional warfare.[20] The peace process, however, came to a standstill in November 2008 following the Pakistani terrorist attacks in India's financial capital, Mumbai. Bangladesh, too, has to some extent come to see the ill effects for its own society of supporting militant activity against India through giving sanctuary to anti-Indian insurgent groups.

In these respects, the impact of globalization through turning the South Asian states to integration with the world economy has been positive. It has engendered a shift away from the earlier primacy of geopolitics by elevating the importance of economics and mutual economic cooperation among South Asian states. This impact need not, however, be exaggerated; like markets and states, globalization and geopolitics are based on different logics; one is therefore not likely to replace the other. Turmoil and war in Afghanistan and in Pakistan's tribal belt can still spread and engulf the region. While there has been some realization of the threat to Pakistan itself from terrorist groups that Pakistan created or nurtured, Pakistan still takes them to be "strategic assets" in reserve for its larger political aims in relation to India and Afghanistan.

Acceleration of Economic Growth

One key impact of globalization has been—at least until the world's financial turmoil in 2008—the acceleration of economic growth, in considerable part because it attenuated the capital, foreign exchange, and market constraints. It is most evident in the case of India, where integration with the world economy led to a break with the "Hindu" rate of growth of 3.5% or lower, to about 6% in the 1980s and 1990s and to over 7% later (Table 5.1). Particularly spectacular has been the growth in the five years from 2003 to 2007, when the rate was close to 9%.

This economic performance has been "empowering" for the state in India in three decisive ways. First, the period after economic liberalization saw a secular decline in poverty (no doubt, defined minimally) from about 55% in 1974 to 45% in 1983 and 36% in 1994 and further to less than 28% in 2005. Second, the economic growth has been "enabling"—that is, strengthening—for the state in that the latter has been receiving an economic bonanza through increased revenues. The state has used the mounting revenues to invest—whether wisely or not remains arguable—in the social sectors of health and education, in vast welfare programs (such as guaranteed rural employment), and in enormous, but unsustainable, subsidies to the poor and also to the not-so-poor in the distribution of food, fuel, and fertilizer. Third, the high growth rates increased the self-confidence of national elites, as they did also more generally of the middle classes and entrepreneurial groups, about the economic future. First high inflation and then the worldwide economic crisis during 2008, however, dented this self-confidence considerably.

The pattern of higher economic growth is evident in Bangladesh as well, which saw a growth rate of close to 5% in the 1990s and a little over 5% subsequently; particularly impressive was the growth rate of about 6.5% during the four years from 2004 to 2007. Meanwhile, the proportion of the population below the poverty line declined from 58.8% in 1990 to 40.8% in 2005 (figures in this and the next paragraph are from IMF staff reports of 2007). Nepal presents a mixed picture because of the Maoist insurgency; in the 1990s, its growth rate was about 5%, which declined subsequently to about 3%. During the 1990s, Sri Lanka's growth rate was over 5%. The intensification of the civil war during 2000 and 2001 affected the economy adversely, but after 2002 the growth rate was impressive, being over 6% for the years 2003 to 2007. Sri Lanka, with a per capita income of about US$1,300, outclasses all other South Asian states and is distinguished by its "welfare state" orientation. The ethnic conflict has, however, limited the spread of economic growth; the west and northwest contribute about 60% of GDP while only 16% originates in the former disturbed areas of the north and east.

An oscillation or pendulum-type pattern is apparent in Pakistan's economic development, where military rule correlates with accelerated growth—because of intensification of alliance ties with the United States and the resulting access to economic resources. After the economic deterioration of the 1990s under civilian rule, the military coup in 1999 led to a substantial recovery, especially after 2002, because of the economic bonanza that Pakistan received from the United States and its allies as part of the war against terrorism. As such, the basis of Pakistan's growth was geopolitics, not globalization. Much of its debt was forgiven, and billions of dollars flowed in as aid. Pakistan's heavy reliance on foreign aid has made some term it a "rentier state."[21] Interestingly, FDI inflows expanded more than ten times in the half dozen years up to 2006–07. Pakistan's growth rate was about 7% during the 2004–2007 period. The proportion of the population below the poverty line seesawed from 26.1% in 1990 to 32.6% in 2000 and to 23.9% in 2005. Political turmoil and terrorism in 2007 and 2008 drove Pakistan back to the economic brink and to the IMF. Today, more than ever, Pakistan's economic survival is a function of generous American geopolitically driven largesse.

If the assessment is correct that globalization has served to accelerate the growth rate in most of the South Asian states, then it has been "empowering"

TABLE 5.1 GDP growth: Annual rates and five-year averages (%)

	Bangladesh	India	Nepal	Pakistan	Sri Lanka
1961–1964*	5.5	5.18	3.31	6.68	3.62
1965–1969	2.60	3.04	1.88	6.87	5.50
1970–1974	-0.18	2.13	2.07	4.65	3.13
1975–1979	3.22	3.72	3.13	5.03	5.32
1980–1984	3.24	5.58	3.3	7.31	5.12
1985–1989	3.19	6.21	4.86	6.43	3.17
1990–1994	4.59	4.86	5.50	4.55	5.58
1995–1999	5.01	6.53	4.27	3.41	4.94
2000–2004	5.43	5.94	3.64	4.33	3.98
2005–2006**	6.34	9.22	2.3	6.76	6.69
1990	5.94	5.81	4.47	4.46	6.40
1991	3.34	0.91	6.64	5.06	4.60
1992	5.04	5.27	4.34	7.71	4.40
1993	4.57	4.87	3.50	1.76	6.90
1994	4.08	7.46	8.56	3.74	5.60
1995	4.93	7.65	3.30	4.96	5.50
1996	4.62	7.39	5.34	4.85	3.80
1997	5.39	4.48	5.26	1.01	6.40
1998	5.23	5.99	2.94	2.55	4.70
1999	4.87	7.13	4.50	3.66	4.30
2000	5.94	4.04	6.10	4.26	6.00
2001	5.27	5.21	5.63	1.98	-1.55
2002	4.42	3.73	-0.60	3.22	3.96
2003	5.26	8.39	3.38	4.85	6.02
2004	6.27	8.33	3.71	7.36	5.45
2005	5.96	9.23	2.71	7.29	6.03
2006	6.71	9.20	1.88	6.23	7.35

SOURCE: World Development Indicators.
*Reflects four-year average.
**Reflects two-year average.

for these states since higher growth makes for—after the pattern described for India—increased revenues for the state. The higher growth can be said to be further empowering for the state insofar as better economic performance adds to support for the state from groups that benefit from it. However, higher economic growth is a double-edged sword, for it may generate dissatisfaction and alienation among those left behind. This aspect constitutes a serious challenge for the state, particularly since evidence has been mounting that economic growth under globalization has been "inequalizing."

Increased Social Mobilization

If the conclusion on the acceleration of economic growth is accurate, then it follows that the pace of "social mobilization" must have also speeded up as a result. The advancing social mobilization has been further pushed by the parallel revolution in communications because of the explosion in mass media and mobile telephony. India exemplifies the expansion in mobile telephony; from almost none a decade earlier, the number of its mobile telephones rose to over 233 million by the end of 2007. The story is repeated in country after country in South Asia. From literally nothing at the beginning of the 1990s, the number of mobile phone subscribers per 1000 people had by 2004 risen immensely: Bangladesh 19.98; India 43.81; Nepal 4.39; Pakistan 33.03; and Sri Lanka 113.74.[22]

Samuel Huntington's employment of Karl Deutsch's concept of social mobilization[23] posits that this process makes for a change in the mindset of the affected population, with the resultant political awakening leading to demands for participation in governance. That is a positive contribution, for modern societies are politically participant societies. But increased social mobilization is also likely to lead to greater dissatisfaction, discontent, and alienation when the higher demands on the state from a more politically involved public with higher expectations remain unmet or are met only poorly. It is apparent that globalization has a double-barreled impact on state capacity. On the one hand, it is empowering for the state because it places greater resources at its disposal as a result of accelerated economic growth. On the other hand, the same growth generates increased social mobilization and, therefore, higher expectations among the populace. There are, as a consequence, greater pressures on the state to meet the expanding demands for internal security and delivery of public goods. It will thus remain a race between the increased resources generated by globalization for the state and the higher demands placed on the state by the quickened pace of social mobilization—in other words, a race between the empowerment of the state and the empowerment of citizens. In considerable part, the outcome of the race will likely depend on the condition of the state's institutions and their effectiveness in supplying public goods. Institutional capacity thus remains critical.

Political Institutions and the Supply of Public Goods

The earlier discussion provides a rough idea of the comparative condition of political institutions in the various South Asian countries. Some authoritative surveys add greater precision, questionable perhaps, to that assessment. The World Bank furnishes data on multiple aspects of governance, aggregating information from various surveys on perceptions of governance on the part of different groups of respondents. What stands out in Table 5.2 is the sparseness of positive scores, of which there are only three and even these are quite low, the remaining twenty-seven for South Asia being negative; two of the positive scores are for India and one for Sri Lanka. Note, by way of comparison, that for Australia all the scores are positive, with five of them at or above 1.45 even as that state outperforms the United States on all indicators.

In terms of comparison within South Asia, while the picture is almost uniformly negative across the board, India shines relative to the other states;

TABLE 5.2 Governance indicators, 2006

Indicator	Bangladesh	India	Nepal	Pakistan	Sri Lanka	China
(1) Voice and accountability	- 0.52	0.35	- 1.15	- 1.17	- 0.35	- 1.66
(2) Political stability and absence of violence	- 1.60	- 0.84	-2.26	- 1.92	- 1.61	- 0.37
(3) Government effectiveness	- 0.81	- 0.04	- 0.89	- 0.51	- 0.36	- 0.01
(4) Regulatory quality	- 0.87	- 0.15	- 0.56	- 0.39	- 0.11	- 0.14
(5) Rule of law	- 0.86	0.17	- 0.68	- 0.82	0.01	- 0.40
(6) Control of corruption	- 1.29	- 0.21	- 0.75	- 0.93	- 0.29	- 0.53

SOURCE: Daniel Kaufman, Aart Kraay, and Massimo Mastruzzi. "Governance Matters VI: Aggregate and Individual Governance Indicators 1996–2006." <www.worldbank.org>.

it literally ranks number one on each of the measures (it is behind Sri Lanka on "regulatory quality" but the difference is nominal). In other words, even though it may be a case of the one-eyed being king among the blind, and even while Indians themselves are terribly dismayed by the deterioration in governance, India is the most democratic, the most stable, the most effective, almost the highest in regulatory quality, the most abiding by the rule of law, and the least corrupt among the states of South Asia.

At the other end from India is Bangladesh, which ranks number 5 on three measures and 2, 3, and 4 on the other three; its relatively better ranking on voice and accountability, and on political stability and absence of violence, must have see-sawed subsequently because of political volatility, including military intervention. Sri Lanka follows immediately after India, ranking first or second on five measures and third on one (political stability and absence of violence). Nepal and Pakistan are about tied in their performance, doing better than Bangladesh but worse than Sri Lanka.

The hierarchy that is evident among the states is confirmed by other surveys using different criteria. The *Failed States Index 2008*[24] ranks 177 states, 60 of which are failing, with the first 20 termed "critical" and another 20 "in danger"; Somalia with a score of 114.2 out of 120 ranks first while Norway is at the bottom (16.8). The failed or failing states are not confined to Africa, however; South Asia is hugely present among them, indeed in the "critical" group. If Afghanistan is 7 (105.4), then Pakistan at 9 (103.8) is not very far from it; Bangladesh is at 12 (100.3), Sri Lanka at 20 (95.6), and Nepal at 23 (94.2). The distance between this set of states and India (rank 98, score 72.9) stands out. The hierarchy is similar also to that emergent from the *Economist*'s "democracy index" for 2006. It corresponds as well to the rank order in the "corruptions perception index" by Transparency International. On corruption, the common perception in South Asia is that of the rapaciousness of political elites, who seek to capture the state in order to plunder it.

In terms of trends, the picture that emerges for South Asia from the World Bank's database for the 1998–2006 period is not very reassuring. Perhaps later developments, such as democratic elections in Bangladesh, Nepal, and Pakistan, may offer a more positive gloss on it, but they are still embedded in uncertainty. Except for India, which showed either improvement—as in government effectiveness, regulatory quality, and control of corruption—or not much change, the other states of South Asia largely saw deterioration in respect of most of the indicators. Bangladesh, Nepal and Sri Lanka witnessed deterioration in 5 out of 6 indicators, and some improvement or little change in one. Pakistan offered a mixed picture, with deterioration in three key indicators (voice and accountability, political stability and absence of violence, and rule of law), some improvement on two indicators (government effectiveness and regulatory quality), and no significant change in respect of control of corruption.

The poor profile of South Asian states in respect of political institutions is reflected in their poor performance in supplying public goods. Here, attention is directed at internal security and the social sectors, as these two areas are significant indicators of outcomes from state capacity for the public.

Internal Security

One important measure in assessing state performance in respect to internal security is the incidence of terrorism. It is a disturbing revelation that South Asia is, of all the regions of the world, the most afflicted by terrorism, when measured in terms of fatalities in 2008; compare its 5,826 deaths with the figure of 292 for the most populous region of East Asia and the Pacific and the world's total of 15,765.[25] Among individual countries, with 2,293 terrorism-related deaths Pakistan ranked number 2 in the world (preceded by Iraq with 5,016 deaths) while India with more than five times its population had 1,113 deaths (rank 5) and Sri Lanka with 325 deaths ranked 9. Two years earlier, the numbers and ranks were somewhat different: India 1,256 fatalities (second), Sri Lanka 627 (fifth), Pakistan 387 (ninth), and Nepal 261 (eleventh).

That South Asia as a whole is the worst-affected region of the world underlines the patent failure of South Asian states to provide adequate physical security, to a greater or lesser extent, to protect their citizens from terrorist attacks. Multiple insurgencies of varying strength are able to inflict horrendous havoc on large sections of the general population, while the state appears helpless in protecting them. The insurgents seem, in effect, to mock the lack of capacity of the states to provide law and order; indeed, the extent of organized violence and the large size of areas where insurgents exercise de facto control, especially at night time, point to the limited nature of sovereignty possessed by these states.

Though elements of the broader process of globalization may be involved in the higher incidence of organized violence in recent years—through easier and faster communications aggravating the sense of relative deprivation and through stimulating emulation of terrorist activity elsewhere—fundamentally, the problems of internal security are rooted in domestic society, where they have persisted over decades, long before globalization. In the ultimate analysis, the explanation for the increased incidence of organized violence in the South Asian states lies in the internal makeup of their societies in the form of ethnic heterogeneity, further aggravated by failure in governance in addressing economic and social grievances of specific groups. To be fair to the leaderships in charge, the management of ethnic conflict is no easy matter either.

Social Sectors

Although absolute expenditures on the social sectors may have been increasing, the states of South Asia are, with one exception, a testimony to poor performance in this area as well, as evidenced in UNDP's human development report for 2007/2008 (based on 2005 data). The best performer is Sri Lanka, which ranks 99th with a human development index (HDI) value of 0.743 (with life expectancy at 71.6 years and adult literacy at 90.7%) (Table 5.3); its performance comes close to that of China's. Some question the authenticity of Sri Lankan data since they do not cover the disturbed areas.[26] Sri Lanka is followed by India, ranking 128th with HDI value of 0.619 (63.7 years; 61.0%). The rankings of other states are Pakistan, 136th with HDI value of 0.551 (64.6 years; 49.9%); Bangladesh, 140th with HDI value of 0.547 (63.1 years; 47.5%); and Nepal, 142nd with HDI value of 0.534 (62.6; 48.6%).

The supply of public goods in the social sectors can also be examined through data on state expenditures. Taking health first, *total* expenditures as a share of GDP in 2004 were the highest in Nepal (5.60%) and India (5.00%);

TABLE 5.3 Human development index: South Asia

Country	HDI		Life Expectancy		Adult Literacy	
	Rank	Value	Rank	Years	Rank	%
Sri Lanka	99	0.743	82	71.6	55	90.7
India	128	0.619	125	63.7	114	61.0
Pakistan	136	0.551	123	64.6	124	49.9
Bangladesh	140	0.547	128	63.1	128	47.5
Nepal	142	0.534	131	62.6	126	48.6
China	81	0.777	68	72.5	54	90.9

SOURCE: UNDP, *Human Development Report 2007/2008* <http://hdr.undp.org>. HDI is a composite figure for the three indicators of life expectancy, educational attainment, and income.

however, *individuals* incurred the major portion of them, especially in India (Table 5.4). Thus, the role of the *state* in India, while not the lowest, was certainly minimal, a mere 0.86%, even as it was mediocre in quality. The best performer in terms of state expenditures on health was Sri Lanka (1.96%), while the worst was Pakistan (0.43%), which also had the lowest total expenditures (2.20%). Bangladesh did better than Pakistan in both total (3.10%) and public expenditures (0.87%).

The data on public spending on education (Table 5.5) are incomplete, but they provide enough information to make a tentative evaluation. In terms of public spending as a share of GDP, India outspends all other South Asian states even as Sri Lanka outperforms India by a large margin in literacy (Table 5.3). Perhaps the explanation for that paradox lies in India's public spending having been skewed in favor of higher education, benefiting the urban middle classes. Surprisingly, as in the case of health, Nepal spends a considerable share of GDP on education. Pakistan has done less well, having fallen behind Bangladesh. Overall, the combination of low state expenditures and,

TABLE 5.4 Health expenditures, private and public (% of GDP)

	2001			2002		
Country	Total	Private	Public	Total	Private	Public
Bangladesh	3.10	2.31	0.79	3.00	2.24	0.76
India	4.50	3.64	0.86	4.80	3.95	0.85
Nepal	5.30	4.07	1.23	6.00	4.28	1.72
Pakistan	2.30	1.81	0.49	2.30	1.71	0.59
Sri Lanka	3.90	2.14	1.76	3.90	2.21	1.69

	2003			2004		
Country	Total	Private	Public	Total	Private	Public
Bangladesh	3.10	2.24	0.86	3.10	2.23	0.87
India	4.90	4.06	0.84	5.00	4.14	0.86
Nepal	5.60	4.27	1.33	5.60	4.13	1.47
Pakistan	2.10	1.72	0.38	2.20	1.77	0.43
Sri Lanka	4.10	2.41	1.69	4.30	2.34	1.96

SOURCE: World Development Indicators

TABLE 5.5 Public spending on education, total (% of GDP)

	Bangladesh	India	Nepal	Pakistan	Sri Lanka
1998	..	3.63	..	2.03	3.05
1999	2.42	4.49	2.89	2.61	..
2000	2.38	4.41	2.98	1.84	..
2001	2.46	..	3.71	..	..
2002	2.32	..	3.38	..	..
2003	2.38	3.66	3.38	1.97	..
2004	2.25	3.75	..	1.97	..
2005	2.46	..	..	2.25	..
2006	..	..	..	2.59	..

SOURCE: World Development Indicators

more importantly, their ineffectiveness because of the state's deficient delivery systems testify to the faltering of the state in the social sectors in South Asia.

If one were to be bold (or foolhardy) enough to make a summary assessment on the supply of public goods, it would be that South Asia does poorly in comparative terms, and that this outcome is related to the poor quality of governance. Continuing on this path of boldness (or foolhardiness), one can extend this assessment to differences in performance within South Asia and maintain that, barring an exception here or there, the ranking among its states is a function of the quality of their institutions.

Conclusions

A combination of geopolitics, colonial inheritance, ethnic heterogeneity, and slow economic growth had made for weak state capacity, to a greater or lesser extent, among the states of South Asia over the three to four decades before globalization. Not all the states were alike in their institutional makeup, however. Two contrasting models are discernible. One model is that of the unitary, majoritarian, often authoritarian state basically identified with a single ethnic group, whether religious or linguistic—as in the case of Pakistan, Sri Lanka, Nepal, and Bangladesh. The other model is that of the federal, pluralistic, and constitutionally secular state, with a bargaining political culture—as in India. While the second model has not been without considerable problems in practice, it has been able to manage the challenges issuing out of diversity somewhat better and has proved more responsive to changes in society and to shifts in public opinion. It, no doubt, faced several crises, but it avoided breakdown. On the other hand, the first model continually faced, and still continues to face, severe problems in managing diversity and has suffered breakdowns intermittently, and even civil war (Pakistan, Sri Lanka, and Nepal).

The fundamental geopolitical fault line in the subcontinent has been that between India as the preeminent power, on the one hand, and the relatively smaller states, on the other, even though some of the latter are substantial powers in their own right. In its foreign policy posture, India differed from the other states over intervention in the subcontinent by extra-regional powers, which it found unacceptable, while the others encouraged such intervention, tacitly if not always openly, as a way of counterbalancing India. In the economic arena, South Asian states more or less followed mercantilist policies, but differed in their treatment of the private sector. Several favored socialistic policies (India over the longest stretch, but also Sri Lanka and Bangladesh intermittently) while some preferred the private sector as the engine of growth (Pakistan). The dominant pattern in economic performance was that of slow growth (India, Bangladesh, Nepal), but some demonstrated considerable economic growth (Pakistan and Sri Lanka).

By the early 1990s, all South Asian states had shifted to the liberal path and as a result have become substantially, if not overly, integrated with the world economy. The impact of globalization on South Asia has been mostly positive for state capacity. Two effects are particularly noteworthy: one, externally, the softening somewhat of earlier geopolitical antagonisms and historical animosities in favor of regional economic cooperation and social interaction among the states and their populations; and, two, internally, the acceleration of the economic growth rate. Both of these have been empowering for the states of South Asia through lowering interstate tensions and augmenting state treasuries with increased revenues for the state. Besides, growth acceleration has made a considerable dent in the incidence of poverty and has perhaps thus mitigated even greater alienation on the part of the poor.

At the same time, growth acceleration has quickened the pace of social mobilization, which has been further amplified by the communications revolution engendered by the explosion in mass media and mobile telephony. As a result, the sense of relative deprivation has intensified among large sections of the population, especially in the context of growth under globalization having been "inequalizing." This development presents the South Asian states with severe challenges in the areas of internal security and the social sectors. Despite the globalization-induced growth having been empowering for the state, the performance of the states has been appalling in these areas. That performance is a reflection of the continued weak institutional capacity of South Asian states.

Globalization has, however, not significantly changed the rank order among the states in their overall state strength and performance except that, by its high growth rate in recent years, India has further widened the distance between itself and the other states; a rough ordering of state strength and performance among the South Asian states would be India, Sri Lanka, Pakistan, Bangladesh, and Nepal. This globalization-driven distance is likely to be reinforced, in turn, by the kind of geopolitics that it engenders in the form of recognition by the major powers, as exemplified by the India-U.S. nuclear deal, now endorsed internationally. On the other hand, that very prospect may make India an even greater target for unconventional warfare by its adversaries.

Notes to Chapter 5

I would like to thank Professor Jagdish Handa for his critical review of an earlier version of this chapter.

1. Baldev Raj Nayar, *Globalization and Nationalism* (New Delhi: Sage, 2001), chapter 1.

2. Linda Weiss (ed.), *States in the Global Economy* (New York: Cambridge University Press, 2003), chapter 1.

3. Geoffrey Garrett, *Partisan Politics in the Global Economy* (Cambridge: Cambridge University Press, 1998); Stefan A. Schirm (ed.), *Globalization* (London: Routledge, 2007), pp. 9, 16; Baldev Raj Nayar, *The Myth of the Shrinking State* (New Delhi: Oxford University Press, 2009).

4. World Bank, *World Development Indicators* (Washington, DC: The World Bank, 2008).

5. Baldev Raj Nayar and T. V. Paul, *India in the World Order* (Cambridge: Cambridge University Press, 2003).

6. Lt General A.I. Akram, "Security and Stability in South Asia", in *The Security of South Asia*, ed. Stephen Philip Cohen (Urbana, IL: University of Illinois Press, 1987).

7. Husain Haqqani, *Pakistan: Between Mosque and Military* (Washington, DC: Carnegie Endowment for International Peace, 2005); Ahmed Rashid, *Descent into Chaos* (New York: Viking, 2008), pp. xxxix, xliii, 33, 47, 51, 220–221.

8. Wayne A. Wilcox, "India and Pakistan," in *Conflict in World Politics*, ed. Steven L. Spiegel and Kenneth N. Waltz (Cambridge, MA: Winthrop Publishers, 1971), pp. 240–260; T. V. Paul, *Asymmetric Conflicts: War Initiation by Weaker Powers* (Cambridge: Cambridge University Press, 1994).

9. Haqqani, *Pakistan*, p. 275.

10. Haqqani, *Pakistan*, pp. 294, 297; Rashid, *Descent*, pp. xliii, 32–33, 38, 41, 47, 50, 219–223.

11. Arun Shourie, *Government and the Sclerosis That Has Set In* (New Delhi: ASA/ Rupa & Co., 2004), pp. 12–13.

12. Haqqani, *Pakistan*, p. 270.

13. Ramesh Chandra and Rajiv Kumar, *South Asian Integration* (New Delhi: ICRIER, 2008), p. 21.

14. Nira Wickramsinghe, *Sri Lanka in the Modern Age* (London: C. Hurst & Company, 2006), p. 316.

15. T. Louise Brown, *The Challenge of Democracy in Nepal* (London: Routledge, 1996); Mahendra Lawoti, *Towards a Democratic Nepal* (New Delhi: Sage, 2005).

16. Wickramsinghe, *Sri Lanka*, p. 254.

17. Ali Riaz, *Islamist Militancy in Bangladesh* (London: Routledge, 2008).

18. K.M. de Silva, *Reaping the Whirlwind* (New Delhi: Penguin Books, 1998); A. Jeyaratnam Wilson, *The Break-Up of Sri Lanka* (London: C. Hurst & Company, 1988).

19. Baldev Raj Nayar, "When Did the 'Hindu' Rate of Growth End?," *Economic and Political Weekly* 41, no. 19 (May 13, 2006), pp. 1885–1890.

20. Haqqani, *Pakistan*, p. 267; Rashid, *Descent*, pp. 32, 51, 219, 221.

21. Haqqani, *Pakistan*, p. 323.

22. World Bank, *World Development Indicators*.

23. Samuel P. Huntington, *Political Order in Changing Societies* (New Haven: Yale University Press, 1968).

24. Foreign Policy and Fund for Peace, "Failed States Index 2008," *Foreign Policy*, July–August 2008, pp. 69–73.

25. U.S. National Counterterrorism Center, *Report on Terrorist Incidents—2006* (Washington, DC:2007), pp. 14–15, 24–25, and *2008 Report on Terrorism* (Washington, DC: 2009), pp. 19, 24.

26. Wickramsinghe, *Sri Lanka*, p. 310.

6 Symbiosis and Fracture

Civil Society and Weak States in South Asia

Mustapha Kamal Pasha

The underlying causes of state incapacity, as contributors to this volume propose, are heterodox, implicating domestic political structures as well as the regional environment (especially the absence of a shared normative framework for conflict management and resolution). Other factors, unequally distributed across the region, have also been highlighted, including diminished legitimacy in the face of societal demands; low levels of socio-political cohesion and unity in largely multiethnic and multisectarian polities; and the presence of secessionist or irredentist groups. To varying degrees, all South Asian states share these common features. Spawning a "crisis of governability"[1] or oscillations between societal and statist directions,[2] the assertion of "strong societies"[3] has exacerbated domestic and regional insecurity. In other contexts, nation and nationalism have failed to come together.[4] With lineages in processes of state formation and consolidation, weak state capacity has acquired a structural and institutional character. Unlocking the insecurity predicament, therefore, appears fairly complex and difficult.

Against the image of state weakness, however, the promise of civil society to produce domestic and regional security has also entered public consciousness. With reduced confidence in the ability of the state—a sentiment shared by large sections of the populace—civil society increasingly appears a panacea for South Asian ailments, ranging from mitigating the development crisis and ameliorating welfare retrenchment to the production of alternative thinking and processes for resolving long-standing regional conflicts and the perennial insecurity predicament. On this broad template, civil society presents not only a different pathway to materialize societal values but a *preferred* route to produce regional security and peace. The presumed inadequacies of the state, it is suggested, can be overcome through reliance on an assertive civil society. This appeal largely rests on the shoulders of disillusionment with the state and the expectation that popular and populist societal projects can help unfreeze bureaucratic inertia and rigidity often linked to statist imaginings. Popular among growing sections of the urban intelligentsia, sections of the media, and both advocacy and development-oriented nongovernmental organizations (NGOs) and their international sponsors, the attraction of civil society competes with established statist thinking. An aspect of the new mood is a conviction that social forces in the civil societies of South Asia provide autonomous historical trajectories for releasing the national imagination from mutual antagonism in favor of tolerance, mutuality, and peaceful coexistence. Hence, the empowerment of civil society is assumed to simultaneously compensate for state incapacity and offer better futures.

As subsequent discussion will show, competing images of civil society inform the largely cheerful mood regarding its competences and strengths. The absence of any common understanding of what constitutes civil society, perhaps, may be a contributing feature of the new mood against the assumed failures of the state. Without a centralizing analytical core, different protagonists can deploy the concept to their own liking, attributing elements found to be more attractive and rescinding the ones that seem disagreeable. Hence, civil society can escape the burden of paradox, tension, or contradiction. A rival to the excesses or malfunctions of the state, civil society acquires a normative edge.

This chapter questions the claim that civil society represents a viable alternative either to compensate for state weakness or to instigate successful projects for peace building and regional security. The strengthening of civil society does not necessarily create the conditions for enhanced security and in some instances may even generate impediments toward achieving regional security. This argument is illustrated mainly in reference to the South Asian regional security complex.[5] The principal claim that civil society does not offer an *autonomous* trajectory may also be extended to the entire region, but a more modest goal is sought here, namely to tease out the dependence of civil society on the state with a focus on the two principal regional protagonists: India and Pakistan. This dependence reflects the inability of the state to allow the consolidation of an autonomous civil society, but it also shows that the fractured character of civil society perpetually haunts state capacity.

A modulated variant of this argument is that the complex interplay between security and civil society in both India and Pakistan presents mixed pathways for *both* deepening insecurity and releasing new options to overcome insecurity. The domineering (dominant, not hegemonic)[6] presence of the state has sharply curtailed civil society. On the other hand, civil society has bypassed the state in mounting its own projects aiming either to produce regional security or to undermine it. In the first instance, the imprint of the state on civil society is palpable—in terms of political discourse, nationalist regurgitations and ascriptions of patriotism and sacrifice, and the circulation of images and symbols in the media, especially in interstate conflicts, from Kashmir to Kargil. The alternate voice of civil society comes from those sites where the state has failed to colonize society effectively: writers and poets, artists with defective nationalist loyalties, and intellectuals with the ability to trespass, to see the "other side" and absorb commonalities, shared hopes, and tragedies. To be sure, the state has also been bypassed in nihilist projects of death and destruction seeking to undo feeble possibilities of tolerance and coexistence. The arrival of the neo-puritans to the South Asian scene from the post-Afghan conflict in Pakistan is a case in point. Extraterritorial, this new force in civil society poses, perhaps, the biggest threat to regional peace and stability, as well as undermining the already stretched capacities of the state to provide protection under the guise of law or order.

Within national spaces, civil society has allowed particularistic sentiments to coalesce, often in the shape of sectarian and communal projects of social purification and the consolidation of exclusivist ideologies. The rise and consolidation of Islamist social forces in Pakistan is offered as an illustration. Similarly, the communalization of civil society in India presents a comparable, if distinct, picture. At the regional level, extremists have severely tested a fragile normative environment, as the November 2008 attacks in Mumbai demonstrate. Civil society cannot escape the historical and structural constraints imposed by the character of the postcolonial state in South Asia. These constraints involve the mutual constitution of state and civil society within imaginaries of conflict, distancing, Otherness, and exclusion. To the degree that nationalist impulses reside in *both* the state and civil society, the insecurity dilemma in South Asia is a product of a complex array of cultural forces that have been deeply politicized over time. The aspiration that civil society can release vast populations in India and Pakistan from the fetters of mutual antagonisms and fear is, therefore, misplaced. This chapter, accordingly, questions the notion that civil society is coterminous with enhanced security.

Background

To contextualize, three separate sentiments converge in recent analyses as vital elements in diagnosing the current political health of South Asia: anxieties about the deepening of market relations in the political economy of virtually all regional states; heightened aspirations of an assertive civil society, presenting new challenges and opportunities for social transformation; and an assumed pathology of state weakness in the face of these developments, characterized by the inability of the state to deliver basic services and materialize primary values, including security and welfare. Often taking the form of moral critique of a decaying social order, without the assurance of an alternative, these sentiments highlight the image of a great transformation in a region previously condemned to an image of temporal inertia.

The expansion of market relations and the rearticulation of social relations in its shadow appear as the triumph of neoliberalism in the South Asian context, once notorious for statism in its various guises: License Raj; developmentalism; or planning.[7] In the second instance, the expansion of the market appears as the general effect of globalization and its inducements to reorient economy and society away from insular conceptions of social engineering toward brave, new frontiers of borderless opportunity. In the third instance, the spread of the market is seen as the propitious combination of the two at a historic juncture that accounts for the unleashing of the capitalist genie in South Asia. Yet, this expansion is producing unprecedented stress on polities conditioned to the insolence of bureaucratic whim.

The assertiveness of civil society comes from a variety of sources: social differentiation and the rise of new social forces; rapid urbanization that is drastically changing the character of material and cultural life in South Asia; and the burgeoning of a "middle class" with fresh claims on the economy and society.[8] With the unleashing of new desires and interests, associational life and sociability outside the traditional arenas of the family or community have materialized. The declining efficacy of the state has also opened up, perhaps by default, new spaces for interest articulation outside the purview of state capacity.

In some accounts, state capacity[9] or the ability of the state "to carry out its objectives with adequate societal support"[10] remains palpably fragile, giving birth to scenarios of eventual failure in some instances, collapse in others.[11] This apparent weakness, it is sometimes argued, emanates principally from an inability to integrate diverse populations, homogenize difference, and create uniformity. Others suggest that state weakness is linked to market expansion and an assertive civil society. Numerous other factors are often added to the list as desirable explanations. These include institutional decay, corruption, ethnic conflict, democratic distemper, an illiberal political culture, an authoritarian proclivity, a feudal social consciousness, and military intervention in civilian affairs.[12] Against the ideal-typical image of successful (Western) liberal states, South Asia appears as a laggard. The putative inability of South Asian states to replicate the Western business of state-building scores them as potential losers.

For some scholars, the problem of state weakness is inherent to the Third World condition, captured in the language of modernization:

> Very few of the newly emergent Afro-Asian states can be considered as nation-states in the nineteenth-century European sense. They are artificial legacies of colonial empires: a ramshackle alliance of heterogeneous groups of people, often linguistically, religiously and racially disparate, who were put together for administrative convenience. These people temporarily united together in their struggle for emancipation from foreign rule but the unity was largely based on xenophobia and was therefore superficial. It was therefore not surprising that the unity, forged in the anti-colonial struggle, withered with the disappearance of the foreigner. The common problem in Africa and Asia today is that having found a state, the people are now struggling to forge a nation.[13]

On this settled view, the general effect of state weakness has not only generated domestic insecurity but invited regional insecurity as well. Ayoob sums up this argument quite unambiguously:

> The principal problem that seems to distort a great deal of Western analysis of the security of the Third World states is the tendency to compare states (that is, industrialized states with developing ones) that are unlike each other in many respects. This is especially so in relation to the crucial variable of state making, where the commonality is simply that both are in formal possession of juridical statehood. This, however, does not preclude the possibility of Third World states eventually approximating more closely the ideal type of the modern in-

dustrialized state (which is the reference point of most security analysts), given an adequate time to complete the prerequisite twin processes of state making and nation building.[14]

State weakness has fanned irredentist tendencies; enhanced ethnic, religious, sectarian, or communal tensions; and contributed vastly to generalized ontological insecurity. For some scholars, security at home would yield not merely the minimum threshold of orderly social life but other dividends as well. Without security, the modernist dream of societal development could never be realized.[15] Once security at home could be established, this would also solicit a climate of greater trust, amity, and peace within the region.

In nearly all cases, competing explanations direct inquiry into the nature of civil society in different national contexts; divergence between the state and civil society; and the increasing impotence of the state to either absorb or to stem the rising tide of societal demands within civil society. The embrace of civil society is ubiquitous, from the political opposition in illiberal polities to sectors within the state itself. Civil society has served as the mantra of alternatives in the international development industry, advocacy NGOs, and their vigorous state and market sponsors, both global and local.[16] In more recent times, however, it is more than a mantra; it is a metaphor for alternative development, governance, and autonomy.[17] Social actors of various hues and sizes, self-help organizations, religious centers, and think tanks have all accepted obligatory state-bashing and the romance of civil society as a marker of their identity and self-worth. A new cottage industry of eager protagonists of civil society now sprawl the policy and academic worlds, ranging from social activists, academics, and leaders of NGOs, to new converts within the establishment. Not to be overrun by the discourse of civil society, donor-dependent intelligentsia have been the vanguard of this new mood. Common sense equates civil society with any form of voluntary associational life.[18]

For the main protagonists of civil society, the state is often portrayed as the adversary, an obstacle either to democratic aspirations or regional peace. Generally, this portrayal does not entertain the notion that the state may be the principal condition of possibility for civil society. The historical experience suggests that the postcolonial state in South Asia has been quite successful in reducing autonomous spaces of alternative social and political action. At the same time, however, the state has also created the terrain for particular instantiations of civil society. Against the burden of this historical experience, can civil society compensate for state weakness? What are the links between state weakness and civil society, when "weakness" permeates both?

Revisiting Civil Society

The resurgence of interest in civil society enjoys an elective affinity with the loss of faith in the state's capacity to mount development, democracy, welfare, or security.[19] Trajectories of resurgence are varied across regions, but they all seem to underscore a new phase in the civilizing process of humanity, reversing the Hegelian sequence between state and civil society. In part, this reversal fulfills the liberal dream of an "open society" secured by the expansion of the "empire of civil society"[20] and the dismantling of dirigiste forms of economic and political dispensation.

Since the 1980s, the mounting fortunes of civil society have been linked to processes of successful democratization; resistance to dictatorship and the return from authoritarian to representative rule; the collapse of communism and the undoing of the Soviet Union; the spread of liberal values on a world scale and the "end of history"; and the widening of the political domain to allow voice to new social forces. On another register, civil society has arrived to compensate for the ills of the state as an economic actor—providing welfare goods and social services where the state has mysteriously disappeared. Self-help conceived as the voluntary organization of society has softened the impact of state retrenchment.

Various traditions of civil society draw from social theory, historical experience, and contingency. The rediscovery of civil society after two centuries of uninterrupted sleep had a distinctly antistatist element to it, energized by the East and Central European underground. From its origins in the Scottish Enlightenment in the last quarter of the eighteenth century, to German Idealism, and to de Tocqueville, the study of civil society took a fairly circuitous route, traversing multiple avenues of investigation. Once civil society reaches the Global South (the former "Third World"), it sheds old meanings and acquires new ones, largely in response to the development crisis, which has now been disaggregated into a myriad of crises: sustainability, governance, accountability, or state-building. From the timid perspective of the ex–Third World, the crisis, above all, remains one of development with familiar accoutrements. In brief, the rise of civil society discourse is in large measure spawned by the deepening of the "development" crisis, reworked under globalizing conditions. A distinctive feature of these changed times is a growing *depoliticization* of both state and civil society. Managerial governance increasingly replaces politics. The relation of civil society to the security problematic, therefore, requires new modalities of analysis.

To be certain, different conceptions of civil society yield alternate pathways. Straddling idealization and rejection are three constellations of the concept of civil society. First, civil society is viewed as an intermediate sphere between the state and the market, spawned by *modern* social relations. This is the sense in which Classical Political Economy deployed the idea. Crucial to this conception is the necessity of both a capitalist economy and a liberal state. Second, civil society has been seen as associational life. Originating in de Tocqueville's reading of democracy in America, this conception now pervades most popular applications of the term. Lastly, there is the equation of civil society and civilized society, a notion based on the Enlightenment's dualistic conception of humanity in the Occident and the Orient. Often, the unruly state of affairs in society is read as the absence of a civilized or civil society, a favorite elitist trope of representing particular social distempers.[21] All three variants of the idea can be discerned in the discourse on civil society in South Asia, with de Tocqueville's notion enjoying hegemony.

Specifically, in the South Asian context, the image of civil society is typically associated with NGOs and a domain of pluralistic interests or as resistance to the state, and in most cases a combination of the two. The popular conception of civil society, therefore, combines an antistatist dimension with a self-sustaining sphere of associational life. This vast terrain allows the possibility to include several disparate social agents "inside" civil society: media, lawyers, business groups, and NGOs of all hues as well as trade and labor unions, pressure groups, and elements linked to political parties. This broader image contrasts sharply with the historically received representation of civil society in Enlightenment thought as a distinct realm of sociability premised on the emergence of capitalist relations, on the one hand, and the rise of the modern liberal state on the other. Neither Hegelian theoretical leanings nor Marxist exhortations inform the dominant image in South Asia. Instead, a variant of de Tocqueville's characterizations of voluntary associational life enters the analytical fray.[22] The defining feature of received images of civil society in South Asia is of a *society-generated* realm, autonomous from the market and the state. The notion of civil society as a *market-generated* society, historically contingent and structurally distinct, is obviated in favor of a borderless universe of voluntary sociability accommodating heterodox social forces. The failure to specify the analytical boundaries of civil society feeds into the romance of its potential to offer alternatives to the state.

The contrast between a societal and a market-driven civil society offers the analytical possibility of demarcating boundaries. Clearly, the two images are interlinked, but they cannot be collapsed under an amorphous conceptual umbrella, which appears to be the case in the prevailing discourses. Civil society is a determinate sphere of sociability, linked both to the market and the state:

> At a minimum, the rise of a civil society (in contrast either to political society, a realm of non-state action or a civilized society with a necessary normative superiority) is contingent upon the development of a certain type of political economy with distinct social practices, including the following: 1) a new social division of labor coextensive with an expanding exchange realm and a self-regulating market which differentiates society, but especially the labor process; 2) the creation of a new sphere of social institutions and interests linked to the former (realm of exchange); and 3) a system of rights linked to the complex apparatuses of coercive power, both serving as a check on the latter's global reach in society *and* providing an alternative channel for interest articulation. The essence of a system of rights is captured in the idea of *legality*, which provides protection to this new sphere both against the arbitrariness of the state and the caprice of private want satisfaction. To stabilize civil society, therefore, the state's role is crucial; a weak state lacking legitimate authority is likely to devour civil society, or the state merely becomes its extension.[23]

To be analytically precise, the rise of civil society is contingent upon the development of a certain type of political economy with distinct social practices. Actually existing civil societies in postcolonial societies are typically hybrid in form, housing conflicting interests and alternative discursive strategies to engage the state. However, the recognition of an inextricable bond between civil society and capitalism, on the one hand, and the modern state, on the other, averts the tendency to equate all associational life with civil society.

Civil Society and Its Limits

The preceding general argument can now be linked to historical and regional specificity with reference to Pakistan and India. First, the set of "conditions of possibility"[24] for civil society in South Asia, one that mirrors the idealized worlds of Enlightenment thought, is increasingly frail due to the emergence of violence as one of the principal forms of political engagement. The received idea of assigning violence anomic space within an otherwise normalized societal order appears tenuous: the symbiosis between normalcy and liberal democratic arrangements can be challenged. A condition of normalcy, violence has entered the public space despite, or because of, the opening up of the political system. Perhaps its cathartic presence in the present has historical antecedents: repressed political desires; unresolved tensions; combustible social interactions between communities of difference; or the sheer incompetence of the state or its crisis of governability[25] and absence of legitimacy. Available answers inevitably collapse into the stubborn counterfactual that recognizes legitimacy as a false apostle, a liberal invention designed to conceal the latent exclusionary practices of the state. Alternatively, the cause-and-effect relationship easily lends itself to a more dialectical operation in which political legitimacy itself may provide the clue to the crisis of governability. Hence, the institution of rules of political engagement, while democratically engineered, may contribute toward alienation and virtual disenfranchisement of communities and groups who do not square comfortably with the circle of Liberal Reason. On their face, democratic arrangements and constitutional frameworks might portend inclusion; their real effect can be the opposite. Violence may also become the source of establishing authority, terrorizing adversaries, and incapacitating opposition. Domestic political order and violence do not necessarily show divergent tendencies, but symbiosis. Civil society is often formed on the crucible of violence, which in the South Asian case does not easily slip into the zone of invisibility. An aspect of the civilizing process is precisely the transition from visibility to invisibility, one that relates violence to the zone of invisibility.

Social forces seeking political dominance in South Asia, as elsewhere, have increasingly embraced violence as an essential ingredient to effect political change—from jihadist extremists in Pakistan wanting to build a transnational virtual City of God; Tamil Tigers in Sri Lanka using violence as a solicitation for participation into the power structure; or Hindu fundamentalists yearning for a purified national space sans minorities, especially, Muslims. Neither atavistic nor pathological, violence in these disparate settings is inextricably interwoven into the modernist narrative of national space. Civil society has furnished the principal elements both to construct exclusionary nationalisms and to materialize them within the horizons of secular temporality.[26]

Empowerment within civil society, as in the case of India, premised on social mobility for certain groups or communities and consequent fissures in life conditions for others, has often translated into ambitious schemes to transform the state and its collective identity. Hindutva is partly explicable on these grounds. The case of Pakistan appears to be radically different, but upon closer scrutiny, the strengthening of the religious fundamentalist current is a product of the expansion of civil society in Pakistan, allowing new entrants, as well as their perceived estrangement from the power structure despite periodic sponsorship from the state.

Second, civil society bears the imprint of a national security imaginary, particularly in the case of Pakistan and India.[27] The presumed autonomy of civil society is highly questionable:

> In South Asia, as elsewhere, in the postcolonial Third World, not only does the state cast a long shadow on civil society, but civil society itself is the site of the reproduction of statist projects. Despite its apparent innocence, civil society in South Asia shows the imprint of the historical constitution of the state. As a moment of the modern state, with its complex structures and practices, civil society is fully implicated in how the state constructs the social world. National security is no exception.[28]

The legacy of the Partition,[29] the perceived vivisection of India on the presumed basis of religious difference, and conflict over the "unfinished business" of the Partition—Kashmir—have been important correlates for producing nationalist imaginaries in the two countries.[30] The statist predilection for exclusionary cartographies has decidedly informed civil society. Postcolonial states in South Asia have been largely unable to embrace autonomous imaginaries.

Yet, it would be reckless to hang the character of postcolonial civil society entirely on received historical narratives. The crucial element is the refurbishment of the nationalist imaginary with renewed and reinvigorated processes of expansion of the public sphere, implicating the media and seemingly apolitical zones of opinion-making within civil society. Hence, patriotism has been forcefully reconstructed in times of national emergency with the active involvement of social actors within civil society—on film, television, print and electronic journalism, and in the public arena in general.

Third, civil society is exposed to cross-border currents, combined with diasporic imaginings of the homeland or influence peddling from international NGOs, shaping the terms of political discourse, but also conditioning the tenor of the modern. Cross-border influences are pivotal in the remaking of Pakistan, not only as a sequestered national homeland but as a porous site to launch new identities either as a cultural condominium between the Gulf States and South Asia or as a transnational zone of Central/South Asian partnership. The former is consummated with material processes of labor migration and remittances; the latter is afforded by the "blowback" from abetting the crusade against the "Evil Empire" and the newly forged arc of Islamism. Once its principal sponsor, the state now becomes the main victim of terror and violence produced by forces ill at ease with secular renderings of society. Yet, paradoxically, Islamism draws its inspiration from secular ambitions of power, rationalized by scripture and precedent. The nationalist imaginary in Pakistan has become vulnerable to a newly formed scopic regime of neo-Pan-Islamism that extends to Afghanistan in the North and to the Gulf States in the West. Unlike its predecessor from the last century, neo-Pan-Islamism rests on the impulse to reshape the center.

Fourth, a weak state is unlikely to produce a strong society. The prevailing sentiment in certain quarters that building robust civil societies in South Asia would produce democratization, security, or welfare neglect the centrality of the state. As Peter Evans notes:

> The fate of civil society is inextricably bound to the robustness of the state apparatus. Deterioration of state institutions is likely to go hand in hand with the disorganization of civil society. Sustaining or regaining the institutional integrity of state bureaucracies increases the possibility of mounting projects of social transformation.[31]

The character of the state and the character of civil society are mutually constitutive in all the states in South Asia. States provide settings in which discourse can be conducted. DeVotta's comment on Sri Lanka also applies to other instances:

> . . . a state's political structure can influence what civil society groups demand and how they go about making those demands. Sri Lanka's political structure has enabled particularistic and ethnic-based groups to hold sway—leading to ethnocentric groups triumphing over interethnic and inclusive groups to generate adverse political change and illiberal governance.[32]

Against this background, a somewhat closer scrutiny of some aspects of civil society in Pakistan and India may be in order. The intent here is to illustrate the principal claim regarding the nexus between civil society and the production of regional insecurity. A comprehensive analysis, however, is beyond the scope of this chapter.

Cultural Fracture: Pakistan

Four distinct features mark the character of civil society in Pakistan.[33] First and most significantly, civil society in Pakistan has largely been shaped by an undemocratic state.[34] The instability of civil society is directly proportional to the arbitrary nature of the political dispensation. Second, civil society in Pakistan has developed in the shadow of national security and its institutional imperatives and ethos. In this context, civil society may not require state patronage to the degree that national security has been embraced by large sections of civil society.[35] Third, the relative autonomy of civil society reflects the relative autonomy of capital. To the extent that capital in Pakistan has largely failed to evolve autonomously without state patronage, preferring a rentier existence, civil society reveals those features. Fourth, fracture, on sectarian, ethnic, regional, and class lines, remains the dominant characteristic of civil society in Pakistan. Sectarianism is directly linked to the consolidation of Islamist influence in the subaltern sectors of society. In this vein, it is a by-product of the growing cultural and class chasm in Pakistan.[36] To this element one can add the proliferation of Islamist social forces, emergent in the aftermath of the war in Afghanistan, especially during the 1980s and 1990s.[37]

Received analyses of the rise of Islamist groups in Pakistan highlight the centrality of the Afghan war and the proliferation of religious schools. The instrumental use of "ideological Islam" as a legitimating force has also been recognized. Pakistan's insertion into the wider vortex of transnational Islam through linkages with the Gulf States and Afghanistan has also been noted. However, from a sociological perspective, the character of civil society itself has been left out of the equation. In this regard, the cultural fracture in Pakistan acquires greater salience. What are the principal features of this fracture?

Unlike ethnic and regional divisions that have been scrutinized with sustained attention, the divide between dominant and subaltern social forces has been neglected. The latter are inextricably linked to a vernacular idiom long repressed in strategies to forge a nation. Islamization from above has been replaced by Islamization from below. Ironically, once its progenitor, the state now finds itself as a victim of processes it set into motion but that it no longer has the capacity to manage. At a deeper level, the cultural divide in Pakistan is linked to the divergent paths social forces have taken within the framework of a weakened state.

The expansion of the market has produced the need for cultural defense in one instance and more assertive attempts to reshape public morality and consciousness in others. However, Islamism is not merely a reaction to modernizing or globalizing impulses but is a social force with agency. A number of factors have contributed to the spread of Islamist tendencies, including the advent of the electronic media, the emergence of rival centers of cultural production, and also the democratization of religious authority with the emergence of "lay" imams and televangelists. The role of religious schools (*madrassahs*) should be seen in this broader context, both as centers of religious production and as competitors in a highly heterodox cultural market. This point does not suggest reducing Islamism to market-driven processes but instead means recognition of the need to place Islamization from below within a stream of social action in part instigated by market forces.

To be certain, the world of Islamism is a bifurcated world: fully integrated into the expanding field of market relations but constructing an alternative public and private morality. The limits of the secularization thesis become fully exposed here; modernity need not secularize. Hence, for example, the nuclearization of the family has been accompanied not with lesser forms of patriarchy but actually more intensified forms of gender inequality, rationalized by certain variants of the faith. The symbiosis between the expansion of the public sphere and restrictive spaces for gender equality challenges received wisdom. The inability of the state to produce a "national" framework to instill a new public morality also becomes transparent. Instead, the state merely echoes the anxieties found in discourses of cultural defense.

To be sure, the Islamist current must be placed within a wider context of contestations between state and society in Pakistan. The expansion of market-driven social relations has also given birth to vibrant media, both print and electronic, as well as an efficacious lawyer's movement. Paradoxically, the media in Pakistan have grown to be the strongest in South Asia despite the authoritarian leanings of the state. In turn, the lawyers' movement has challenged erstwhile conceptions of elite bias, especially in reference to the suspension of the chief justice of the Supreme Court, Iftikhar Muhammad Chaudhry, by the quasi-military government of Pervez Musharraf on March 9, 2007.

The lawyers' movement began in earnest in response to a declaration of Pakistan's Supreme Court Bar Association, condemning the suspension of the chief justice and supporting his refusal to comply with the order. After massive street protests by the lawyers, human rights activists, the media, and students, the Supreme Court of Pakistan restored Chaudhry as chief justice in July 2007. However, Pervez Musharraf imposed a state of emergency in November 2007 and dismissed Chaudhry again, alongside sixty other judges. Continued rallies and protests ensued, ultimately leading to the political demise of Pervez Musharraf, who was forced to step down in response to the restoration of civilian rule in Pakistan after an election in 2008. The new civilian government resisted demands to restore the judges, including Chaudhry, but eventually succumbed to pressure after a "Long March" in March 2009 led by the lawyers. A combination of sustained media pressure and street protest underscored the inability of the state to quell dissent and stifle democratic aspirations.

Unprecedented in scope, the lawyers' movement clearly redefines the terms of political discourse in Pakistan. However, it is important to balance this inference with an appreciation of deep social rigidities that prevent the consolidation of a democratic temper. Rasul Baksh Rais captures this point quite well:

> Pakistan's social and political worlds present two contrasting pictures: one that shows remarkable change, while the other remains more of the same, rather it has witnessed decline and decay in leadership, legitimacy, social connectedness and in its other manifestations. While society has changed a great deal with the emergence of new social forces, their dynamism and eagerness to change politics, the political side presents more of the same: preservation of the dynastic, mainly feudal elite and their subordinate, subsidiary layers of local networks.[38]

Equally salient is a disjuncture between social forces seeking democratic ideals and their relative insignificance in relation to the regional security complex. While some business associations in Pakistan have sought more amicable ties with their eastern neighbor, the terms of discourse pertaining to India have been deeply impacted by either nationalist fervor or religious extremism. In the latter instance, the growing importance of *jihadi* groups as a "spoiler" element cannot be exaggerated. With rhetoric and action, these groups have severely conditioned the larger political mood, producing a comparable response across the border in raising the temperature of animosity and mistrust. The impasse on the Kashmir problem has been strengthened with the growing interjection of religious consciousness within Pakistan.

State weakness in Pakistan has further ensured that *jihadi* groups now operate with impunity, as recent attacks in both Mumbai and in Lahore show. The brazen assaults in early 2009 on the Sri Lankan cricket team and the Police Academy in Lahore, and the "Pakistani" Taliban's de facto capture of the Swat Valley before Islamabad's military action to reverse the trend, reveal the symbiotic relation between insecurity and elements within civil society.[39]

Communalization of Civil Society: India

Commentators generally recognize the robustness of civil society in India, underlining its dynamism, but they also note its contradictory character:

> On the one hand, the uncivil elements occupying the civil society space have successfully communalized Indian politics at the macro and meso levels to further their agenda of establishing India as a Hindu nation....On the other hand, a large section of civil society, working primarily at the micro level, presents an alternative vision of justice and development that is embedded in the discourse of empowerment, rights and democracy.[40]

No singular image captures the complexity of civil society in India. Caste, ethnicity, religion, community, and region forcefully structure the content of associational life. The consolidation of the middle classes has clearly produced a bourgeois realm, but the linkages between subaltern classes and political society have also matured. As Chatterjee notes:

> What I do know is that the practices of democracy have changed in India in the last four decades, that the project of state-led modernization has been drastically modified, and that forms of involvement of the subaltern classes with governmental activities as well as with representative institutions have both expanded and deepened.[41]

Contradictions within any civil society are neither unique nor unprecedented. However, the key site to link the question of insecurity to civil society is the consolidation of communal tensions with a regional impact. Increasingly, the heterodox and fluid character of civil society metamorphoses into homogeneous and fixed zones. The principal effect of *Hindutva*[42] lies precisely in producing an unbridgeable space between the majority and the minority.

Civil society's active involvement in conditioning contra-discourses of state-building and repudiating the Nehruvian secularist compromise cannot be exaggerated. However, the setting for these contra-discourses has been chiseled by the modernist state.

Similarly, a recent nationalist resurgence in the wake of Pokhran and Kargil offers a determinate illustration of the symbiotic relationship between the Indian state and civil society.[43] Patriotic fervor may appear spontaneous, but its genealogy suggests otherwise. The relative comfort of the transition from state ideology to popular sentiment is an important warning against hasty celebrations of the emergence of "autonomous" spheres of societal action. The rivalry between India and Pakistan casts a lengthy shadow on internal processes of classification of degrees of patriotism. Large sections of India's civil society have been conditioned by the character of that rivalry. Communal tensions are closely intertwined with perceptions of patriotism. Although the defeat of the Bharatiya Janata Party (BJP) in the last general elections shows the nonlinear character of politics in a vast and complex country like India and the limits of communal politics, the nexus between insecurity and communalism in terms of its impact on the regional security environment remains entrenched in the political unconscious.

India's associational life offers multiple trajectories and alternatives, given the country's scale and diversity. Perhaps it is more pertinent to speak of civil societies, as opposed to a monolithic conception of civil society. The expansion and consolidation of market relations and the assertion of new social actors also offers heterodox possibilities. Yet, these possibilities can be easily compromised by statist discourses, but also by exclusivist claims emerging within civil society. The events of late 2008 in Mumbai illustrate the fragility of peace in a regional environment that can rapidly deteriorate with heightened tensions. The role of the popular media—institutions within civil society—in reproducing enmity appeared more crucial than statist discourse in both India and Pakistan.

Conclusions

The discourse of state weakness feeds into the narrative of mutual hostility as much as does the idea of an assertive civil society shaped by exclusionary predilections. Particularistic civil society cannot escape the burdens of modernist cartographies of inside/outside in which Otherness provides nourishment to sustain fictions of integration in multiethnic or multireligious states. The so-called autonomous realm of civil society has no *autonomous* imagination; the state has ensured that its version of pasts and futures persists. Perhaps this formulation is too extreme, but the converse offers a romanticized view of the possibilities of civil society.

The rediscovery of civil society as a site of alternative social and political action in South Asia is linked to the declining fortunes of statism. Public confidence in the state is low. Expectations that the state can play its historic role as an agent of social transformation have also dwindled. Civil society presents itself as a normatively superior alternative under these conditions. However, this prospect is swiftly confronted by probing whether civil society can compensate for presumed state weakness.

First, the autonomous spaces of civil society are heavily circumscribed by statist constructions: development, democracy, or progress. These are modernist constructs that follow the logic of linearity, historicism, and civilizational progress. In general, civil society has not been able to liberate itself from the entanglements of post-Enlightenment modernization thinking. Alternatives to the latter are either too feeble or readily dismissed as utopias, whether Gandhian economics or nonelitist politics. National mega-projects have ensured the relegation of alternatives to the margins or zones of irrationality in which survival rests on values of competitiveness, modern science, and exploitation of the commons.

Second, civil society is conditioned by statist discourses of patriotism, national identity, purity, and danger.[44] In both India and Pakistan, patriotism has been conceived in terms of hostility toward its respective neighbor. The wellsprings of "love of country" have dried up in favor of exclusivist nationalism. Popular culture, once open to multivocality and tolerance, has succumbed to nationalist frenzy, especially in times of "national" crisis.[45] Neither of these South Asian states is unique in this regard, against the backdrop of an established affinity between Hollywood and American empire. The central point, however, is the complicity of civil society in fulfilling nationalist dreams.

Third, the symbiotic relationship between state and civil society may be the principal agent of fracture. Committed to the production of homogenized space, the postcolonial state has strived to create civil society in that image. As this logic has played out, civil society has grown more intolerant. To the degree that the production of homogenized political space remains the hegemonic paradigm in effecting social arrangements or transformation, or in gauging degrees of state success or failure, the prospects for the region may not improve significantly. On this view, the idea of "national integration" may only create new fractures and conceptual fault lines.

Perhaps the biggest challenge to insecurity comes from the spillover of state weakness in Pakistan, and the failure of the state to bridge deepening cultural fissures. The "Talibanization" of both the North and Northwestern regions, as well as the growth in extremist violence, reveal the increasing inability of the state to forge either a national social compact or to reduce profound social and political rigidities. Despite the expansion of civil society, political society, unlike India, remains inaccessible to the subaltern classes in Pakistan. The source of alienation, hence, is both cultural and political, with vast regional effects. State weakness across the region offers enormous possibilities for local and national alienation, but particularly for its violent expression to acquire a regional character. The emergence of a fractured and unstable regional environment, therefore, cannot be ruled out.

In sum, the relationship between state and civil society is in a state of flux in South Asia. Unprecedented change brings new problems and solutions. However, the biggest problem lies not in facing the unknown but in the refusal to abandon received spatial and temporal imaginaries for organizing political life. Against the stubbornness of these imaginaries, civil society may offer no more than the state.[46]

Notes to Chapter 6

1. Atul Kohli, *Democracy and Discontent: India's Growing Crisis of Governability* (Cambridge: Cambridge University Press, 1991).

2. Lloyd I. Rudolph and Susanne Hoeber Rudolph, *In Pursuit of Lakshmi: The Political Economy of the Indian State* (Chicago: University of Chicago Press, 1987). Cited in Partha Chatterjee, "Democracy and the Violence of the State: A Political Negotiation of Death," *Inter-Asia Cultural Studies* 2, no. 1 (2001), p. 7.

3. Miller, this volume.

4. Christophe Jaffrelot, ed., *Pakistan: Nationalism without a Nation* (London: Zed Books, 2002).

5. Barry Buzan and Gowher Rizvi, eds., *South Asian Insecurity and the Great Powers* (Basingstoke, UK: Macmillan, 1986).

6. Ranajit Guha, *Dominance without Hegemony* (Cambridge, MA: Harvard University Press, 1998).

7. Mustapha Kamal Pasha, "Liberalization, State Patronage, and the 'New Inequality' in South Asia," *Journal of Developing Societies* 16, no. 1 (2000), pp. 71–85.

8. Leela Fernandes and Patrick Heller, "Hegemonic Aspirations: New Middle

Class Politics and India's Democracy in Comparative Perspective," *Critical Asian Studies* 38, no. 4 (2006), pp. 495–522.

9. On state weakness, see Robert I. Rotberg, "The Failure and Collapse of Nation-States: Breakdown, Prevention, and Repair," in *When States Fail: Causes and Consequences*, ed. Robert I. Rotberg (Princeton: Princeton University Press, 2004), pp. 1–45; and Joel S. Migdal, *Strong Societies and Weak States: State-Society Relations and State Capabilities in the Third World* (Princeton: Princeton University Press, 1988).

10. Paul, this volume.

11. The potentially grave consequences of state collapse have provoked considerable debate in International Relations. Some have even suggested changing the core foundational principles of the world order. See for example, Stephen D. Krasner, "Sharing Sovereignty: New Institutions for Collapsed and Failing States," *International Security* 29, no. 2 (Fall 2004), pp. 118–119. A similar mood can be found in James D. Fearon and David D. Laitin, "Neotrusteeship and the Problem of Weak States," *International Security* 28, no. 4 (Spring 2004), p. 43.

12. Hasan Askari Rizvi, *The Military and Politics in Pakistan* (Lahore: Progressive Publishers, 1974); and Ayesha Siddiqa, *Military Inc.: Inside Pakistan's Military Economy* (London: Pluto Press, 2007).

13. Gower Rizvi, "Pakistan: The Domestic Dimensions of Security," in Buzan and Rizvi, *South Asian Insecurity*, p. 84.

14. Mohammed Ayoob, "The Security Problematic of the Third World," *World Politics*, 43, no. 2 (January 1991), p. 265.

15. As Ayoob notes, "the greater the security that the Third World state possesses and can provide to its populace the greater will be the chances for successful transformation, economic growth and redistribution." Mohammad Ayoob, "The Third World in the System of States: Acute Schizophrenia or Growing Pains?" *International Studies Quarterly*, 33, no. 1, (March 1989), 67–79. For an extensive treatment of this theme, also see Ayoob, *The Third World Security Predicament* (Boulder, CO: Lynne Rienner, 1995).

16. Bishwapriya Sanyal, "NGOs' Self-Defeating Quest for Autonomy," *Annals of the American Academy of Political and Social Science: The Role of NGOs: Charity and Empowerment*, 554, no. 1 (Nov. 1997), pp. 21–32; and Shelley Feldman, "NGOs and Civil Society: (Un)stated Contradictions," *Annals of the American Academy of Political and Social Science: The Role of NGOs: Charity and Empowerment*, 554, no. 1, (Nov. 1997), pp. 46–65.

17. Others have seen prospects of involving civil society directly in building peace. See Camilla Orjuela, "Building Peace in Sri Lanka: A Role for Civil Society?" *Journal of Peace Research* 40, no. 2 (March 2003), pp. 195–212.

18. On common sense, see Antonio Gramsci, *Selections from Prison Notebooks*, ed. Quintin Hoare and Geoffrey Nowell Smith (New York: International Publishers, 1971).

19. The literature on civil society is extensive. For a theoretical exposé of the concept, see Jean L. Cohen and Andrew Arato, *Civil Society and Political Theory*

(Cambridge, MA: MIT Press, 1992); Sudipta Kaviraj and Sunil Khilnani, eds., *Civil Society: History and Possibilities* (Cambridge: Cambridge University Press, 2001); John Keane, ed., *Civil Society and the State: New European Perspectives* (London: Verso, 1988); Adam Seligman, *Civil Society* (New York: Free Press, 1992); Charles Taylor, "Modes of Civil Society," *Public Culture* 3, no. 1 (1991), pp. 95–118; Edward Shils,"The Virtue of Civil Society," *Government and Opposition* 26, no. 1 (1991), pp. 3–20. A critical review of this literature is offered in David L. Blaney and Mustapha Kamal Pasha, "Civil Society and Democracy in the Third World: Ambiguities and Historical Possibilities," *Studies in Comparative International Development* 28, no. 1 (Spring 1993), pp. 3–24.

20. Justin Rosenberg, *The Empire of Civil Society* (London: Verso, 2000).

21. For a critique of this thinking, see Asef Bayat, "Un-Civil Society: The Politics of the 'Informal People,'" *Third World Quarterly* 18, no. 1 (March 1997), pp. 53–72.

22. Alexis de Tocqueville, *Democracy in America*, 2 vols., trans. John Keane (New York: The Colonial Press, 1990).

23. Mustapha Kamal Pasha, "The Hyper-Extended State: Civil Society and Democracy," in *State, Society and Democratic Change in Pakistan*, ed. Rasul B. Rais (Oxford: Oxford University Press, 1997), pp. 186–187.

24. Michael Hardt, "The Withering of Civil Society," *Social Text*, no. 45 (Winter 1995), pp. 27–44.

25. Kohli, *Democracy and Discontent.*

26. Ashis Nandy, "The Political Culture of the Indian State," *Daedalus*, 118, no. 4 (Fall 1989), pp. 1–26.

27. I have explored this theme in greater detail in "Security as Hegemony," *Alternatives* 21, no. 3 (July–September 1996), pp. 283–302.

28. Ibid., p. 284.

29. For a counterintuitive reading, see Sankaran Krishna, "Oppressive Pasts and Desired Futures: Re-Imagining India," *Futures*, 24 (1992), pp. 858–866.

30. On Kashmir, see Raju G.C. Thomas, ed. *Perspectives on Kashmir: The Roots of Conflict in South Asia* (Boulder, CO: Westview, 1992). For a broader perspective on Indo-Pakistan rivalry, see T. V. Paul, ed., *The India-Pakistan Conflict: An Enduring Rivalry*, (Cambridge, MA: Cambridge University Press, 2005). For an alarmist account, see Sumit Ganguly and Devin Hagerty, *Fearful Symmetry: The India-Pakistan Conflict in the Shadow of Nuclear Weapons* (New Delhi: Oxford University Press, 2005).

31. Peter Evans, *Embedded Autonomy* (Princeton: Princeton University Press, 1995), p. 249.

32. Neil DeVotta, "Sri Lanka: Ethnic Domination, Violence, and Liberal Democracy," in *Civil Society and Political Change in Asia: Expanding and Contracting Democratic Space*, ed. Muthiah Alagappa (Stanford, CA: Stanford University Press, 2004), p. 292.

33. For a useful background, see Iftikhar H. Malik, *State and Civil Society in Pakistan: Politics of Authority, Ideology and Ethnicity* (London: Macmillan, 1997).

34. The notion of democracy here is generic in terms of procedural facts of rep-

resentation. For detailed analysis of the "undemocratic" character of Pakistan's state, see Aqil Shah, "Pakistan: Civil Society in the Service of an Authoritarian State," in Alagappa, *Civil Society*, pp. 357–388. Also see Zulfiqar Gillani and Anita M. Weiss, eds., *Power and Civil Society in Pakistan* (Karachi: Oxford University Press, 2001). For an analysis of general trends, see Stephen Phillip Cohen, *The Idea of Pakistan* (Washington, DC: Brookings Institution Press, 2004); and Lawrence Ziring, *Pakistan: At the Crosscurrent of History* (Oxford: Oneworld Publications, 2003).

35. A similar trend in India is noted by Neera Chandhoke, "The 'Civil' and the 'Political' in Civil Society: The Case of India," in *Civil Society in Democratization*, ed. Peter Burnell and Peter Calvert (London & Portland, OR: Frank Cass, 2004), pp. 143–165.

36. Muhammad Qasim Zaman, "Sectarianism in Pakistan: The Radicalization of Shi'i and Sunni Identities," *Modern Asian Studies* 32, no. 3 (1998), pp. 689–716.

37. Husain Haqqani, *Pakistan: Between the Mosque and the Military* (Washington, DC: Carnegie Endowment for International Peace, 2005); and C. Christine Fair, *The Madrassah Challenge: Militancy and Religious Education in Pakistan* (Washington, DC: United States Institute of Peace Press, 2008).

38. Rasul Bakhsh Rais, "New Social Forces," *The Friday Times*, 19, no. 50 (February 1–7, 2008).

39. For an excellent analysis of the wider implications of the Islamic militant threat to Pakistan's domestic security, see C. Christine Fair, "The Educated Militants of Pakistan: Implications for Pakistan's Domestic Security," *Contemporary South Asia*, 16, no. 1 (March 2008), pp. 93–106.

40. Amitabh Behar and Aseem Prakash, "India: Expanding and Contracting Democratic Space," in Alagappa, *Civil Society*, p. 191.

41. Chatterjee, "Democracy," p. 20.

42. On Hindutva, see Christophe Jaffrelot, *The Hindu Nationalist Movement in India* (New Delhi: Viking, 1993) and Ashis Nandy, et al., *Creating a Nationality: The Ramjanambhumi Movement and the Fear of Self* (New Delhi: Oxford University Press, 1995).

43. Chandhoke, "The 'Civil' and the 'Political,'" offers a forceful analysis of this trend.

44. As Chandhoke notes, "even as this genre of nationalism seeks to cast a long shadow of suspicion on the minorities within the country, it dismisses those who question the shape of this nationalism as anti-national. Overtaking civil society in India, this nationalism—both exclusive and insular to a frightful degree—strongly bears the imprimatur of the state. Narrow in scope, chauvinistic in content, stereotypical in form, and constructed around the homogenizing impulse, cultural nationalism attempts to accomplish two feats. It seeks to construct majorities and minorities out of a plural, heterogeneous and loosely articulated society, and it seeks to institutionalize fissures between two constructed groups on the basis of stereotypes and stigmata." Ibid, p. 154.

45. Notice the tenor of films made on the heels of the Kargil war, or premised on the Indo-Pakistan rivalry.

46. As Chatterjee succinctly writes, "history, it would seem, has decreed that we, in the post-colonial world, shall only be perpetual consumers of modernity. Europe and the Americas, the only true subjects of history, have thought out on our behalf not only the script of colonial enlightenment and exploitation, but also that of our anti-colonial resistance and post-colonial misery. Even our imaginations must remain forever colonized." Chatterjee, "Whose Imagined Community?" p. 521.

PART III
THE REGIONAL STATES

7 Polity, Security, and Foreign Policy in Contemporary India

David Malone and Rohan Mukherjee

> External affairs will follow internal affairs. Indeed, there is no basis for external affairs if internal affairs go wrong.
>
> *—Jawaharlal Nehru, in a speech to the*
> *Constituent Assembly of India on March 8, 1948*[1]

Sixty years ago, at the dawn of independence, modern India's first prime minister and foreign minister acknowledged the importance of domestic forces in the shaping of a country's security environment and foreign policy. This chapter confronts a paradox: India is riven with internal conflicts that challenge state legitimacy and levels of routine violence, often politically manipulated, that astound foreign observers. These sources of insecurity sometimes flow across its international borders, in both directions. Yet India presents to the world, altogether credibly, the face of a rising economic and geostrategic power. It is today, well into India's seventh decade, hard to question its overall national cohesion as an international actor.

The image of India is shifting, perhaps excessively, from one of numbing poverty feebly combated by inept governments at various levels to one of an economic powerhouse rising to challenge China and perhaps one day the United States as a global actor of growing significance. But, on closer examination, is this the whole, or even an accurate, story? What of India's continuing crushing rural poverty, its growing economic inequalities (mirroring those in much of the rest of the world), its communal divisions often expressed through sudden and shocking violence, its murderous insurgencies, its terrorist outrages, and its increasingly fractured politics? Are these mere footnotes to the "India Shining" narrative promoted breathlessly by India boosters both within the country and internationally?

In his introduction to this volume, T. V. Paul characterizes India as a "strong-weak" state. In other words, it is harder to conclusively identify the Indian state as either strong or weak, especially when compared to other countries in the region that fall more readily into the "weak" category. One can understand India's relative position based on Paul's definition of state capacity. Whereas the Indian state has done well to secure its citizens from foreign threats, its record is far murkier on domestic order and welfare provision. While there is no doubt that (unlike neighboring states such as Nepal or Sri Lanka) the Indian state successfully claims the right to speak for the Indian people in international affairs, it faces multiple domestic legitimacy challenges from different corners of its territory. Moreover, the state's effectiveness in implementing policy untrammeled by internal or external actors is highly questionable. India's record on state capacity is therefore decidedly mixed and nuanced. The heart of the paradox lies in the fact that although internationally India is emerging as a strong state that is increasingly tilting the global balance of power in Asia's favor, it is domestically a relatively weak state, compared to other great powers, with multiple security challenges.

This chapter argues that India's strong-weak state capacity is a common intermediate cause of both its domestic insecurity and international strength. The underlying forces behind the Indian state's weakness are structural, relating largely to the nation's social composition and political architecture. The influence of these factors, mediated by the state, has ensured that India is simultaneously strong and weak. At home, deep social divisions and a democratic federal polity contribute to the rise of various subnational movements that challenge state legitimacy and hinder the state's ability to respond effectively to security challenges. In terms of foreign policy, however, the resulting domestic political fragmentation since the 1980s has opened up the space for post-Nehruvian ideas of India's role in the contemporary world. This trend mirrors the decline of single-party government in India, and in the absence of any clear winning ideology, an approach rooted in pragmatism has become the de facto lowest common denominator of India's foreign policy. This has helped India shed its moral baggage on the international stage and embrace strategic relationships with a diverse range of countries, from the United States to Iran. India's international stature has concomitantly grown since the early 1990s.

As a result, in spite of tensions often rooted in security concerns with several of its neighbors, India is refocusing its foreign policy beyond these regional concerns to the global level, seeing its interests today as more globally economic and (to an extent) geostrategic than a foreign policy focused primarily on neighbors would allow. This is potentially encouraging for South Asia, but in some senses worrying for India's neighbors, as the region's anchor and powerhouse is moving beyond them to engage more than in the past with the great powers. The sustainability of this arrangement depends on how India manages its regional relationships and the extent to which India can rediscover a moral basis for projecting its power and influence globally.

Structural Determinants of State Weakness in India

To even the most superficial observer, the dominant characteristic of Indian society is diversity. Modern Indian society is primarily differentiated along regional and religious lines. The Constitution of India recognizes twenty-two official languages, each with a broadly distinct geographical coverage.[2] Of the major world religions, Hindus make up the majority of the population (80.5%), followed by Muslims (13.4%), Christians (2.3%), Sikhs (1.9%), Buddhists, Jains, and others (together adding up to 1.9%).[3] It is a testament to the absorptive capacity of Indian society that the Hindu religious tradition over the centuries has exhibited pluralistic tendencies that have in some form or another absorbed non-Hindu ideas and religious practices.[4] Thus, while religious conflicts did occur at times during India's earlier history, the broad trend has been one of coalescence and assimilation. However, the Hindu practice of stratification between castes has played a major role in creating social cleavages in modern India, and the recent political enfranchisement of the lower castes is today reshaping India's politics. Another critical factor has been the rise of *Hindutva*, a political brand of Hindu nationalism that is in constant tension with India's multicultural character and often attempts to resolve this dissonance through bouts of severe violence against religious minorities, particularly Muslims.

Although India is a federal republic, the Union government holds greater power than state governments and has the authority to remove state governments in times of emergency. The scale of India's security incidents (terrorist and separatist) is such that situations of emergency (by any international standards) abound, beyond the equally frequent political deadlocks produced by fragmented politics at federal and state levels. The 1990s witnessed the emergence of "identity politics," whereby identity, be it of caste, religion, or region, is equated with interest in the political sphere. Identity politics introduces new elements and levels of volatility—all too often with associated violence—into India's constant negotiation with itself.[5]

Playing into this maelstrom, generally positively, several key sets of national actors should be mentioned: civil society organizations that have started to exert pressure on the state to fulfill its commitments to economic reform and development; India's vibrant media—television, print, and electronic—which play an important role in articulating public opinion for policymakers and facilitating debate on vital issues; the Indian bureaucracy, celebrated and reviled in equal measure, which plays a central role in implementing government policy; and the Indian judiciary, an institution that has risen to the challenges of governance in India with considerable vigor, filling a vacuum often created by political instability and state incapacity. The Indian polity emerges as a complex arrangement of institutions, networks, and relationships alternately cooperating and contending with each other in democratic government against a backdrop of deep social cleavages.

Although economic liberalization since the early 1990s has resulted in unprecedented levels of economic growth,[6] that growth has been uneven (regionally, and among sectors of society with agricultural productivity growth largely stagnating of late). Its unevenness has produced new tensions in society and new threats of unrest, as large numbers of rural men migrate to the urban centers where they hope to find better-paying jobs. They are sometimes targeted, for example in Mumbai in 2008, as expatriate interlopers and undesirables.[7] Meanwhile, the rural poor, better informed than in the past through India's impressive telecommunications revolution, are keenly aware that very little of the money allocated to their needs by various levels of government ever reaches them. While the "trickle down" effect does operate in India—in some regions more than others—and the rising tide has lifted many boats into the burgeoning middle class, dissatisfaction with government is rife, as expressed in India's very strong "anti-incumbency" electoral culture. These factors create new sources of volatility and insecurity.

Social Cleavages and Political Fragmentation
Social heterogeneity and a federal polity combine with the sheer geographic and demographic challenges of administering a nation of India's size to create conditions for the emergence of subnational identities. Some of these identities take the shape of social or political movements. Others that fail to achieve their objectives politically turn to violence as a means of bringing the state to the negotiating table. Both phenomena create significant challenges

for the state apparatus, both in terms of a constant string of challenges to its legitimacy and in terms of hindering effective state responses to armed insurgencies. The preponderance of local or regional influences in Indian politics often complicates the exercise of central authority. Thus, for example, in the case of Assam the support for the United Liberation Front of Asom (ULFA) among the Assamese people was a major stumbling block in the way of an effective central government response to the insurgency. It was only during the 1990s as public support for the movement began to wane that the state could begin to make gains against the ULFA. Similar examples can be found in other states of Northeast India, a region particularly known for its multiple subnational identity conflicts.

Insurgency aside, the political mainstream too has witnessed a steady fragmentation of power and authority since the 1980s, particularly as numerous regional and caste-based parties have cultivated pockets of influence in the Indian polity. Sociologist Dipankar Gupta highlights the "closed" nature of stratification in the Indian caste system, where differences are predicated on invisible qualitative characteristics and mobility depends on one's ability to ideologically question the very fundamentals of the system.[8] When it comes to the distribution of economic gains in conditions of scarcity, there can hardly be any defensible intrinsic justification for such a system (despite religious doctrine). Therefore it is justified externally: hierarchy is imposed on qualitative differences using power that derives not from within the social system but through other means, notably sheer political clout. It therefore falls upon those lower down the order, if they wish to improve their conditions, to attain political power through ideologically charged appeals to their group members.

This group-based competition has been ongoing. The federal nature of the Indian polity creates spaces where local groups can vie for the power to exercise the autonomy afforded by the system. The existence of the single-member simple plurality electoral formula, combined with the stratified nature of social institutions, allows regional identity-based parties and coalitions to effectively preclude larger national parties (like the Congress and Bharatiya Janata Party [BJP]) from gaining majorities at state and local levels. Local political actors thus develop electoral bases that can be activated even during federal elections to gain a small degree of representation at the center, which gains significance as parties form alliances. The cost of influencing national electoral outcomes is therefore relatively lower for smaller identity-based parties than it would have been in a single-member plurality system without social stratification.[9] The traditional culture of personality-oriented politics and the lack of intra-party democracy (mainly in the Congress Party, less so in the BJP) prevent existing national parties from incorporating new sociopolitical movements into their fold. If new sociopolitical movements were coopted by the existing machinery of the large parties, it is likely that the impact of new social cleavages on the Indian polity would be diluted. In the absence of this phenomenon, however, new movements find their expression and vitality in challenging the existing social and political structures. Together, these factors contribute to the politicization of social cleavages in an environment of socioeconomic inequalities.

Against a backdrop of strong regional identities and the organization of states along linguistic lines, a range of regional political parties has emerged. The party system since the early 1990s has seen a proliferation of parties that appeal exclusively or mainly to ethnic or linguistic identities (as well, in a narrower range of cases, to caste). In the 2004 general elections, state-based parties won 30% of the seats in the lower house (Lok Sabha) with approximately 29% of the vote. Consequently, India's major national parties (Congress and BJP) have found it difficult to obtain majorities in Parliament, and coalition governments have become the norm over the last two decades. Small regional parties with even a handful of members in Parliament are able to obtain key cabinet positions by taking advantage of the prevailing electoral calculus, sometimes holding the cabinet to ransom on issues potentially and actually undermining national security or the government's stated foreign policy (e.g., on Sri Lanka).

The picture of India that emerges is one of a heterogeneous society, a fragmented yet functioning polity, and a burgeoning yet lopsided economy. As India's economy has grown, its social diversity has manifested itself in the form of socioeconomic inequalities, including the uneven distribution of gains from development. These inequalities, combined with certain features of the political system, have led to the political mobilization of hitherto excluded groups, including through the agency of new region- and caste-based political parties relying on the politics of identity. Witnessing the success of their political strategies, parties continue to rely on identity politics, which results in the deepening of social cleavages.[10]

The resulting domestic scene is a fluid and unstable morass of shifting social and political alliances that complicates as much as facilitates democratic policymaking. The fragmented nature of India's political system diminishes the state's ability to effectively maintain law and order and provide public goods, particularly in the face of strong patronage pressures from various identity groups. Various subnational movements and armed insurgencies continue to challenge the legitimacy of the state and cause grievous harm to government property and personnel. The net effect of these phenomena is a decline in overall domestic security as the state grapples with Maoists in Jharkhand, militants in Kashmir, rebels in Nagaland, and insurgents in Assam, to name a few. Particularly intractable are those situations where domestic challengers to the Indian state develop linkages with broader threats in India's security environment.

External and Internal Actors

Aside from sources of state weakness that are intrinsic to India's social and political structure, a major constraint on the Indian state's capacity is its inability to function in a manner untrammeled by internal or external actors. When the objectives of internal and external actors align, or when internal and external actors find common cause against the Indian state, India is presented with a serious security challenge. Here we briefly discuss the major identity-related sources of insecurity emanating from within India itself, and their linkages with the South Asian neighborhood. It quickly becomes evident that many of India's domestic security challenges also grow out of its basic structural feature of being a socially heterogeneous and politically fragmented nation.

Ethnic Identity

Three kinds of domestic factors relevant to ethnic identity influence India's policies toward its neighbors.

Transnational Ethnic Groups. Indian populations in border regions tend to share a common ethnic and sometimes religious bond with populations in adjacent countries. This is true of Tamils and Sri Lanka, Indian Punjabis and Pakistani Punjabis, Indian Kashmiris and Pakistani Kashmiris, Indian populations bordering the Tarai region of Nepal, and even Malayalis (the people of Kerala) and the Gulf countries. By corollary, and extending the concept to religion, it is also true of the Hindu minorities in Bangladesh and Pakistan, and Muslims in India with respect to some neighboring countries and communities.

The broad territorial division of ethnic groups within India and the strength of regional ethnic identities ensure that Indian policy toward the countries in question is always attentive to the preferences of domestic actors in these regions. This has been evinced by the sustained and vociferous support of the Tamil people and the Tamil Nadu government to the separatist movement of Tamils in Sri Lanka until the early 1990s, a fact that caused the Indian government to be heavily and sometimes unhappily involved in the ongoing conflict at various times, to the point of acquiescing in the armed tactics of the LTTE,[11] launching a disastrous peacekeeping mission in Sri Lanka, and refusing military aid to the Sri Lankan army.[12] More recently, in 2008, New Delhi bent to political pressure from Tamil Nadu to intervene with the Sri Lankan government, at a time when it was in military ascendance against the LTTE, to provide calming assurances. Similarly, the International Crisis Group, regarding the Madhesi movement for autonomy in the Tarai region of Nepal, reports that there is "widespread sympathy" in Indian border regions and "most politicians and bureaucrats do not hesitate to express moral support" for the cause.[13]

Secessionist Movements and Insurgencies. Due to its vast size and heterogeneous society and polity, India has been the subject of various conflicts between subnational regions and the central government. Scholars particularly attribute this to the failure of the Indian state to ensure "substantive democracy and equitable development" for large swathes of society.[14] This, they argue, has resulted in the discrediting of state-sponsored nationalism and, inter alia, the rise of movements aimed at establishing separate sovereign status from the Union. The history of modern India is replete with such movements, many of which are still in progress.

Movements in border areas are particularly problematic because they become flashpoints with neighboring countries, mainly due to three factors. First, secessionist movements, especially armed movements, are likely to use the territories of adjacent countries to stage their attacks on the Indian state. This has negative consequences for the security of India's neighbors and makes India diplomatically vulnerable to allegations of not doing enough to prevent its domestic conflicts from destabilizing the border regions of neighboring countries. Second, and more importantly, the cross-border activities of secessionists create obstacles to neutralizing these movements. Third, secessionist movements allow neighboring countries with an interest in destabilizing India to interfere in its internal affairs in an adverse manner. These number among the considerations that have influenced India's policy toward

Pakistan in the case of the Khalistan movement;[15] toward Myanmar, Bhutan, China and Bangladesh in the case of multiple secessionist movements in the Northeast;[16] and toward Nepal in the case of the Naxalite (Maoist) movement. The existence of domestic groups of insurgents and separatists therefore significantly complicates India's security environment in South Asia.

Migration: New Ethnic Groups. The cross-border movement of large populations, although a version of the transnational ethnic group conundrum, presents a conceptually distinct challenge because it involves the large-scale migration of individuals into Indian territory, transforming an international affair into one with significant domestic ramifications. The mass migration of such populations either at one time or over time results in the creation of new ethnic groups in the border (and other) regions of India, with the potential of creating security problems, particularly in relations with respective originating countries. Two examples stand out in this regard—the limited migration of Buddhist Tibetans escaping Chinese persecution and the much larger and steady inflow of Muslim immigrants (legal and illegal) from Bangladesh into West Bengal and the Northeastern region of India. The creation and expansion of two new ethnic groups (Tibetan Buddhists and Bengali Muslims) to which postindependence Indian society was not accustomed has impacted the domestic reaction to these migrations, not least given suspicions attaching to the purported connections between some recent terrorist attacks in India and Bangladeshi elements, and consequently impinged on India's relations with China and Bangladesh, respectively.

In the case of China, India has walked a tightrope between official recognition of Tibet as an integral part of China and granting asylum to the Dalai Lama and his followers in Indian territory. This is largely because Tibetan migrants are relatively small in number and representatives of a globally recognized struggle (yet one that the Indian government cannot officially endorse). Also, Buddhism is accepted as a native faith in India, albeit nowadays a very minor one numerically. By contrast, the domestic sociopolitical response to Bangladeshi Muslim immigrants has been much less forgiving, partly due to their faith and partly the purely economic motive driving the migrants onto Indian soil. The reaction has been particularly violent in Assam, where riots against migrant Bengalis date back to the 1960s and 1970s. Despite some progress toward normalization of bilateral relations with Bangladesh, complicated by a host of other issues, the migration question remains a thorn in India's side. A manifestation of the domestic impulse was the Indian decision to construct a 4000 km concrete fence along the Indo-Bangladeshi border in 1984, a project that carries on today and has created controversy between the two countries.[17]

Religious Identity

The importance of religion as an integral component of the Indian worldview cannot be understated. Various commentators have highlighted the weight that Indian foreign policymakers attach to the religious opinions and sentiments of India's sizeable Muslim population, which by many accounts is the second largest in the world.[18] C. Raja Mohan describes India as an "Islamic nation" with a national culture deeply influenced by Islam.[19] Other members of the Indian intelligentsia have highlighted West Asia as a priority area for India not just for strategic reasons but also due to the spiritual and religious needs of India's Muslim population. Indeed, the fear of alienating this population is cited as a major reason for the lack of a noticeable Indo-Israeli relationship until the 1980s.[20] India also has the second largest Shia Muslim population in the world, which makes its ties with Iran, a Shia state, particularly relevant and sensitive. The fate of Indian Muslims is keenly followed by Iran and plays an important part in cementing a long-term relationship between the two countries.[21]

The impulse to accommodate the sensitivities of India's Muslim community on at least some foreign policy issues derives more recently in part from a growing recognition that not all terrorism involving Muslims in India is likely to be directed from Pakistan or Bangladesh. Thus, while India's Muslim community is viewed by some political movements as already a Fifth Column within the country that will respond only to a firm government hand, others believe it short-sighted to alienate in any unnecessary way a community so large within a state so fragmented (and one with a fairly weak internal security apparatus, judging by its inability to track down the perpetrators of most recent terrorist attacks). The actual and potential interplay between some Indian Muslims and radical Muslim forces outside India has worried many in the security establishment for some time, but no consistent policy in this regard has arisen under any recent Union government.

No other country has figured more prominently in the interplay of religion and India's security than Pakistan. (In this regard, religion is more fundamental to the political identity of India than some observers recognize.) India's secular polity was forged as a conscious refutation of the idea that religion should be the basis of nationality, an idea more commonly referred to as the "two-nation theory." While the progenitors of Pakistan considered partition to be primarily a religious phenomenon, India's leaders viewed it as an instance of territorial self-determination.[22] This basic divergence lies at the root of India's policy toward Pakistan and India's position on the Kashmir issue. While Pakistan views the status of Indian-controlled Kashmir as abhorrent to the idea of Muslim nationhood (i.e., a Muslim-majority state in a Hindu-majority nation), India views the Kashmir valley and surrounding territory as an integral part of its territorial identity. Moreover, Kashmir stands as a crucial test of India's secular character—a move toward independence for Kashmir or, worse still, its accession to Pakistan, would undermine India's religious plurality while adding credibility to the two-nation theory. This could have "far-reaching, reactionary and undemocratic effects" in India.[23]

The rise of *Hindutva* in the early 1990s was from this perspective disconcerting for many Indians. Its political philosophy sought to establish India as a Hindu nation, thus inadvertently legitimizing the two-nation theory. However, when leading a coalition in power in New Delhi, 1998–2004, the BJP proved surprisingly pragmatic. Demographic and constitutional realities dictated that, in power, it could not exclude other religions, and it maintained India's traditional line on Kashmir. Moreover, the BJP, while playing on communal issues (as do, all too often, other Indian parties) when these offered easy pickings, mostly contested elections not on religious grounds but on issues of democracy and governance. Indeed, its prime minister, Atal Bihari Vajpayee, was instrumental in reaching out to the Pakistani leadership in an effort to initiate a peace process, which bore some fruit despite major setbacks.

Nonetheless, the specter of religion as a vexing intervening variable in India's security calculations continues to haunt its political and policymaking elites. The BJP's own domestic actions with regard to the organized demolition of a prominent mosque (the Babri Masjid) on disputed land in 1992 and the massacre of Muslims in Gujarat under BJP (state and federal) governments in 2002 did nothing to allay these fears, particularly as a domestic backlash from India's Muslim minority became evident through the activities of the Students' Islamic Movement of India (SIMI).

National Identity
Transcending factors of disunity and paralysis affecting India's foreign and domestic policies at times, and enhancing its cohesion in times of challenges, is an overriding sense of national identity to which polling suggests India's Muslim community also strongly subscribes. In the realm of foreign policy,

some scholars have found helpful the concept of "state nationalism," or the state-sponsored idea of a nation with specific goals and a conception of how they can be achieved.[24]

State nationalism in India was strong in the initial years of independence, when the ideals of freedom from oppression and of anti-imperialism carried over from the freedom struggle. Nehru's India projected a very strong sense of national identity, reflected in some key foreign policy decisions that defined the course of India's interactions with the world. Bhiku Parekh notes that Nehru gave India a "distinct moral voice" in the world, derived primarily from his and Mahatma Gandhi's leadership of the anti-colonial struggle. In contemporary times, Parekh notes that India has developed a new identity that is a deliberate reaction to Nehruvian nationalism. It seeks to break from the Indian tradition of "poverty, moralizing and isolation" to focus more on economic and military power in foreign policy.[25] This accords with most contemporary writing on Indian foreign policy, which describes it as pragmatic, realist, and a departure from the rhetorical idealism of the past. The new pragmatism, however, threatens to erode the moral basis of India's state nationalism. Without a strong moral thread to bind the identity of its citizens, the Indian state risks undermining its own cohesiveness and security. There is, however, little sign that those who formulate India's security policies are capable of bringing any level of cohesion into the numerous conceptions of Indian identity that interact (and often clash) within the Indian polity.

Policymaking and Implementation

As T. V. Paul argues in the introduction, the ability of a state to develop and implement policies to provide collective goods such as security, order, and welfare is a vital component of state capacity. Although India boasts the third largest army in the world in terms of manpower and a highly trained foreign policy bureaucracy, its capacity to pursue strategic objectives in the South Asian region or internationally is not commensurate with its technical capabilities. Yet in classic strong-weak state form, at times of crisis India has displayed the military will and might required to defend its territory and advance on adversaries if required. India's policymaking and implementation challenges lie partly in the structural factors discussed in previous sections and partly in the nature of the policymaking and implementing institutions themselves. Here we explore the institutional aspects of low state capacity that India has exhibited time and again in the everyday conduct of strategic affairs and diplomacy.

The Indian official institutions of foreign and national security policy-making broadly encompass the cabinet, the prime minister's Office (PMO), the Ministry of External Affairs (MEA), the Indian Foreign Service (IFS), the Ministry of Defence (MoD), the Indian Parliament, and various manifestations of the defense and intelligence establishment (including the armed forces, the Defence Research and Development Organization, the nuclear establishment, the Research and Analysis Wing, and the Intelligence Bureau). While the defense of India's territorial sovereignty is viewed as paramount by virtually all of these areas, the defense establishment in particular has chosen understandably to focus on immediate threats from within India's neighborhood. Historically, it has therefore played a selective role in wider foreign policymaking (except at times of military crisis). The broader conduct of diplomacy that spans the gamut of inter-state relations (and more recently, a range of instruments underpinning India's "soft" power) has traditionally been the domain of the PMO, MEA, and IFS, who are accountable to Parliament through various channels. With domestic political life ever more fractured and fractious, the latter's focus on fundamental strategic issues has declined over the years, with little attention being devoted to debating the larger goals of Indian diplomacy (a notable exception being the topic of India–U.S. relations since 2005).

Aside from the traditional concerns of interministerial and intraministerial coordination, two main issues stand out with regard to the contemporary foreign policy establishment, described next.

Principal-Agent Problem

It has often been noted that officers of the IFS, when in international forums, sometimes pursue actions that are contrary to the predefined objectives of Indian foreign policy.[26] This was an acute problem soon after the end of the cold war, when the Indian foreign policy bureaucracy found it hard to shed its ideological baggage and traditional diplomatic attachments and to accept the changed circumstances of the international order.[27] In contemporary times, it has been exemplified by unseemly turf battles between high-ranking members of the foreign policy establishment, whose bureaucratic politics at home at times impact their behavior abroad.[28]

Likewise, members of the defense establishment in India (the senior civilian and military retirees more than active service personnel) promote a number of their own policy preferences and flog their bêtes noires in the media with great skill and tenacity. Notable among these is China, which they continue to see as the principal threat to India (not least given its friendly ties with Pakistan). The run-up to the visit of Chinese President Hu Jintao to India in November 2006 was marked by near-hysterical attacks from these quarters and their political allies in the media against Beijing's trustworthiness as a neighbor, eventually spilling over into an unattractive debate in Parliament. Not surprisingly, the visit proved only a moderate success.

Capacity

At a time when specialization is highly prized in the administration of foreign affairs in many capitals, some analysts believe that Indian officials, though often highly talented, are too frequently compelled to be generalists, since they are spread all too thinly across the spectrum of Indian diplomacy.[29] Indeed, the shortage of Indian government trade negotiators is such that in recent years New Delhi has increasingly and sensibly resorted to private sector lawyers and sectoral experts to buttress the bureaucratic cadre. Inevitably, the limited number and capacity of personnel, combined with a plethora of international and multilateral demands and commitments, results in "the best [having] unbelievable demands placed upon them," yielding an overworked, underpaid, and under-appreciated bureaucracy.[30]

A challenge of a different order arises from the questionable performance of both India's internal intelligence apparatus (mainly, the Intelligence Bureau) and the once-fabled external intelligence operatives of the Research and Analysis Wing (RAW), the leadership of which increasingly became an embarrassment in 2007-2008. The failure of Indian intelligence to anticipate a number of murderous terrorist attacks within India, notably in Mumbai in November 2008, or to apprehend most of those responsible over the years, speaks not just to weak, undermotivated, and underequipped police forces but also to dubious intelligence capabilities.

The diffusion of authority between leading institutions (the PMO, the National Security Council, the MEA, and the MoD) exacerbates the challenges of decision making faced by the foreign policy establishment, which were critically highlighted in its handling of the Kargil crisis with Pakistan.[31] Indeed the disproportionate concentration of authority within a small PMO relative to other actors, a reflection of wider international trends, in India's case may be problematic as New Delhi juggles more diplomatic and security-related issues than do all but a very few capitals.[32] That said, the creation of a National Security Adviser providing forward impetus and in a position to arbitrate differences between other foreign policy actors has doubtless been helpful and, as India emerges as a relevant player on the geostrategic stage, indeed indispensable.

But bureaucratic factors as well as political distraction are largely behind a sense among Indian authors (and some others) that the country lacks effective coordination at the international level and has produced a foreign policy and security strategy that some view as reactive and bereft of strategic vision, highlighted in charges of "ad hocism" and "drift."[33]

Structural Determinants of a New Foreign Policy

The history of the modern Indian society and polity can be viewed as one long struggle to accommodate extreme heterogeneity. Social cleavages, translated into socioeconomic inequalities and supported by certain constitutional features of the Indian polity, have led to fragmentation of the political space since the end of the Nehru era. There is no doubt that the Indian state has grown stronger over the last six decades, particularly in its ability to devise and implement successful economic policies, but the structural constraints it faces have to a considerable degree dampened the potential pace of change in other areas and contributed to overall domestic insecurity. One would expect a reasonable concomitant of state weakness to be the Indian state's inability to project any credible threat or power beyond its boundaries. Yet the central paradox of India's development, one that we explain here, is precisely the dichotomy between India's domestic insecurity and growing international power.

The logic behind this is as follows. Although political fragmentation diminishes state capacity, the emergence of multiple small yet powerful players creates space for alternative foreign policy ideologies. As fragmentation proceeds, eventually a point is reached where the multitude of voices results in a cacophony and consequently foreign policy becomes devoid of any single guiding principle or ideology. Faced with uncertainty and an ideological vacuum, decisionmakers rely on a policy or set of policies that is least likely to offend any powerful actors and that does not favor any one ideology over others. The most expeditious policy is that which is predicated on interests rather than ideology, whose outcomes can be measured easily and whose gains those in power can share. By default, this becomes the lowest common denominator policy—even if parties cannot agree to anything else, they do not at least disagree on this policy. This policy is then pursued irrespective of who is in power, and gradually the state develops a comparative advantage in its implementation. Consequently state capacity is augmented along this one dimension, though in other aspects the state may remain weak. If it so happens that this policy has wider impacts on other dimensions of state capacity, then it might result in a virtuous circle that enhances state strength both at home and abroad. If not, then the state remains weak at home while becoming powerful abroad. The latter scenario better approximates the Indian condition, as explained below.

Political Fragmentation and Ideological Incoherence

Beginning in the 1980s, the decline of single-party dominance and the emergence of alternate national governments facilitated the articulation of alternative worldviews within the policymaking establishment. Diverse foreign policy ideologies such as the "genuine non-alignment" of the 1977 Janata government,[34] or the "Gujral Doctrine" of the late 1990s,[35] or the "Hindu Rashtra" of the BJP at the turn of the century,[36] came into play as soon as the political space began to fragment. Even Rajiv Gandhi deviated from the policies of Indira Gandhi in the 1980s by prioritizing better relationships with India's neighbors.

A fairly direct result of the diffusion of power and the proliferation of views within India's political space was the growing ideological incoherence of Indian foreign policy, which manifested itself in a number of incremental shifts by successive Indian governments substantially modifying established policy or completely reversing it. A trace of this is evident in the Indian response to the Soviet invasion of Afghanistan in 1979. Having recently ousted Indira Gandhi, the Janata government reacted with strong disapproval of Moscow's actions in the United Nations. A month later, Indira Gandhi regained power and, more committed to India's relationship with the USSR, substantially toned down the Indian stand in the UN.[37]

Similarly, Rajiv Gandhi's approach to regional cooperation led him to pledge an Indian Peacekeeping Force (the IPKF) to oversee the devolution of power to the local Tamil government as part of the Indo-Sri Lanka Agreement of 1987. Subsequently, the V. P. Singh government in 1989 ordered the immediate withdrawal of the IPKF from Sri Lanka. This resulted in a power vacuum as India withdrew, leaving the LTTE rebels to fill the political space vacated by the Indian forces.[38]

India's biggest reversal, however, occurred during the second Gulf crisis of 1990–91. Under Prime Minister V. P. Singh and Foreign Minister I. K. Gujral, India initially took a strong stance in the UN in September 1990, counter to the United States' unilateral action against Iraq and to the UN's related decision-making process. By November, the Singh government had been replaced by another minority coalition led by Chandra Shekhar. The new government immediately condemned Iraq for its actions and, in a highly controversial decision, allowed American and Australian airplanes to refuel on Indian territory en route to the Gulf.[39]

Arguably, as a result of the incoherence that characterizes a fragmented political system, Indian foreign policy has become largely reactive in nature. It is criticized at home and abroad for lacking vision and a unified strategy for India's role in the world.[40] While some Indians argue that the country needs an ideological basis on which to project its power, there is no prospect of wide agreement on what such an ideology should contain.

Decision Making and the National Interest

The lack of an agreed on framework for India's international relations among its principal political actors has affected decision making in Indian foreign policy. But the persistence of coalition government (even in the current loosely bipolar setup of two large blocs) and the tortuous nature of foreign policy decision making within the government have steepened the political and institutional cost of significant departures from existing foreign policies. The barriers to significant change were highlighted by the tumultuous negotiations and then early implementation of the Indo-U.S. nuclear agreement of 2005–2008. In practice, at best the establishment aims for incremental change. At worst, decisions are based on the lowest common denominator, which can be nothing but an ill-defined appeal to national interest (seen through a variety of lenses in today's India). However, there is one element of the national interest that most foreign and domestic actors agree on, and that is the logic of economics.

India's former Finance Minister P. Chidambaram in 2007 had the following to say about India's emergence as an economic power:

> India is respected not because it has acquired the capacity to launch rockets or satellites, or because of the size of its population, or because of its dominant presence in Asia. The world respects India because of its capacity to emerge as an economic powerhouse.[41]

In the new century, the pursuit of economic growth has displaced previous Indian foreign policy ideologies. The nation's rapid and positive response to liberalization since 1991 has unleashed social, political, and of course economic forces that many believe make India "unstoppable" (temporary market-driven reverses such as those of 2008–2009 notwithstanding). Political parties of all stripes agree, albeit for different reasons, that economic growth is a good thing for India (although rising inequality is uniformly critiqued by parties of the left). From a foreign policy perspective, economic prosperity (the "tide that lifts all boats")[42] is now seen as the key to India's attainment of great power status, and it is the driving argument behind India's current worldview. No longer willing to lead the poor nations of the Third World in a struggle against imperialism, and no longer wishing to project its power merely within the conflicted confines of its own neighborhood, India is pressing its suit on the world stage, not least within the World Trade Organization, in the company of such other rising, essentially "emerged" powers as Brazil and South Africa, and partly egged on by the worryingly faster pace of Chinese development.[43]

Indeed, trade and bilateral economic cooperation have become the cornerstones of India's relations with the world, even with China. India no longer discriminates significantly between Russia, America, Israel, Iran, and the ASEAN countries (although restrictions on Chinese investment remain significant, driven by security considerations). It is formally willing to do business with all, even those in its neighborhood, through the South Asia Preferential Trade Arrangement (SAPTA). Both moralizing and power politics on the international stage are now viewed as potentially bad for business, whereas economic linkages are seen to promote stability. Thus India is currently engaged in promoting economic development in Africa, securing oil fields in Central Asia, promoting trade and nuclear cooperation with the United States, receiving remittances from its 3.5 million workers in the Gulf, and acting as Israel's biggest arms market.

This is not to say that ideology and power politics are no longer important. India still accords priority to security issues and retains its nuclear weapons option. However, at the 2006 NAM summit in Havana, Prime Minister Manmohan Singh's speech focused on antiterrorism, "inclusive globalization," nuclear disarmament, energy security, and investing in Africa—issues that are vital to India's global agenda but not necessarily top priorities for developing countries worldwide. On balance, it is clear that modern India prefers to articulate and prioritize its own national interests over the collective interests of developing countries.[44]

More importantly, the nature of Indian concerns is morphing from those of a captious regional power to those of a more confident global power that derives its stature from economic success. As its economic stake in the international regime grows, India is increasingly choosing strategic cooperation over competition or confrontation in its relations with other nations (along the lines of China's contemporary approach). Today, India's foreign policy can be described, in Pratap Bhanu Mehta's words, as one of "unprincipled moderation."[45] While most countries practice double standards in expressing their values, India is notable for expressing few principles beyond that of noninterference in the affairs of others (actually practiced less selectively by Delhi than it is in many other capitals).

In this manner India has steadily honed its economic diplomacy skills and strengthened its hand in the international system. However, this has not so far had any impact on the Indian state's ability to effectively deliver on domestic order or welfare without interference from internal or external actors. If anything, India's success when converted into a larger military budget continues to exacerbate regional insecurities and invite external intervention. Unless India's economic gains are put to good use in augmenting state capacity either through policies that alleviate inequalities within India or policies that promote interstate economic interdependence in South Asia, India's rising star may well be eclipsed by the specter of a deeply unsettled region.

Conclusion

Social heterogeneity and political fragmentation have over the years been the underlying causes of numerous challenges to India's state capacity (particularly in the present era of high yet uneven economic growth). Through the political process, they have also complicated the management of India's domestic and external security environments. Yet by impinging on the ability of India's foreign policymakers to forge a coherent ideological foundation, they have also led India's foreign policy down a more pragmatic path and (almost by default) anchored it on the imperatives of economic diplomacy. The overriding driver of foreign policy has emerged as pragmatism in support of the "national interest," most widely seen today as rooted in the economy. Therefore although India's continuing domestic insecurity and growing international stature may seem incongruous to many observers, there is no fundamental tension between the two trends. Both are products of the same background conditions and political processes. Indeed, India's potential as a global economic powerhouse is viewed by many domestic leaders as the surest way of improving domestic security (understood broadly) through greater and more equitably shared prosperity.

Nevertheless, a foreign policy rooted exclusively or even primarily in economics may not work indefinitely for India for three reasons. First, as was obvious in 2008 and 2009, greater integration into the world economy is likely over time to render India more vulnerable to global shocks and imbalances. Second, although current levels of growth, if sustained, can take India a long way toward becoming a major power, it is quite likely that future economic growth may not be sustained at the levels witnessed in the years 2006–2007. Third, no matter how well the Indian economy fares, it is not likely in the decades immediately ahead to be as productive as that of its neighbor China.

Without a more unified vision and strategy for its international role, encompassing more than policies designed to enhance and capitalize on economic growth, India may find it hard to achieve a seat at the high table of international relations. Without a concurrent political agenda, a comprehensive defense policy with effective humanitarian reach, and a clearer vision for India's place in the world and what it wishes to contribute to the rest of humanity, economic growth and integration are unlikely alone to produce a winning foreign policy.

It is in this light that the potential of India's developing relationship with the United States may best be appreciated. Although cast domestically in terms of national interest, the focus in Washington on shared values in the relationship associated with liberal constitutional democracy may offer India a wider canvas on which to sketch its global aims for developing influence and projecting power on a global scale.

Whether India's fractious domestic scene can credibly support such a strategy of course remains to be seen.

Notes to Chapter 7

1. A. Appadorai, ed., *Select Documents on India's Foreign Policy and Relations 1947–1972*, vol. I (Oxford: Oxford University Press, 1982), p. 18.

2. For more on India's languages, see Census of India, "Abstract of Speakers' Strength of Languages and Mother Tongues," Part A and Part B, 2001, http://www.censusindia.gov.in/Census_Data_2001/Census_Data_Online/Language/Statement1.htm

3. Census of India, "Religious Composition, 2001," http://www.censusindia.gov.in/Census_Data_2001/India_at_glance/religion.aspx.

4. T.N. Madan, "Religions of India," in *Handbook of Sociology in India*, ed. Veena Das (Oxford: Oxford University Press, 2004), pp. 203–222.

5. Sudipta Kaviraj, "The Nature of Indian Democracy," in Das, *Handbook*, pp. 451–470.

6. Atul Kohli, "Politics of Economic Growth in India, 1980–2005, Part I: The 1980s," *Economic and Political Weekly* 41, no. 13 (April 1–7, 2006), pp. 1251–1259.

7. Angus Deaton and Jean Dreze, "Poverty and Inequality in India: A Re-Examination," *Economic and Political Weekly* 37, no. 36 (September 7–13, 2002), pp. 3729–3748.

8. Dipankar Gupta, "Social Stratification," in Das, *Handbook*, pp. 120–141.

9. This analysis is based on Pradeep K. Chhibber, *Democracy Without Associations: Transformation of the Party System and Social Cleavages in India* (Ann Arbor: University of Michigan Press, 1999), p. 15, as contributing factors in "keeping concerns local."

10. As discussed by E. Sridharan in "The Fragmentation of the Indian Party System, 1952–1999: Seven Competing Explanations," in *Parties and Party Politics in India*, ed. Zoya Hasan (Oxford: Oxford University Press, 2002), pp. 475–503.

11. J. N. Dixit, *Across Borders: Fifty Years of India's Foreign Policy* (New Delhi: Picus Books, 1998), pp. 182–193.

12. Arun Swamy, "India in 2000: A Respite from Instability," *Asian Survey* 41, no. 1 (January–February 2001), pp. 91–103.

13. International Crisis Group, "Nepal's Troubled Tarai Region" (Asia Report No. 136, July 9, 2007), p. 22.

14. Sugata Bose and Ayesha Jalal, eds., *Nationalism, Democracy and Development* (Oxford: Oxford University Press, 1997).

15. J. N. Dixit, *Across Borders*, 146. See also K. Shankar Bajpai, "India in 1991: New Beginnings," *Asian Survey* 32, no. 2 (February 1992), pp. 207–216. Bajpai writes (at p. 215), " . . . howsoever limited the extent of Pakistan's physical or logistical support to the Sikh extremists, the Pakistani nexus gave the problem an enlarged dimension; the very fact that they could look to a foreign power made the extremists infinitely harder to deal with."

16. For a detailed account of the various secessionist movements in the northeast, see Wasbir Hussain, "Ethno-Nationalism and the Politics of Terror in India's Northeast," *South Asia: Journal of South Asian Studies* 30, no. 1 (April 2007), pp. 93–110.

17. Roland Buerk, "Villagers left in limbo by border fence," *BBC News*, January 28, 2006, http://news.bbc.co.uk/2/hi/programmes/from_our_own_correspondent/4653810.stm.

18. Carin Zissis, "India's Muslim Population" (Backgrounder, Council on Foreign Relations, June 22, 2007), http://www.cfr.org/publication/13659/indias_muslim_population.html. According to the U.S. Department of State, however, India, with its 138 million Muslims, ranks third behind Indonesia (205 million) and Pakistan (162 million). See U.S. Department of State, "Background Notes," http://www.state.gov/r/pa/ei/bgn.

19. C. Raja Mohan, *Crossing the Rubicon: The Shaping of India's New Foreign Policy* (New Delhi: Viking, 2003), p. xvii.

20. Rajendra M. Abhyankar, "India's West Asia policy: Search for a Middle

Ground," in *Indian Foreign Policy: Challenges and Opportunities*, ed. Atish Sinha and Madhup Mohta (New Delhi: Foreign Services Institute, 2007). It is also asserted that the Palestinian cause remains popular among Indian Muslims.

21. Harsh V. Pant, "India and Iran: An 'Axis' in the Making?," *Asian Survey* 44, no. 3 (May–June 2004), pp. 369–383.

22. A. Appadorai and M. S. Rajan, *India's Foreign Policy and Relations* (New Delhi: South Asian Publishers, 1985), p. 17.

23. Ibid.

24. For a discussion of state nationalism in the Indian context, see Dawa Norbu, "After Nationalism? Elite Beliefs, State Interests and International Politics," in *International Relations in India: Theorising the Region and Nation*, ed. Kanti Bajpai and Siddharth Mallavarapu (New Delhi: Orient Longman, 2005), pp. 85–116.

25. Bhiku Parekh, "The Constitution as a Statement of Indian Identity," in *Politics and Ethics of the Indian Constitution*, ed. Rajeev Bhargava (Oxford: Oxford University Press, 2008), pp. 43–58.

26. K. P. Saksena, "India's Foreign Policy: The Decisionmaking Process," *International Studies* 33, no. 4 (August 1996), pp. 391–405.

27. Sumit Ganguly, "Indian Foreign Policy Grows Up," *World Policy Journal* (Winter 2003/04), pp. 41–47.

28. For an instance of this, see George Iype, "War in MEA Cripples India's Battle for World Support," *Rediff News*, July 14, 1998, http://www.rediff.com/news/1998/jul/14bomb4.htm.

29. Devesh Kapur, "India in 1999," *Asian Survey* 40, no. 1 (January–February 2000), pp. 195–207.

30. Pratap Bhanu Mehta, "Not So Credible India," *Indian Express*, April 24, 2008.

31. Kapur, "India in 1999," p. 206.

32. Saksena, "India's Foreign Policy," p. 9.

33. Harsh V. Pant, "Four Years of UPA: Foreign Policy Adrift," *Rediff News*, May 12, 2008, http://www.rediff.com/news/2008/may/12guest.htm.

34. This was articulated as a course-correction in reaction to the tilt in Indian foreign policy toward the Soviet Union under Indira Gandhi.

35. This was primarily based on the idea of nonreciprocity in India's relations with its neighbors, on the principle that as the state with the greatest stake in maintaining South Asian stability, India should be willing to give more than it receives in its bilateral relations with neighbors.

36. This was premised on the political goal of shaping India into a Hindu nation.

37. Dixit, *Across Borders*, pp. 134–138.

38. Ibid., p. 187.

39. See J. Mohan Malik, "India's Response to the Gulf Crisis: Implications for Indian Foreign Policy," *Asian Survey* 31, no. 9 (September 1991), pp. 847–861.

40. See C. Raja Mohan, "Peaceful Periphery: India's New Regional Quest" (Center for the Advanced Study of India. 24 May 2007). Also see Mehta, "Not So Credible India," and Pant, "Four Years of UPA."

41. P. Chidambaram, "India Empowered To Me Is," in *A View from the Outside: Why Good Economics Works for Everyone* (New Delhi: Penguin, 2007).

42. Ibid.

43. India's stance on trade issues is arguably shaped as much by domestic political considerations as purely economic ones. Standing up to the (largely indefensible) U.S. and EU positions on agricultural trade within the Doha Round WTO negotiations in mid-2008 was a domestically no-lose proposition, not least following a crisis in food security globally and within India, earlier that year. India's talented and charismatic trade minister at the time, Kamal Nath, did his political party more good by confronting the main trading blocks than in seeking to compromise with them (as did Brazil). But political considerations also had the upper hand in EU and U.S. calculations.

44. Full text of speech available at LP News Team, "Text of Manmohan Singh's Speech at NAM Summit," September 16, 2006,

http://www.canadaupdates.com/news/text_of_manmohan_singhs_speech_at_nam_summit-24018.html

45. Pratap Bhanu Mehta, remarks at the International Development Research Centre, Ottawa, October 22, 2008.

8 Weak State, Failed State, Garrison State

The Pakistan Saga

Lawrence Ziring

Conceptualizing a Weak State

States have a fictitious air of inevitability about them. Once created, it is assumed they were meant to be—in fact, have always been, and will always remain. Unlike animate beings that pass through their stages of existence arrive, linger, and pass on, states are viewed as mystical objects, immortal, abstract, and self-succeeding. States, no matter how designed or possessed, no matter how prominent or obscure, encompass the whole, give succor to generations of humans, demand their allegiance, and oftentimes insist on their blood sacrifice in the perpetuation of their demeanor. Curiously, however, states are nothing in the absence of the humanity that imagines, spawns, and sustains them. States therefore are inseparable from their subjects and are potent only to the extent that they are revered and extolled. Indeed, states live through the mechanism and mindset of a transient humanity that passes its legacy and belief systems to those who succeed them and from them to others, and then still on to others. States in effect gain their immortality through the love and affection, that is, the patriotism, of their human component without which they neither can thrive nor sustain themselves. States, in the final analysis, are a contrivance, a human expression made real only in the identity they afford their anthropomorphic component.

No state is born complete, perfect, or omniscient, nor is its destiny foreordained. In the world of the twenty-first century, states generally form two

categories: first, those whose history winds through the annals of human experience, whose roots draw from a well-spring of ancient activity; and second,
those emerging from the last great era of global restructuring, most of all from
the detritus of vanquished dreams. The former are nurtured by centuries of
civilization, of acknowledged accomplishment, and of sustained contributions
to the human condition. The latter formed from the former in the crucible of
great conflict and tragic adventure, despite their connection to vaunted pasts,
too often fail to draw from the evolutionary character of the former and remain inchoate statements of what might have been. Pakistan is such a state.
Born a flawed and weak state, Pakistan was an unlikely answer to the British
retreat from empire.

This is not to question the existence of the states of the modern era but
rather to recognize that states emerge as a consequence of forces that are
seldom the result of self-realization, despite all the ceremony and ritual that
mark their awakening. The idea of a reborn independent Muslim sovereignty
within the subcontinent was driven more by European expressions of self-
determination and nationalism than by latent Muslim desires to revisit a celebrated past. Pakistan was imagined before it was given a name, and indeed
in that context there were competing imaginings, only one of which was
acknowledged and given credence by Great Britain and therefore the only
one with the capacity to realize its objective. The Muslim League's proximity to the Indian National Congress and Mohammad Ali Jinnah's parallel
life alongside Mahatma Gandhi were key factors in the ordaining of Pakistan. The British decision following World War II to quit India provided the
catalyst for a colonial transfer of power. Jinnah impressed the British just
as he mesmerized his followers. His reconstituted Muslim League skillfully
charted the rough waters of partition, in the end achieving an objective that
months earlier seemed impossible. Pakistan's emergence as an independent
state in 1947 was less a consequence of British absentmindedness and more a
conscious decision by Jinnah to take advantage of Britain's retreat from empire. A self-governing Muslim state within the subcontinent ultimately captured the attention of the withdrawing Europeans, and Pakistan was judged
necessary to satisfy abstract concepts of justice and equity. Its independence
marked the divide between a rapidly fading European colonial experience
and the globalization of the Western nation-state system. The aftermath of
this monumental decision, however, never received the serious consideration

it deserved, and the result sowed the seeds of a chaotic beginning that carries into the twenty-first century.

The Central Theme

This chapter argues that Pakistan emerged as an independent state in weak condition, not only because it had yet to register its bona fides as a coherent political expression but also because its mentors on all sides of the equation failed or ignored to acknowledge the errors that marked their decisions. Created in substantial haste at a time of great upheaval, Pakistan joined an unfolding family of national states without the rudiments of an integrated community or civil society, without the required sinews of a performing government, and indeed without the basic territorial design that at first glance gives meaning to the nature of the state being created. Pakistan's inauspicious beginning as a weak state was never transcended, and weakness only begot deeper infirmity and propelled its passage from crisis to crisis and finally to civil war and dismemberment.

The weak state metamorphosed into a failed state, but the failed state was not allowed to pass. Resurrected and deemed to be more coherent than its predecessor, the post-1971 Pakistan faced virtually all of the same issues that burdened the original Pakistan, and although the second coming was assumed to enjoy more of the elements of nationhood it too proved long on expectation but short on results. The new Pakistan was neither more at peace with itself nor with its neighbors. Weaknesses were all too evident in ethnic rivalry and in the failure to erect and sustain workable political, social, and economic institutions, even if these troubles had roots also in the clash of personalities and mindsets. Choosing between religious or secular identity remained as much if not more a conundrum for the people of the reconstituted Pakistan as it had for its predecessor.

Moreover, the military institution that had early on dominated the Pakistan scene sustained its grip on the nation in the altered Pakistan. A veritable garrison state had evolved that bridged the two Pakistans, drawing and consuming much of the state's resources and dominating all aspects of Pakistani life. On the one side, judged the defender of the Pakistan ethos, the garrison state on the other became the indispensable arbiter of a nation-state that could not cope with its ruptured destiny. This chapter frames the torturous course of Pakistan's short history in an effort to better understand its current impact on itself, on all of South Asia, and indeed on the extended world.

Genesis

Pakistan's territorial design was a consequence of inept and failed diplomacy. Although Muslims resided in communities that stretched the length and breadth of the subcontinent, no consideration was given to the in-gathering of the masses of believers, and if a Muslim state was to be carved from British India, the formula for the intended surgery would be determined by regions harboring Islamic majorities. Moreover, the persons responsible for frontier demarcation were not those destined to live in the new states. Outsiders, they revealed little if any concern for the consequences of their actions. Once consecrated, however, the lines separating Pakistan from India could not be undone. Whatever loose ends remained after the ceremonial passing of the torch would become the responsibility of those empowered to speak for the new dominions. Nor were the leaders of the two states prepared for the multiple problems that ensued at the moment of partition. Neither government was prepared to cope with the communal strife that cut deep wounds in the body politic. Neither government was prepared for the influx of millions of people seeking shelter from indiscriminant bloodletting. Neither government was prepared for war with the other over territory coveted by each but left unresolved by the departing authority.

Pakistan was a weak state from the beginning, made weaker by its formation in two parts separated by a thousand miles of Indian domain. The collapse of the two-winged state hardly more than twenty-three years after independence was not unanticipated, but the slaughter of the innocent in a grotesque civil war was testimony to an intrinsic human failure of the soul, the clearest evidence that a state erected solely on a foundation of spirituality could not survive the vicissitudes of multiethnicity and disparate cultures. Political organization, so vital to the formation of coherency and good governance, proved impossible across a vast geographic divide, and most notably among people whose perceptions of life experience was ordered along lines of family, clan, kinship, and tribe. Indeed, the impossibility of bridging the distance between the eastern and western regions of the subcontinent was replicated in the inability to integrate the different nationalities and subgroups of what remained of Pakistan following the end of the 1971 civil war. Pakistan emerged as a sovereign state in 1947 without the evolutionary elements needed to construct civil society, and little was learned from the traumatic loss of East Bengal that might rally the people inhabiting the remaining regions of Pakistan. An inherently weak state grew progressively weaker in the aftermath of the civil war while its institutional underpinnings never gained popular acquiescence.

Personalities and the Weak and Failed State

The weak state, like the failed state, is an abstraction, so much hyperbole in the discourse of inanimate actors. Weakness and failure, however, are outcomes of human behavior and performance, and states are weak and hence fail when the personalities who claim to speak for them are unprepared for national leadership. In the final analysis, Pakistan did not fail; rather, it was the people responsible for the formation and operation of the state who must be taken to task. Pakistan was not gifted with a surfeit of clairvoyant, let alone selfless, leaders. It came into existence with the coterie at hand, far short of the idealized cadres that fill the pages of fictional tomes. Mohammad Ali Jinnah had no significant counterparts or disciples. His passing within a year of the country's independence left a vacuum that would never be filled. Indeed, the run-up to independence required a different form of leadership from that responsible for actualizing the processes of government. Moreover, Jinnah's vision of a pluralist, secular, Muslim-dominant state had yet to mesh with a population diverse in character and culture and, more importantly, lacking exposure to the overriding features of modern twentieth century life.

Ethnicity and provincialism did not contribute to the shaping of new national mentors, and all subsequent political personalities, despite their claim to represent the larger polity, represented little beyond their immediate kin. Bereft of national constituencies, political leaders grasped for power that belied their real intentions: to amass personal eminence and influence at the expense of their rivals. Rural mindsets and feudal experience obscured efforts at building cosmopolitan society, and although the metropolitan areas expanded in concert with burgeoning population growth, the fundamental relationships between superior and inferior went unaltered. Moreover, the stunting of the educational experience guaranteed the continuation of primitive behaviors and bolstered ancient regimes. The political and social vacuum created by these conditions explains the revitalization of politicized fundamentalist beliefs and the subsequent expanding influence of the religious divines throughout the country. Social malaise, political ineptitude, and moral decay opened channels to the clerical members of society. Their call for a cleansing of the spirit, for a renaissance of believers, for a substitute to the artificially contrived character of modern government registered with rank and file members of Pakistani society. The secular state on which so much of the future was vested failed its citizens, and the rush to find an alternative deeper in the religious experience assumed new priority.

The Garrison State

Garrison states are responses to weakness, not strength. Pakistan's failure as a sovereign political actor was apparent in the run-up to partition, and the events that have long tracked the state reaffirm the argument that there is more to statehood than a declaration of independence. The former colonial overlord did not leave the subcontinent before assuring the multitude of reigning princes that their satrapies would remain intact despite the new emphasis given to nationhood and national integration. The hundreds of local monarchs were deemed to be self-sustaining, and nothing was done to suggest their days were numbered and that they might quietly exit the scene. It was left to the two dominions of India and Pakistan to deal with the potentates in their midst, and in the former, New Delhi moved with lightening speed to absorb the many kingdoms and pension off their rulers. Pakistan, with only a fraction of the royal houses to deal with, proceeded more gingerly, and its forbearance was answered with resistance from the more tribal relics of princely India. Balochistan was a case in point. The Khan of Kalat took his independence seriously, and when he resisted the incorporation of his land within the new Pakistan province of Balochistan, it required the forceful action of the Pakistan army to quell the rebellion.[1] Although less dramatic, similar military campaigns were organized to ensure that the sundry rulers of the frontier and northern regions accepted the new order stemming from the central government in Karachi.

Pakistan was early on forced to come to grips with Afghanistan's quest for an outlet to the sea on the one hand and Kabul's claim to speak for the entire Pashtun nation on the other. Afghanistan did not welcome a brother Muslim state on its eastern frontier. The Durand Line, drawn by the British in 1893 to separate Afghanistan from British India, split the Pashtun nation between the two states. Partition made it the permanent and legal boundary between Afghanistan and Pakistan, despite Kabul's insistence that the border be renegotiated. In rejecting Afghanistan's plea, Pakistan argued that the transfer of power had made it the legitimate successor to arrangements in force during the imperial epoch. Reluctant to find a diplomatic settlement, Pakistan not only confronted a bitter adversary, but it also had to contend with an indigenous movement led by the Khudai Khidmatgar (KK) for the creation of an independent Pashtunistan. The Khudai Khidmatgar found a willing ally in Kabul, and the latter too joined its voice to the chorus calling for a self-governing Pashtun state.[2] Confronted with what it judged renegade movements in other areas of the frontier, the Pakistan army did not hesitate to challenge the writ of the Fakir of Ipi, whose legions were more inclined than those of Abdul Ghaffar Khan's KK to resort to arms in pursuit of their territorial quest.[3] Ordered to crush the holy man's cry for jihad, Pakistani forces, with assistance from rival tribal groups, eliminated the threat and in return Karachi offered the tribes even greater autonomy. But even more so than the turbulence in Balochistan or along the tribal North West Frontier, the struggle for Kashmir proved the ultimate test for the nascent Pakistan army. It also became the central issue in the development of Pakistan as a garrison state.

The conflict over Kashmir emerged from the process of independence. Given its overall Muslim majority, the Muslim League had reason to believe Kashmir, contiguous with the North West Frontier Province and Punjab, would be granted to Pakistan. The British, however, also had the Indian National Congress to contend with, and in the lead-up to independence, Congress leaders, most notable among them the Kashmiri Pandit and India's first prime minister, Jarwaharlal Nehru, insisted on the division of Punjab. Punjab provided the land bridge to Kashmir from northern India; all the other significant roads to the Himalayan state trailed by way of Pakistan's North West Frontier. Moreover, because Kashmir was ruled by a Hindu maharaja with ties to India, the British made the fateful decision of awarding Punjab's northernmost Gurdaspur district, heavily populated by Muslims, to India. Thus, when the Hindu prince confronted an invasion of his kingdom by Pashtun tribesmen, he was quick to call New Delhi for assistance, and the conflict over who controlled Kashmir instantly consumed the newly independent states.[4]

Pakistan and India engaged in formal war at the very moment of their establishment. Moreover, India received the bulk of the British Indian army and virtually all the arms transferred from imperial warehouses. Pakistan, by contrast, raised its armed forces from the remnants of the empire and far fewer cohesive army units came under Karachi's command. Furthermore, much of what became the Pakistan army was needed for border security or the protection and management of refugees flooding into Pakistan from India. Waging war in Kashmir with a relatively intact Indian army was also hampered by New Delhi's refusal to divide the military stores with its Muslim neighbor. Nonetheless, Pakistani troops matched Indian forces in tenacity, and with Pakistan's greater logistical access to the Himalayan state, a virtual stalemate ensued with Pakistan seizing and holding the western and northern areas along with the region that became Azad or Free Kashmir. India, however, occupied and dominated the Muslim-dominant Kashmir Valley as well as Jammu.[5]

The Kashmir conflict became Pakistan's war of independence. Compared with India, which drew its independence movement from the 1857 mutiny and pitted Indians against the British Raj, Pakistan's independence was measured by the struggle to free Muslims from Hindu control. The struggle over Kashmir therefore was the essential test of the Muslim country's emergence as an independent state. Believing they held the moral high ground, Pakistanis insisted on gaining the Muslim-dominant territory that had been denied them at partition. Moreover, the Pakistani army, comprised predominantly of Punjabis and Pashtuns, was eager to demonstrate its bona fides in the struggle with India. Kashmir was not only geopolitically contiguous to and intertwined with Pakistan's Punjab and North West Frontier Province; it inspired a form of patriotism that gave particular meaning to Jinnah's emphasis on what had been cast as a "two-nation theory."

The Pakistan army therefore loomed large in the first hours of Pakistan's independence. Pakistan's survival rested not so much on the success of its political and administrative structure but on its men in uniform who were called to defend the country's honor as well as its territorial integrity, and even more so to ensure the stability and future of the new state. Partition and independence had given the erstwhile protectors of the empire, who once served as members of the same military force, a new challenge. Called to confront their counterparts not as former brothers in arms but as adversaries, Kashmir defined the relationship between the two neighbors. It also ensured a role for the Pakistan army that made it an active player in the political life of the new nation.[6]

Emerging in the early years of the cold war that pitted the United States against the Soviet Union, Pakistan sensed the opportunity to acquire the weapons its army desperately needed in its face-off with India. Mindful of its shortcomings and the advantages India enjoyed in trained troops and arms, Pakistani leaders aggressively moved to close the military gap with New Delhi, and India's critical posture toward the United States' actions in Asia opened the way for Pakistan's entreaty to Washington. Following Prime Minister Liaquat Ali Khan's extended visit to the United States in 1950, and his appointment of Mohammad Ayub Khan to command the Pakistan army, Pakistan made its decision to stand with the Americans. Between 1953 and 1954, Pakistan sealed its relationship with the United States, and Washington, in turn, made Pakistan a key recipient of American arms. In 1954 Pakistan not only entered into a mutual security arrangement with the United States but it also agreed to join the American-promoted South East Asia Treaty Organization (SEATO). By joining this Western alliance and still another in 1955 (the Baghdad Pact, subsequently CENTO) the Pakistan army was ensured substantial transfers of military supplies that in time enabled it to challenge India's military prowess. Linkages with the United States also made Pakistan the recipient of economic aid, and in the years that followed the American role in Pakistan was ubiquitous, bolstering Pakistani defenses and, most important, contributing to the expansion of the country's armed forces. Indeed, the stage was set for the Pakistan army's entry into the political arena.

Garrison State: Union or Disunion

Pakistan's external concerns and foreign policy decisions contributed significantly to the formation of the garrison state, but the country's domestic challenges were no less instrumental in the growth of the military complex. The externalities of the Pakistani experience in fact had a positive effect on the country's emergence as an independent entity. Given the state's appearance in two distinct parts separated from one another by culture, language, history, and geography, the Pakistani army was cast as the essential unifier. With the exception of religion, however, Bengalis shared almost nothing with their brethren in the far western regions of the subcontinent. On the one hand, therefore, the army represented the bridge between the two wings; on the other, it was an army predominantly comprised of non-Bengalis, and the Bengalis had no intention of repeating their earlier colonial experience. Moreover, the soldiers from West Pakistan failed to acknowledge Bengali culture or aspirations and seemed to deny the local inhabitants mastery of their own destiny.

Military recruitment policy followed the lines established by the British, who judged Bengalis among the "non-martial races."[7] In the end, the army was little more than a coercive unifier and hence a key instrument in the alienation of the Bengali people.

Denied control of their lives, the Bengali rebellion took several forms, the most symbolic being the 1952 language riots. Provoked by the central government's myopic attempt to make Urdu the lingua franca of the polyglot nation, Bengali students led the charge to make Bangla a national tongue alongside Urdu. Moreover, the Bengalis were more numerous than the combined ethnicities of Western Pakistan, and more Pakistanis spoke Bangla than Urdu. West Pakistan's hesitation in acknowledging Bengali demands prompted almost daily displays of dissatisfaction with the central authority in Karachi, and subsequently in Islamabad, but it was the language issue that came to symbolize Bengali separatism and ultimately waxed into Bengali nationalism. The 1954 provincial elections in East Bengal that ended Muslim League dominance in the province only added to the alienation. Karachi's arbitrary denial of the election results and its ill-fated declaration of Governor's Rule further embittered a population already passionately committed to secessionist maneuver. West Pakistani fears that Muslim Bengalis had yielded to the influence of the province's significant Hindu minority were mirrored in army performance, and given the numerous episodes in which the troops were commanded to suppress riotous street demonstrations, the soldiers soon came to see the Bengalis as anti-Pakistani and anti-Islam.[8]

General Mohammad Ayub Khan's seizure of the Pakistan government in 1958 began the long train of army takeovers. Ayub postured himself an architect of change and reform, but after ten years of personal rule he failed to bridge the divide between the two wings. Unable to contain his opposition, Ayub passed his mantle to General Mohammad Yahya Khan, whose efforts at pacifying the country ended in the costly civil war. The 1971 slaughter of hundreds of thousands of Bengalis by the Pakistan army speaks volumes about the weakness and failed nature of the Pakistan state created in 1947. Moreover, the vast killing of Muslims as well as non-Muslims destroyed the notion that Pakistan could be a tolerant Muslim community. Mohammad Ali Jinnah's vision of a modern Muslim state, a state representative of the best in the Islamic tradition, but nevertheless secular and hence responsive to the needs and aspirations of all its citizens, could not be translated into action programs by his successors.

Jinnah was a man of his time, hardly one for all time.[9] Though succeeding generations of Pakistani leaders would remind their followers of Jinnah's role in the creation of Pakistan, none among them could transcend the more narrowly defined political cultures of their constituents. Moreover, the establishment of a state on the basis of religion ultimately had to confront the role of the country's traditional religious elites. A state whose ethos was reflected in its religious experience would have difficulty in explaining the emphasis on secularism or the need to treat all citizens with equanimity and justice. Pakistan's clerics, the spokesmen for the Islamic State, although sidelined in the run-up to independence, could not be ignored or silenced as the country passed from crisis to crisis in search of answers to its existence.

With the predominance of tribal and feudal orders and ethnicity over social integration, the Islamic religion, not the garrison state, came to be seen as the binding element in the Pakistani mix. But it did not take long to recognize that it was the Pakistan army, locked in a contest with India, and reinforced by U.S. military assistance, that deemed itself the mortar in the solidification of the Pakistan experience. The garrison state was made of such stuff. The formation of Pakistan was initially a failure of the British imperial system, a failure that extended to those inheriting the transfer of power. In the final analysis, however, Pakistan's army was a foreign presence in eastern Bengal, and after the loss of that distant province, it also would become anathema to much of what remained of Pakistan.

The Islamicizing of the Garrison State

Ethnicity remained a problem after the loss of the Bengali wing. Shorn of its eastern province, Pakistan was a contiguous and perhaps more coherent territorial state following the civil war, but the several western regions comprising the country were no more unified than in the earlier epoch. In fact, the loss of Bengal not only had made the Punjab the most populous province, it also had intensified its aggressiveness. The Punjab loomed large in the reconstituted Pakistan, and its overwhelming presence prompted concerns among non-Punjabis that the Punjab's superior status denied them equal opportunity in the acquisition and distribution of national resources.[10] Moreover, the Pakistan army was more glaringly composed of Punjabis, and it was their will and their policies that prevailed in any contest of strength and influence. Coupled with the belief that Punjabis were the most genuine among the Pakistanis, or that Pakistan held greater significance for Punjabis, Pakistan's minority ethnic groups, like the Bengalis before them, sensed their second class status in a society still seeking community. Pashtunistan was an old issue, so, too, Sindh for the Sindhis and Balochistan for the Baloch; nor did these voices diminish after the loss of East Pakistan.

The Pakistani army, humiliated in defeat following the disastrous 1971 war with India, reluctantly yielded its claim to political rule after thirteen years of relatively absolute power. Humbled and shaken, it deferred to the civilian government of Zulfikar Ali Bhutto, who negotiated the release of the thousands made prisoners of war in the great debacle. Bhutto, a Sindhi, temporarily inspired his fellow Sindhis to eschew their call for a separate state, but his Kashmir policy ran counter to the machinations of the army elite. The garrison state had taken hard blows, but its lower profile in no way implied its dismantlement, and as much as Bhutto sought to remove the dragon's fangs, to subordinate the army to his ruling party, it remained intact and vital, ever ready to regain the spotlight. Bhutto's agreement with Indira Gandhi at Simla in 1972 pointed to a shift in fundamental policy toward India.[11] Most important, Pakistan appeared to yield ground on the status of the Kashmir Valley. An immediate consequence of Bhutto's diplomacy was New Delhi's agreement not to try Pakistanis for war crimes, and tens of thousands of Pakistan's soldiers were released from custody. Subsequent restoration of relations between New Delhi and Islamabad followed, but all of these seeming accomplishments did not satisfy a garrison state that was determined to reclaim its lost pride and in so doing reestablish its bona fides.

Acknowledging the need to repair its ego and needing time to restore its reputation, the Punjabi-dominated Pakistani army turned its attention even more forcefully to Kashmir. Ignoring Bhutto's efforts at burying the hatchet with New Delhi, the Punjabi-led garrison state, now clearly a state within a state, had set its sights on reigniting the Kashmir dispute. Indeed, it intended to make Kashmir the raison d'être of the reborn Pakistan. Understanding that it could not challenge India's supremacy in conventional battle, the Pakistan army nevertheless refused to give up the fight, and its new strategy pointed to the deployment of clandestine units mentored by the Inter-Services Intelligence Directorate (ISI). The ISI had operated in relatively minor circumstances since its origin during the Ayub Khan era, and Bhutto had seen it merely as an instrument to bolster his rule in tandem with his newly created

Federal Security Force (FSF). But by centering attention on the FSF, Bhutto left the ISI to engineer its own plans.

The ISI therefore underwent reorganization and was at liberty to divert considerable material resources, and in a period of U.S. retreat, to attract significant support from Pakistan's Muslim but predominantly oil-rich Arab neighbors. With almost no oversight, the ISI plotted its assault on the Indian occupation of the Kashmir Valley. Secretly recruiting, training, and supplying guerrilla bands of zealous young Muslims, the ISI assembled the surrogates needed to carry the struggle to its major adversary. Most significant, the ISI moved away from the army's American dependence. Moreover, in the decade following the 1965 war, and in the aftermath of the 1971 civil war, a new generation of army leaders filled key positions. More motivated by matters of faith, they found renewal in the commitment of their brethren to continue the fight against the infidel. It was in this context that the ISI began building a jihadist network, and it was not long before operations were launched in Kashmir against the Indian army. Indeed, the sundry guerrilla bands that were mobilized for the cause, Jaish-e-Muhammad and Lashkar-i-Tayyaba among them, operated as phantom groups, seemingly self-contained and bearing no connection to Islamabad.[12] Indian intelligence services early on exposed the roots of Islamabad's jihadist movement, but it did little more than label Pakistan a terrorist state.

Bhutto's overthrow in 1977 and subsequent execution by the military junta led by General Muhammad Zia-ul-Haq opened a broad thoroughfare for the garrison state's reentry on to the Pakistan political scene. Hardly six years after presiding over the state's dismemberment the garrison state again imposed its will on the nation. Moreover, the garrison state had metamorphosed into a quasi-religious expression. Not only were its personnel more dedicated to Islamic notions of political experience, but the military edifice linked forces with obscurantist religious organizations, not the least of which was the Jamaat-e-Islami. Linked with ISI strategy in aiding and abetting clandestine Muslim groups, the religious cause became central to the rehabilitation of the armed forces.

Greater Pakistan also required reorientation, however. In the aftermath of the demoralizing 1971 conflict with India, Pakistan was called to renew its ethos, to bring its reality into balance with essential theory. General Zia did not hesitate to call an end to politics as usual, most notably to competitive political parties. His Islamization program centered on penetrating the thin veneer of sophisticated Pakistani society to embrace the unwashed masses whose articulation of faith remained unaffected by the fashions of the modern era.[13] Zia's garrison state was designed to impose limits on the country's elite, but it allowed ample opportunity for people of strong faith to spread their influence in all sectors of Pakistani society. Islamization was viewed by the country's literati as a tactic to ensure the permanence of military power, but for newly enfranchised theocrats it opened wide avenues for power sharing. Ultimately, Islamization focused attention on the reordering of the failed state along chaste religious lines.

The Soviet army's invasion of Afghanistan in December 1979 reinforced the bona fides of the garrison state. With the Soviet Union pressing its influence up to the Pakistan frontier, Pakistan assumed both frontline status in the cold war and confirmed the Islamization of the garrison state. The ensuing contest pitted believers against nonbelievers, and even the United States, having distanced itself from the region, returned to confirm the need to frame the overall struggle as one between godless atheism and righteous religious order. After a period of hesitation, U.S. military supplies again began flowing into Pakistan. The Reagan administration came to agree with key operatives in the ISI that Pakistan's best defense was a forward policy engaging the most dedicated and committed of Afghanistan's religiously inspired organizations. Virtually overnight, Pakistan became Washington's chief proxy in the ongoing struggle with international communism. Moreover, Pakistan's harboring of Afghan resistance groups meant Islamabad determined which among them received the weapons needed for protracted war. Linkages between the ISI and the American CIA became intimate, while the deepening of Islamization was a direct outcome of their joint endeavor.

The ISI-prompted guerrilla campaign in Kashmir not only spilled over into Afghanistan, it assumed even greater credibility given the contest with the Soviet Union. Jihadist organizations proliferated in both Afghanistan and Pakistan, and in an atmosphere favorable to religious portrayals of human destiny, Pakistan's Islamist organizations gained strength and legitimacy. At the same time, ISI, directing Islamist militant networks, now lay at the heart of the national security establishment. With a strategy aimed at avoiding conventional war, and with all sides in the Afghan struggle stressing limited conflict, Pakistan effectively played the role of the quasi-innocent bystander while doing everything possible to service the resistance.[14]

Pakistan became the main conduit for the transfer of weapons to the Afghan *mujahidin*. Moreover, Islamabad, with assistance from Saudi Arabia,

Egypt, and other Arab states, encouraged recruitment of volunteers, and Pakistan became the transit point for a global movement of jihadists to Afghanistan. So-called Afghan Arabs led the Islamist militants filtering into Afghanistan from Pakistan, and the combined *mujahidin* forces, operating in small bands of dedicated warriors, harassed and deflected the Soviet advance, took a heavy toll on Red Army personnel and equipment, and in time brought the conflict to a stalemate. Moscow's reluctance to expand its force levels in Afghanistan meant the steady flow of *mujahidin* could sustain their effort almost indefinitely, and after almost ten years of bloodletting, Moscow decided to bring its adventure to a close.[15]

Pakistan would never be the same following the Soviet-Afghan War. The last Soviet soldier left Afghan soil in February 1989, and the huge behemoth of the north self-destructed two years later. The fading of Soviet power in Central Asia and the reappearance of sovereign Muslim states there seemed to offer Pakistan opportunities not heretofore contemplated. Moreover, Afghanistan had been torn asunder and lay exposed to foreign manipulation. Islamabad sensed the moment had arrived to develop a strategy ensuring the neighboring state would not only fall within its orbit, but if carefully crafted would provide Pakistan with the defense in depth it long sought in its contest with India. Most important, Islamabad wanted closure on the Pashtunistan issue. Islamabad now entertained linking its Pashtun area with the related tribes of Afghanistan. Success in such operations would not only alter the long-standing Durand Line, in time it would allow for the merger and formation of a sedentary Pashtun nation. Indeed, Islamabad's influence would spread to Kabul and beyond, thwart the ambitions of Afghanistan's competing ethnicities, most notably the Uzbeks and Tajiks, and allow Pakistan to move its defenses vis-à-vis India toward Central Asia.

Such strategic thinking was already in play during the Soviet invasion, with Pakistan's sponsorship of the more militant and extreme Islamist organizations, such as Gulbuddin Hekmatyar's Hizb-i-Islami, as opposed to the Tajik-led Northern Alliance of Ahmed Shah Masud. Moreover, the Islamization of the Pakistani army meant that Sunni Pashtuns were favored over Shia Tajiks in any future Kabul government, and indeed, the Afghan leadership assembled in the wake of the Soviet withdrawal raised critical questions for Pakistani policy. Thus, it was Islamabad that engineered the military assault on Jalalabad with the objective of bringing down the communist government still in place in Kabul. The failure of that venture caused the ISI to alter its tactics, but the Soviet Union's sudden demise allowed Masud's forces to remove the communists and seize Kabul. The ISI, however, was not done. Hekmatyar and his ISI cohorts appealed to Pashtuns on both sides of the frontier not to cooperate with Masud's Northern Alliance.[16] The result was the unleashing of a protracted and costly civil conflict that made a functioning coalition Afghan government impossible.

American involvement in Afghanistan had ended with the Soviet retreat. So too, just months after signing the agreement gaining the Soviet withdrawal, General Zia, in power for more than a decade, was assassinated. Explosives secreted aboard his aircraft detonated, killing all aboard, including the American ambassador and most of the highest-ranking officers in the Pakistani army. Although responsibility for Zia's death was never revealed, and prevailing opinion centered on the work of the communist Afghan Khadamat-e Etela'at-e Dawlati (KHAD) intelligence agency, Zia's passing gave the ISI an even greater hand in shaping the future of Afghanistan. Challenged by sustained internecine warfare in Afghanistan, the ISI seized the opportunity to reinforce its allies as well as isolate and eliminate its adversaries.

Islam Trumps Nationalism

During the protracted Soviet-Afghan War, Pakistan had become the principal place of refuge for several million Afghan refugees, predominantly women and children. With international aid slow in materializing, the Zia government turned to the Arab states, and in particular to Saudi Arabia, to provide the resources required to settle and care and feed the destitute population. Riyadh did not disappoint nor hesitate in offering assistance, and in tandem with the effort to recruit *mujahidin* from among the varied Muslim states, it provided the funds needed to sustain the refugees. Moreover, the refugee camps were converted into small villages, replete with mosques, dispensaries, and schools. In the latter effort, young Afghan boys were exposed to religious education that largely followed the Saudi interpretation of Islamic jurisprudence, Wahhabi Islam.

Wahhabi Islam, the most conservative of the orthodox divisions of Sunni Islam (drawn from the Hanbali tradition), contrasted with the Afghan's historic association with the more liberal Hanafi and Sufi schools of Islamic exegesis. But given the intensity of the conflict with the Soviet Red Army, as well as the imposition of Communist rule in Kabul, matters of faith assumed new importance. Moreover, Pakistan's Pashtuns intermingled with the refugee community, and given their own encounter with "Hindu India," most significantly in Kashmir, their sense of religious calling was also heightened by the more austere religious orders, not the least of which was the radical Deobandi expression. Wahhabi Islam therefore found fertile ground along Pakistan's frontier, and with Saudi largesse a prominent factor, the Pashtuns accepted the teaching and proselytizing of their Arab brethren as congenial and welcoming.

The ten-year-long Soviet incursion into Afghanistan provided Saudi missionaries and their Pakistani partners with ample opportunity to expose an entire generation of Afghan children to their version of Islam. Moreover, Saudi wealth financed the building of *madrasahs* throughout Pakistan, and Wahhabi religious instruction became available to Pakistani youth.[17] Following in the footsteps of the jihadists recruited to fight the infidel, young Muslims migrated to Pakistan for extensive training in the meaning of faith. Nor was it long before the ISI realized it possessed a cornucopia of religious zealots who when trained and armed could serve the cause of the Pakistan military establishment.

The ISI saw the continuing turmoil in Afghanistan as both a threat and an opportunity. As a threat, the ISI had to confront non-Pashtun Afghans determined to order their future free of Islamabad's influence. As an opportunity, the ISI intended to remain a major actor in supporting Pashtun objectives, especially Pashtuns eager to deny Tajik, Hazara, and Uzbek aspirations in postwar Afghanistan. Pashtuns from both sides of the Durand Line were enlisted in the effort to neutralize the non-Pashtun presence in Kabul. Moreover, the ISI could not ignore the Muslims, foreign and domestic, studying and passing through the frontier *madrasahs*. How the order was generated or who was most responsible for the policy is immaterial. Arrangements were made, resources were allocated, leaders were identified, and the Taliban or "student movement" was born amid the chaos of fraternal infighting between rival armed groups, all seeking control of Afghanistan's destiny. Pakistan, its garrison state, and most important the ISI, were all active and connected players. Islamabad had invested considerable energy and resources in Afghanistan and it was not inclined to let its objective slip away. Afghan warlords had to be contained and isolated. Armed with austere Islamic teachings, the newly formed Taliban were trained, armed, and directed to take up the cause of faith over nation.

The Taliban emerged from the frontier areas between Pakistan and Afghanistan but it was publicized as an Afghan student reform movement with its headquarters in Kandahar. The Mullah Omar, a showy personality with a somewhat mythical reputation in the war against the Red Army, appeared as its mentor and supreme leader. From its outset the Taliban argued the need to transform Afghanistan into an Islamic Emirate, a Holy State from which Muslims the world over could draw strength in the building of community. It was a movement founded not on nationalism but on faith. Islamabad carefully nurtured it and now pressed it into battle.[18]

The Taliban's dependence on Pakistan's garrison state was a given. Even the resumption of civilian-led government in Pakistan that followed Zia's death did nothing to alter the policy in train. Neither Benazir Bhutto nor Nawaz Sharif did anything to deflect the course taken in Afghanistan. Moreover, the United States, although distancing itself from what it determined to be an Afghan civil war, seemed to welcome the arrival of a third force. Thus with major military assistance supplied by Islamabad, and sufficient reserves to swell the ranks of the Taliban, the so-called student movement cut through the many Afghan rivalries, defeated one group after the other, and in 1996 entered Kabul.[19] From Kandahar and Kabul the Taliban proceeded to subdue the remnants of warlord armies and in relatively short order occupied most of the country, with the exception of the northern areas where Masud's forces refused to yield to their new foe. While the world looked on in relative indifference, Pakistan, Saudi Arabia, and the United Arab Emirates recognized the Taliban regime as the new sovereign force in Afghanistan. Islamabad's garrison state and its aggressive ISI seemed to have achieved its most lofty goal.

Blowback

Islamabad nevertheless confronted a condition that challenged its writ in the neighboring state. Appearing to have vanquished its competition, the ISI-influenced Taliban veered away from its nurturers and soon realized that its message, not Pakistan's military support, was the key to its success. Although a contrived phenomenon, the Taliban was at the same time both the outward representation of historic Pashtun aspirations and the fulcrum of a broad Islamic awakening.[20] Protected by the high mountain ranges that overlooked the great land routes of Eurasia, the Taliban elicited and nourished Muslim yearnings from all over the Islamic world. The Red Army retreat and, in short order, the fall and breakup of the Soviet Union addressed the coming of a new Islamic age. The emergence of the Taliban was quickly perceived as both divine intervention and a consequence of popular will. Although not itself the instrument of the Soviet demise, the Taliban were nonetheless the legatees of an historic moment, and what success the Afghan people achieved in beating back the intruders ultimately came to rest at their feet. People believe what they wish to, and in the case of the Taliban they saw the student movement as the natural as well as the spiritual outcome of the *mujahidin* resistance. Osama bin Laden read the success of the Taliban in similar fashion, and his decision to return to Afghanistan, to free the Taliban from Islamabad's influence, and to make real the dream of an Islamic renaissance, cannot be attributed to happenstance.

Bin Laden's embrace of the Taliban had its roots in his perception of the Pashtuns and their place in Islamic history.[21] It also was the Saudi's epiphany. Wahhabi to the core, bin Laden connected the fall of the northern superpower to the tenacity and spiritual underpinnings of a people virtually untouched by modernity. In bin Laden's eyes, the primitive Pashtuns became the instrument for the revival of Islamic passion and purpose, for the much desired counterpoint to European-cum-American culture and global dominance. Fearless and wanting little material comfort, Pashtuns, for bin Laden, were the untarnished representation of the Islamic spirit, especially contrasted with the circumstances of his motherland in the Arabian Peninsula, where even Bedouin life had changed beyond recognition. The Taliban, therefore, was the genuine representative of born-again Islam. Thus al-Qaeda found its home in the Pashtun areas of Afghanistan, and whereas the Taliban projected the metamorphosis of a single region, in league with al-Qaeda it was destined to play a role that transcended time and place. With Taliban assistance, it became the task of al-Qaeda, mentored by bin Laden, to not only protect and reinforce their corporate endeavor but to carry the message of resurgent Islam throughout the world.[22]

The combination of the Taliban and al-Qaeda was more than Pakistan's garrison state had contemplated. Instead of the Taliban becoming an instrument of Pakistan's military establishment, the student movement became one with al-Qaeda, their union portrayed in the betrothal of the bin Laden and Mullah Omar children. More important, however, al-Qaeda and the Taliban became one in soul and purpose. If it was the Taliban's objective to realize the chaste Islamic State, it was al-Qaeda's task to remove the remaining obstacles to rejuvenated Islam. The nation-state was never the choice of Muslims; indeed, for the followers of the austere Islamic tradition the nation-state system was of alien character, its secular and competitive sovereignties given to divisiveness and bitter interaction. Islam, the great unifier, bringing together the spiritual and mundane, could never realize its true purpose constrained within a system that divided the community of believers from one another while providing advantages to its sworn enemies. Bin Laden therefore projected the demise of American power.

Osama bin Laden was not alone in emphasizing the need to reconstitute the world of Muslims. Nor did the Taliban operate in a vacuum. Al-Qaeda and the Taliban addressed the central themes of Islamic experience. Rather than aberrations, both were products of troubled times, and each responded to another dimension of the larger experience.[23] The paradox that they both addressed was an Islamic environment pulsating with activity while at the same time constrained by alien forces that sought to change its character. For Muslim true believers, non-Muslim stress on assimilation and conformity meant continued subordination to alien machinations and ultimately to the neutralizing of their tradition. Imperialism and colonialism were too recent phenomena to ignore. For the preachers of Islamic supremacy, failure to veer away from the course determined by the non-Muslim world could only mean the continuation of Muslim subordination. The joining together of al-Qaeda and the Taliban therefore was more than fortuitous. Seen for what it was, it elevated the Islamic spirit, gave focus to rehabilitated Muslim consciousness, and promised a new age of Islamic assertiveness.

Operating from remote locations in Afghanistan, on September 11, 2001, al-Qaeda struck symbolic but nevertheless deadly blows on the United States. The destruction of the World Trade Center in New York City and the damage inflicted on the Pentagon in Washington by suicide bombers linked to al-Qaeda demonstrated in the most dramatic fashion that a sea-change had occurred in the Islamic world. Moreover, the earlier forecast of a pending clash of civilizations was no exaggeration.[24] Given the Bush administration's impatience for launching retaliatory assaults on al-Qaeda in Afghanistan, it was Pakistan that was called to reevaluate its strategy in the neighboring state. Having become a nuclear weapons power in 1998, and having experienced still another army coup in 1999, Pakistan's garrison state was challenged to take sides. Having sustained his support of the Taliban despite rising concern in the outside world over its repressive tactics, General Pervez Musharraf, the coup leader, was not oblivious to the Taliban's al-Qaeda connection, nor could he sidestep American pressure.

Musharraf cleared the way for the Americans to put troops on the ground in Afghanistan. Washington's intention was to link forces with the Northern Alliance, the Taliban's remaining Afghan nemesis. Confronting his greatest challenge, Musharraf was torn between his comrades supporting ISI operations and others believing the intelligence agency had placed the country in an untenable position. Musharraf, therefore, was forced to abandon the garrison state's strategy in Afghanistan or run the risk of identifying Pakistan with the September 11 terrorists. In choosing the former, Musharraf provided the bases from which American air power not only struck al-Qaeda but also began the disassembling of the Taliban regime.[25]

Musharraf not only abandoned a long-held and deeply rooted policy, he also embittered those among his countrymen who had committed themselves to the purification of the Islamic experience. Moreover, India remained a mortal enemy and the Kashmir issue continued to fester. Washington offered no quid pro quo in finding a solution to that sustained dilemma. Many therefore interpreted Musharraf's actions as anti-Pakistan and anti-Islam. The religious parties that the general courted in redesigning Pakistan's political process turned against him. The tribal Pashtuns who had sacrificed so much to spread their influence into Afghanistan, and who were instrumental in the creation of the Taliban, registered their dissatisfaction by challenging government writ. Pakistan's garrison state confronted new challenges from alienated and disaffected tribesmen, and the American presence in the border region saddled Islamabad with still another internal war.

The U.S.-Northern Alliance coalition that swept the Taliban from power in Kabul would not have succeeded without cooperation from Islamabad. Pakistan, however, was not made more secure by the success of the American-orchestrated campaign. Indeed, the Northern Alliance had been Islamabad's sworn enemy and a principal reason for assembling the Taliban. While the Taliban scattered to havens in the eastern and southern areas of Afghanistan, many more were at home in Pakistan's tribal Pashtun region and Balochistan. Taliban foot soldiers found succor and protection throughout Pakistan's tribal belt, and the Pakistan army looked aside as they melted into the general population.[26] Al-Qaeda too, although forced to withdraw from its bases in Afghanistan, filtered across the Durand Line and settled among the different Pashtun and Baloch tribes. Al-Qaeda operatives also sought and received shelter throughout the provinces of Pakistan, and some obtained asylum in the country's metropolitan areas. It was only with American prodding that Musharraf cooperated in seizing some of the more flamboyant al-Qaeda functionaries, but bin Laden was not among them. Although the Pakistan–United States association in the "war on terror" was significant, Musharraf saw his once formidable powers ebb away. On most counts Pakistan too had much to lose and little to gain. Not only was the garrison state's Taliban policy in shambles, the Taliban had metamorphosed into an unrequited adversary.

From Here Where?

Born a weak state, the Pakistan of the new millennium is a compendium of weaknesses and failures. Held together not by nationalism or religion but rather by the instrument of the garrison state, Pakistan as a nuclear weapons power has yet to demonstrate that such status implies strength over weakness, success over failure, and, most important, security over the apocalypse.

The paradox that describes Pakistan as a nuclear weapons power but nonetheless a state unable or unwilling to invest in the development of its people raises questions of global as well as regional proportions. Despite a thin veneer of accomplishment and the existence of an educated and sophisticated fraction of the population, Pakistan as a nation remains poor, segmented, mired in superstition, and unable to cope with the vicissitudes of modern life.[27] Seeking a reason for being, in religious experience and performance, Islam has proven to be both a unifier and a divider. On the one side the country must contend with extraterritorial Islam, while on the other it has never been able to demonstrate that religious practices promote national identity, and its concomitant, national community. No matter how strong matters of faith are represented, seldom has Pakistan's focus on religion produced the integrative facets so vital to the melding of disparate social and cultural units. Religious fervor has its moments, but the building of national substance requires the sustained endeavor that enhances cooperation and accommodation among diverse players, and the latter has yet to become the focal point of national strivings.

Nor has the exaggerated emphasis given to military expansion, growth, and posturing produced the kind of Pakistan envisaged by its founders. Pakistan burst upon the scene through the efforts of its Quaid-e-Azam, or "Great Leader." But Jinnah failed to articulate the sentiments of the people who suddenly became Pakistanis. His representation of South Asian Muslim aspiration, for all its power, did not mirror the lives or the wishes of a people made citizens of a country that little resembled their notion of freedom, let alone statehood. Moreover, his death, so early after the transfer of power, left little more than a name to cling to. Given the incompetence and demise of his immediate political successors, Pakistan for a brief period was sustained by the remnants of the former colonial bureaucracy, and when they faltered, the task of managing the country was assumed by the armed forces, most notably the Pakistani army. Made powerful in no small measure through foreign alliances and the machinations of cold war, military rule was legitimated by the country's face-off with its menacing larger neighbor. The nurturing of intense and unyielding rivalry with India ensured a permanent role for the nation's guardian class.

Civilian leaders have made their momentary appearances on the Pakistani stage but have been forced to acknowledge the long shadow cast by the military institution. Long made subordinate to military power, their inability to manage effective government has too often prompted army intervention. Moreover, elections are hardly sacred tests of popular will and are just as likely to end in calamitous consequences. Indeed, Pakistan's first national election in 1970 ended not in the glorification of democratic practices but in the hideous resort to civil war. In the 1970 elections, Zulfikar Ali Bhutto's claim to popular legitimacy was silenced on the gallows of a military prison. His daughter's eventual succession, interrupted twice by army intervention, was terminated permanently by assassins in the run-up to the 2008 balloting. Civilian leaders continue to grope for political power, and civilian control of the armed forces may be a fundamental requirement of democratic government, but Pakistan is not now and never has been a workable democracy. Nor are civilians chiefly responsible for the unstable nature of Pakistani society. Pakistan's men in uniform have long dominated Pakistani life, and it is they who must assume responsibility for much of the state's record of failure.

The garrison state has presided over all the significant failures: from the failure to force India from Kashmir in 1965 to the debacle of civil war and the loss of East Pakistan in 1971, and from the fashioning of the jihadist network in Kashmir and Afghanistan to the formation of the Taliban and the housing and unleashing of terrorist forces worldwide. In the final analysis, the garrison state stunted Pakistan's development. Under military rule, civilian leadership atrophied, civil society went unattended, and the flotsam and jetsam of the country's humanity slipped more under the influence of obscurantist religious divines whose task in life traditionally gives more credence to bombast than to healing.[28]

Union between the garrison state and the more radical Islamist organizations illustrates the extent of state failure. Only a weak state, unsure of its past or future, could have taken up policies that threatened the country's national purpose. Only a failed state could have formulated policies that made fear the centerpiece of state actions and expression. The Pakistan of 1947 died amid the ashes of civil war. The Pakistan emerging from that horrific past was a different Pakistan from that envisaged by its founders. Born as a by-product of the garrison state's humiliation, the new Pakistan had little to celebrate other than its survival.[29] The acquisition of nuclear weapons stands as the most notable if not the most terrifying achievement of this new Pakistan. Having failed on virtually every other front, the central question raised by this chapter is whether Pakistan retains the capacity to purge the demons that possess it before it is devoured by them.

Notes to Chapter 8

1. Mir Khuda Bakhsh Bijarani Marri Baloch, *Searchlights on Baloches and Balochistan* (Karachi: Royal Book Company, 1974), pp. 225–249.

2. D.G. Tendulkar, *Abdul Ghaffar Khan: Faith Is a Battle* (Bombay: Popular Prakashan, 1967), pp. 56–60.

3. Ibid., p. 465.

4. Aziz Beg, *Captive Kashmir*, 3rd ed. (Lahore: Allied Business Corporation, 1958), pp. 25–31.

5. Ibid., pp. 141–142.

6. Hasan Askari Rizvi, *The Military and Politics in Pakistan* (Lahore: Progressive Publishers, 1974), pp. 161–165. See also Pervaiz Iqbal Cheema, *The Armed Forces of Pakistan* (New York: New York University Press, 2002).

7. See A.K. Nazmul Karim, *The Dynamics of Bangladesh Society* (Dacca: Nawroze Kitabistan, 1980).

8. Anthony Mascarenhas, *The Rape of Bangladesh* (Delhi: Vikas Publications, 1971), pp. 111–120.

9. M. A. H. Ispahani, *Qaid-e-Azam Jinnah: As I Knew Him* (Karachi: Din Muhammad Press, 1966), p. 236.

10. See Prakash Tandon, *Punjabi Century, 1857–1947* (New York; Harcourt, Brace and World, 1961).

11. Mubashir Hasan, *The Mirage of Power: An Inquiry into the Bhutto Years, 1971–1977* (Karachi: Oxford University Press, 2000), p. 157.

12. Lawrence Ziring, "Pakistan: Terrorism in Historical Perspective," in *Pakistan:*

Democracy, Development and Security Issues, ed. Veena Kukreja and M. P. Singh (New Delhi: SAGE, 2005), pp. 195–198.

13. Kavita R. Khory, "The Ideology of the Nation-State and Nationalism," in *State, Society and Democratic Change in Pakistan*, ed. Rasul Bakhsh Rais (Karachi: Oxford University Press, 1997), pp. 142–147.

14. Rasul Bakhsh Rais, *War Without Winners: Afghanistan's Uncertain Transition after the Cold War* (Karachi: Oxford University Press, 1994), p. 243.

15. Ibid., pp. 121–127.

16. Ibid., p. 184.

17. Laurent Murawiec, *Princes of Darkness: The Saudi Assault on the West* (New York: Rowman and Littlefield, 2003), pp. 71–73.

18. See Charles E. Butterworth and I. William Zartman, *Between the State and Islam* (Cambridge: Cambridge University Press, 2001).

19. Neamatollah Nojumi, *The Rise of the Taliban in Afghanistan* (New York: Palgrave, 2002), p. 151.

20. Ibid., pp. 224–226.

21. Bin Laden's exposure to the Pashtuns was a consequence of the Soviets in Afghanistan, but he also had ample opportunity to follow the literary history of the tribes. Travelers to the region have spoken eloquently of the Pashtun character and exploits and the following works require new reading. See James Spain, *People of the Khyber: The Pathans of Pakistan* (New York: Praeger, 1962); Olaf Caroe, *The Pathans* (London: Macmillan, 1958); W. K. Fraser-Tytler, *Afghanistan: A Study of Political Development in Central Asia* (London: Oxford University Press, 1950); T. H. Holdich, *The Indian Borderland, 1880–1900* (London: Methuen & Co., 1901).

22. Jean-Charles Brisard, "Terrorism Financing: Roots and Trends of Saudi Terrorism Financing," (New York: United Nations, December 19, 2002), cited in Murawiec, *Princes of Darkness*, p. 100.

23. Antony Black, *The History of Islamic Political Thought: From the Prophet to the Present* (New York: Routledge, 2001), pp. 321–324.

24. See Samuel Huntington, *The Clash of Civilizations and the Remaking of World Order* (New York: Simon and Schuster, 1996).

25. Lawrence Ziring, *Pakistan: At the Crosscurrent of History* (Oxford: Oneworld Publications, 2003), p. 292.

26. William Maley, *The Afghanistan Wars* (New York: Palgrave, 2002), p. 266.

27. Lawrence Ziring, *Pakistan in the Twentieth Century* (Karachi: Oxford University Press, 1997), p. 72.

28. Anthony Shadid, *Legacy of the Prophet: Despots, Democrats, and the New Politics of Islam* (Boulder, CO: Westview, 2001), pp. 14–20.

29. Lawrence Ziring, "A Historical Perspective on Ethnicity, Tribalism, and the Politics of Frontier Policy in Pakistan," in *Democracy, Development and Discontent in South Asia*, ed. Veena Kukreja and M. P. Singh (New Delhi: Sage, 2008), pp. 204–233.

9 Afghanistan

A Weak State in the Path of Power Rivalries
Rasul Bakhsh Rais

Afghanistan is a remarkably old country, founded as a kingdom by the Pashtun tribal chiefs exactly two centuries before the birth of its immediate southern neighbor, Pakistan, and the independence of India. The Pashtun tribes had a strong martial tradition, serving in the armies of a stream of invaders and conquerors from Persia and Central Asia, and from within their own territories, marching on the plains of the subcontinent. The tribes played a major role in building the successive Muslim empires in the region. When the latest empires they served, the Persian and Mughal, were on the decline, a gathering of Pashtun chiefs in the vicinity of Kandahar selected Ahmad Shah from the Abdali tribe as the first king of the Afghans in 1747.[1] But there was no Afghanistan at that time with definite boundaries, and there could not be one, given the fluid situation of internal and external conquests on which the Afghans repeatedly embarked. It was roughly one and a half centuries later when, in different circumstances, the boundaries of modern Afghanistan were established.

What really helped found the Afghan kingdom? Was it the valor or wisdom of the Pashtun tribal chiefs or some other factors that played a role? There is no doubt how shrewdly the Pashtun chiefs took advantage of the disarray in Persia following the death of Nadir Shah and of the chaotic conditions in Mughal India. Perhaps the Afghans could not dream of a kingdom with their own king without a propitious geographical condition: remoteness. Their lands had been on the margins, not at the center of competing ancient empires. Equally important were the warrior traditions of the Pashtun tribes, their history of invasion southward and their conquests, and a fierce spirit of independence, not accepting masters.[2] The frontier character of the Afghan people and their lands was perhaps the most salient factor in the declaration of the kingdom.

With such an auspicious beginning more than a quarter of a millennium ago, Afghanistan remains seventh on the Failed States Index.[3] In 2009, it had a NATO-led International Security Assistance Force (ISAF) and American forces fighting a war, with its survival in the balance.[4] Even after seven years of massive security and economic assistance in the tens of billions of dollars, re-building and stabilizing Afghanistan remains as distant a goal as it was when these forces marched in to "free" Afghanistan from the scourge of the Taliban.

The central question in this chapter is this: Why has a country and a peo-ple so ancient and so independent minded failed to transform from a king-dom to a modern nation-state? Why has the Afghan state remained weak in the post-colonial era? What internal and external forces have caused the fail-ure and ultimately the collapse of the Afghan state? What factors have inter-rupted Afghanistan's struggle for modern statehood? Our answers to these questions rest on the following propositions:

1. Afghanistan's progress toward establishing a modern state started late with a meager institutional endowment and a convenient "rentier" mindset.

2. The "frontier" character of the state placed limitations on what the Afghan nation-builders aspired for and narrowed the scope of their efforts to what realistically could be achieved in a highly constraining environment.

3. Afghanistan has been on the path of multiple power rivalries (domes-tic, regional, and global) that have destabilized the country, creating an odious nexus between internal power groups and external forces trying to change its regime and ideological complexion to make it normal and to fit into their vision of an acceptable state.

The running thread in my analysis of the Afghan state is the thirty-year cycle of endless war that has wiped out the accumulated institutional and po-litical heritage of Afghanistan, disrupting its natural evolution as a historical entity. I also probe the motives and interests of the Afghan groups and foreign actors involved in the conflict and how they have attempted to define and shape the future of Afghanistan according to their own respective power, security, and strategic interests.

The struggle for reordering Afghanistan has involved two interventions by the two superpowers of modern times and several bouts of internal struggle and civil war amongst various Afghan factions that had a stake in the future of the country. Why has the character of this state been such a contentious issue, and why shall it remain troublesome for the present and future coalitions? Why has it been so difficult to evolve a consensus among the Afghans about the kind of a state they would like Afghanistan to be? Why have foreign powers been so interested in determining the future of this historically isolated country? We will answer these questions with reference to domestic and international contestation over Afghanistan. Luckless Afghanistan has been concurrently on multiple paths of internal and external power rivalries. The parallel interests of domestic and foreign actors, including nonstate actors, have found many converging points during the past three decades, leaving Afghanistan nothing but a symbolic expression of a state. Wars over such a lengthy period of time have wiped out the infrastructural and political capacity of the Afghan state. This makes reordering of the Afghan state and society complex and difficult, as their natural historical flow and the social capacity for balancing competing interests have been lost. This partly explains the dilemma of the international community in trying to revive the Afghan state within a modernist framework—building state capacities to deliver security, economic, and political goods—after forcing the Taliban out of power.

The Making of the Frontier State

The idea of frontier that we intend to use with regard to Afghanistan is a geopolitical conception with the following characteristics: a relative condition of statelessness in the vast periphery, self-governing tribal and agrarian social formations, the syndrome of nominal or symbolic central authority, and the country's place on the margins of regional and global systems.

There is another crucial dimension to the frontier character of Afghanistan: its ethnic groups are shared by at least six neighboring states. It is perhaps the only state in the world that has majorities of the ethnic groups that comprise it living across the borders of neighboring states. Afghanistan retains only a rump of them. The ethnic fault lines of Afghanistan that were once overshadowed by mythical Afghan nationalism and a long, though fragmented, history of the state have clearly emerged very strongly with the civil war. All ethnic groups have evolved close, strategic ties with the neighboring states to position themselves better against their local competitors. The neighboring states have used these dependency linkages with Afghan social groups to play their miniature "great game" in the region.

The areas which now comprise Afghanistan were always at the crossroads as well as at the frontiers of ancient empire-building in the region; Afghanistan was both a gateway to foreign armies as well as a source of invasions. These areas changed hands with the rise and fall of the Turko-Mongol and Persian empires. Around the middle of the eighteenth century, the Afghans found the two neighboring Muslim empires, the Mughal and Persian, dying. With the loss of imperial control and domination, the successive rulers of these empires found little strength to assert power over rebellious provinces and populations. It was much in the tradition of old empires that their weakening encouraged ambitious local chiefs to carve out their own fiefdoms or build rival centers of political power. The Pashtun territories had all the conditions that would support their separateness from the disintegrating empires. It would be a high-risk game to take their territories back into the empires because of difficult terrain and the warrior traditions of the Pashtun. Some of the Pashtun tribes had continuously revolted against the Mughal Empire in the previous decades. More important was the political vision and will to form a political union of tribal chiefs. At the critical juncture, they sunk their rivalries and gave up power feuds to found their own kingdom and went on expanding it in all directions.

In the ethos of that time, Afghanistan was a kingdom founded, expanded, and valiantly defended by the Pashtuns. In this quest, they subjugated their ethnic rivals in the proximate neighborhood—the Uzbeks, Tajiks, and Hazaras. Early state-building in Afghanistan was as violent and as driven by the idea of internal conquest as in many European nations before the Peace of Westphalia in 1648.[5] However, the kingdom of Afghanistan was qualitatively different from the Westphalian state system in two fundamental respects. First, the boundaries were neither fixed nor were they mutually respected by its neighbors, equally primitive states. Territorial fluidity with frequent opportunistic expansion, mostly in the direction of the subcontinent, and retraction when successfully challenged, kept the kingdom undefined externally and unstable internally due to the power political games of the royal family and frequent revolts by tribes and minority ethnic groups.

Second, the regions around Afghanistan remained politically infirm and very much in the mold of ancient kingdoms and empires ruled by local chieftains and kings. The political landscape of Central, Southwest, and South Asia was somewhat chaotic, with its political authority structure decentralized and generally fragmented. The ideas and institutions that were shaping the state system in Europe at that time were quite absent in the region. The space vacated by weakening empires was captured by ambitious local rulers who founded their own mini-kingdoms, like the Punjab, that extended to the borders of Afghanistan. The political evolution of this part of the world remained quite stagnant, old-fashioned and feudal, and oligarchic in character.

Perhaps the feudal principalities and relatively larger kingdoms taking shape on the territories vacated by the Persian and Mughal empires could have evolved into modern nation states, but their journey was disrupted by the advent of British and Russian imperialism. Interestingly, Afghanistan, once an invading base and on invasion routes, found itself in the middle of two expanding empires from the north and south. The Russian conquest of Central Asia had a great impact on the future territorial shape of Afghanistan. Britain became greatly alarmed over the Russian advance southward, fearing that Moscow would use Afghanistan as a base to encroach upon its Indian empire. The Russians were equally fearful of British intentions about expanding their empire to Russia's Central Asian colonies. A climate of mutual fear fed into imperial rivalry, which shaped the "great game" between the imperialist powers.[6] Afghanistan found itself on the path of two jealous and expansionist giants fiercely suspicious of each other and fearful that the other could bring the country under its control or influence to damage the colonial interests of the rival power.

While playing the "great game" of cloak and dagger, the two competing empires avoided the temptation to use Afghanistan as an invasion bridge. They had enough on their colonial plates to chew and wanted to consolidate their power more than to engage in a high-risk game of evicting each other from their respective colonial holdings. They took great caution in not becoming territorially connected to each other, which they feared could spark a conflict. Afghanistan became very significant in their understanding of how to avoid military confrontation. The two great powers decided to keep Afghanistan as a buffer between them, which would keep them separate.

Their suspicions of each other, however, never died out, and they remained vigilant of each other's moves. Unlike Russia's geographical proximity, Britain's home base was distant, and it invested greatly to defend its Indian empire from possible Russian invasion. Two aspects of British strategy had a great impact on Afghanistan. First, the "forward" deployment policy took the frontiers of its Indian empire right to the present-day borders of Afghanistan. The British annexation of all the regions that now comprise Pakistan was dictated by its desire to take the defensive perimeters of the empire as far as it could push. Second, fearful that the Afghan kings, so weak and vulnerable, could be induced by the Russians to become allies, Britain decided to control Afghanistan's external affairs after realizing that its internal control would be costly and untenable. Britain had tried that option in its first war with Afghanistan (1839–1842) and had miserably failed in subduing the Afghans. Later, British India formally settled the eastern and southern frontiers of Afghanistan in 1893,[7] after firmly establishing imperial domination over Afghanistan at the end of its second war with the Afghans (1878–1880).

Afghanistan won full sovereignty in 1919 after a brief war with British India. The timing of asserting control over its external affairs was favorable. The First World War had dissipated the energies of Britain to start new regional wars, and the Russians were still preoccupied with consolidating their revolution. Bolshevik Russia, however, was the first to recognize Afghanistan's independence, offer it assistance, and enter into a treaty of friendship.[8] The British also accepted Afghanistan's independence as a fait accompli and formalized it by concluding a new treaty at Rawalpindi the same year.[9] A number of European states began to assist Afghanistan in the interwar period, but the foreign aid was not enough to support the modernization program that country's new modernist ruler Amanullah Khan had embarked upon. The program included modern educational institutions, bureaucracy, and social reforms, which lacked domestic support.[10]

Tribal Kingdom or Nation-State

Afghanistan essentially remained a weak state even by the standards of the early twentieth century. The authority structure of the state and its institutions were rooted in vertical social hierarchies. Traditional legitimacy allowed the Afghan kings absolute power, but they made very little use of that power to develop the capacity of the state in any significant area of national security or social development. Unlike the European monarchs, the Afghan kings did not demilitarize local chieftains and thus failed to establish a monopoly of violence.[11] Nor was there any effort to root the state in society through a system of representation or political participation. The state, largely confined to the capital city, did not expand by providing services, nor by extending its rule through police and other services to replace allegiance of the local communities to their chieftains. Consequently, the governing infrastructure of the Afghan state remained essentially weak and primitive.

Afghanistan's status in Britain's estimation was nothing more than an exalted princely state. Such states in British India had some internal autonomy, but they were closely guided and supervised by British agents. Even such states fared better in the British Indian Empire than Afghanistan did in terms of economic infrastructure, communications, and state institutions like the army and bureaucracy.

Sadly, while Afghanistan suffered the loss of its sovereign self under indirect colonialism, it did not gain any positive benefits, as India had under direct British rule. Modern education, new professions and functional specialization, industry, capital accumulation and a long political struggle for independence against the Raj created dynamic social, political, and economic sectors in Indian society, which aided the process of state formation. Afghanistan was not positively affected by these fundamental transformations next door. But the absence of direct colonial rule protected and promoted among the Afghans other qualities—independence and the will to resist attempts by outsiders to shape its destiny.

International diplomacy and contact by the Afghan state with the international system were not of much help in rooting the state in the society either. The foreign assistance that came its way in the postwar period from diverse countries had more or less the same crippling effect on the structure of state-society relations as in other weak developing states where the state became autonomous. An autonomous Afghan state in its quest to develop itself became largely divorced from its society.[12]

The patterns of interaction between the state and society remained more or less tribal and feudalistic due to the low capacity of the state to deliver services and the absence of the idea of citizenship. Afghan individuals interacted with the state not as citizens in any modern sense of the word but as members of primordial social formations such as tribe, ethnic community, religious sect, and other kinship networks. These traditional institutions maintained their own political space and allowed the state limited access to its members. A political culture based on the autonomy of the tribes and other social groups constrained the growth of the state.[13] Therefore, the Afghan state never emerged as a focal point in the Afghan individual's identity.[14] The growth of governing institutions—administrative, legal, extractive, and coercive organizations—that form the core of the Weberian state remained stunted.[15]

A real change in the development of the Afghan state took place during the cold war years when it found tremendous support from rival Soviet and American powers. But the massive foreign aid transformed Afghanistan into a "rentier" state depending heavily on foreign resources and thus was not helpful in redefining its relationship with society.[16] Overall, there was growth in the coercive and administrative capacity of the Afghan state as the foreign powers invested in its security apparatus, physical infrastructure, and economic development. It, however, remained weak in its political capacity to penetrate society through the extraction of resources or in building its legitimacy through public support. Perhaps mindful of this deficiency, or to accommodate voices for political reform, King Zahir Shah took a first step toward political modernization by promulgating a constitution in 1964. It was not really intended to create a constitutional monarchy or limit the absolute powers of the king but to create a political safety valve to leak out pressure for political change. The political experiment opened up Afghan politics, marking the beginnings of a relatively free debate on national issues. It facilitated the emergence of political groups, allowing them to publish magazines and newspapers that had a deep imprint of their ideological leanings. In the process of parliamentary elections, these groups became polarized along leftist and Islamist lines. Neither electoral politics nor urban-based loose ideological camps made any difference as far as the distribution of power in the Afghan state and society was concerned.

Remarkably, the traditional power structure of Afghanistan remained unaffected by both the free debates in the parliament and its criticism in the press. Elections only legitimized the power of the tribal chiefs, monarchists, oligarchs, and to some extent the Islamic clergy. In the 1969 parliamentary elections, out of the 216 elected members, 146 were tribal leaders, and, next, to them, religious leaders constituted the largest professional group.[17] The monarchy retained all the powers of the state. The king had veto power over all laws passed by the parliament, which reduced the elected assembly to a debating forum.

The Afghan state system revolved around the monarchy and royal family and sustained itself through an oligarchic network of patron-client relationships. Only socially significant individuals commanding the loyalty of some social group were in the power network and served as a link between the local population and the monarch. The Afghan state, instead of developing institutions to reach out to the masses, used the traditional mechanism of socially significant local power holders.[18] The legitimacy, stability, and maintenance of this traditional political order depended on power sharing among elite groups. It was a closed system in which the spoils of power remained within the ruling class. Even the recruitment to higher administrative positions and the allocation of political roles was restricted to influential members of the patrimonial elite.

The traditional power groups, satisfied with the distribution of power and autonomy in their local affairs, remained loyal to the system. Their overlapping participation in religious and social networks further promoted their integration into the power arrangements at the top. The ruling oligarchy of Afghanistan, like any other in the Third World, had a stake in preserving the lopsided distribution of power and privileges in society, which came through bloodline rather than personal merit or success. In part, it was through the underdevelopment of civil society, evident in the absence of any organized protest, that the traditional institutions, and the groups operating them, maintained their monopoly over social and political control.[19]

One of the common characteristics of weak states is that autonomous structures of local authority exist parallel to state institutions and perform statelike functions, such as maintaining local order and providing dispute resolution.[20] Universally, they have debilitating effects on the growth and development of the capacities of the state. In the case of Afghanistan, local authority structures have blocked the access of the state to the local populations. Competition and polarization between state-associated power and local authority frustrated the attempts of the Afghan state to integrate itself with the fragmented society. The resistance to the state was quite stubborn and mostly came from the way in which social and political power was organized in the vast and autonomous periphery of the country. The *mullahs* (clerics), landlords, and tribal chiefs have exercised far greater influence than the state. Blood ties, kinship, tribal links, and the hold on local economies have immensely contributed to the power of nonstate societal elites. The local patron-client relationships and the exercise of authority, though within the bounds of tradition, have been socially accepted and generally perceived as benevolent compared to an alien and intrusive image of the state.[21]

Another important reason for the weakness of the Afghan state is the political economy of agricultural production. Since arable land and water resources are limited and scattered, agriculture has remained largely subsistence-oriented with very little to trade within or outside Afghanistan's boundaries.[22] Underdeveloped infrastructure further added to the fragmentation and localization of the agricultural economy. With the construction of a few highways and the introduction of mechanized cultivation on a limited scale, agriculture began to commercialize in the 1960s and 1970s. But changes in the agricultural economy were restricted to few areas and its benefits confined to influential landowners who had easy access to the government-sponsored loans.[23] The modern sectors of the economy, such as industry, commerce, and finance, did not show any growth either. The important thing to note is that the political economy, based on agricultural production, could not generate enough resources for the state to strengthen its authority structure and institutions.[24] Afghanistan faced a classical dilemma of weak states in failing to sink its roots into society through the two-way traffic of taxes and service delivery.

Dependent State-Making and Intervention

The cold war and the ensuing strategic rivalry between the Soviet Union and the United States in the 1950s created a somewhat better external environment for countries on the edge of the Communist world. Pakistan's decision to join the Western alliances pushed Afghanistan closer to the Soviet Union. Kabul found Moscow quite generous in extending much-needed economic and military assistance to build its state infrastructure and perform social development functions. Even more significantly, Afghanistan received the diplomatic and political backing of the Soviet Union against Pakistan, supporting its claims against Islamabad. From Moscow's point of view, Afghanistan was an important element in its strategy toward the Muslim countries and also for a broader expansionist strategic reach in the wider Central-Southwest Asian region.

The United States understood the importance of Afghanistan as a historic buffer, now between the "free" developing world and communist expansionism, but it refused to inherit the British legacy, except in the more diffused manner of a containment strategy. It engaged with Afghanistan in a positive sense to help develop its social and agricultural sectors. Though Washington provided considerable developmental assistance to Afghanistan, it did not match the growing influence of Moscow in the important areas of training and the supply of military equipment.[25] The United States was more sensitive to Pakistan's concerns about arming Afghanistan because of the latter's irredentist posture and thought Pakistan was a more important strategic ally and more willing to play its cold war game than was Afghanistan.[26]

Afghanistan's heavy dependence on external sources can be seen in the fact that from 1955 to 1987 the Soviet Union alone gave $1.27 billion in economic and $1.25 billion in military aid, while the United States poured in economic assistance worth $533 million.[27] Afghanistan used foreign assistance in developing state institutions and economic infrastructure. It established new educational institutions, mostly in Kabul and other major towns, developed road and communication networks, and trained state administrators. A new postkingdom nation-state was finally taking shape, mostly in rentier fashion. The heavy flow of foreign economic and military assistance contributed to a significant expansion of the apparatus of the state, mainly in military power and an infrastructure with which it could move around its coercive firepower.[28]

Afghanistan's close security connections with the Soviet Union had disastrous effects on the country and the region. The Afghans made many mistakes, but nothing would be more destructive for their state and nationhood than allowing the Soviet Union to penetrate its vital policy and security institutions.[29] Without its intelligence links with the Afghan military officers trained in its military academies, or its involvement in the political affairs of the country, the Soviet Union could not have marched into Afghanistan in December 1979. Moscow defended its fateful military intervention as the protection of the communist government which it had helped install in April 1978. What exact role the Soviet Union played in the coup is a contested issue, but what followed confirms the point that it wanted to bring Afghanistan under its domination and to restructure its domestic and foreign policy as a satellite state.

The April 1978 revolution was a change through a military coup that the Soviet-trained officers had staged. These officers had links with Soviet intelligence as well as with a small group of Afghan Marxists. There was no popular constituency of support for the coup-makers or their textbook revolutionary allies. Political survival being their first instinct, the Afghan Marxists increasingly turned to the Soviet Union for further economic and military assistance. Their first appearance on the Afghan political scene after the murder of Sardar Daoud and members of his family provoked public contempt. Alienated from their own people, the new Afghan rulers became political hostages to the ideological and strategic vision of the Soviet Union. The new political and social order which they wanted to build would not be possible without massive economic and security commitments from Moscow.

The Soviet Union sparked off a new conflict by violating the buffer status of Afghanistan. The Soviet move was quite baffling to almost every observer of the region. The debate is still inconclusive as to why the Soviet Union invaded and occupied Afghanistan, the effects of which seeded new and more dangerous conflicts. There is also another legitimate question to debate: whether it was the Soviet invasion or the regional and international reaction in supporting the Afghan *mujahidin* that finally destroyed the Afghan state.

The Soviet motives were not as fuzzy as they appeared to be at that time. They were rather mixed, with immediate attention to saving the fragile Marxist regime against a highly mobilized national resistance. In planning the military intervention, the Soviets did not fear any countermove by the United States, as Washington's security arrangements in Southwest Asia had collapsed with the success of the Islamic revolution in Iran.[30] The Soviet leaders wrongly assumed that military action could stabilize the puppet regime and save the faltering Afghan state.

Resistance to the Marxist State and Its Collapse

The Soviet leaders were wrong in their calculations about their forces' ability to fight a long war of attrition and about the reaction their adventure would provoke within Afghanistan and in the larger international community. Pakistan, Iran, the Islamic states of the Middle East, and the Western powers were outraged by the Soviet invasion of Afghanistan and saw its move as essentially aggressive and expansionist. Pakistan was more concerned than any other state because of the fear that it could be the next target, as it occupied the only landmass that stood between the Red forces and the Indian Ocean. The Soviet military presence across the Khyber Pass changed the buffer status of Afghanistan, making Pakistan's security environment more complicated and less predictable than it had been before.[31]

Pakistan was more than willing to become the "front-line" state in an international effort to roll back the Soviet aggression from Afghanistan. With the inflow of refugees, even well before they came in large numbers, Pakistan extended whatever support it could to the *mujahidin*. Islamabad's decision to stage a counter-intervention was influenced by a host of factors—geopolitical considerations, the prospects of economic and military assistance from the United States and other sources, and ending the international isolation of the military regime.[32]

Contrary to Soviet assumptions and expectations, the Afghan and international response to its aggression was very severe. The United States viewed the Soviet move as a threat to the security of the adjacent areas that it regarded as strategically important for the economies of the industrialized West. To uplift the sagging morale of regional allies shocked by the success of the Islamic revolution in Iran, Washington declared that "any attempt by outside force to gain control of the Persian Gulf region will be repelled by any means, including military force."[33] The Afghan Marxists and their Soviet sponsors were mistaken in their thinking that what happened was an affair between two states and that no other party would be concerned about it. The conflict in the frontier state became internationalized, much to the consternation of the Afghan Marxists. From now on the Afghan state became a victim of not only its internal confrontations but also of the geopolitical conditions that war had created throughout the region.

The Soviet forces did what all imperial forces do. They used massive force to overwhelm the civilian population. As the resistance grew stronger and more stubborn, the invading forces went on destroying rural populations along with the agricultural infrastructure. That forced millions of Afghans to seek refuge in Iran and Pakistan. The entire Afghan nation rose up to fight against the Soviet forces. Soviet involvement in support of the Kabul regime had a very adverse impact on the legitimacy of the state, which most Afghans regarded as adversarial and occupied by a foreign power. The resistance forces targeted every symbol of the state, destroying whatever capacity it had developed. The objective of pacifying the country had quite the opposite effect, resulting in a highly inflamed Afghan nationalism and the Islamic character of the resistance. Both these forces have had a lasting impact on the stability and security of the region.

The Afghan resistance against the Soviet forces had no parallel in ferocity and determination to liberate the country. After failing to expand control beyond the cities despite protracted counterinsurgency campaigns, Moscow decided to cut its losses and seek a way out of the Afghan quagmire.[34] Political changes within the Soviet Union, especially the new leadership of Mikhail Gorbachev, who committed to openness and restructuring, added to the previous urgency to end a war that was unpopular at home and had become too costly to sustain any longer.

We may perhaps fail to understand the real reasons for the collapse and failure of the Afghan state without comprehending the linkages between Afghanistan's internal conflicts and its geopolitical environment. Three factors may explain this interplay: the dependence of the Afghan state and the forces countering it on external powers; the convergence of the political and strategic interests of the Afghan groups locked in the power struggle and those of their foreign supporters; and the involvement of transnational ideological groups.

The Afghan-Soviet war is one modern war in which it is very difficult to determine clearly who won. This was rather one of those wars in which every actor involved lost, sooner or later: the Soviet Union collapsed, the Kabul regime withered away with Communism, and the *mujahidin* factions fought for years and paved the way for the Taliban. The United States faced the attacks of September 11, 2001; the Taliban were in turn forced from power, and Pakistan continues to face its legacies in terrorism and in the Taliban insurgency in the tribal regions.

The biggest casualty of the Soviet war was the Afghan state, because the conflict had devastating effects on the state's institutions and its relationship with society. Almost everything that Afghanistan had built with foreign assistance and through its own meager national resources was destroyed. The conflict washed off the Weberian state qualities, which were still evolving. The Afghan state could no longer perform any of its fundamental functions and quickly melted away in the midst of war. The failed state syndrome[35] created warlords and brought in foreign elements that benefited from political and ethnic fragmentation. The rise of the Taliban was one of the disastrous outcomes of the conflict that continues to trouble Afghanistan even today.

The political and security effects of the Afghan war went beyond its borders and have spilled over into Pakistan, Central Asia, and the Middle East. The tens of thousands of young men who volunteered to fight on the side of the Afghan *mujahidin* went back home with war hardiness and training to launch military attacks against their own regimes. They also embraced a radical Islamic ideology and opted for armed struggle to change the traditional political order according to a vision of Islam that is anti-modernity, anti-West, and obscurantist. Their imprints are too visible in acts of terrorism and violence throughout the region today.

The Taliban, Civil War, and the State

Whatever was left of the Afghan state following the Soviet withdrawal was completely eliminated with the rise of the Taliban and the ensuing fresh bout of civil war, with its new polarity between the Pashtun Taliban and ethnic minorities grouped into the Northern Alliance. With the caving in of the state, which had historically maintained some kind of balance and peace among different communities, the struggle for autonomy, power, and influence became so desperate that it resulted in the worst communal violence the country had ever seen. Afghanistan's history is replete with violent outbursts, but what it experienced during the rise and reign of the Taliban was perhaps one of its most tragic periods both in its incivility and human degradation as well as in terms of its long-term effects on ethnic and social relations and on the security of surrounding regions, like the tribal areas of Pakistan which are now in the grip of a Taliban insurgency against both the Afghan and Pakistani states.

The phenomenon of the Taliban is one of the most misunderstood political troubles of Afghanistan, because commentators overplay the religious character of the movement. With the popular perception of the Taliban as a religious movement driven by the zeal of Islamic fundamentalism, its ethnic undertones have largely been ignored. Even for the ethnic minorities that confronted the Taliban, the religious militia was both a symbol of Islamic conservatism as well as a reflection of Pashtun ethnic chauvinism that aimed at recapturing political power and reasserting the traditional dominance of their social group. It is hard, therefore, to ignore the ethnic dimension of the Taliban movement in understanding the civil war under the Taliban regime.

At first the Taliban appeared to be a nonpolitical force seeking to rid the country of thugs and warlords and establish peace, stability, and justice. Most Afghans, sick and tired of warlordism and chaotic conditions, found the agenda and political innocence of the Taliban attractive. Many Afghans, even on the other side of the ethnic divide, for a while welcomed the emergence of the movement as long as it was confined to the Pashtun territories.[36] But that sentiment did not last very long. When the Pashtun tribes put their support behind the Taliban and began their march toward Kabul, the ethnic minorities and the *mujahidin* government realized the grandiose political aim of the Taliban was to establish an Islamic state under their strict, totalitarian control.

The ethnic minorities did not lose much time in closing their ranks and gathering all their energies to confront a common adversary. They contested the Taliban's claims of forging national unity and establishing peace and stability as false and deceptive, resolving to fight back to reclaim their territories and stake an equal claim to power in Afghanistan. The civil war further eroded the social capacities of the ethnic groups for rebuilding a devastated state and society.

Before ending this section it is necessary to make a brief comment on the nature of the Taliban regime, its leadership, and its ideological makeup to show how Afghanistan lost its sense of direction and the traditional balance of power among various groups. The Taliban attempted to create an entirely new Afghan state according to their *Wahabi*[37] interpretation of Islam, which has become ingrained in Pashtun Islamic practices. In doing so, they focused on the centralization of political order, which they tried to implement through a dreadful security machine, dispensing quick justice along with their adversaries.

The Afghan state under the Taliban was weak in all aspects other than security through strict Islamic justice. The order it created was based more on fear than habitual compliance or respect for the new system. Mullah Omar, the chief of the movement, sat on the top of the vertical hierarchy of the Islamic state, and all orders flowed from him to the lower rungs of the clerical organization and the regime's functionaries. The Taliban ideology was rigidly conservative in outlook and anti-modern and anti-West in ethos and beliefs. The Taliban movement took a regional character in attracting all kinds of militants from Central Asia, Pakistan, and the Middle East. The foreign militants were part of the Taliban's victory march toward Kabul and beyond. They all thought that the Taliban regime could play a vanguard role in supporting Islamic movements in other countries. Each foreign militant group in Afghanistan found the regime supportive of their respective religious and political struggles. Afghanistan became the home of the most dangerous radical Islamic forces around the world, providing them sanctuary, training grounds, war experience, and intergroup linkages.

It was no surprise that all Islamic states in the neighborhood of Afghanistan became increasingly apprehensive about the fallout from a stable Islamic state under the Taliban. Their fears about insurgency by the Islamist groups operating from Afghanistan were not unfounded.[38] Therefore, they persistently raised questions about the wisdom of Pakistan's support to the religious militia, which Islamabad continued to deny in the face of considerable evidence.[39] Pakistan's interest in Taliban-controlled Afghanistan outweighed the dangers the same movement would later pose it, as it does today to Pakistan's national security in the Federally Administered Tribal Areas (FATA) region and farther into the major cities.

Ethnic Fragmentation

Wars leave a great impact on the social, political, and economic life of a society, and long wars have much deeper and long-lasting effects on all dimensions of human life. One of the important effects of the endless wars in Afghanistan is that they have drastically altered the balance of power and influence among the traditional social and political forces in the country. Supplies of foreign arms, money, and patronage, along with the illegal economy of drug trafficking and warlordism, have created new forces. The ethnic and social forces of Afghanistan are more conscious of their separate identities today than any time in the history of the country. The responses to the Communist regime and the Soviet invasion were organized more or less on an ethnic and local basis. By ousting the Communist state and its functionaries from their regions, the Afghans established a sort of self-government under their own ethnic leaders. Even the *mujahidin* groups that had strongly challenged the Soviet forces were polarized along ethnic lines, some more so than others. These divisions influenced their power struggles once the country was free of the Soviets.

Afghanistan's multipolar civil war acquired dangerous sectarian and regional dimensions and gradually transformed itself into an ethnic conflict between the Pashtuns, fearing loss of power, and the coalition of Uzbek and Tajik groups from the North who had gained greater political influence in Kabul, which had been traditionally dominated by the Pashtun elite. In the absence of democratic institutions, the Afghan factions were unable to resolve their differences peacefully or maintain stable coalitions, which undermined national unity. The differences between the Pashtun majority groups and the minorities on the one hand and the political rift between the parties professing traditional and revolutionary Islam on the other widened among the *mujahidin* groups after the fall of the Marxist regime.

The Taliban movement, which sought reunification of the country through military conquest, established a highly centralized state apparatus run by a rigid theocratic line with clear Pashtun ethnic undertones. Their military offensives were directed against minorities who felt pushed to the wall and decided to fight back with the support of neighboring countries. After September 11, 2001, these minorities aligned themselves with the United

States and the international coalition to overthrow the Taliban, their ethnic and sectarian nemesis.

The Bonn process to rebuild the Afghan nation and state and the ensuing political arrangements favored greatly the ethnic minority groups from the northern parts of the country. With the new constitution and elections for the parliament and provincial councils, Afghanistan's political system is gradually becoming more representative. But the question of identity and regional interest will take a longer time to settle. How long it will take the social groups of Afghanistan to strike a new balance within a unified state that satisfies all of them is a difficult question to answer. The Pashtuns feel a sense of deprivation and have a minority syndrome that may continue to have an influence on state and nation-building until they feel accommodated.

Regime Change and Nation-building

The Taliban have been on the Afghan scene for years, and their power and international connections come from the *mujahidin* resistance that the Western world supported to defeat the Soviet Union. Following this, the United States also left Afghanistan—a country badly fractured, divided and stateless—in a condition of civil war, attending to other world issues. Once again, Afghanistan was a remote frontier state on the margins of new world order. The United States and other Western powers first saw in the Taliban some vague prospects for stability but soon realized the dangers of helping a militant Islamic movement that had the potential to spell disaster throughout the region.[40] It took them longer than it should have to recognize how dangerous Afghanistan had become under the Taliban. Not even the attacks on the U.S. naval vessel USS *Cole* and two embassies in East Africa caused any major shift in U.S. policy, except lobbing cruise missiles in August 1998 at Osama bin Laden's hideout and seeking Pakistan's collaboration to capture him. The U.S. security establishment was never clear about the ability of bin Laden and his underground network of transnational militants to strike at the symbols of its power and prestige on home ground.[41]

The tragic events of September 11, 2001, established beyond doubt two facts of international life in the emerging post–cold war world order. First, ungoverned spaces in failed or collapsing states can become secure and comfortable zones for terrorists to wage their wars against the West and other states opposing their worldview if they are not filled with credible authority.

Second, the United States, leading the Western world, can no longer define security in traditionally narrow terms or confine its strategy to defending certain strategic zones against states; it needs to extend defense to nonstate actors in distant places and employ its forces to change regimes and replace them with effective state- and nationhood.

Whether or not such an ambitious objective, requiring the long-term commitment of forces and funds, is achievable, it became part of a complex American strategy when Washington decided to invade Afghanistan to remove the Taliban regime. Eight years after the U.S. forces landed in Afghanistan, it is nowhere close to completing the major task of state and nation-building. Along with NATO, the United States continues to fight an insurgency mainly in the Pashtun regions close to the border with Pakistan. There are troubling questions about a strategic failure in Afghanistan and how it will adversely affect the stability and peace of the neighboring states.[42] Afghanistan, with all the international security and economic assistance that it has been receiving for the past several years, still remains within the zone of uncertainty. The peace and security with an effective, functional state that the Afghans expected to achieve are not within reach yet. Economic and political gains are only partial, and the reconstruction process is too slow. There are genuine difficulties in building peace and reconstructing Afghan state and society, which cannot be described entirely as a postconflict situation, as limited, unconventional war and counterinsurgency operations still continue.

Afghanistan has acquired a strategic position in countering terrorism and the Taliban movement throughout the region more for its weaknesses than its strengths. The future stability and peace of the region hinge a great deal on the success of a stable and unified Afghanistan. Therefore, leaving the business of state and nation-building unfinished is not a rational or prudent option. However, there can be a debate about setting the priorities of reconstruction, the choice and adequacy of means, the cultural or social relevance of policies, the nature and extent of the inclusion of social groups, the questions of power sharing, and the internal contestation in the process.

The Revival Framework

The challenge for the Afghan leaders and the international community trying to rebuild the country is how to achieve peace and stability and normalize a society that has experienced one of the most devastating conflicts of our time.

They are trying to reconstruct Afghanistan's political institutions, structure of governance, infrastructure, and rural economy. The reconstruction model has ingredients of modernity with a focus on human development, representative institutions, and an effective statehood. This is the vision that the silent majority of Afghans, tired of a vicious cycle of violence, would like to pursue, and these might be the qualities that would rebuild the Afghan state and through it reconstitute its nationhood.

There is a realization among Afghan leaders and ordinary people that they need international assistance to overcome their difficulties, notably the stubborn legacies of the conflicts that continue to haunt them in the form of warlords, drug cartels, and remnants of the Taliban. There cannot be any two opinions about peace and stability being fundamental requirements for reconstruction. Conversely, progress on the reconstruction of infrastructure and state institutions will have credible demonstrative effects on populations and wean them away from the warlords and the Taliban movement.

Rebuilding societies and states after longer periods of internal strife and external intervention is a difficult task that requires a long-term commitment and regular flow of resources until national leaders and their institutions can take care of themselves. One of the major obstacles in the way of reconstruction has been, and continues to be, the Taliban insurgency in the majority Pashtun regions. The Taliban attacks on NATO and the Afghan security forces and the counterinsurgency operations against them have delayed the rehabilitation of populations and the revival of normal life patterns. One of the casualties of the growing conflict is the diminishing trust between ISAF and local communities because of the collateral damage caused to civilians.[43] The issue of winning the support of the civilian population through reconstruction and security programs remains as important as ever before. The coalition forces face enormous odds in delivering these programs in a state of lawlessness in the Pashtun regions. The resurgence of the Taliban has slowed the pace of reconstruction somewhat, but the movement has not acquired the capacity to reverse the process and change the dynamics of politics in its favor.

Military action and counterinsurgency operations in situations such as Afghanistan are essential but have to be linked to peace building, negotiations, and conflict resolution through a shared vision for the good of society and by integrating the interests of all vital stakeholders. A political solution to the conflict, aiming at reconstituting broad and legitimate power arrangements, would be credible only if it gathers the support of all the important

Afghan groups. Reviving the internal social and political energies of Afghanistan would be crucial for preventing a reversal back to chaos and civil disorder, which would wipe away the gains made thus far.

Postconflict state building in the fractured polity of Afghanistan might remain slow unless those engaged in a struggle for power, and the outsiders wishing to defuse it, seek new relationships among all the constituent groups—ethnic, regional, and religious. Any attempt to structure a powerful centralized authority within the framework of the nation-state model would be self-defeating. Decentralization, regional autonomy, and the revitalization of traditional patterns of authority would all strengthen accommodation. Political restructuring may not make much progress and the state in Afghanistan may not be revived, nor acquire significant capacities to face the great challenge of security and reconstruction if the friction among its social groups continues. To make the process of state building more effective and make it stand on strong foundations, the delivery functions and institutional capacity of the state needs much more investment in material and political capital than what has been provided for during the past eight years. Rebuilding Afghanistan may remain a big challenge for the world community, particularly for the United States, but not confronting this challenge would return Afghanistan to a condition of statelessness—a disaster for regional and global security.

Notes to Chapter 9

1. See Louis Dupree, *Afghanistan* (Princeton: Princeton University Press, 1980); Monstuart Elphinstone, *An Account of the Kingdom of Caubul and Its Dependencies in Persia, Tartary, and India* (Karachi: Oxford University Press, 1972, first edition 1815).

2. Bernhard Dorn, *History of the Afghans*, translated from the Persian of Neamet Ullah (Lahore: Vanguard Books, 1999), p. vi.

3. Foreign Policy and the Fund for Peace, "Failed States Index 2008," *Foreign Policy* (July/August 2008), p. 67.

4. ISAF, as of February 2009, had 56,420 personnel from forty-one different countries. Britain and the United States are the largest contributing nations. The United States also had 17,100 troops under Operation Enduring Freedom as of December 2008. BBC News, "Q&A: ISAF Troops in Afghanistan," February 19, 2009, http://news.bbc.co.uk/2/hi/south_asia/7228649.stm.

5. Charles Tilly, "War Making and State Making as Organized Crime," in *Bringing the State Back In*, ed. Peter B. Evans, Dietrich Rueschemeyer, and Theda Skocpol (Cambridge: Cambridge University Press, 1985), pp. 169–186.

6. On the "Great Game," see Subash Chakravarty, *Afghanistan and the Great Game* (Delhi: New Century Publications, 2002).

7. The Durand Line is the present boundary between Afghanistan and Pakistan. An accord to draw this boundary was signed between Britain and Afghanistan in 1893. After the creation of Pakistan, Afghanistan insisted on re-demarcating this boundary, which Pakistan has claimed to be final. Pashtunistan is the Afghan title for the tribal territories around the Durand Line that form part of Pakistan. Afghan rulers have, from time to time, demanded either the inclusion of this territory in Afghanistan or the creation of an independent Pushtunistan. These two issues caused considerable friction between the two neighboring states in the 1950s and 1960s. Afghanistan's position changed considerably in 1976–1977 when President Sardar Daoud decided to improve relations with Iran and Pakistan. These issues lost significance with the civil war, the Soviet invasion, and Pakistan's support for the liberation of Afghanistan. Whether or not the future rulers of Afghanistan will take up old quarrels with Islamabad is yet to be seen. On the historical origins of these disputes, see, S. M. Burke and Lawrence Ziring, *Pakistan's Foreign Policy: A Historical Analysis* (Karachi: Oxford University Press, 1990), pp. 68–90; Ainslee T. Embree, ed., *Pakistan's Western Borderlands*, (Durham, NC: Carolina Academic Press, 1977), Mehrunisa Ali, *Pak-Afghan Discord: A Historical Perspective, Documents 1853–1979* (Karachi: Pakistan Study Centre, Karachi University, 1990); Saedduddin Ahmad Dar, ed., *Selected Documents on Pakistan's Relations with Afghanistan 1947–85* (Islamabad: National Institute of Pakistan Studies, Quaid-i-Azam University, 1986).

8. S. Fida Yunas, *The Durand Line Border Agreement 1893* (Peshawar: Area Study Centre, University of Peshawar, 2003), pp. 1–45.

9. Ibid, pp. 93–94.

10. Leon Poullada, *Reform and Rebellion in Afghanistan, 1919–1929: King Amanullah's Failure to Modernize a Tribal Society* (Ithaca: Cornell University Press, 1973).

11. On European state making, see Tilly, "War Making."

12. A state is "autonomous" when it pursues goals and objectives "that are not simply reflective of the demands or interests of social groups, classes, or society." Theda Skocpol, "Bringing the State Back In: Strategies of Analysis in Current Research," in Evans, Rueschemeyer, and Skocpol, *Bringing*, p. 9.

13. *Jirga* (a grand assembly of elders and notables) and provincial councils of sardars (chiefs) were two traditional institutions that, along with the religious establishment, played important roles in confirming the legitimacy of the Afghan kings and approved constitutional and legal changes in the country. The *jirga* also functioned at local levels to adjudicate disputes between individuals and tribes. Looking at the evolution of the Afghan state, particularly its early phase and central system of governance, one can hardly miss the point that it rested on the consent of the tribes and other socially influential groups. Their allegiance to the state was conditioned by the unwritten but well-respected tradition of local autonomy. On this point see A. Olesen, "Afghanistan: the Development of the Modern State," in *Islam: State and Society*, ed. K. Ferdinand and M. Mozaffari (London: Curzon, 1988), pp. 155–169; Jolanta Sierakowska-Dyndo, "The State in Afghanistan's Political and Economic System on the Eve of the April 1978 Coup," *Central Asian Survey* 9, no. 4 (1990), pp. 85–86. Leon B. Poullada has argued that

"[o]riginally the central government was in effect an emanation of a tribal confederation and the Amir was considered a paramount chief, a *primus inter pares*, by other tribal chiefs." Other factors that contributed to the autonomy of the tribes are geographic location, a tribal culture of defiance, dynastic quarrels and the impact of the "great game" between Britain and Russia, which, in particular, promoted the pugnacity of the Pushtun tribes. See Poullada, "Political Modernization in Afghanistan: The Amanullah Reforms," in *Afghanistan: Some New Approaches*, ed. George Grassmuck, Ludwig Adamec, and Frances Irwin (Ann Arbor: University of Michigan Press, 1969), p. 117.

14. On the evolution and identity of the Afghan state and its relationship with civil society, see Barnett R. Rubin, "Lineages of the State in Afghanistan," *Asian Survey* 28, no. 11 (November 1988), pp. 1183–1209; M. Nazif Shahrani, "State Building and Social Fragmentation in Afghanistan: A Historical Perspective," in *The State, Religion, and Ethnic Politics: Afghanistan, Iran and Pakistan*, ed. Ali Banuazizi and Myron Weiner (Syracuse: Syracuse University Press, 1986), pp. 23–74.

15. Max Weber, *Economy and Society*, ed., Guenther Roth and Claus Wittich (New York: Bedminster Press, 1968, originally 1922), vol. 2, chapter 9.

16. On the rise of "rentier" state, see Amin Saikal, *Modern Afghanistan: A History of Struggle and Survival* (London: I.B. Tauris, 2004), pp. 117–132.

17. Fred Halliday, "Revolution in Afghanistan" *New Left Review*, no. 112 (November/December 1978), p. 19.

18. Three types of leadership may be identified that used links with the state to enhance their local power: elders of tribes and ethnic groups, *ulema* (scholars of Islam), and *rohanyun* (saintly figures), which included pirs (spiritual leaders), and *hazrats* (respectable on religious grounds). See Nabi Misdaq, "Traditional Leadership in Afghan Society and the Issue of National Unity," *Central Asian Survey* 9, no. 4 (1990), pp. 109–112.

19. Although social class distinctions existed in Afghanistan, the basic identity of the common man in the villages was with a clan or tribe. The mystique of kinship relations prevented the emergence of any challenge to the traditional authority.

20. On the nature of the political system of Afghanistan and its social and historical roots, see a pioneering study by Richard S. Newell, *The Politics of Afghanistan* (Ithaca: Cornell University Press, 1972).

21. For this analysis I have benefited from David Gibbs, "The Peasant as Counter-Revolutionary: The Rural Origins of the Afghan Insurgency," *Studies in Comparative International Development* 21, no. 1 (Spring 1986), pp. 37–45.

22. Estimates of arable land vary. But it is generally believed that land area where something can be grown is about 12 percent, but only 4 percent is cultivated, mainly because of insufficient irrigation. Louis Dupree, cited by Gibbs, in Ibid., p. 38.

23. Douglas G. Norvell, *Agricultural Credit in Afghanistan: A Review of Progress and Problem from 1954 Until 1972* (Kabul: Agricultural Division, United States Agency for International Development, 1972), pp. iii, 1.

24. Despite the largest share of the agriculture in Afghanistan's economy, the government's farm-generated revenues were nominal. It is difficult to find statistics on

this issue. Just to give an idea, government's revenues in 1971–1972 from agriculture were only 1.2 percent. Klaus Glaubitt, Fawzi Saadeddin, and Bernd Schafer, "Government Revenues and Economic Development of Afghanistan," *Afghanistan Journal* 4, no. 1 (1977), p. 1.

25. In 1947 and then in 1955, the Afghan government had requested the military aid from the United States. But Kabul's disputes with Pakistan complicated the affair. However, the United States supplied Afghanistan with $800 million in economic assistance between 1946 and 1978. The military assistance during this period amounted to only $5.6 million. Milton Leitenberg, "United States Foreign Policy and the Soviet Invasion of Afghanistan," *Arms Control* 7, no. 3 (December, 1986), pp. 272–273.

26. On this point see Henery S. Bradsher, *Afghanistan and the Soviet Union* (Durham, NC: Duke University Press, 1985).

27. Barnett R. Rubin, *The Fragmentation of Afghanistan: State Formation and Collapse in the International System* (New Haven: Yale University Press, 2002), pp. 63–68.

28. H. Sidky, "War, Changing Patterns of Warfare, State Collapse, and Transnational Violence in Afghanistan: 1978–2001," *Modern Asian Studies* 41, no. 4 (2007), p. 854.

29. Amin Saikal notes that "by the turn of the 1970s, no major Afghan political decision could be taken or military operation initiated without the knowledge of Soviet advisers and embassy," Amin Saikal, "Russia and Afghanistan: A Turning Point?" *Asian Affairs* 20, no. 2 (June 1989), p. 173.

30. On December 8, 11, 15, 17, and 27, 1979, the United States conveyed its serious concern to the Soviet Union about the movement of its troops around Afghanistan. But the U.S. capability to prevent the impending Soviet invasion or retaliate effectively was not taken seriously by Moscow. See: *East-West Relations, op. cit.,* pp. 111–21.

31. Theodore L. Eliot, Jr., and Robert L. Pfaftzgraff, Jr., eds., *Red Army on Pakistan's Borders* (Washington, DC: Pergamon-Brassey's, 1986); Francis Fukuyama, "The Security of Pakistan: A Trip Report," Rand Report N-1584-RC (Santa Monica: Rand Corporation, September, 1980); Lawrence Ziring, "Soviet Policy on the Rim of Asia: Scenarios and Projections," *Asian Affairs* 9, no. 3 (January/February 1982), pp. 135–146; Robert G. Wirsing, "Pakistan and the War in Afghanistan," *Asian Affairs* 14, no. 2 (Summer 1987), pp. 57–75.

32. See, Omar Noman, *Pakistan: Political and Economic History Since 1947* (London: Kegan Paul International, 1990), pp. 120–125; Shahid Javed Burki, ed., *Pakistan Under the Military: Eleven Years of Zia ul-Haq* (Boulder, CO: Westview Press, 1991).

33. On the American response, see Richard P. Cronin, "Afghanistan: Soviet Invasion and US Response," IB 80006 (Washington, DC: Congressional Research Service, Library of Congress, November 24, 1981); U.S. House of Representatives, "Hearing: East-West Relations"; Zalmay Khalilzad, "Afghanistan and the Crisis in American Foreign Policy," *Survival* 22, no. 4 (July/August 1980), pp. 151–160; William E. Griffith, "Superpower Relations after Afghanistan," *Survival* 22, no. 4 (July/August 1980), pp. 146–150; U.S. Department of State, *Soviet Invasion of Afghanistan*, Special Report No. 70 (Washington, DC: US Government Printing Office, April, 1980).

34. For an analysis of shifts in the Soviet approach to negotiations, see an excellent study by Riaz M. Khan, *Untying the Afghan Knot: Negotiating Soviet Withdrawal* (Durham, NC: Duke University Press, 1991), pp. 242–284.

35. Gerald B. Helman and Steven R. Ratner, "Saving Failed States," *Foreign Policy* (Winter 1992–1993), p. 3.

36. Kamal Matinuddin, *The Taliban Phenomenon: Afghanistan 1994–1997* (Karachi: Oxford University Press, 1999), pp. 22–34.

37. The sectarian lineage of the Taliban goes to the nineteenth century movement of Mohammad Bin Abdul Wahab to purge Islam of rituals and practices that had crept into it. Its puritanical version was adopted by the Deobandi Ulema in India. The Wahabi influence on the Taliban came through the Deobandi religious movement from India, which now has very strong roots in Pakistan.

38. The Islamic Movement of Uzbekistan had links with the Taliban. Its military leader, Juma Namangani, took refuge in Afghanistan, where he was killed after the ouster of the Taliban. See the testimony of R. Grant Smith in the Committee on March 13, 2002, "Terrorists or Mujahideen" (editorial), *Daily Times*, March 22, 2004.

39. Ahmed Rashid, "Pakistan and the Taliban," in *Fundamentalism Reborn? Afghanistan and the Taliban*, ed. William Maley (London: Hurst & Company, 2001), pp. 72–89.

40. The initial view about the Taliban in the United States was that the religious students could serve positive objectives. See Richard Mackenzie, "The United States and the Taliban," in Maley, *Fundamentalism Reborn?* p. 96.

41. Anonymous, *Through our Enemies' Eyes* (Washington, DC: Brassey's, 2003), p. xviii.

42. "Afghan Failure May Lead to Regime Change in Pakistan: UK Generals," *Daily Times*, July 16, 2007.

43. Luke Baker, "Taliban Growing Stronger in Afghanistan: UK Report," *Dawn*, July 19, 2007.

10 Sri Lanka

Challenges in State Consolidation and Minority Integration

Sankaran Krishna

Sri Lanka today is a weak state inexorably on the path toward becoming a failed state. If we define state capacity as "the ability of a state to develop and implement policies in order to provide collective goods such as security, order and welfare to its citizens in a legitimate and effective manner. . . ."[1] it is obvious that the Sri Lankan state has had a serious deficit of legitimacy almost from independence in 1948. The primary reason for this lack of legitimacy and its continued erosion in the decades since is that nation-building has become equated with remaking a once plural and hybrid space into one where the ethnic majority (the Sinhala-speaking Buddhists) has the pride of place, and the others (the largely Hindu Sri Lankan Tamils, the Estate Tamils who emigrated to Sri Lanka in the nineteenth century, the Muslims, the Burghers, and the Veddas or aboriginal groups) are seen as secondary actors in deservedly minor roles. This consolidation of ethnic majoritarianism has occurred largely because of the working out of a competitive electoral process in which the two main political parties have tried to gain the votes of the Sinhala-Buddhist majority by equating the latter with the nation. Thus, rather than seeing "ethnicity" as an undesirable and regrettable detour on the way to arriving as a nation, I argue that it is one of the dominant means by which the nation makes sense to the people in a postcolonial setting. This makes the task of overcoming "bad" ethnicity and achieving "good" national citizenship a more fraught and difficult process than we have hitherto realized.

In the first section of this chapter, I elaborate on the ethnic-majoritarian character of the postcolonial Sri Lankan state. I show how six decades of independence have led to the consolidation and strengthening of ethnic identities, rather than that of national citizenship, on the part of both the majority and minority communities. I also demonstrate how even among the more astute and progressive works on Sri Lanka's modern politics, there is an inability to see beyond a narrow, enumerated and ethnically fractionated notion of democracy and nationhood. In the second section, I investigate the complex contribution of regional factors, especially the role of its huge neighbor India, in the crisis of the Sri Lankan state. On the one hand, I argue that the "minority complex" of the Sinhala majority in Sri Lanka leads them to exaggerate the links between the Sri Lankan Tamils and the Tamils in the neighboring Indian state of Tamil Nadu. On the other, I argue that the presence of co-ethnics across national boundaries has served as an important tool in the foreign policy arsenal of South Asian state elites and their efforts to destabilize their neighbors. In brief, my argument is that it is not the presence of co-ethnics across national borders that represents a real threat to the security of the region, but rather it is the expedient use of the presence of such co-ethnics by state elites in their domestic and foreign policies that is the real reason for insecurity. Two significant events separated by a decade—the assassination of Rajiv Gandhi by a Sri Lankan Tamil female suicide-bomber in May 1991 and the attacks of September 11, 2001—altered the regional and international equation to the detriment of the main militant group spearheading the Sri Lankan Tamil movement for secession, the Liberation Tigers of Tamil Eelam (LTTE). In the final section, I examine the comprehensive military defeat of the LTTE and the physical elimination of its entire leadership in May 2009 by the Sri Lankan Army. The months since the defeat of the LTTE have represented an unprecedented opportunity for the Sri Lankan state to transcend its ethnic majoritarian character and emerge as the legitimate embodiment of the nation as a whole. This opportunity to reconstitute the nation on a pluralist and inclusive basis is being squandered, as the normalization of war has over-developed the state's capacity for repression and coercion while simultaneously reducing its concern for democratic norms and the allegiance of minority sections of society. For the region as a whole, building state capacity and allaying insecurity through joint actions will remain daunting tasks.

Ethnic Majoritarianism, Electoral Democracy, and State Crisis

At the time of its independence from Britain in 1948, Sri Lanka (or Ceylon as it was then known) seemed uniquely poised among developing countries to be a success story. It had gained universal franchise as early as 1931, the first society to have it in all of Africa and Asia. For a variety of historical reasons, it had a welfare state before such a term was invented, and the grinding poverty and famines that characterized the rest of South Asia during the centuries of colonial rule were unheard of there. Benign state intervention and a matriarchal tradition in many parts of the island also meant that its level of literacy, public health, and women's empowerment were off the charts in comparison to the rest of the developing world. The state's organizational and bureaucratic capacity to collect revenue and to deliver public goods was also impressive in relative terms. The movement for independence was led by a multiethnic and cosmopolitan elite, one that moreover had an opportunity to learn and perfect the arts of liberal democratic governance and factional give-and-take over a fairly peaceful and elongated process of decolonization. When Howard Wriggins noted in 1961 that of all the Asian countries, Sri Lanka stood "the best chance of making a successful transition to modern statehood,"[2] it was a prediction that rested on sound empirical grounds.

The first step toward civil war in Sri Lanka was taken immediately after independence with the disenfranchisement of the Tamil plantation laborers of recent Indian origin.[3] They were targeted for repatriation to India, though the vast majority of them, by that point, had been born in Sri Lanka. The disenfranchisement was enacted by the Sinhalese-dominated political parties with the support of leftist parties, trade union leaders, and sections of the Sri Lankan Tamils, including the Ceylon Congress. Thereafter, the process of ethnic othering spread to the Sri Lankan Tamils with the critical steps being the declaration of Sinhala as the sole official language of the nation (1956); that it was the duty of the state to foster and protect Buddhism (1972); strategies of economic development, especially the giant irrigation schemes involving the expansion of newly cultivable lands and their settlement by the majority community; and policies designed to redress the incongruence between ethnic proportions and public goods, especially in access to higher education and professional courses. At each step, the consolidation of the nation was accompanied by girding it more firmly to a Sinhala-Buddhist core, and rendering Tamil, Muslim, Christian, Burgher, mixed, and other identities as less than equal.

The fact that the first mobilizers of ethnic identity as a way to gain political power were cosmopolitan, Western-educated, English-speaking modernizers in Sri Lanka should tell us something. If any group should have been thoroughly imbued with the idea of a supra-ethnic national citizenship, it was the cosmopolitan leaders of these parties. And yet, it was the Bandaranaikes, Jayewardenes, Senanayakes and their ilk (literally) who appealed to the idea of the Sinhala-Buddhist as the model Sri Lankan. The consolidation of ethnic identities was not an aberration or departure from the emergence of democratic politics and modern institutions of governance but intrinsic to them.

The evidence since independence points to a hardening of ethnic identities in this once-hybrid island. In his many works on Sri Lankan Tamil nationalism, A. Jeyaratnam Wilson depicts how the Tamils' early desire for a form of federalism and provincial autonomy was repeatedly betrayed by Sinhala majoritarianism and its refusal to countenance any but a unitary state. By the mid-1970s, the moderate Tamil demand for a federal polity led by the likes of Chelvanayakam stood discredited in the face of this intransigence, clearing the space for the emergence of extremist groups like the LTTE.[4]

Neil DeVotta has shown how Sri Lanka was characterized by a process of ethnic outbidding by the two main political parties of the Sinhala majority— the United National Party (UNP) and the Sri Lanka Freedom Party (SLFP)— at the expense of the minorities. His summary of the process encapsulates Sri Lanka's postcolonial trajectory:

> Outbidding stems from politicians' desire and determination to acquire and maintain power and may be practiced in varied contexts. Yet whenever it incorporates race or ethnicity it marginalizes minority communities, exacerbates interracial or polyethnic tensions, and undermines the state's ability to function dispassionately. When a government in a polyethnic state utterly disregards minorities' legitimate preferences and instead cavalierly institutes policies favoring a majority or other community, which is precisely what ethnic outbidding engenders, those marginalized lose confidence in the state's institutions. This could easily promote reactive nationalism among those disfavored and create a milieu conducive to ethnic rivalry and conflict . . . If the marginalized group is territorialized, and thereby has claims to a historical homeland, they could mobilize to seek a separate existence. This is indeed the setting for Sri Lanka's sad ethnic saga.[5]

The hardening of Sinhala identity was accompanied, DeVotta argues, by a process of "institutional decay" as the army, security forces, police, state

bureaucracy, and other significant institutions have been thoroughly Sinhal-
ized over time. His statistics regarding the rapidly declining Tamil representation in institutions of governance bear repetition: "while thirty per cent
of the Ceylon Administrative Service, fifty per cent of the clerical service,
sixty per cent of engineers and doctors, forty per cent of the armed forces
and forty per cent of the labour force were Tamil in 1956, those numbers had
plummeted to five per cent, five per cent, ten per cent, one per cent and five
per cent respectively by 1970."[6] Depicting a similar process of the hardening
of religious-ethnic identity, Ameer Ali argues that trapped in the political
quagmire of the conflict between the Sri Lankan Tamils and the Sinhalese,
the Muslims of Sri Lanka have asserted their religious distinctiveness, and the
conflict has "once again reinforced the need to hold on to the religious identity even more tightly."[7]

In the early decades after independence, state-sponsored irrigation
schemes especially impacted the eastern province. The settlement of largely
Sinhalese peasants in newly cultivable lands brought the wary Tamils and
Muslims somewhat closer together. As Denis McGilvray hails the multiethnic
eastern province as the "crucible of conflict," noting that:

> For the rural, rice-cultivating Tamils and Muslims on the east coast of the island
> . . . it was above all else the massive post-independence resettlement of Sinhala
> farmers on internationally funded irrigation projects adjacent to older Tamil-
> speaking districts that steadily deepened their sense of marginalization and
> political disempowerment. The Accelerated Mahaweli Development Scheme, a
> massive hydroelectric and peasant-resettlement project, launched in 1977, that
> invoked nationalist visions of the ancient Sinhala Buddhist hydraulic civiliza-
> tion, further exacerbated Tamil anxieties on a national scale.[8]

If "national development" comes to be tainted as ethnic, as the ambitious
hydraulic resettlement programs indeed were, the very process of nation-
building becomes also one of national unmaking.[9] As the civil war in Sri
Lanka gathered momentum after the pogrom of July 1983, and especially
after the ascendancy of the LTTE from 1987 onwards, the Muslims of the
North and especially of the Eastern province have coalesced strongly around
their religious identity and downplayed their "Tamil-ness." Tamil-Muslim
relations have seen incredible violence since 1990, including efforts by the
LTTE to ethnically "cleanse" the Northern province of Muslims and LTTE-
conduced massacres against the Muslims in the Eastern province as well.

This process of hardening of subnational identities continued unabated through the first decade of the new millennium. In the elections to the Parliament held in April 2004, the PA (the Peoples Alliance, led by President Chandrika Kumaratunga of the SLFP) campaigned on a far more hard-line policy toward the ethnic question than the incumbent regime of Prime Minister Ranil Wickramasinghe of the United National Front (UNF). The PA reasserted its commitment to the unitary state, charged the UNF with irresponsible negotiating, and ousted the latter through its alliance with the ultranationalist JVP, the once-Maoist group. The latter expanded its presence in parliament from 16 in the 2001 elections to 40 in 2004. For the first time in Sri Lanka's independent history, an all-Bhikku political party, Jatika Hela Urumaya (JHU—the National Heritage Party), ran as many as 260 candidates for office and won 9 seats in the 225-member Legislature. Like the JVP, the JHU stands committed to a unitary state, opposes any idea of devolving power to the North or the East, and essentially denies that Sri Lanka has an ethnic problem. Instead, it sees it as having a "terrorist problem" deserving a military solution. The JHU, along with other hard-liners in the JVP, wanted the speedy exit of the Norwegian peace mediators who were seen as partial to the LTTE, and the establishment of a Buddhist "dharmarajya" or righteous state in Sri Lanka.[10] In the Northern Province, in the same elections, the Ilankai Tamil Arasu Katchi (ITAK), a pro-LTTE formation, won eight of nine seats in Jaffna with only one being won by the anti-LTTE formation led by Douglas Devananda, the EPDP. Overall, the ITAK won 22 seats indicating that the LTTE retained its hegemony over the Sri Lankan Tamils into the mid-2000s.[11]

In the November 2005 presidential elections, Mahinda Rajapakse of the United People Freedom Alliance, with the support of the hard-line JVP and JHU, won. The UPFA regime prioritized a military solution to the ethnic conflict and believed in "maximum devolution within a unitary state." It has essentially "cast Sri Lanka's debate on power-sharing several decades back in time."[12] Across the board then, Sri Lanka has seen a steady strengthening of ethnic identity rather than the consolidation of national citizenship. Furthermore, such hardening has resulted from processes that are constitutive of the postcolonial nation-building project: elections based on universal mass franchise; economic development programs such as irrigation schemes; and affirmative action programs to redress ethnic "imbalances" and disproportions in access to public goods.

The difficulty we have in imagining a way out of this postcolonial bind between ethnicity and nation is amply illustrated in some of the best recent works on Sri Lanka. Our understandings of democratic representation, fairness, and equality in a multiethnic society remain trapped in a discourse of majorities and minorities rather than citizenship. This is a complex issue and one that relates directly to the reasons for the crisis of state capacity and legitimacy in contemporary Sri Lanka, and therefore it merits further investigation.

In her excellent book *Sri Lanka in the Modern Age*, Nira Wickramasinghe observes that changes in admissions policies of higher educational institutions after independence,

> ... led to disillusionment and despair among the youth of the North [Tamils] whose economic mobility was hampered. In *real terms* Tamils were still *overrepresented* in the faculties of medicine and engineering, but the drop in the admission rate of Tamils to the national universities was so dramatic it was viewed as a *loss of rights* rather than a *loss of privilege*.[13] (my emphasis)

Wickramasinghe's case rests upon certain tacit assumptions regarding the content of postcolonial society. The most salient would seem to run as follows: Since Sri Lankan Tamils represent about 13% of the national population, they should properly be entitled to a similar proportion in universities, professions, security forces, the parliament and legislatures, state jobs, and other collective goods in the nation. Any "excess" in terms of their access to such goods amounts to an "over-representation." Moreover, they ought not to protest against state policies that seek to bring the distribution of collective goods in society in line with the pattern of ethnic/social cleavages because, if they do so, they are trying to hang on to *privileges* rather than their legitimate *rights* in society.

Wickramasinghe's use of the word "privilege" also has to do with the fact that the overrepresentation is widely seen as a legacy of Sri Lanka's colonial past, which by definition is a discredited and inauthentic past characterized by alien rule. In a recent essay that characterizes Sri Lanka as a particular variant of a weak state, namely a "fragmented state," Erin Jenne echoes Wickramasinghe. She explicitly adduces the historical fact of colonialism for Tamil overrepresentation as she notes:

> Anti-minority sentiment in the post-independence period was also fueled by the fact that the British had favored ethnic Tamils as functionaries in the colonial government. Indeed, under British colonial rule, Tamils were *over-*

represented in universities and the civil service and held a *disproportionate share of the wealth.*[14] (my emphasis)

Jenne expands the ideas of appropriate entitlement or access to educational opportunities or positions in the state bureaucracy now to "wealth" as well. In other words, if Tamils are 13% of the population they ought to own no more than a similar percentage of national wealth, however measured. This expansion of the idea or proportionality from access to state-provided resources to (mostly privately) generated wealth amounts to a deepening of a majoritarian vision of postcolonial society.

In similar vein, Neil DeVotta locates the origins of Tamil privilege in colonial times when he notes that

> The British had marginalized the Buddhist religion, which most Sinhalese adhere to, and also showed a preference for hiring Tamils into the civil service. The alacrity with which young Tamils embraced the English language was a major reason for this British preference, though the fact that this also enabled the British to effectively marginalize the majority community was considered a strategic bonus. The upshot, however, was that the Tamils benefited *disproportionately* under British colonialism. For example, in 1946, just two years prior to independence, Tamils comprised thirty-three per cent of the civil service and forty per cent of the judicial service. . . . They also accounted for thirty-one per cent of the students in the university system. Such disparities had to be *rectified*, and linguistic nationalism in the post-independence era became the symbolic mechanism by which to do so.[15] (my emphasis)

Redressing (or "rectifying," to use DeVotta's phrase above) colonially inherited privilege becomes a part of the task of postcolonial nation-building. In fact, I would argue that it is precisely this mandate of the postcolonial nation-state to redress colonial legacies that is being translated in specific circumstances into riots and pogroms that attack Tamil-owned businesses and neighborhoods. Wealthy Tamil homes, neighborhoods, or individuals stand as testament to their "disproportionate" assets, given their status as a minority. The anti-Tamil riots that have punctuated the postcolonial history of Sri Lanka (1956, 1958, 1977, 1981, and 1983) may be seen as efforts by the majority community—and not just their political leaders—to actively participate in the construction of the post-colonial nation and to "rectify" colonial anomalies. Tracing Tamil "over-representation" to colonial machinations also serves to locate the Tamil as less of a native and more of an outsider.

It sanctions postcolonial nation-building as the effort of the majority community to achieve its "rightful" place at the top of the social order and the minorities to understand their "proper" place in that same order.[16]

If the enterprise of postcolonial state- and nation-building is primarily seen as a redress of inherited imbalances and unearned privileges, it is difficult to see how a unified nation can emerge from this process. It is more likely to create disaffected minority groups, and when such minority groups also happen to be concentrated in specific territories, the possibility of demands for secession increases.

Is a society in which the distribution of collective goods is in direct proportion to the enumerated fractions of various identities (ethnic, religious, or linguistic) possible or even desirable? It would be an impossible task of social engineering to attempt to bring the distribution of all collective goods into strict congruence with societal fragments. At the same time, histories of deprivation, discrimination, and neglect against social groups are all too real. "Affirmative" action that redresses such historical wrongs is both ethical and worthy of support. Yet the creation of policies for increased access for such groups adversely affects those, such as the Tamils, who have a greater number of those with the skills necessary to gain access to such goods on a narrow and ahistorical definition of "merit." What, in such a context, constitutes a "fair" distribution of collective good in relation to the proportion of ethnic fragments in a society?

I do not claim there are any easy answers to such questions of fairness and equity, and the question of the right balance (if there is such a thing at all) to be struck between redressing historical discriminations and ensuring a contemporary meritocracy. In the context of our discussion of state weakness and capacity, certain points seem to be salient, however: (a) under conditions of rapid economic growth it is perhaps more likely that the gains of a particular community are less likely to be perceived as coming at the expense of others, and the zero-sum character of gains and losses is likely to be diminished; (b) in defining the postcolonial national project, a balance has to be struck between the redress of historically derived inequalities through state-mandated affirmative action programs and that of moving forward into the future as a meritocratic society with equal opportunity for all citizens based on their Sri Lankan-ness; and (c) the state has to act and be perceived as a legitimate embodiment of all Sri Lankans and not one that is weighted or colored in proportion to the distribution of various ethnic majorities and minorities in the nation. These are daunting and yet inescapable requirements if Sri Lanka is to avoid further descent down the spiral from a weak to a fragmented to a failed state. As I show in the last section of this chapter, however, such a debate on the content of democracy, on the tension between ethnicity and nation, and on the means to produce a Sri Lankan rather than a Sinhalese state, has been decisively put on the back burner thanks to the resounding military defeat of the LTTE by the Sri Lankan Army in the first half of 2009.

Regional Factors in Sri Lanka's Ethnic Conflict

In the literature on failed or weak states, the presence of kindred ethnic minorities or groups across state borders is commonly cited as an important reason for their difficulties in state consolidation and minority integration. Thus, Pakistan is accused of harboring, training, and inducting militants into Kashmir to fuel the fires of a nationalist struggle there against the Indian state, just as it was seen as aiding the Taliban in emerging and consolidating their hold on Afghanistan during and after the Soviet occupation. India aided Bengali nationalists in East Pakistan, culminating in the successful secession of Bangladesh from Pakistan in 1971, and is often accused by its neighbors of supporting various minority groups in their nations as part of its regional foreign policy. Besides the support of the regional states for so-called ethnic kin populations in neighboring countries as a part of their foreign policy arsenal, it is also argued that nonstate linkages between ethnic kin communities across interstate borders can promote secessionist movements and contribute to regional instability and conflict.

In the case of the Indo–Sri Lanka border, both these factors—state support for an ethnic kin community and societal linkages between trans-border kin communities—are held responsible to varying degrees for the crisis of the Sri Lankan state. In this section, I briefly summarize the role both of governments (the state government of Tamil Nadu and the Indian central government) as well as society (specifically the supposed co-ethnic Tamils in Tamil Nadu) in terms of their contribution to the crisis in Sri Lanka. I make two main points: firstly, the role of the so-called ethnic kin community in Tamil Nadu in aiding and abetting the rise of a secessionist movement in Sri Lanka has been greatly exaggerated, and it was, at best, a trivial contributor to the ethnic conflict. The overwhelming responsibility for the rise of Sri Lankan Tamil nationalism rests with Sinhala majoritarianism. Secondly, the period from about 1980 to 1991, which saw the explicit involvement of India in Sri

Lankan affairs, was driven mainly by central leaders in Delhi who used Tamil co-ethnicity as an alibi for their intervention.[17]

For a variety of reasons, various Sri Lankan academics and politicians—both Sinhalese and Tamil—have tended to exaggerate India's, and specifically Tamil Nadu's, role in the rise of a secessionist movement amongst Sri Lankan Tamils. For the Sinhalese, attributing extra-national inspiration and resources to the Tamil struggle was important in delegitimizing the latter. For the Tamils, exaggerating the support of Tamil Nadu and India to their struggle was a natural outcome given their marginalization by Sinhala majoritarianism, and often more an expression of hope than of reality. The sociocultural, linguistic, and religious affinities between the two Tamil communities were undoubtedly real and thick. But such affinities do not necessarily or automatically translate into a convergence on political aims.

Dravidian nationalism in Tamil Nadu lost its secessionist bite almost immediately after independence. The breakup of the once-secessionist Dravida Kazhagam and the emergence of an explicitly political and electoral party in the Dravida Munnetra Kazhagam (DMK) under the leadership of C. N. Anna Durai in 1948–1949 was an early indication of this. Once the idea of linguistic states was conceded by Nehru and the DMK became the ruling party of the state in 1967, it became even more willing to work the federal system to its advantage. Foreign policy in India, as in every country, is a central subject, and it would be a rare regional party or state government that would act autonomously of the center in this regard. The overblown rhetoric of DMK and AIADMK about both the Sri Lankan Tamils and, on occasion, the Estate Tamils, and their grand-standing on these matters in the national parliament, the Tamil Nadu legislature, or in the streets of Tamil Nadu, often became grist for the mill of many in Sri Lanka who were interested in exaggerating the role of the "foreign hand." Yet, such rhetoric by the Dravidian parties was more a sign of weakness than of strength. Having given up early on their claims for a separate nation, they distinguished themselves from Congress in Tamil Nadu by their claims to speak for a larger worldwide "Thamilakam." In terms of their actual (as distinct from symbolic) politics, going beyond the central government's writ on foreign policy and colluding with the leaders of the Sri Lankan Tamils without the center's tacit approval could result in the swift ouster of a state government and the declaration of president's rule. Such ousters of non-Congress state governments occurred repeatedly under Prime Minister Indira Gandhi's terms in office (1966 to 1977 and 1980 to

1984) and it would be a serious misunderstanding of DMK and AIADMK to accord them such impunity.

The only period in which one could credibly argue that regional (Indian) factors impacted the state crisis in Sri Lanka was from the beginning of Prime Minister Gandhi's second term in office (1980) to the end of the Rajiv Gandhi administration (1989). The UNP and President Jayewardene seemed to go out of their way to antagonize Gandhi when she was out of office from 1977 to 1980. UNP foreign policy moved Sri Lanka closer to the United States and ASEAN, and away from nonalignment, which was deemed by Gandhi to be against India's regional interests. From the beginning of her second regime in January 1980, Prime Minister Gandhi decided that Jayewardene had to be cut to size, and Sri Lankan foreign policy reverted back to the line followed by Sirima Bandaranaike—and that the instrument for doing this would be the burgeoning Tamil militant movement there.

Today, we know that Indian intelligence agencies provided sanctuary and training to Sri Lankan Tamil militants from sometime in the early 1980s all the way until a "hot" war broke out between the Indian Peace Keeping Force (IPKF) and the LTTE in October of 1987, and perhaps even beyond. In such covert support and training, the "secessionist history" of Tamil Nadu and the fact of co-ethnicity served as the perfect alibi for the Indian central government's policy. Yet, it was the central government that took the lead in aiding and training the Tamil militants in Sri Lanka during the 1980s; the DMK and AIADMK were bit players doing the center's dirty work for it when needed.

Gandhi's actions in Sri Lanka were from the same playbook she used in Punjab, Assam, and Kashmir: aid extremist groups to discredit opposition parties and moderates and then run on a platform of the Congress being the sole party committed to national security and stability.[18] Her son and successor Rajiv Gandhi was more well meaning and earnest but also naïve. His regime inaugurated a twin-track policy in Sri Lanka whereby the militant prong would be used to pressure the Jayewardene administration to forego a military approach to the ethnic question, while the diplomatic prong (represented by the efforts of Natwar Singh, P. Chidambaram, and others) would encourage Sri Lanka down the road of provincial autonomy, a federal political dispensation, and recognizing itself to be a pluralist and multiethnic society.

The twin-track strategy seemed to have succeeded with the signing of the Indo–Sri Lanka Agreement of July 29, 1987. However, the main stumbling block emerged in the shape of a group and its leader who had been gravely underestimated by the Indians—LTTE and its chief, Velupillai Prabhakaran. As has happened innumerable times, the militant group refused to remain its sponsoring state's puppet and turned on its master. A war between the LTTE and the IPKF broke out in October 1987. By 1989, the strategy lay in tatters as the IPKF was trapped in a counterinsurgency war against a guerrilla group on its own terrain. None of the other Tamil militant groups that India aided could stand up to the LTTE which, after 1989 and Jayewardene's exit, was now being supported by the new president of Sri Lanka, Ranasinghe Premadasa, whose animosity toward the Indians exceeded even that toward the Tamil militants.

When the IPKF left Sri Lanka in March 1990, the twin-track policy had reached a dead end. Even before the assassination of Rajiv Gandhi in May 1991 by a Sri Lankan Tamil suicide bomber, India's foreign policy toward Sri Lanka had returned to what it had been for the period from 1947 to 1980—one that I would largely describe as committed to its sovereignty and territorial integrity over the interests of Sri Lankan Tamils or the Estate Tamils. The "Tamil Nadu" factor remains as irrelevant to the fortunes of Sri Lanka's Tamils as it ever was, except for that brief moment in the mid-1980s when it was expediently used by the center as a cloak for its own covert actions in Sri Lanka.[19]

In the years since 1991, the equation between India and Sri Lanka changed to the detriment of the LTTE. The role of the latter in Rajiv Gandhi's assassination, and the defeat of the IPKF, seemed to bring home to India the dangers of supporting ethnonationalist movements in neighboring countries. More importantly, it eroded the sympathy of Tamil Nadu for the LTTE without diminishing their support for the rights of the Sri Lankan Tamils. India has watched the ebb and flow of negotiations and wars between the LTTE and the Sri Lankan government, and the role of external mediators, with guarded interest. It has come to the aid of the Sri Lankan government in its war against the LTTE on occasion and has expressed its commitment to the territorial integrity of that country.

The isolation of the LTTE increased greatly in the post–9/11 world, and earlier distinctions between "terrorists" and "national liberation movements" are no longer as salient. These developments have freed the hands of states pursuing a hard line against ethnonationalist insurgencies within their borders, be it the Sri Lankan state against the Tamils or the Russians vis-à-vis the Chechens or the Chinese state against the Uyghurs. With the LTTE's activities banned and its declaration as a terrorist outfit in India, the United States, the European Union, Canada, Australia, and a number of other nations, the LTTE has found it difficult to mobilize public support and financial resources as before. The human rights violations of the Sri Lankan Army and state against the Tamils tended to produce less of an outrage in the Western or Indian media and society after September 11, 2001, especially in comparison to the 1980s. This period, a moment in the re-girding of state sovereignty globally vis-à-vis terrorism, was used to devastating effect by the Sri Lankan regime of Mahinda Rajapakse, as detailed in the next section.

The case of Indo–Sri Lankan relations has some interesting implications for state capacity and the role of regional factors in producing insecurity. First, it indicates that we sometimes tend to exaggerate the role of so-called ethnic kin across territorial boundaries and assume that cultural, social, religious, or linguistic (in other words, "ethnic") overlaps between communities in different nation-states must necessarily produce shared political aims or a desire to create a separate nation-state. Whether ethnic kin communities across interstate borders actually behave in this way seems more dependent on the actions of state leaders, rather than a predestined outcome.

Second, it appears that the supposedly dangerous proclivities of transborder ethnic communities also create opportunities for regimes to destabilize their neighbors regionally and to discredit regional political parties and leaders by tarring them with the secessionist or communal brush. In other words, co-ethnics across borders represent both danger and opportunity for the production of state sovereignty and for the conduct of domestic and foreign policy.

While the idea that the states in a region should cooperate with each other in maintaining collective security and stand united against insurgent or militant groups is an oft-repeated piety, the truth is that the presence of such insurgencies and their expedient use by regimes in the region are an inseparable part of the conduct of everyday politics in South Asia. In such a context, it is plausible to argue that regional insecurity arises less from the presence and actions of ethnic kin communities across interstate borders and more from the actions of state elites determined to exploit this fact in their domestic and foreign policies.

The Normalization of Endless War and State Capacity

In 2006, Mahinda Rajapakse of the SLFP was elected to the presidency in alliance with the extremist Sinhalese parties of the JVP and the JHU. At the outset, he stated that Sri Lanka had a terrorist, not ethnic, problem deserving of a military, not political, solution. He averred that any talk of devolution or a political solution to the ethnic issue had to follow the military defeat of the LTTE. Under his presidency, the Sri Lankan Army doubled in size and became far better equipped and trained than before. Rajapakse coordinated a diplomatic united front before commencing his all-out attack on the LTTE, securing the cooperation and military assistance of India, China, and Pakistan, among others. Such a front would have been inconceivable in the period prior to 9/11. Coinciding as this did with international developments that have worked to the detriment of the LTTE, the Sri Lankan Army cornered the LTTE within a tiny area in the northeastern part of the country by April 2009, and in May of that year launched a final assault that ended in the slaughter of the top LTTE leadership, including Prabhakaran.

The decisive military defeat of an insurgent outfit that had existed for over 25 years cannot be minimized and has not happened often in post-colonial South Asia. In its prime, the LTTE governed much of the Northern and Eastern provinces and had many of the attributes of "state-ness," such as its own police and judiciary; border control, including the issuance of visas; its own navy and a small but effective air force; tax collection both within its territory in Sri Lanka and from a global diaspora of Sri Lankan Tamils; and it had successfully faced down the Indian Army, from 1987 to 1990, and the Sri Lankan Army for a quarter of a century. The defeat of the LTTE by the Sri Lankan state is one of those moments when a more nuanced discussion of state capacity and strength/weakness is merited. The Rajapakse regime pursued the military defeat of the LTTE with a single-mindedness that revealed an acute appreciation that the international and regional conjuncture was greatly in its favor and to the detriment of the LTTE. If this warrants a momentary appreciation of the strength of the state and its capacity in the realm of coercion, as the following paragraphs reveal, the reasons for its current success in this domain may also underlie the erosion of its legitimacy and descent into a failed state in the future.

The United Nations estimates that as many as 7,000 civilians, overwhelmingly Tamils, were killed in the final assault on the LTTE between January and May 2009, and a further 13,000 were injured. The foreign ministers of the European Union have demanded an independent inquiry into possible war crimes and violations of human rights during the final push by the Sri Lankan Army. In the aftermath of the war, more than 300,000 Sri Lankan Tamils have been herded into refugee camps. In late May 2009, after a visit to some of the camps, the UN Secretary General Ban Ki Moon called conditions therein shocking and urged the Sri Lankan government to speedily rehabilitate the internally displaced Tamils and allow them to return home. More than five months later, only a few thousands have been allowed to leave the camps, while the overwhelming majority of them remain in squalid conditions. The Sri Lankan government has said that its main priority is to ensure that no LTTE cadres escape the camps and that the speed at which refugees are rehabilitated will be dictated by that priority. The government has proven itself quite immune to international pressure to either speedily dismantle the camps or improve conditions for the refugees therein.[20]

From the beginning of the latest war against the LTTE, the Sri Lankan state strictly controlled all media coverage of the war, and the defense secretary (who happens to be the brother of the president) has criticized Western media outlets (such as the BBC and CNN) for their (in his view) biased coverage. Echoing former President George W. Bush, Gotabaya Rajapakse noted that when it came to terrorism there was no room for gray: you were either with the terrorists or opposed to them. Any attention given by the media to civilian casualties, attacks on hospitals, and alleged human rights violations would, he said, lead to their expulsion from the country. Sri Lanka has become one of the most dangerous places in the world to be a journalist. An attack on the largest private television station in 2009 led to millions of dollars in damage, and similar attacks on the media by party goons and unknown assailants are increasingly common. Sixteen journalists have been killed in Sri Lanka since 1992, and others have been imprisoned, tortured, or exiled.[21]

In August 2009, Tamil journalist J. S. Tissainayagam was sentenced to twenty years of hard labor in prison on grounds that he incited racial hatred and supported terrorism. The government alleged, and the court upheld, that he had obtained funds from the LTTE, though the evidence for the latter charges remain dubious to say the least. The world's leading organization of journalists, the International Federation of Journalists, has come out in strong opposition to what it considers a vendetta against Tissainayagam for doing his job, for highlighting the violations of human rights on the part of the Sri Lankan military and state. His sentencing has occasioned protests from human rights organizations from all over the world and figured in a speech on freedom made by U.S. President Obama.[22] However, Tissainayagam's sentencing has had a chilling effect on Sri Lanka's vibrant civil society, with its many organizations committed to human rights, minority rights, social justice, and democracy.[23]

The chauvinism that has often accompanied the victories in recent months by the Sri Lankan army does not augur well for the future. President Rajapakse promised a fair and equitable political solution to the ethnic question in the aftermath of the victory, but no proposals or initiatives have been forthcoming. Instead, the situation in the resettlement camps and the everyday humiliations faced by the Tamils continue unabated. Even if a political settlement is attempted in the aftermath of this victory, it will not strike the Tamils as either fair or legitimate and will sow the seeds for another round of conflict. Irrespective of the short-term fortunes of the LTTE, given what we know about such conflicts elsewhere, unless the material conditions that produce ethnic majoritarianism and minority discrimination are transformed, a militant Tamil movement in Sri Lanka will not die out.[24]

Prolonged conflicts—be they civil wars or interstate—enhance those aspects of state capacity that emphasize coercion over consent, secrecy over transparency, personalization of power over decentralization, and corruption over general development. In the long run, the normalization of conflict threatens the democratic order of society. Nearly all these general propositions regarding the impact of continuous war on state capacity are proven in the case of Sri Lanka. The routinization of war over twenty-five years has created its own political economy, and this cannot be firewalled from discussions of state capacity. As Darini Rajasingham-Senanayake notes

> A variety of politicians as well as members of the defense industry and paramilitary groups have used the armed conflict to acquire personal and political profit. In the war zones, violence by paramilitary groups and military forces alike has become routine and includes torture, rape, massacres and summary executions. The war itself has become a "dirty war," reaching across ethnic and national boundaries, undermining civil-military relations and democratic practice, eroding multicultural social structures, and creating hidden economies of taxation and terror.[25]

In this context, it is not surprising that there has been no decrease in defense expenditures in the aftermath of the LTTE's defeat, and the head of the

Sri Lankan Army has said that he would like to augment the current level of troops by another 50% in the year ahead.[26]

Conclusions

In many ways, the present conjuncture in Sri Lanka is even worse than what prevailed in prior times in terms of the devolution of power or imagining a plural Sri Lanka. The period of July–August 1987 around the signing of the Indo–Sri Lanka agreement, the unilateral initiatives towards devolution taken by the Kumaratunga government in the mid-1990s, and the period immediately after the announcement of the cease fire agreement between the Sri Lankan government and the LTTE in 2002, were moments when some renegotiation of a majoritarian state seemed under way. Ironically, on each occasion the threat of peace seemed to destabilize the protagonists, who soon retreated into the predictability and protocols of armed conflict.

It is difficult to be optimistic about enhancing state capacity and regional security in South Asia after a close analysis of Sri Lanka. Six decades of independence and postcolonial politics have diminished state capacity and witnessed serious institutional decay, except in those areas inimical to democracy and human security. The institutions of democracy and development have been used by cosmopolitan elites to establish an ethnocratic, rather than an inclusive and pluralist, state. This has delegitimized the state in the eyes of significant sections of the population. The routine use of ethnic kin populations by the various regimes in South Asia as an instrument in their domestic and foreign policies complicates the idea of a regional security arrangement to jointly combat insurgencies and reinforce the sovereignty of the various states. It is for this reason that I apprehend that Sri Lanka is a weak state on a trajectory that will culminate in a failed state.

It is perhaps a truism that strong and democratic states that command the allegiance of all sections of their society will make for peaceful and cooperative regions. In that sense, the first order of business for Sri Lanka would be the creation of a democratic, pluralist nation-state in which no single ethnic group is seen as more equal than others. Yet, that envisaged future will have to be one in which Tamil (or Muslim or Sinhala or Burgher) over-representation, disproportion, or privilege is regarded as an unremarkable fact. Our difficulty in conceiving such a future is testament to the distance that separates where we are from where we would like to be.

Notes to Chapter 10

1. See T. V. Paul, Chapter 1, "State Capacity and South Asia's Perennial Insecurity Problems," p. 5.

2. Howard W. Wriggins, "Impediments to Unity in New Nations: The Case of Ceylon," *American Political Science Review* 55, no. 2 (June 1961), p. 316, quoted in Neil DeVotta, "Civil Society and Non-Governmental Organizations in Sri Lanka: Peacemakers or Parasites?" *Civil Wars* 7, no. 2 (Summer 2005), p. 173.

3. For a recent essay that surveys the emergence of ethnic mobilization and the incipient fractures in a unified idea of Ceylonese citizenship, in the last three decades of colonial rule itself, see Harshan Kumarasingham, "A Democratic Paradox: the Communalisation of Politics in Ceylon, 1911–1948," *Asian Affairs* 37, no. 3 (November 2006), pp. 342–352.

4. A. Jeyaratnam Wilson, *Sri Lankan Tamil Nationalism: Its Origins and Development in the 19th and 20th Centuries* (Vancouver: University of British Columbia Press, 2000); Wilson, S.J.V., *Chelvanayakam and the Crisis of Ceylon Tamil Nationalism, 1947–1977* (Honolulu: University of Hawaii Press, 1994); and Wilson, *The Break-Up of Sri Lanka: the Sinhalese-Tamil Conflict* (London: C. Hurst and Co., 1988).

5. Neil DeVotta, "From Ethnic Outbidding to Ethnic Conflict: the Institutional Basis for Sri Lanka's Separatist War," *Nations and Nationalism* 11, no. 1 (2005), p. 142.

6. DeVotta, "From Ethnic Outbidding," p. 151.

7. Ameer Ali, "The Muslims of Sri Lanka: an Ethnic Minority Trapped in a Political Quagmire," *Inter-Asia Cultural Studies* 5, no. 3 (2004), p. 372.

8. Denis McGilvray, *Crucible of Conflict: Tamil and Muslim Society on the East Coast of Sri Lanka* (Durham, NC: Duke University Press, 2008), pp. 4–5.

9. For more on the point that the liberalization of the Sri Lankan economy after 1977, and the partial dismantling of its strong welfare state thereafter, has accentuated the discrimination faced by ethnic minorities and the disaffection of rural, educated Sinhala youth, see Jennifer Hyndman, "The Securitization of Fear in Post-Tsunami Sri Lanka," *Annals of the Association of American Geographers* 97, no. 2 (2007), pp. 361–372.

10. For more on the JHU, the reasons for its rise, and its intransigence on even limited ideas such as the devolution of powers to provincial councils, a federal set-up and the softening of the unitary state in Sri Lanka, see Neil DeVotta and Jason Stone, "Jatika Hela Urumaya and Ethno-Religious Politics in Sri Lanka," *Pacific Affairs* 81, no. 1 (Spring 2008), pp. 31–51.

11. See Rajat Ganguly, "Sri Lanka's Ethnic Conflict: at a Crossroads Between Peace and War," *Third World Quarterly* 25, no. 5 (2004), pp. 903–918.

12. Jayadeva Uyangoda, "Ethnic Conflict in Sri Lanka: Changing Dynamics," *Policy Studies Paper # 32* (Washington, DC: East-West Center, 2007), p. 26.

13. Nira Wickramasinghe, *Sri Lanka in the Modern Age: a History of Contested Identities*, (Honolulu: University of Hawaii Press, 2006), pp. 278–279.

14. Erin K. Jenne, "Sri Lanka: a Fragmented State," in *State Failure and State*

Weakness in a Time of Terror, ed. Robert I. Rotberg (Washington, DC: Brookings Institution Press, 2003), p. 225.

15. Neil DeVotta, "From Ethnic Outbidding," p. 148.

16. For an insightful argument regarding this characteristic of postcolonial Sri Lanka, see Jayadeva Uyangoda, "Ethnicity, Nation, and State-Formation in Sri Lanka: Antinomies of Nation-Building," *Pravada* no.3 (1994), pp. 11–17.

17. I have made both these arguments at length in at least three works: *Postcolonial Insecurities: India, Sri Lanka and the Question of Eelam* (Minneapolis: University of Minnesota Press, 1999); "India's Role in Sri Lanka's Ethnic Crisis," Marga Monograph Series on Ethnic Reconciliation, no. 3 (Colombo: Marga Institute, 2001); and "Divergent Narratives: Dravidian and Tamil Eelamist Nationalisms," in *Collective Identities Revisited*, Volume II, ed. Michael Roberts (Colombo: Marga Press, 1998), pp. 315–346. This section summarizing India's role in Sri Lanka's ethnic conflict relies heavily on these earlier works of mine.

18. Prime Minister Gandhi's disastrous policies in Kashmir, Punjab, Assam, and Sri Lanka, and more generally her paranoid style of politics and its horrific consequences both domestically and regionally, are only now being fully appreciated in India. While there are many works that critically examine her political legacy, I would mention in particular Paul Brass, *The Politics of India Since Independence* (Cambridge: Cambridge University Press, 2008), and Inder Malhotra, *Indira Gandhi* (New Delhi: National Book Trust, 2006). For a detailed examination of the similarities between Mrs. Gandhi's policies in Kashmir, Punjab, Assam, and Sri Lanka—and their uniformly disastrous outcomes—see my *Postcolonial Insecurities*.

19. This limited relevance has diminished even further in contemporary times. A clear indicator of this is the fact that the LTTE leadership was decimated in May 2009 alongside thousands of civilian casualties and hundreds of thousands of internally displaced Tamils at a time when general elections to the Indian Parliament and assembly elections to the state government were occurring just across the Straits. The defeat of the LTTE had little political reverberations in Tamil Nadu, and one of the politicians in the state who has tried to make a career of espousing their cause, Y. Gopalasamy, was resoundingly defeated in his parliamentary constituency. The Sri Lankan issue figured only marginally in the electoral platforms of the leading contenders for parliamentary or assembly seats in the state of Tamil Nadu, be it the DMK, AIADMK, or the Congress.

20. See Anbarasan Ethirajan, "Winning the Peace in Sri Lanka," *BBC News*, May 19, 2009. http://news.bbc.co.uk/2/hi/south_asia/8056734.stm (accessed September 19, 2009).

21. See Miranda Leitsinger, "Sri Lanka's Media Faces Growing Pressure," CNN.Com.Asia News, February 5, 2009. http://www.cnn.com/2009/WORLD/asiapcf/02/01/srilanka.media/index.html?iref=newssearch (accessed September 21, 2009).

22. BBC News. "Jail Term for Sri Lankan Editor," August 31, 2009. http://news.bbc.co.uk/2/hi/south_asia/8230067.stm (accessed September 19, 2009).

23. There has been very little independent and reliable media coverage of these issues from within Sri Lanka due to the hostility of the government.

24. The majoritarian impulse in Sri Lanka runs deep and wide. In a recent interview, General Sarath Fonseca, now a war hero after the defeat of the LTTE, observed that "I strongly believe that this country belongs to the Sinhalese but there are minority communities and we treat them like our people . . . We being the majority of the country, 75%, we will never give in and we have the right to protect this country . . . They can live in this country with us. But they must not try to, under the pretext of being a minority, demand undue things." Quoted in Mukul Kesavan, "When Will Peace Return to Serendip," *LiveMint.com & The Wall Street Journal*, May 29, 2009, http://www.livemint.com/articles/2009/05/29004656/When-will-peace-finally-return.html?pg=1 (accessed September 19, 2009).

25. Darini Rajasingham-Senanayake, "Dysfunctional Democracy and the Dirty War in Sri Lanka," *Asia-Pacific Issues* 52 (Honolulu: East-West Center, Honolulu, 2001), p. 1.

26. Charles Haviland, "Sri Lanka's Expanding Peacetime Army," BBC News, June 29, 2009. http://news.bbc.co.uk/2/hi/south_asia/8121385.stm (accessed September 21, 2009).

11 Bangladesh

A "Weak State" with Multiple Security Challenges

Ali Riaz

This chapter intends to problematize the notion of the "weak state," drawing on the experience of Bangladesh, which, on the one hand, has achieved remarkable successes in many critical sectors, while, on the other hand, demonstrates weaknesses symptomatic to weak states, including a host of security challenges.

It is my contention that extant conceptions of state capacity and security are inadequate in understanding the current situation of the Bangladeshi state, its implications for society, and its future trajectories. The dominant conceptualization of state capacity has an institutional bias; that is, these conceptualizations privilege institutions such as the government. The bias is greater toward those institutions that "determine the articulation and implementation of state policies."[1] Thus it is often argued that the stronger the institutions, the greater their capacity, and by extension, the stronger the capacity of the state to achieve distinctive outcomes including maintaining law and order and delivering political goods. I argue that neither the conventional indicators of state capacity nor the dominant conceptualization of security challenges as "military threats" are helpful in examining the Bangladeshi case. This chapter problematizes these notions and offers an alternative analysis to the complex political ecosystem of the country. The chapter's central argument is that extant theories of state capacity ignore the role of state as a social actor, that the state is also an agent of hegemony and a source of ideology. The state plays a role in creating an environment within which institutions can play their assigned roles, and this role of the state is intrinsically bound up with its legitimacy. Within the context of this discussion, the legitimacy of the state is more than a juridico-legal legitimacy; it is also a combination of the trust its institutions enjoy from the citizens and the ideological hegemony it succeeds in achieving.

Six sections follow the introduction: the second section provides a background on Bangladesh; the third section examines the weaknesses of extant state capacity theories; the fourth section weaves together the issues of legitimacy and state capacity, drawing on the Bangladesh case. Building on the arguments of the fourth section that the ideological weakness of the Bangladeshi state is eroding the capacity of the state and thus making it vulnerable to various security challenges, the fifth section examines both traditional and nontraditional security challenges to Bangladesh. The chapter concludes with a summary of the arguments.

Background

Since 2004, concerns regarding the erosion of governance and the future of democracy in Bangladesh have been expressed by many analysts.[2] These concerns were followed by the inclusion of Bangladesh in the contentious list of twenty countries featured in the "failed states index" by the organization Fund for Peace and *Foreign Policy* magazine. In 2005, the country was ranked seventeenth in the index.[3] A vigorous debate ensued within the country as to whether the country was heading toward becoming a "failed state."[4] A Bangladeshi analyst, who vehemently opposed the characterization of Bangladesh as a failed state, concluded that:

> While the country most certainly cannot be branded as a 'failed state' or a 'rogue state,' at least not yet, one perhaps cannot completely rule out the apprehension that the state apparatus is increasingly weakening under the dead weight of multiple crises of governance. Few observers of the recent developments in Bangladesh would disagree that the obsolescence of almost all state institutions is more than palpable. Worse still, all of them seem to be malfunctioning simultaneously, often betraying a sort of competitive bid to outdo each other.[5]

The events leading to the declaration of emergency on January 11, 2007, have given credence to concerns regarding the future of democracy in Bangladesh.[6] Additionally, the presence and proliferation of radical and militant groups with distinct political agendas have drawn the attention of almost all observers of Bangladeshi politics. The most prominent of these groups, who have demonstrated their presence throughout the country, are the Islamists. However, the increase in violence is not entirely an Islamist phenomenon per-petrated by clandestine groups posing challenges to the law and order of the country. Instead, there are other sources of violence. A number of so-called leftist groups have also thrived in the southwest parts of country, and the mainstream parties have also resorted to violence in greater measure. Al-though not entirely a new trend, the Bangladeshi state has been engaged in extrajudicial killings with impunity during the past decade.

In contrast to this bleak picture, glimmers of hope are discernable. Despite the lack of good governance, the Bangladeshi economy has made progress, and a number of social indicators such as population control, education, and pov-erty show positive developments in recent years. For example, even the country profile of the Failed States Index in 2007 acknowledged that the GDP growth rate of Bangladesh has remained steady at 5–6% during recent years. The country's success in increasing access to education for children, particularly for girls, is considered exemplary. Infant mortality has declined significantly, at an annual rate of 5% according to the UN Development Programme.[7]

Bangladesh, therefore, presents conflicting scenarios. On the one hand, the country demonstrates severe weaknesses even in maintaining law and order, while on the other hand it possesses strengths to address some vital problems with significant successes. These pictures have serious implications for understanding the state's capacity and strengths and raises the question as to whether the Bangladeshi state should be described as a "weak" state.

State Capacity: When Is a State "Weak"?

The indices commonly used to measure the capacity of the state are as conten-tious as the definitions of the state and are intrinsically related to the norma-tive question: what is the state supposed to do? One can utilize a Lockean, Weberian, or structural-institutional framework to understand the nature of the state, and consequently its capacity.[8] For example, in the Lockean frame-work, the state is to fulfill the social contract, and therefore any shortcom-ings in so doing represent its weakness. If, as in a Weberian view, the state is seen to be a set of institutions with the capacity to exercise a monopoly on the legitimate use of violence within its territory, the existence of any parallel authority in this regard is a testimony to the state's weakness. For those who consider the legal capacity of the state as the defining feature, any wavering on the part of state institutions or institutional challenges to that capacity is considered a sign of the state's weakness. These conceptualizations may not be mutually exclusive, but they do advocate different sets of indicators to measure the state's capacity.

The theories related to the state often attempt to conceptualize it as some combination of its functions, purposes, activities, personnel, organizational contours, legitimacy, legal norms, rules and machinery, sovereignty, coercive monopoly, and territorial control. In any combination of the preceding elements, three aspects are incorporated in understandings of the state: apparatus, power, and authority. State apparatus, in this context, means the complex set of institutions staffed by a professional bureaucracy and armed forces, specialized to some degree or other, which together ensure the formulation and execution of policies. Second, the state represents a concentration of economic and political power. In most cases, it is the largest single such concentration in a particular social formation. Third, it also represents a concentration of authority. This means, in the ideological sense, it is able to give legitimacy to the actions of those who act in its name, or at least it claims to do so. A fundamental question remains to be answered: Is there a hierarchy of order in determining the capacity? In other words, should one feature of the state be privileged against others?

Despite the apparent comprehensiveness of the conceptualization, one important aspect of the state is left out: What does the state do? From the normative perspective the question is, what is the state *supposed* to do? This question goes to the heart of the capacity issue; if the state is unable to do what it is supposed to do, either it lacks the capacity or is failing to perform at an optimal level. For decades the question of what the state is supposed to do has remained central to policy debates in connection with development issues in the Third World and has influenced the policy undertakings of governments, international agencies, and nongovernmental organizations. Two different views in this regard are discernable according to Khan.[9] The first insists that the primary role of the state is to provide a range of services, in particular, law and order, public goods, social security, welfare-oriented redistributions, and market regulation. The second view contends that the state has a more critical and problematic role—the transformation of the precapitalist and preindustrial societies into dynamic and essentially industrial capitalist models. The first is identified as the service delivery model and the second is called the social transformation model. Importantly, these two are not mutually exclusive: "historically, success in service delivery has depended in most cases on the success of states in pushing social transformation rapidly in the direction of viable capitalist economies."[10]

Discussions of state capacity, at least to date, have put very little weight on an important role of the state, particularly in the "developing" countries, that is, the state's role as an agent of hegemony and its production of ideology. It is worth recalling here the omnipresence of the state in the lives of ordinary people in the developing world and the importance of the state as a *social actor*. Peter Evans appropriately noted, "from the poorest countries of the Third World to the most advanced exemplars of welfare capitalism, one of the few universals in the history of the twentieth century is the increasingly pervasive influence of the state as an institution and social actor."[11] Yet, often discussions on the state are skewed toward institutions and their capacity in delivering tangible goods. The state is central not only in terms of its economic activity (measured by a share of GNP, employment, national investment, consumption, savings, and so on) but beyond that to those functions that are essential to the economic process (such as determining and upholding the legal and statutory forms necessary for commodity exchange, stabilizing the growth of the national product, and determining the choice of the development model) and as an agent of hegemony/domination.

It is nothing new to say that the capitalist state produces and reproduces capitalist social relations not only at the economic level but also at the political and ideological level. Gramsci taught us that the capitalist state is the "organizer of consent" in the bourgeois hegemonic system.[12] But in the case of peripheral societies, classes are formed in a distinctly different way compared with advanced capitalist societies, and the class formation processes, at times, prevents the emergence of a hegemonic bourgeoisie. Under these circumstances, the state is utilized by the ruling classes, whoever they may be, as the agent of hegemony/domination. Through it, a new ideology (or value system), assumed to be superior to all others, is imposed. This accords the state apparatus a new significance. I insist that the issues of hegemony and ideology require urgent attention, especially as we are witnessing the rise of what is often inaccurately described as the fundamentalist movement in the Third World. States in various countries—from Iran to India to Sudan to Bangladesh—have played an instrumental role in producing or accommodating confessional ideologies.[13] If we continue to disregard this crucial role of states in the developing world, such as Bangladesh, we risk missing a very important impact of the state on society.

The progressive attenuation of the capacity of the state, often displayed in developing societies, results from its inability and/or failure to be the crucial agent of hegemony. The impact of the state on society underscores the need to adopt what Joel Migdal has advocated as the "state-in-society" approach[14] or what Evans has described as the examination of the "embeddedness" of state.[15] Migdal suggests that we use four parameters to understand the strengths of the state: "the capacities to *penetrate* society, *regulate* social relationships, *extract* resources, and *appropriate* or use resources in determined ways" (emphasis in original).[16] Within this framework, the state that fails to perform any or all of the tasks, or performs them poorly, should be seen as weak compared with the society within which it is located. While the framework is helpful, it only tells us the relative strength of the state; it is not an objective assessment of the state.

The perspectives we have examined thus far operate with the assumption that the strengths/weaknesses of the state are entirely a domestic matter. The global interstate system within which a state operates seldom features in these discussions.

Economic globalization has had phenomenal impact in the past decade, resulting in the gradual circumspection of state power. But the state has always been subjected to the influence of the global political economy and hegemons, both global and regional. The sovereignty of the state, particularly in the developing world has been, and is, partly a fictional idea. Thus to speak of a state which operates at will and where strengths and weakness are determined exclusively by domestic compulsions is devoid of reality. Such states are influenced, if not shaped, by extramural forces. Therefore, it is erroneous to attribute weakness of the state to domestic forces alone.

The notion of a weak state, which has gained salience among Western governments since the frightful events of September 11, 2001, primarily as an early warning system of potential trouble spots, is often considered part of a fourfold categorization of states advocated by Rotberg:[17] weak, failing, failed, and collapsed.[18] But it should be borne in mind that this is not a unidirectional phenomenon; not all states that display weakness are destined to fail and collapse. T. V. Paul has aptly noted this point: weak states need not be "failed states," since a weak state may exhibit better capacity in some of these areas [i.e., security, participation and infrastructure] and deficiencies in others.[19]

The forgoing discussion demonstrates that the concept of the weak state, profusely used by academics and policymakers alike in recent years, has yet to resolve the definitional problem. Furthermore, most of these discussions dwell upon the symptoms of the weak state instead of the causes. If we are to agree that state weakness means deficiencies in security, participation, and infrastructure[20] and lack of legitimacy,[21] these concepts do not tell us what causes these deficiencies.

This is not to suggest that capacities of the state do not vary; they do. But the crucial question is, which of these capacities are key to understanding the nature of the state?

Bangladesh: Unpacking the Paradox

T. V. Paul has argued in his introductory chapter that "the characterization of weakness has to be seen in relative terms, as most states have some elements of strength. A state may be weak in some areas while in others it may show relative strength."[22] Bangladesh provides an excellent example in this regard. But, this begs a question at the analytical level: should the relative strengths of a state receive closer attention than the weaknesses?

In recent years, the country has drawn enormous attention from both the international media and the international community due to unbridled corruption,[23] poor governance, and confrontational politics hindering the institutionalization of democracy. Adding to this grim picture are the rise of violence and the presence of militant organizations with potential connections to transnational terrorist groups challenging the state's monopoly of violence. There are other indications that reveal weaknesses in the state's capacity to govern and provide services to its citizens. These include the near absence of the rule of law and an ever weakening law enforcement apparatus, corrupt courts at the local level, unaccountable public service providers, insecurity of life and property, and violation of human rights, including religious persecution, to name but a few. In many ways the state has shown its inability or reluctance to protect citizens' constitutional rights. Undoubtedly, by all accounts, these are symptomatic of a weak state.

But it would be erroneous to suggest that the Bangladeshi state leaves the marginalized and vulnerable sections of the society at the mercy of the private sector or market. Budget documents and five-year planning documents show that the government has not only reiterated its commitment to the poorer population but has attempted to live up to its promises, even if not entirely. Various kinds of welfare programs (for example, Vulnerable Group Feeding and Food for Works) have been included in these documents as measures to address poverty, and many of these programs have been implemented whether the country is governed by a military or a civilian regime. Additionally, infrastructure development, the absence of which is considered as a key indicator of a state's weakness by Rotberg, has remained a top priority of the regime.

The Bangladeshi state has demonstrated significant success in some key areas. Take, for example, economic growth. The economic indicators of 2003–2007 show positive trends on many fronts (see Table 11.1). Throughout the 1990s, the country established a sustained credible growth record within a stable macroeconomic framework. Beginning with 1.9% in the early 1990s, the rate reached above 4.5% in the mid-2000s (Figure 11.1). Equally impressive is its achievement in reducing poverty. Data from various sources demonstrate that despite variations in estimates, the trend is very clear: poverty has been reduced in the last decade (Figure 11.2). Similar success is noticeable in reducing the child mortality rate.

TABLE 11.1 Bangladesh: Economic indicators, 2003–2007

Economic Indicator	2003	2004	2005	2006	2007
Per capita GNI ($)	400	400	470	480	--
GDP growth (% change per year)	5.3	6.3	6.0	6.6	6.5
CPI (% change per year)	4.4	5.8	6.5	7.2	7.2
Unemployment rate (%)	4.3	--	--	--	--
Fiscal balance (% of GDP)	-3.4	-3.2	-3.3	-3.2	-3.2
Export Growth (% change per year)	9.5	15.9	14.0	21.5	15.8
Import Growth (% change per year)	13.1	13.0	20.6	12.1	16.6
Current account (% of GDP)	0.3	0.3	-0.9	1.3	1.4
External debt (% of GNI)	34.3	33.7	30.0	31.4	--

-- = Data not available, CPI = consumer price index, GDP = gross domestic product, GNI = gross national income.

SOURCES: ADB. 2008. Asian Development Outlook 2008. Manila; World Bank. 2008. Global Development Finance Online; World Bank. 2008. World Development Indicators Online.

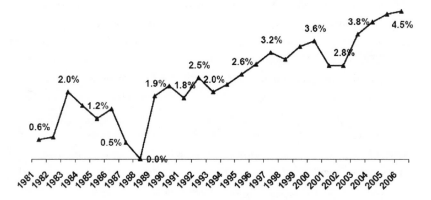

FIGURE 11.1 Bangladesh growth accelerated after 1990.

SOURCE: Darryl McLeod, "Is Poverty Increasing in Bangladesh? Reconciling National and Global Monitoring Estimates." Final report to UNDP-BDP Poverty Group (New York, 2007), mimeo, 6

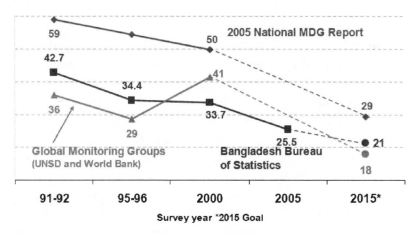

FIGURE 11.2 Bangladesh poverty trends.

SOURCE: Darryl McLeod, "Is Poverty Increasing in Bangladesh? Reconciling National and Global Monitoring Estimates." Final report to UNDP-BDP Poverty Group (New York, 2007), mimeo, 8

The education sector, in the 1990s, made dramatic progress; net primary school enrollment increased from 74% in 1991 to 87.27% in 2001. Bangladesh has also achieved gender parity in primary school enrollment—one of the key Millennium Development Goals (MDG)—and made female education free up to the twelfth grade to ensure gender parity in secondary and tertiary education.

The economic indicators cannot be underestimated; instead they should be taken seriously because as Rotberg (in his contribution to this volume) has forcefully argued, economic indicators "provide clear, timely and actionable warnings" of a state's impending failures. Conversely, they can indicate the hindrances toward creeping failures. In the context of Bangladesh, these successes are signals, if not decisive proof, that state failure is not a looming issue. Equally important is the contextualization of these successes. Here we must look at two larger issues: Are these indicative of the state's role as a transformative agent? Do they hide a growing pattern of weakness?

The achievements of the past two decades should be partly credited to the plurality of "drivers of development" or, in other words, multiple sources of providers, both public and private sector. Many analysts credit the success to the policy of economic liberalization adopted in the 1980s and vigorously pursued in the 1990s. This is a testimony of the state's successful role as an institution of social transformation. Within the framework proposed by Mushtaq Khan,[24] this is a vital role of the state. Thus, from a long-term perspective, the Bangladeshi state is demonstrating some characteristics which cannot be ascribed to a state labeled as "weak."

If leading the public and private partnership to achieve development goals has demonstrated the strengths of the state, it has also sowed the seeds of its weakness. In the wake of the state's perceived inability to provide services to its citizens effectively and in a transparent manner, donors have increasingly used nongovernmental organizations (NGOs) to replace the government as development contractors for the delivery of their aid, particularly to the poorer sections of the society.[25] The trend, which originated in the late 1980s when Bangladesh was ruled by a military autocracy, has intensified in the 1990s, a period of democratically elected governments. The donors, euphemistically called "development partners," including the United States and the United Kingdom, are now keener to induct civil society organizations (CSOs) in the development process and improve their standing as an alternative to the state. These efforts are packaged under the rubric of "good governance," accountability, and transparency, all of which are essential for the effective functioning of the state. Such efforts are justified on the grounds that civil society must act as a watchdog to protect and preserve the rights of the people. This is a testimony to the fact that the state's capacity is not only determined by domestic imperatives but also by external compulsions.

It is also necessary to examine whether this trend might eventually contribute to what Geoffrey Wood has described as the "franchise state"—a state that only serves a small clique and leaves the larger segment of the society to the vagaries of international capital and the compassion of the NGOs.[26] Whether or not we call it the franchising of the state, the scenario obviously suggests an absence of the state. Such an absence, either in certain geographical areas (e.g., rural areas) or in regard to certain social services (e.g., education), would obviously accentuate the crisis of governance. The absence of the state is bound to create a void, which, in turn, leads to the establishment of a parallel structure of authority. One can easily see this coming to pass in various parts of rural Bangladesh, where militant Islamist groups have a strong influence.

Robert Rotberg and other political scientists have often insisted that one of the key features of the weak state is a lack of, or hindrance to, participation. Many weak states have displayed this characteristic. But if participation is the defining criterion of the nature of the state, Bangladesh will confound analysts. Bangladesh "has a long tradition of high political participation," observed Peter Bertocci, about a quarter of a century ago.[27] This tradition is reflected in two elements of Bangladeshi politics: the high voter turnout in elections and the existence of numerous political parties. Since 1991, the country has had four free and fair general elections, in which the opposition party secured victory rather than the incumbents. Opposition parties have also demonstrated enormous power in organizing popular agitation. However, the political developments since 1991 in Bangladesh raise questions about the nature of democracy there. Success in regularly conducting an election, a sign of the formal aspect of democracy, indicates a major achievement, while lack of substantive democracy represents the weakness of the Bangladeshi political system.[28]

The paradoxes of the Bangladeshi scene are not only necessary to comprehend the complexity specific to Bangladesh but also to appreciate that all too visible features are not always sufficient determinants of the capacity of the state. Instead, certain less visible facets of political dynamics are germane to an assessment of the extant nature and the future trajectories of governance in any country. In the context of Bangladesh, two such elements are trust and legitimacy, which have received less than due attention. I argue that, notwithstanding institutional weaknesses, the lack of trust in public institutions and the weak legitimacy of the state have been instrumental in limiting the state's capacity to address some long-term problems, particularly security issues.

Surveys conducted by Transparency International Bangladesh (TIB) and other organizations show that the citizens of Bangladesh have very little trust in state institutions such as the judiciary, police, and local government.[29] The lack of confidence and trust in state institutions has increased the costs of transactions and enhanced unpredictability, but more importantly, it has created a gap between the citizens and the state. The capacity of the state weakens when it has to employ resources to connect with the people that it is supposed to represent. It is needless to say that distrustful citizens are less likely to obey the law and thus create a hospitable environment for various forms of subversion.

In the juridico-legal sense the Bangladeshi state does not suffer from any crisis of legitimacy, but the legitimacy of any state also depends on its ability to be the dominant source of ideological hegemony. The incessant battle surrounding the identity of the citizens of Bangladesh—Bangladeshi and Bengali—has made the state an ineffective institution of hegemony. These two identities offer two different worldviews and represent two different ideological positions, particularly in regard to the role of religion in politics and society. The pendulum-like swing between these two identities in the past three decades is symptomatic of the deep division within the society and is indicative of the growing salience of religion in public space. Importantly, the Bangladeshi identity, which underscores being Muslim as opposed to being Bengali as the principal social marker, received support from the state for more than two decades. The emphasis on the Muslim identity created the space for adherents of Islamist ideology within the mainstream political landscape. These political forces, in turn, have allowed transnational Islamist ideologies and organizations to proliferate within the country. Thus one element of Bangladeshi nationalism is territory-based, therefore parochially nationalistic, while the other element is open to transnational ideas of Islamism. For decades, the opponents of Bangladeshi nationalism have continued their battle for a secular inclusive nationalism. As the state has become the site of this contestation, it has weakened the state's capacity to govern. The long-term effect of this erosion of capacity is that the security of the Bangladeshi state is increasingly becoming vulnerable.

Security Challenges: Traditional and Nontraditional

The security challenges Bangladesh is facing are multiple: traditional and nontraditional, domestic and regional. Some of them are evident, such as the proliferation of Islamist militant groups within the country, while others are not so palpable, such as ongoing global climate change. Similarly, some have their origins within the borders of the country, while others are beyond the reach of the Bangladeshi state. The combination of institutional weaknesses, the lack of trust, and the weak legitimacy of the state is making it difficult for the Bangladeshi state to address these challenges. The geographical location of the country, particularly the porous nature of its border with its neighbors, India and Myanmar, has not been very helpful either. Two major security challenges discussed below demonstrate that the Bangladeshi state, even at its strongest position, is not able to counter these challenges.

The crucial security challenge to the Bangladeshi state is an increased incidence of violence, particularly growing militancy. This phenomenon has resulted from changes in state ideology. The salience of Islamists within mainstream politics has enabled the militant groups to thrive, at times with the complicity of the state. But the most important and menacing development is that these groups have become part of a larger network of insurgent groups, based on both ideological affinity and tactical necessities, and this network is spread across the region beyond the borders of Bangladesh.

The militant groups in Bangladesh did not grow as a local response to local problems; instead, since their inception, they have drawn inspiration and received support from outside, primarily from the Afghan war. The most prominent of these militant groups is the Harkat-ul Jihad-al-Islami Bangladesh (HuJIB). The HuJIB, the Bangladeshi counterpart of the Pakistan-based HuJI, was established by a small group of Bangladeshi Islamists who volunteered to join the Afghan war effort in the 1980s.[30] In the early 1990s, the Pakistan-based HuJI expanded its operation in other parts of the world. It was during the expansion phase of the organization that the Bangladesh chapter began its clandestine operation. The HuJIB and the homegrown militant group called the Jamaat-ul-Mujahideen Bangladesh (JMB) joined forces in 1998. HuJIB has been involved in a number of audacious operations since 1996, including several attempts to assassinate former Prime Minister Sheikh Hasina of Bangladesh. On August 21, 2004 the HuJIB attacked a public gathering in the capital Dhaka organized by the Awami League, then in opposition. A series of grenade attacks on the gathering cost twenty-three lives, including that of a central leader of the party. Hasina escaped unhurt, although she was the primary target, according to the confessional statements of the key HuJIB leaders.[31] The series of bomb blasts throughout the country on August 17, 2005, followed by a number of suicide attacks by the JMB, has clearly demonstrated that the state is unable to rein in the militants as the line between the state and underground has became blurred, thanks to the presence of Islamists in the ruling coalition since 2001.

The connections between the external militant organizations and Bangladeshi groups are no longer one-way. Instead, members of some of the Bangladeshi militant groups have been found to have engaged in activities in India. For example, the HuJIB is reported to have developed close connections with militants in India. HuJIB operatives arrested in India in 2006 and 2008 have confessed that they received training and funds from Jaish-e-Muhammad and Lashkar-i-Tayyaba of Pakistan.[32] The organization has also trained militants in Bangladesh to engage in subversive activities in India, as three operatives arrested in India told the Delhi police. The confessional statements also indicate that militant leaders from Pakistan had traveled to Bangladesh to recruit, organize training, and disburse funds.

The connection between Pakistan-based Islamist militants and their Bangladeshi counterparts began at the inception of the latter, but this relationship was cemented when the Bangladeshi militants became the bridge to rebel groups in Myanmar, thanks to the topography of the southeastern hill tracts of Bangladesh that border Myanmar. The region was already restive and was witnessing a low-intensity war between the Bangladeshi military and a rebel group called the Shanti Bahini. The Shanti Bahini, the military wing of the ethnic tribal groups, received support from the Indian authorities. Rebel organizations claiming to represent the Rohingyas (Muslims from the northern Burmese state of Arakan, who fled the persecution of the Myanmar military junta) established their bases on the southeastern hill tracts within Bangladesh in the 1990s. The Rohingya Patriotic Front (RPF), the Arakan Rohingya Islamic Front (ARIF), and the Rohingya Solidarity Organization (RSO) received moral and material support from the Bangladeshi government. The impassable hill areas became a safe haven for militants.

The links between militants from Myanmar and those from Bangladesh (both the Shanti Bahini and the Islamists) were established with ease because of the proximity of their bases to each other in the 1980s. In the 1990s, connections between these groups began to emerge as a network as all of them became part of a chain of arms procurement from illegal sources largely originating in Southeast Asia. Soon various insurgent groups from India, who had been receiving support from the Bangladeshi authorities for quite some time, joined the network, especially after the Islamist militants moved to northwestern districts located along the Indo-Bangladesh border.

Sources close to rebel groups acknowledge that by the late 1990s weapons had become the common currency in their world. Rohingyas were trading arms with the Islamist militants in exchange for political protection and for reasons of ideological affinity, and with the Indian rebels for their training. Skills, political protection, and arms were being exchanged among the rebels who had their bases within the hilly southeast region and weakly monitored coastlines of Bangladesh. The movement of weapons from the southeastern regions to other areas of Bangladesh brought criminal gangs within the chain, creating more demand and consequently accentuating the proliferation of light arms throughout the country. Adding to this are the homemade or recycled small arms that are turning up in Bangladesh from neighboring Indian states through the porous borders. Between 1991 and 1998, Bangladesh was transformed into "a destination state from a transit state of small arms."[33]

It is not only the unscrupulous, profit-seeking merchants of death who are engaged in the business of selling weapons to these rebel and insurgent groups, but also governments, especially intelligence agencies. The Small Arms Survey 2002 noted, "Government patronage appears to be the leading source of arms, funds, and training for the vast majority of non-state actors . . . Nearly every region of the world has experienced this phenomenon."[34] Both the Indian Research and Analysis Wing (RAW) and Pakistan's Inter-Services Intelligence Directorate (ISI) have been using Bangladesh as a transit point for small arms.[35] The most dramatic example of Bangladesh being used in the transit of weapons is the discovery of a massive quantity of weapons and ammunition in two trawlers in the jetty of the Chittagong Urea Fertilizer Factory in April 2004. This chance discovery was described by Jane's Intelligence Review as "one of South Asia's largest ever seizures of illicit weaponry."[36]

However, these developments should not obscure the fact that domestic politics in India and the failure of the Indian government to address the issue of insurgency in the northeastern states contribute to the security threat to Bangladesh. Some analysts have suggested that the instability of India's northern region is primarily the government's making. The delay with which the Indian government addresses these concerns may provide a hospitable environment for militant groups to find a receptive audience. Indian neglect of concerns on the part of the Muslim population and the rise in Hindu nationalism in recent years have increased and spurred ethnic tensions between the majority Hindu population and minority groups of Muslims, separatists, and immigrants. India has been accused of placing the blame for attacks, largely attributable to localized politics, on foreign terrorist groups, claims which have subsequently been picked up by the international media.[37]

The emergence of the network of militant groups in and around Bangladesh, a country which is beset by internal political instability, characterized by a fragile democracy and lacking a state capable of addressing domestic problems, poses a serious threat to national security. The Bangladeshi state cannot delay too long in confronting this security challenge. Equally important, this challenge cannot be confronted by the Bangladeshi state alone, however strong a posture it adopts. The regional nature of the problem requires a comprehensive strategy to be developed and shared by regional political actors and supported by extra-regional actors.

As the traditional security threat faced by the Bangladeshi state requires a comprehensive regional (and extra-regional) strategy, so too does the foremost non-traditional security threat that emanates from global climate change. The country's unique geographic location, in the largest floodplain of the world, combined with low elevation from the sea, has made the country exceptionally vulnerable to ongoing climate change. The impact of climate change on Bangladesh, as hypothesized by Working Group II of the Intergovernmental Panel for Climate Change (IPCC) and presented in the fourth IPCC report (published in November 2007) in brief, is as follows:

> A one-meter rise in sea level would submerge one-fifth of the country by 2050–2075. Cyclones would be creeping deeper in the delta because of saline intrusion. Cyclone velocity would increase, and storms would be increasingly more intense. Besides, floods would be more frequent; irregular rainfall would make it difficult for farming; and the North-West would become drier increasing the chances of greater food insecurity.[38]

In a country with a large population living at or below subsistence levels, the decline in food availability will not only make a large section of the society even more vulnerable but is also a recipe for political and social instability. The decline in food production will make the country dependent on the international food market, the volatility of which needs no elaboration after the events of 2008.

Climate change has the potential to be a disruptive factor for the domestic political situation, particularly because of the presence and future migration of a significant number of discontented and marginalized citizens to politically volatile urban areas. These new migrants will largely come from coastal areas due to sea level rise and from rural areas due to a decrease in agricultural production.

The potential for disruptive changes also lies with the fact that increasing frequency of natural calamities will require the mobilization of funds from already meager resources available for development (e.g., infrastructure) and social services (e.g., education and health). The situation after Hurricane Sidr (2007) illustrates this dramatically.[39] Preventive and preparatory measures will also cost the nation dearly. Needless to say, the strain on limited resources is not going to be equally shared by all segments of the society. Therefore, certain sections of society will bear a disproportionate share of the costs.

As we have discussed previously, in the event of resource constraints the state will rely on NGOs to deliver social services, which in turn will reduce the legitimacy of the state. The absence of state agencies creates an opportunity for the growth of parallel authority; the experience of the past decade bears testimony to this.

With an anticipated substantial decline in agricultural crop productivity throughout South Asia, the process is bound to have serious implications for Bangladesh. The most important implication will be the decline, perhaps the demise, of food security.[40] The high dependence on agriculture (about 22.7% of GDP) combined with population increase (1.88% annually) will require diversification of the economy and state intervention to protect the vulnerable sections of society. Emigration to urban areas constitutes the most immediate impact of these climatic changes. Combined with fragile political institutions, a contentious political culture, and preponderance of violence, the possibility of radicalization is very likely. The extant militant organizations will make use of these conditions to their benefit. The huge pool of urban poor, particularly new migrants from rural areas, may serve as a reservoir for a disgruntled army.

The migration, which is already taking place, is not limited to Bangladesh. A growing number of people are crossing the border into India, but the size and scope of the migration remains contentious. The Indian authorities, media, and some political parties tend to present exaggerated numbers and attempt to tie the migration with the increasing number of terrorist activities within the country. In past decades, some Indian political parties, especially the Bharatiya Janata Party (BJP), have alleged that illegal Muslim migration from Bangladesh is changing the demography of India. Citing dubious statistics, the BJP leaders argue that Indian states bordering Bangladesh, such as West Bengal and Assam, are bearing the brunt of the effects of migration, and that this is a well-designed plan to Islamize these states and establish a large Muslim state. The BJP has advocated an uncompromising approach to dealing with the illegal immigration problem. Consequently, India has identified illegal Bangladeshi immigrants as a security threat. In 2003 the then Deputy Prime Minister of India, Lal Krishna Advani of the BJP, issued a national directive to "take 'immediate steps . . . to identify them, locate them, and throw them out.'"[41] Some Indian sources claim that 20 million illegal Bangladeshis live in India.[42]

Bangladesh continues to deny a Bangladeshi presence within India. Instead it argues that the "illegal" Bangladeshi migrants identified by Indian officials are actually Bengali-speaking Indian Muslims expelled from their homeland and forced upon Bangladesh. As a result, Bangladesh has refused to accept undocumented migrants.[43] The Bangladeshi government has publicly declared that India is making political use of Bangladeshis: "India looks for a 'scapegoat' every time there was [*sic*] a terror attack."[44] Social and political analysts insist that the indiscriminate labeling as terrorists of "illegal Bangladeshi migrants," most of whom can be identified as economic migrants, has engendered a serious "social repercussion" that is breeding "fear and historical ethnic tensions."[45]

Already a politically charged issue, this will strain the Bangladesh-India relationship further. Anti-Indian feelings among Bangladeshis will increase, which usually serves as a legitimating factor for the Islamists (and radical *Hindutva* supporters in India).

The anticipated decline in freshwater availability, especially in the drought-prone northwestern region where an arsenic crisis[46] has already reduced water availability, the long-term water sharing problem with India will take on a new urgency. What can exacerbate the situation are the contested claims to offshore resources, particularly gas and oil fields in the Bay of Bengal. This is equally true in regard to the Bangladesh-Burma relationship.

While militancy and climate change are important and have far-reaching consequences for the existence of the country, they are not the only challenges the Bangladeshi state is facing. However, these two examples show that the nature and magnitude of the challenges are too large to be dealt with by the Bangladeshi state alone.

Conclusions

The preceding discussion on security challenges to the Bangladeshi state underscores several points that warrant further exploration and robust debate. At the theoretical level, the paper argues that a qualitative shift is necessary in discussions regarding the capacity of the state. A Weberian model that emphasizes institutions and their capacity to govern is not sufficient to understand the role of the state in society. This prism completely ignores the state's ability to act as an agent of hegemony and ideology, and therefore it pays little attention to the legitimacy of the state, an important element in determining its success and failure. Additionally, the chapter raises questions regarding the implicit assumptions and hierarchy of indicators in classifying a state as a weak state. One of the key arguments of this paper is that the state's capacity should not be considered as entirely a domestic phenomenon. The global interstate system within which each state operates has received less than its due share of attention. Despite the fact that the post–September 11 security environment has given currency to the notion of the weak state, academics and policymakers are using a framework which is inadequate in addressing some of the security threats faced by states. The preeminence of militaristic notions of security in discussions regarding security threats undermines equally, if not more, significant, nontraditional threats.

At the country study level, the chapter argues that the Bangladeshi state presents a complex and paradoxical picture in regard to its capacity—it demonstrates both strengths and weaknesses. The predatory nature of the state and successes in various socioeconomic sectors paints a picture that is inconsistent with its inability to provide safety and security to its citizens and rein in the growing militancy that threatens the state's monopoly of violence and its existence. It is my contention that the limitations of the Bangladeshi state are the result of a combination of institutional weaknesses, lack of trust on the part of its citizens, and the questionable legitimacy of the state. Analysis of the country's two most crucial security threats bears out the fact that the Bangladeshi state cannot confront these challenges. This is not only because of its lack of capacity, but more importantly because of the nature and magnitude of these challenges. This underscores the need for developing a regional security strategy and greater cooperation among the South Asian nations. The principal threats Bangladesh is facing have not emerged from within the country nor are they going to remain within its political boundaries.

Notes to Chapter 11

1. David Held, *Political Theory and the Modern State: Essays on State, Power, and Democracy* (Stanford, CA: Stanford University Press, 1989), 74. The most glaring example of the institutional bias of conventional paradigm is reflected in the Failed States Index published annually in *Foreign Policy*. Foreign Policy and the Fund for Peace, "Failed States Index 2008," *Foreign Policy*, July–August 2008.

2. Examples include, weekly *Time*'s description of Bangladesh as a "dysfunctional state" ("State of Disgrace," *Time*, April 5, 2004), and the *Economist*'s question, "Is Bangladesh slithering into anarchy?" ("A Bomb Too Far," *The Economist*, August 28, 2004, 37).

3. In 2006 Bangladesh was ranked nineteenth, in 2007 it was ranked sixteenth, and in 2008 it ranked twelfth. For details of these rankings see The Fund for Peace, "Failed States Index 2008," http://www.fundforpeace.org/web/index.php?option=com_con tent&task=view&id=99&Itemid=140 (last accessed on 10 September 2008); for the 2007 ranking of Bangladesh with country profile, see the Fund for Peace, "Bangla-desh 2007," http://www.fundforpeace.org/web/index.php?option=com_content& task=view&id=273&Itemid=43; for 2006 ranking and the country profile, see the Fund for Peace, "Bangladesh 2006," http://www.fundforpeace.org/web/index.php ?option=com_content&task=view&id=54&Itemid=265.

4. A commentary in June 2004 in the leading Bengali daily in Bangladesh *Pro-thom Alo* stirred the debate, which went on for months. For examples of the debate see "Failed State and Bangladesh," *Daily Star*, June 11, 2004 and "The Fault Lies in Politics," *New Age*, September 8, 2004.

5. C.A.F. Dowlah, "The State of Affairs in Bangladesh," *Weekly Holiday*, November 11, 2004.

6. In October 2006, as the incumbent four-party alliance led by the Bangladesh Nationalist Party (BNP) completed its tenure and was required under the constitution to hand over power to a caretaker government (CTG), the country plunged into chaos. The opposition parties, under the leadership of the Awami League (AL), re-fused to accept the immediate past chief justice of the Supreme Court as head of the CTG, for a number of reasons. The opposition parties also demanded that the Election Commission (EC) be reconstituted because the members of the EC were partisan appointees and that the voters list, full of errors and "ghost voters," be scrapped. The president, a political appointee, took over the position of head of the CTG in addition to his role as president, defeating the purpose of a neutral caretaker administration

overseeing the parliamentary election. On October 28, 2006, the low-scale violence and conflict erupted into full-blown street battles between government forces and government supporters on the one side and opposition activists on the other, bringing about a collapse of law and order in the capital, Dhaka. The eleven-member CTG was reshuffled twice, but evidently was being influenced by the former ruling party. Hectic parleys by the diplomatic corps led by the U.S. and UK envoys made some headway in resolving the crisis but failed to convince the opposition parties to join the election, as the administration was clearly tilted toward the BNP, and the possibility of a fair election was slim to none. After weeks of violence, general strikes, and transport blockades disrupting public life, causing damage to public property, enormous economic losses, and above all, the deaths of innocent people in clashes between law enforcement forces and political activists, the election scheduled for January 22, 2007, was cancelled. A state of emergency was declared on January 11, 2007 and a new eleven-member CTG, with the backing of the military, was installed the next day. Thus large-scale bloodshed was avoided, but the nation paid a very high price—the loss of the elected government. The fifteen-year "democratic era" came to an unceremonious end. The country returned to a democratic path in January 2009 with the transfer of power to an elected government after the general election on December 29, 2008.

7. United Nations Development Programme, "Human Development Report 2005: International Cooperation at a Crossroads: Aid, Trade and Security in an Unequal World," http://hdr.undp.org/en/reports/global/hdr2005/.

8. I have deliberately left the Tillyian model out of this discussion, as Tilly is more concerned with how states are formed than how the state functions. In the Tillyian model of state formation, interchangeable with "state-building" and "state-making," it refers to the processes that lead to the centralization of political power over a well-defined territory, and with a monopoly of the means of coercion. Rolf Schwarz, "State Formation Processes in Rentier States: The Middle Eastern Case," paper presented at the Fifth Pan-European Conference on International Relations, European Consortium for Political Research Standing Group on International Relations (The Hague, September 9–11, 2004). Tilly argues for the primacy of warfare as a causal agent in state formation. Drawing on the European experience, he notes that "war made the state." Charles Tilly, "Reflections on the History of European State-Making," in *The Formation of National States in Western Europe*, ed. Charles Tilly (Princeton: Princeton University Press, 1975), p. 42; Tilly, "War Making and State Making as Organized Crime," in *Bringing the State Back In*, ed. Peter Evans, Dietrich Reuschmeyer, and Theda Skocpol (Cambridge: Cambridge University Press, 1985); Tilly, *Coercion, Capital and European States, AD 990–1990* (Oxford: Basil Blackwell, 1990); Tilly, "Entanglements of European City States," in *Cities and the Rise of the State in Europe, AD 1000–1800*, ed. Charles Tilly (Boulder, CO: Westview, 1994). According to the Tillyian model, state formation involves four processes: state making by war making (to neutralize rivals outside the territory); state making by elimination (to eliminate potential challengers within the territory); providing protection to the supporters (to create

an environment for the continued existence of the new structure); and the extraction of resources (to subject the population and territory to continuous taxation for the maintenance and/or expansion of the territory). Tilly, "War Making," p. 181.

9. Mushtaq H. Khan, "State Failure in Developing Countries and Strategies of Institutional Reform" (paper presented at the Annual Bank Conference on Development Economies, Oslo, Norway, June 24–25, 2002).

10. Ibid., p. 1.

11. Peter Evans, *Embedded Autonomy: States and Industrial Transformation* (Princeton: Princeton University Press, 1995), p. 5.

12. Antonio Gramsci, *Selections from Prison Notebooks* (New York: International General, 1971), p. 258.

13. I have addressed this at length in *God Willing: The Politics of Islamism in Bangladesh* (Lanham, MD: Rowman & Littlefield, 2004).

14. Joel S. Migdal, "The State in Society," in *State Power and Social Forces: Domination and Transformation in the Third World*, ed. Joel S. Migdal, Atul Kohli, and Vivienne Shue (Cambridge: Cambridge University Press, 1994). See also Mehran Kamrava, *Understanding Comparative Politics: A Framework for Analysis* (London and New York: Routledge, 2008), pp. 62–68.

15. Evans, *Embedded Autonomy.*

16. Joe S. Migdal, *Strong Societies and Weak States, State-Society Relations and State Capabilities in the Third World* (Princeton: Princeton University Press, 1988), p. 4.

17. Robert I. Rotberg, "Failed States, Collapsed States, Weak States: Causes and Indicators" in *State Failure and State Weakness in a Time of Terror*, ed. Robert I. Rotberg (Washington, DC: Brookings Institution Press 2003), and Robert I. Rotberg, ed. *When State Fail: Causes and Consequences* (Princeton: Princeton University Press 2004).

18. While these four categories have been used by most analysts in recent years, there are other categories in use too. In the 1990s in the African context, scholars used the terms "fragmented" and "archipelago" state in describing states characterized by weak capacity to extract revenues and loss of control over and fragmentation of the instruments of physical coercion.

19. T. V. Paul, this volume, p. 6.

20. Rotberg, "Failed States," also used by Paul, this volume, p. 4.

21. Kalevi J. Holsti, *The State, War, and the State of War* (Cambridge: Cambridge University Press, 1996), pp. 104, 106, quoted in Paul this volume, 4–5.

22. Paul, this volume, p. 6.

23. According to the Corruption Perception Index (CPI) released annually by Transparency International, the level of corruption in Bangladesh was perceived to be the highest in the world from 2001 to 2004. Transparency International, "Corruption Perception Index," 2008, http://www.transparency.org/policy_research/surveys_indices/cpi.

24. Khan, "State Failure."

25. Rehman Sobhan, "Bangladesh in the New Millennium: Between Promise and Fulfillment" (Dhaka: Center for Policy Dialogue, 2002).

26. Geoffrey D. Wood, "States Without Citizens: the Problem of the Franchise State," in *Too Close for Comfort: NGOs, States and Donors*, ed. D. Hulme and M. Edwards. (London: Macmillan, 1996).

27. Peter J. Bertocci, "Bangladesh in the Early 1980s: Praetorian Politics in an Intermediate Regime," *Asian Survey* 22, no. 10 (October 1982), p. 993.

28. "A formal democracy is a genuine democracy insofar as it guarantees, among other things, the right to vote and the freedom of expression. Yet it may not evince all the features of its normative ideal, thus the notion of substantive democracy." Ayesha Jalal, *Democracy and Authoritarianism in South Asia* (Cambridge: Cambridge University Press, 1995), p. 3. Substantive democracy, on the other hand, is about the inclusiveness of the citizens, empowerment of the people as active citizens, and building a culture of accountability and responsiveness.

29. Regarding police corruption, see "Corruption 'Rife' in Bangladeshi Police," *BBC News*, May 27, 2001, http://news.bbc.co.uk/2/hi/south_asia/1354301.stm; for the 2002 TIB report, see the overview by Manzoor Hassan, "Corruption in Bangladesh Surveys: An Overview," n.d., http://unpan1.un.org/intradoc/groups/public/documents/APCITY/UNPAN004880.pdf, and Transparency International Bangladesh, "Corruption in Bangladesh: A Household Survey" April 20, 2005, http://www .ti-bangladesh .org/documents/HouseholdSurvey200405-sum1.pdf.

30. See *Islami Biplob* (Islamic Revolution), a bulletin published from Sylhet. Also see Julfikar Ali Manik, "HuJI Kingpins' Coalition Link Keeps Cops at Bay," *Daily Star*, November 7, 2005, p. 1.

31. "Abu Zandal Confesses to Carrying Out Aug 21 Attack," *Daily Star*, February 21, 2008, p. 1.; and "Aug 21 Attack was Aimed at Killing Hasina: Huji Leader Confesses Before Court," *Daily Star*, April 26, 2008, p. 1.

32. "HuJI Bangladesh Has Connections with Indian and Pakistani Militants, Mursalin and Muttakin Tell Delhi Police" (in Bengali), *Prothom Alo* (Dhaka), May 16, 2008, p. 1.

33. Small Arms Survey, *Small Arms Survey 2002: Counting the Human Cost* (Oxford: Oxford University Press,) pp. 142–143.

34. Ibid. The study provides a long list of countries that provided arms to various nonstate actors.

35. For discussions of RAW and ISI in Bangladesh, see Ali Riaz, *Islamist Militancy in Bangladesh: A Complex Web* (London and New York: Routledge, 2008), pp. 68–80.

36. Anthony Davis, "New Details Emerge on Bangladesh Arms Haul," *Jane's Intelligence Review*, September 2004.

37. Philip Bowring, "India Is Causing Trouble," *International Herald Tribune*, January 22, 2003, http://www.bowring.net/banglaind.htm.

38. Atiq Rahman "Bangladesh Must Learn to Live Thru' Climate Change," *Daily Star* (Dhaka), March 29, 2008, p. 1.

39. A Category 4 tropical cyclone named Sidr hit Bangladesh on 15 November 2007, killing at least 3500 people, making millions homeless and costing billions of dollars. According to a World Bank report, "The accompanying storm surge reached

maximum heights of about 10 meters in certain areas, breaching coastal and river embankments, flooding low lying lands and causing extensive physical destruction. The cyclone's winds of up to 220 kilometers per hour caused further destruction to buildings and uprooting of trees that in turn destroyed housing and other infrastructure inland." World Bank, "Cyclone Sidr in Bangladesh Damage, Loss and Needs Assessment for Disaster Recovery and Reconstruction," February 2008, mimeo. This was the third natural disaster the country faced in 2007. Previously, Bangladesh was devastated by two floods.

40. Some analysts argue that in the medium term (i.e., 2030), climate change may not adversely impact overall rice production, but in the long term food production will be significantly impacted by the water shortage. They argue: "the overall impact of climate change on the production of food grains in Bangladesh would probably be small in 2030. This is due to the strong positive impact of CO_2 fertilization that would compensate for the negative impacts of higher temperature and sea level rise. In 2050, the negative impacts of climate change might become noticeable: production of rice and wheat might drop by 8% and 32%, respectively." I. M. Faisal and Saila Parveen, "Food Security in the Face of Climate Change, Population Growth, and Resource Constraints: Implications for Bangladesh," *Environmental Management* 34, no. 4 (2004), pp. 487–498.

41. Sujata Ramachandran, "Indifference, Impotence, and Intolerance: Transnational Bangladeshis in India" (Global Migration Perspectives no. 42, Global Commission on International Migration, Geneva, September 2005), http://www.gcim.org/attachements/GMP%20No%2042.pdf.

42. Bowring, "India Is Causing Trouble."

43. Ramachandran, "Indifference."

44. "Terror-hit India Looks for Scapegoats: Bangladesh," *Indo-Asian News Service*, August 5, 2008.

45. Arpita Mukherjee, "Bangladeshi Immigrants Spreading Terror in India?" September 9, 2008, http://arpita.instablogs.com/entry/bangladeshi-immigrants-spreading-terror-in-india/.

46. "The Government of Bangladesh estimates that 30 million people are drinking water that contains more than 50 micrograms per liter of arsenic. However, up to 70 million people are drinking water that contains more than 10 micrograms per liter of arsenic, which is the provisional WHO guideline value. After a quick field survey in 2001, the government estimated that 40–50% of the estimated 10 million tube wells were contaminated with arsenic. In some villages that figure was as high as 80–100%. Now there is the problem that some tube wells that were not originally poisoned are becoming so." "Interview with Mahmuder Rahman: Bangladesh's Arsenic Agony," *Bulletin of the World Health Organization* 86, no. 1 (January 2008), p. 11.

12 Rebellion and State Formation in Nepal

Implications for South Asian Security

Maya Chadda

Nine years into the new millennium, Nepal stands at the crossroads of history. By the end of 2008, the king had been deposed and the monarchy—a 250-year-old institution—was abolished. The unexpected Maoist plurality in the constitutional assembly elections had produced the hope that Nepal would find a road map to a constitutional and democratic government. That hope was dashed by the resignation of Prime Minister Pushpa Kamal Dahal, intense infighting among additional political parties, and the rising spate of popular unrest and economic meltdown.[1] To add to Nepal's woes, four Tarai-based armed groups were threatening secession if the interim government did not meet their demands. These developments have been traumatic for the Nepalis, but their regional impact would have been limited given that Nepal—one of the poorest and smallest countries in South Asia—can exercise little or no power over the security calculus in the region. But that is not the case.

Nepal occupies a special place in India's security concerns. In many ways, Nepal stands in a symbiotic relationship to India. They share nationalities, religion, and culture. Nepal's landlocked location requires commerce and trade to be conducted through India. India thus controls the economic lifeline of Nepal. But India's influence in Nepal is not unchallenged. China, the other great civilizational state in Asia, has, from time to time, sought to expand its influence and challenged India's special relationship with Nepal. Nepalis have resented their dependence on India and the sustained influence India has exerted on its domestic politics. Nepal has therefore increasingly emerged as an arena of competition between India and China. It is in this cultural and geo-political context that this chapter examines the issues central to this volume: the implications of weak state capacity and weak interstate cooperative norms on South Asia's regional security.

Why is small, poor, and dependent Nepal a threat to regional security? How do we understand the nature of Nepal's weakness, and what connections does such a state have to India's security interests? In what way does weak regional cooperation jeopardize security and how might we think about Indo-Nepal relations in this context? This chapter examines these questions in light of recent events in Nepal. The purpose is to assess whether weak states and weak regional cooperation norms lead to chronic regional insecurity. This chapter argues that as a first step, definitions of state strength and weakness must be placed into a region-specific context. It then argues that the particular character of state formation in Nepal has indeed contributed to regional insecurity; however, in contrast, state strength would not necessarily produce regional security, especially at the inter-state level. International norms of cooperation are necessary as well, and this chapter contends that Nepal's case highlights the important role of a broader geostrategic context that needs to include China and the United States as important actors in shaping regional security.

Structural Realities of Nepal

At least three structural realities of Nepal need to be considered as a broad context to examine the connections between domestic and regional security. The first noteworthy feature of Nepal is its underdeveloped and India-dependent economy. According to most estimates, Nepal is one of the least developed, most unequal, and economically smallest states in the world. Close to 42 percent of its population lives below the poverty line, and almost 87 percent live in rural areas, a majority among them eking out a meager living from agriculture, which has been largely ignored in state budgets. More than 44 percent of Nepalis own minute plots of land tied in feudal relationship to large landowners who wield oppressive political and economic power over their lives. There are few industries, and although tourism is an important source of revenue, instability and violence have diminished its share of the GDP over the last ten years. Nepal has abundant potential in hydropower, but the development of this industry depends on regional cooperation, particularly with New Delhi. Prospects for foreign trade and foreign direct investment are dim, given the small size of the economy, its technological backwardness, and land-locked geographic location, not to mention the violent rebellion.[2] According to Lawoti, poverty and inequality in Nepal have increased despite developments in some sectors of the economy such as transportation, real estate, trade, and commerce.[3] There is a growing but tiny urban, educated middle class, but the majority of Nepalis live in poverty and want, amid absence of economic opportunity.

The second important feature is Nepal's location between India and China. Because of this, Nepal has assumed an increasingly pivotal position in South Asia's geostrategic environment. Nepal's need for passage to the outside world gave India a particular advantage throughout the 1950s and 1960s, but that advantage came to be increasingly challenged as China rose in economic power and international influence. Nepal's leaders have been tempted to play the two rival Asian states against each other in order to gain greater autonomy for Kathmandu.

The third structural reality is the shared ethnic and religious nationalities between Nepal and India. The majority in India is Hindu, but it is Nepal that has pronounced itself a Hindu state. Instability, poverty, and conflict in Nepal deeply affect the proximate areas of Bihar and Uttar Pradesh in India. Over the years, a huge number of Nepalis have migrated and settled in areas around Darjeeling. Nepali political parties have frequently sought India as a refuge from Nepali monarchs. Indeed, there is a long and close relationship between the Nepal Congress Party and the Congress Party of India. These cultural and societal connections have constrained policies and shaped responses.

An unstable and weak state of Nepal is a tempting opportunity for neighboring states to advance their influence; it is also a source of danger if violence and civil strife spill over across the borders into neighboring regions. The equation between a weak Nepal causing inter-state insecurity is made more complex because all states in South Asia are weak and unstable, although the extent of instability varies from state to state, as do real and potential measures of power. India, though vastly larger and more powerful than Nepal, is also vulnerable to conflicts caused by overlapping ethnicity and disputed borders.

It is against these enduring features that we need to examine the nature of the Nepali state and the sources of its weakness. While it is fairly obvious that a weak Nepal will jeopardize regional security, is the obverse true? Will a strong Nepal enhance regional cooperation? We can give only a conditional answer to this question. A strong Nepal might not enhance security in the region.

Whether weak or strong, Nepal's responses to events are shaped by several intervening variables: geopolitical compulsions, the domestic struggle for power, and the intensity of Nepali nationalism. A stronger Nepal could seek to neutralize India's influence by inching closer to China. This cannot be reassuring to India; nor can it enhance interstate cooperation in South Asia. A stronger and more internally stable, prospering Nepal is no guarantee of peace. The second theme in this volume, namely that weak interstate norms lead to regional insecurity, also needs to be modified. Cooperation among South Asian states alone will not guarantee peace and security. The South Asian region needs powerful external states that have important interests at stake in the subcontinent, namely the United States and China, to cooperate as well. Their actions can easily jeopardize the carefully built edifice of mutual and collective understanding among South Asian states, particularly India and Nepal.

State Weakness and Regional Security: Conditions in South Asia

T. V. Paul argues in this volume that South Asia's multifaceted insecurity is largely a function of two factors: the presence of weak states and weak cooperative interstate norms. This proposition assumes that weak states are a danger to interstate security, particularly if they share cross-border nationalities and are unable to control their nations and territories. In this event, domestic turmoil can spill over across the border and provoke the country at the receiving end to intervene or to take proactive steps.

The state-provinces of Kashmir, Punjab, Assam, and Nagaland in India have been severely affected by developments in neighboring countries. The Sinhala-Tamil conflict in Sri Lanka is another example of ethnic overlap jeopardizing interstate relations. A weak state leading to ethnic separatism and interstate conflict is not, then, an uncommon occurrence in South Asia. While this is true, is the opposite also true? Will there be greater security if South Asian states are strong and in control of their borders and nationalities? Is such a situation likely to produce greater regional cooperation and peace? And how does an asymmetry in economic and military capacity affect this proposition? What if both states are weak but one is stronger than the other, as in the case of India and Nepal? What if the two states under scrutiny are asymmetrical in size, resources, and military power but are strong states in terms of domestic capability?

One might argue that the existence of strong neighboring states does not guarantee peace, nor does an asymmetry of military power lead always to conflict between them. In fact, a close match in material capabilities can lead to conflict. State ideology, ambitions, and national self-perception are important variables in shaping conflict relationships. Two well-matched strong states might induce tensions and war. A close match in power and capability did not spell peace between France and Germany in the nineteenth and early twentieth centuries, but led to a state of perpetual rivalry. According to A.F.K. Organski, war is most likely when a challenger to the dominant power enters into approximate parity with the dominant state and is dissatisfied with the existing system. Similarly, alliances are more stable when the parties to the alliance are satisfied with the power structure.[4] While India and Pakistan are not otherwise similar to nineteenth-century France and Germany, they are relatively close in matched strategic and military strength, and this situation has led to nothing but a perpetual state of tension and three wars between them. As in the case of India–Sri Lanka and India–Nepal, two ill-matched states can also experience serious tensions.

These anomalies bring us to the core questions in this volume: How do we understand "weakness," and what makes for strength? The conventional definition of state capacity, popular during the height of nation-state formation in the nineteenth and early twentieth centuries, was limited to territorial control, fixed boundaries, and governmental authority. A strong state was characterized by the ability to effectively maintain law and order and govern and protect the nation from external aggression. With the dawn of economic interdependence, development in international norms and laws, the spread of democracy, and the global market, this definition has undergone a reevaluation.

A review of international debates on state capacity is beyond the scope of this chapter, but applying the four typologies set forth in this volume, Nepal is a fragile or very weak state with only tenuous territorial control and poor ability to care for its people. This definition corresponds with the general consensus on what constitutes a weak state.[5] Rice and Patrick represent this fully when they contend that weak states "lack the capacity and/or will" to perform the core functions of statehood: "fostering an environment conducive to sustainable and equitable economic growth; establishing and maintaining legitimate, transparent, and accountable political institutions; securing their populations from violent conflict and controlling their territory; and meeting the basic human needs of their population."[6] Measured by the index of weakness, states in South Asia, with the exception of India, score in the bottom quintile among some 140 world states. Nepal ranks 17 from the bottom, indicating its inability in all the areas of the state functions enumerated by Rice and Patrick.

Since popular will is an important element in this definition we might ask: Would more democracy lead to increased security among states within the region? Based on South Asia's structural realities, we cannot be certain that democracy would ensure regional peace. After all, insurgency emerged from an unstable parliamentary democracy (1990–2005) and has strained relations with another democratic country, namely India. We need to then add regionally specific qualifications to the democratic peace theory when applied to South Asia and particularly to Indo-Nepal relations. In multiethnic and deeply divided countries such as India and Nepal, the presence of an electoral democracy does not ensure stability; cultural diversity demands additional provisions of federal autonomy and consociational rights for ethnic communities. South Asia is rife with instances where lack of ethnic compact has derailed the democratic process and brought back the authoritarian option. There have been periods in Pakistan's post-independence history when the alienated ethnic provinces of Sindh and the North-West Frontier Province (NWFP) supported the military governments at the center, contributing to a temporary truce from violence. But this ethnic bargain did not endure. In the long run, there is no substitute for a real democracy built on ethnic agreement to accommodate cultural diversity. In this regard, Nepal and India have followed a distinctly different trajectory of state development, although they share religion and caste-bound social structures.

The index of state weakness ignores the role of culture. It tells us that the state of Nepal currently ranks very low on the ability to protect, safeguard, and provide for its people. What it does not tell us is that in its current and highly mobilized conditions, authoritarian rule cannot survive for long in Nepal and that democratic aspirations are strong and widespread, the ethnic communities assertive and forceful, and rural Nepal anxious to be liberated from poverty and violence. These aspirations for democracy and prosperity, so evident in the collapse of the monarchy, are not captured by the weakness index. However, popular movements represent Nepal's capacity to change into a more democratic and stronger state. The index of weakness is only a snapshot measured by a marker that is blind to culture and history.

Two caveats need to be introduced before we turn to the consequences of state weakness on Indo-Nepal relations. At the minimum, the capacity index presumes the existence of an established state structure that is autonomous from changes in government. But the notion of autonomy which requires separating state from society is problematic in Nepal. Currently Nepal's state is a "work in progress": There is a strong popular impulse to build democratic legitimacy, rule of law, social welfare, and security, but no significant institutional infrastructure exists to articulate these aspirations. In the current transitional phase, the lines between social movement (represented by various ethnic movements and the Maoist movement) and government are blurred. The task of understanding Nepal's future is made difficult by the struggle over the new constitutional template.

The second caveat is Nepal's geopolitical compulsions. Nepal's geostrategic position has implications for Nepal's state capacity: it can impose limits on what Nepal can do, but it can also enable Nepal to gain a degree of leverage by playing India against China.

Modes of State Formation in Nepal

Governments in Nepal have been made and remade four times since the departure of the British from the Indian subcontinent: in the early 1950s, when an India-supported coup replaced the Rana family's regime with the monarchy, which had been usurped by the Ranas earlier in the century; in the mid-1960s when King Mahendra and then King Birendra banned political parties and set up a Panchayat Raj in which all power flowed to the monarch and his supporters; in the early 1990s, when a popular revolution (Jana Andolan) swept away the Panchayat Raj and ushered in a parliamentary democracy under a constitutional king; and in 2007, when the monarchy collapsed under the pressure of Maoist rebellion, leading to the current quest for a new political order and a new constitutional rule. What kind of state did Nepal construct on the anvil of these developments, and why did Nepal's parliamentary democracy and free elections produce a Maoist revolution?

To answer this, we turn next to some salient points of Nepal's history.

Some Distinctive Features of the Nepali State

It might be suggested that Nepal's early history—in terms of the broad processes of state formation—is closer to the history of European nation-states than it is to the developments that created states in South Asia: independent

India, Pakistan, Bangladesh, and Sri Lanka. Unlike the other South Asian states, Nepal was never colonized.

European nation-states were welded as distinct entities by internecine wars and expansion of national markets. While Nepal failed to experience economic and technological revolutions, like European states it was welded together as a kingdom by conquest which was legitimized by the notion of divine right (under Hindu ideology) decreed by its kings.[7] Nepal's expansionist phase came to an end when it came up against the expanding British rule in India: "With the boundaries fixed, the Gorkha elites did not have any other choice but to expand their economic resource base within the realm, with a large standing army . . . playing an important role in the subsequent period of administrative consolidation."[8] Moreover, geographic proximity and economic dependency, what we might identify as the constraining structural conditions of state formation, gave India a central place in Nepal's past and present.[9]

Still, Nepal reflects the continuities of its national borders with two separate but contiguous civilizations, the Tibeto-Mongolian and the Hindu-Buddhist. These two influences have shaped the ethnic, caste, communal, and regional identities in Nepal and divided them as discrete formations. Some among these have remained poorly integrated within the kingdom. As in India, the upper castes—Brahmins, Chetri, and Newars in Nepal—wielded power, but no single ethnic community formed an absolute majority. Society was stronger in Nepal than the state, and its regional, caste-based and ethnic divisions far more enduring than the state-promulgated policies of homogenization.

Hinduization as a Control Strategy

To hold their kingdom together and legitimize their conquest and control, the Shah kings incorporated the Hindu theory of divine rule.[10] The Hinduization of Nepali culture continued under the Ranas, who usurped power from the kings and ruled Nepal until they were replaced in a coup in 1953. The Nepali state asserted the "universal" nature of the Hindu religion, encompassing the diverse communities that constituted Nepal, but there were real limits to how far Nepal's Tibeto-Mangolian communities could be Hinduized.[11] Still, Nepal's ethnic plurality came to be ordered within a holistic framework of "national caste hierarchy."[12] The kings and Ranas had put in place a caste-based vision of a Gurkha kingdom to distribute land, power, and office among the high (pure) castes from which many ethnic and tribal groups were excluded. The caste order was legitimized by the divine power of the Hindu kings; the kings were regarded in popular myth as avatars of Vishnu, the Hindu god of universal preservation.

Caste-Based Order

The promulgation of the first Nepalese Civil Code (Muluki Ain) in 1854 was then a strategy to gain effective control over Nepal's diverse nations.[13] It privileged the Brahmins and Chetris and relegated the Tibeto-Mongolian Magar, Tharu, and Gurung ethnicities to a secondary place. Still, the civil code resonated with the generally accepted rules of social intercourse. It had two purposes: first centralization and then consolidation of the Nepali state under the royal umbrella. Muluki Ain provided Nepal's political classes with the means to extract resources and gain acceptance by building a network of power and patronage. The Hindu religion and caste-based legal order was meant to contain the inter-elite struggle and provide "universal" rules for access to and exercise of power.

But many provisions of the Muluki Ain were not implemented, and the state frequently accommodated ethnic communities through a strategy of co-option. What emerged was a patron-client network that substituted for political parties and channels of legitimate opposition. But patronage-driven strategies discriminated against communities that were reluctant to accept Hinduization, because it compromised their identity and undermined authority derived from their distinctive ethnic culture. The palace's assimilation strategy widened the gulf between the people and the king in Nepal. Although decades were to elapse before this gulf would swallow up the monarchy, the discriminatory nature of the patron-clientism explains why the marginalized communities in rural Nepal, especially the Tibeto-Mongolian ethnic groups, took to a violent rebellion.

Feudal Political Economy

How did the process of marginalization work, and what means did the king and the court employ to achieve exclusive control over offices and material resources? Riaz and Basu observe, "Nepal has been administered through a complex tenurial system of 'state landlordism.' This allowed the ruling class to usurp the territorial domains of the indigenous population and reapportion them as private entitlements to the army and loyal government functionaries. For example, during the Rana regime, a fourfold classification of this tenurial system was created in which land rights were determined by caste and proximity to the court and the king."[14] Most of those privileged by the court were "Ranas, brahmins, Thakuris, and families close to the ruling elites, and the relatives of royal families."[15]

As Madhav Joshi and T. David Mason write, "with any change in the alignment of elite politics in the capital, *birta* [government] land could be "reassigned to supporters of the newly ascendant elite faction."[16] Most peasants throughout the kingdom were reduced to the status of sharecroppers subject to institutionalized oppression that deprived them of tenurial security. This highly feudal and exploitative system became the economic instrument that allowed the state to extract resources, sustain administration, and maintain a large security force that ensured control over subjects and territories.[17] Nepal's economy revolved around the palace and court, first under the kings and then (from 1846 to 1951) under the Ranas, the self-appointed hereditary prime ministers. The Ranas presided over a strong patron-client network extending from the palace to remote villages, but this political arrangement led to underdevelopment and poverty. Nepal became one of the most unequal and poorest countries in South Asia.

Evolution of the Nepali State

Post-Colonial South Asia and Nepal: Phase I

The British withdrawal from the subcontinent and the emergence of independent India in the late 1940s let loose democratic aspirations in Nepal as well, but the struggle remained confined within the top echelons of political elites. The anti-Rana forces, composed mainly of Nepali residents in India who had served their political apprenticeship in the Indian nationalist movement, formed an alliance with the royal family, led by King Tribhuvan (1911–55), and launched a revolution in November 1950. Anxious to ward off interference from any external powers, India struggled to maintain stability and bind Nepal in special relations with New Delhi. A democratic Nepal, spearheaded by the Nepali Congress (NC) under the auspices of a benign monarchy, was India's best bet at the time. Nehru and other Indian leaders pressed for political reforms to defuse internal conflicts.[18] Under the new arrangement brokered by India, the rebels accepted a settlement with the Ranas, the sovereignty of the crown was restored and the revolutionary forces, led by the Nepali Congress Party, rose to power. The Rana regime became the "Rana Oligarchy," but the King was the main figure with full authority.[19] Nehru's motives in brokering an arrangement and promoting democracy were clear when he said, "the fact remains that we cannot tolerate any foreign invasion from any foreign country in any part of the Indian sub-continent. Any possible invasion of Nepal would inevitably involve the safety of India."[20] India helped end the rule of the Ranas, even though, in a compromise solution, a Rana retained the post of prime minister after monarchy had been restored. Nepal had opened up to what India hoped would be a gradual process of democratization presided over by the king, but in the early 1960s events took a turn in the opposite direction. King Mahendra banned political parties and introduced a partyless Panchayat system in Nepal.[21]

The Panchayat Raj: Phase II

The official aim of the Panchayat system was to mobilize rural support for the government by redistributing land and removing glaring inequalities. This was to be accomplished by decentralizing village government without competing party elections. The king had the power to control the election outcome by making sure that only favored individuals were nominated in the elections.[22] Once the loyal local elites were in place, the king was able to control the pyramid of power from village to the national Panchayat. According to Joshi, the Panchayat-era land reform led to redistribution of only 1.5% of the total arable land. "After land reform, 7.8% of peasant household were still landless, whereas 3.3% of households owned about 26.9% of arable land with an average size of 18.3 hectares."[23] He adds, "An especially perverse effect of the 1962 land reform was its impact on communal lands. In particular, the act broke up communal holdings by awarding individual households permanent title to the plots they cultivated. This converted ethnic communities into a class of marginal smallholders. Many soon found themselves unable to produce enough for subsistence because of further fragmentation of family landholdings."[24] Each development was a precursor to the Maoist insurgency that would devastate Nepal and change the balance of power in the country.

Parliamentary Democracy and Rebellion: Phase III

The main features of the Nepali state—autocratic rule, the importance of ascriptive status, centralization of power in the hands of privileged castes and classes, and marginalization of ethnic communities—did not change significantly until the Jan Andolan (People's Movement) of 1990 swept away the arbitrary rule of the kings and ushered in a constitutional monarchy and parliamentary democracy.[25] According to Mahendra Lawoti, political leaders were themselves subject to the power of the palace since in Nepal, the palace was the only "fountain of privileges," and the elected leaders could not overturn the centrality of the monarchy.[26] There were protests, but the king was able to strike a bargain that retained the palace as a symbol of Nepal's unity. Despite parliamentary elections, therefore, which were all too frequent between 1990 and 2005, the patrimonial state endured. This particular mode of state formation explains why Nepal failed to effect an economic transformation and why democratization led to a violent revolution.

Centralization of power had created two kinds of tension by the mid-1990s: within the national elites and between the center and ethnically defined regions. Although elections permitted the state to legitimize the functions of taxation, governance, and coercive control, lack of economic growth heightened tensions among political classes. The second source of tension was the conflict between the privileged classes and peripheral ethnic regions. Denied power in the Hindu civil code and cultural rights for their language, the Rais, Magars, and Limbus saw no alternative but to resist. Both intra-elite and ethnic tensions began to surface with growing ferocity during the democratic era.[27] The reason for this was not hard to identify. Joanna Pfaff-Czarnecka writes that despite the emphasis on social development, ethnic communities lacked access to state welfare and had no political voice. They saw state policies as an attempt at "internal colonization." The newly awakened ethnic communities began to refer to themselves as the Janjatis (indigenous people) which at once identified them as the original inhabitants of Nepal, a nation apart from the Hinduized Nepal and now the target of state oppression.[28]

Still, it might be argued that the monarchy and Hinduism had bestowed a degree of coherence to the Nepali state although it was both unjust and narrowly exploitative. The rise of democratic aspirations in Nepal undermined the monarchy but did not replace the king in the popular imagination. The royal massacre of 2001, however, achieved that. The attempt to impose arbitrary rule by King Gyanendra, who claimed the throne after the massacre, did even more damage. When the Maoists launched an armed struggle to "liberate" Nepal in 1996, the monarchy and traditional political parties were still in the driver's seat. By 2003, the king and the party leaders, including the parliamentary left parties, were pleading with the rebels for a cease fire and negotiated settlement. United in their desire to end the conflict, the king and the parties remained deeply divided over tactics and timing. Each sought to gain in the short term and sided with the Maoists in the hope of weakening its political rival. The result was their mutual weakening. A political vacuum had replaced the central state.

In contrast, the Maoists gained control over more and more districts of Nepal. The liberated areas were secured by empowering the peasants, confiscating lands, and eliminating the old ruling class.[29] In 2005, King Gyanendra dropped all pretenses at democratic constraints and usurped power. Shisir Khanal writes, "a divided state that was weak, a lack of functioning democratic institutions and a power struggle between the palace and political parties also helped in the rise of the insurgency."[30] But it was because of the promise to redress the social and economic ills of Nepal that the Maoists achieved success. The expansion of "liberated" zones diminished the state to the point where it could no longer govern, protect, or ensure the safety of its own people.[31] Once the Maoists had acquired a territorial base, set up a parallel government, and driven the Nepali royal army from these areas, they overturned Nepal's post–Jan Andolan parliamentary democracy and ultimately the monarchy. The rebellion was supported by recruits from ethnic communities that had been marginalized in the previous decades. The Janjatis of Nepal came to be the mainstay of the revolution.

The Nation and State in Transition: Phase IV

It is, however, important to distinguish between state collapse of the kind that took place in the Soviet Union and state collapse in Nepal. In Nepal, the idea of the Nepali nation has survived, and arguably strengthened, as a result of intense popular discourse about the shortcomings of current regimes and the desire for a democracy. The Nepali nation is not about to disintegrate; but the administrative base of the state that traditionally performs the core functions all states have to perform has weakened to the point where it endangers Nepal's political integrity.

Dilemmas of a Revolutionary Movement

Nepal is an intensely mobilized country with no national consensus and few effective channels that can translate popular demands into legitimate and enduring authority. Despite Goodwin and Skocpol's faith in the power of democracy, "[t]he ballot box" has clearly *not* "proven to be the coffin of [the] revolutionary movement"[32] in Nepal. The rapid-fire rise and fall of more than fourteen governments between 1990 and 2005 and the steady deterioration in the abilities of the state to perform its core functions point to a possibility of real collapse. The May 2009 crisis precipitated by the resignation of the Maoist Prime Minister Dahal points to a serious disagreement over integration of the Maoist cadres into the Nepali regular army and the division of power and responsibilities between the prime minister and the president. Behind this public disagreement lurks the intense struggle for power among Nepal's political parties and leaders. The Maoists have mobilized their supporters in the streets as leverage in the competition over the prime ministerial office and government. There are other issues at stake as well. Not least among these is the accommodation of the ethnic armed groups in Tarai who have banded together to demand a better deal in the emerging balance of power in Kathmandu.[33] The Maoists have not pulled out of the government (as of this writing), but they face a difficult dilemma: compromise might lose them the image of a revolutionary party; refusing to compromise will lead to deadlock from which no one can benefit. This is why they have conducted these negotiations against the impending threat of resuming armed struggle.[34]

Nepal needs to resolve the conflict over who should govern, how, and how long; it needs to also figure out the distributional question about who should get what, when, and how. The first concerns political design, the formal institutions of government and informal arrangements based on tacit rules of political competition. The second concerns the deeper issues of equitable distribution of power and resources: access to jobs and education, land reforms, the mix of public and private ownership, state services, and above all, popular access to the policy-making process. In the intensely mobilized Nepal of today, these two conflicts have fused together and produced a deadlock.

The main players, the Maoists and the traditional and ethnic parties, are in fundamental disagreement over questions of ideology, agenda, and the design of the future Nepal. Ethnic parties seek a highly devolved state that would afford them autonomy and self-rule within the sovereign frame of a democratic Nepal; the Maoists and the traditional political parties would have to adjust to this against their own preference for greater centralization. In other words, the design of the central Nepali state and its federal structure will require negotiations between the Maoists and the traditional parties and the Janjatis. Second, any broad compromise will have to revolve around special treatment and provisions to level the playing field between the weaker sections of the society—Dalits, women, ethnic minorities—and the general population. This too requires a negotiated agreement, because there may be disputes over who should and should not be included in the special protection provisions. There is likely to be a dispute over the distribution of power between the executive and legislative branches of the future government.

The compromise will be shaped by how traditional political parties and the Maoists assess their future prospects and how ethnically based parties see this competition affecting their own prospects. In the absence of the king, the president's office has potentially huge powers, as evident in the rupture between the prime minister and president over the decision to sack the army chief. The resolution of these questions will depend on how rapidly the Maoists transform their role in politics and society and give up the option of armed revolt.

As made evident by the fallout over the army chief, a central problem of this transition is the integration of the hard-core Maoist combatants and militias in Nepal's regular army.[35] The Army Integration Special Committee (AISC)—which comprises representatives from the Maoist party and the main opposition Nepali Congress party—is yet to lay down the ground rules for proposed integration. Many in Nepal's army are reluctant to admit the rebels to their ranks for fear of affecting the morale and command structure of the military; they also fear being sidelined in favor of the new entrants. The Maoists cadres are equally reluctant to lose their revolutionary identity and importance.

The traditional parties—the NC and the Communist Party of Nepal (Marxist/Leninist), in short the CPN-ML—prefer a mixed economy, although the latter would have less problem with intervention and state regulation of markets. Still, given the conditions of poverty and underdevelopment, not to mention damage caused by a decade-long rebellion, Nepal needs a long-term and comprehensive agreement on balancing growth and distributive justice. The new Maoist-led government has ceded to market forces and globalization but the precise role of the state in regulating its scope remains uncertain. The Maoists will insist on carrying forward land reforms, but that legislation will run up against opposition from entrenched forces in rural Nepal—many among these support the traditional parties. Land reforms might then threaten the fragile coalition and force the Maoists to choose between their political ideology and the survival of their government. Similarly, efforts to create jobs will run up against a paucity of investment, economic dependency, and inadequate infrastructure. There will be disagreements about where to invest and who should be the first target group to receive benefits. Nepal's dependence on India points to perhaps the most contentious area of disagreement among its ruling elites. In this regard, the Maoists and the traditional political parties need to decide how best to balance Nepal's relations with India and China.

Implications for Regional Security

Given the fragile state of the current elite bargain, a broken economy, and a divided security force, the Nepali state is unable to fulfill its core functions of protection, law and order, and effective governance. While an unstable Nepal is a problem for the region as a whole, its greatest impact is on India and the triangular balancing among Nepal, India, and China. An unstable Nepal jeopardizes India's political security in two ways: military-strategic and domestic-political.[36] India's domestic political vulnerability has caused severe strains between the two countries in the past. Although India is several times larger and more powerful than Nepal, the "hegemonic stability" framework does not adequately explain their relationship and sense of mutual vulnerability. This has prevented India from exercising the dominance it could have if we are to simply compare its power attributes with those of Nepal. India has nevertheless tried to shape events in Nepal to ward off adverse fallout of instability there and to prevent Kathmandu from edging closer to China. The best way to achieve this was to tie Nepal in a strong bilateral relationship that guaranteed mutual security and forged close political, economic, and cultural links.

On balance, at least four ground realities have shaped India-Nepal relations. The first is the existence of a treaty between the two countries (1950) that underwrites the open border between them. Article 1 of the treaty states that "there shall be everlasting peace and friendship between the Government of India and the Government of Nepal," and that both will "acknowledge and respect the complete sovereignty, territorial integrity and independence of each other."[37] Under Article 2, Nepal and India agreed to share information about "any serious friction or misunderstanding with any neighboring state likely to cause any breach in the friendly relations subsisting between the two governments.'"[38] Article 5, which states that Nepal "shall be free to import from or through the territory of India, arms, ammunition, or warlike materials and equipment for the security of Nepal,"[39] has meant that India can exercise control over the kind and source of military supplies Nepal obtains. In return, India offers Nepal nondiscriminatory treatment of its citizens in economic and commercial affairs.

The second defining condition to shape Indo-Nepal relations is Nepal's landlocked geographical situation and dependence on India for trade and transit facilities. The 1951 Trade Treaty includes transit facilities for Nepal's trade with both India and a third country. This treaty has witnessed several modifications, each more liberal to the Nepali side than before.[40] Facilitating trade, transit, open borders, and economic opportunities on an equal footing is the quid pro quo New Delhi offers in exchange for Nepal's promise not to jeopardize India's security.

The third ground reality in Indo-Nepal relations is the dominance of the Indian economy over Nepal's small and poor economy. While this is a cause for concern among Nepal's nascent business and commercial community, it is also an opportunity for India and Nepal to develop a common market closely tying together the proximate regions of Bihar, Uttar Pradesh, and Uttaranchal in India and Terai in Nepal. The shape of such a common market will depend largely on the political will and common objectives of governments in each capital. Still, trade and transit issues as well as the need for open borders have led to frequent disagreements and tensions between India and Nepal.

The fourth political condition is closely tied to the third, namely the presence of millions of ethnic Indians in Nepal's Terai region, largely from the Indian states mentioned earlier. These constitute close to 30 to 40 percent of Nepal's population. Similarly, millions of Nepalis have migrated and settled in the Darjeeling area of India.[41] Their geographic concentration in areas around Darjeeling has led to a demand for a separate state of Gorkhaland in India. The emergence of a restive Nepali population within India poses a challenge to Indian federal integration and domestic security.

The rapid expansion of the Indian economy, particularly since 1990, has encouraged poor Nepalis to migrate across the border by the thousands in search of jobs, education, and livelihood. But an expanding economy requires larger inputs of energy and water resources. As a lower riparian state, India is dependent on Nepal for river waters, and the management of these waters is a source of tension and recrimination between the two states. India and Nepal have signed several treaties for sharing waters and developing water resource management. Their importance to India and Nepal's food security and flood management can hardly be overstressed. Nepal is convinced that it has got the short end of the stick in these and other landmark treaties with India.[42]

The rise of the violent Maoist insurgency in Nepal since 1996, and in large swaths of India's eastern regions around the same time, has further complicated the strategic and domestic interconnections between the two states. They have made Nepal's domestic instability inseparable from India's ability to exercise political and territorial control within its own borders. In July 2001, nine South Asian Maoist parties met in West Bengal and formed a Coordination Committee of Maoist Parties and Organizations of South Asia (CCOMPOSA).[43]

The Maoists' success in Nepal has dangerous demonstrative implications for the radical left in India. The Maoist ascent compelled India to support their inclusion in the government in August 2008, since that was the best way to control the fallout of insurgency across the border and secure a stable Nepal. But the course of future events in Nepal is likely to seriously impact the fate of the violent Naxalite movement in areas stretching from Andhra to Jharkhand and Bihar in India.

At the minimum, India would like the Nepali Maoists to abandon revolution and follow a neutral policy between Beijing and New Delhi. And although the new Maoist government had pledged policy equidistance from its two neighboring giants, India remained deeply suspicious and apprehensive of the Maoists within the governing coalition. These suspicions deepened whenever Nepal made anti-India statements or was perceived as courting China. Prime Minister Dahal's first state visit to attend the 2008 Beijing Olympics caused consternation in New Delhi. [44]

The China factor has been critical since the 1960s and has assumed increasing importance as India's own sense of vulnerability has intensified. India has been apprehensive of China constructing the trans-Himalayan highway, the signing of a Nepal-Tibet trade treaty, the growing Chinese economic aid to Nepal and an intelligence-sharing agreement of the late 1980s.[45] The latter proved to be the proverbial last straw on the camel's back. India responded by imposing an economic blockade in 1989–1990 that undermined the monarchy and unwittingly ushered in democratic change. Once parliamentary democracy was restored and a pro-India NC came to power in Kathmandu, India renegotiated the Treaty on Trade and Transit with Nepal, offering substantive economic concessions. In 1996 India and Nepal signed the Mahakali Treaty that defined their mutual obligations to distribute and manage the Mahakali River waters.[46]

Although China has been pragmatic in its relations with Nepal, preferring to maintain state-to-state relations rather than revolutionary camaraderie with the Maoists, it is far from pleased about the increasing American and Indian cooperation to combat terrorism in Nepal after September 11, 2001. Since then, Nepal has been drawn in a new way into the regional security calculus. The 1999 Kathmandu hijacking of Indian Airlines flight IC 814 by Islamic extremists underlines a new way in which a weak Nepal can threaten India's security.[47] It is evident that Pakistan's Inter-Services Intelligence Directorate has been active in Nepal since the outbreak of turmoil in Kashmir and war in Afghanistan. India's security will be in serious jeopardy if Nepal were to become a safe haven for anti-India Islamic, revolutionary or separatist movements. As a weak state, Nepal has always made India vulnerable, not least because India has been weak in establishing state control over its nation and territory and because Nepal's stability is inseparable from India's political stability.

Future Trajectories

The mode of state formation in Nepal—from monarchy to anarchy—has made it highly dangerous to regional security, particularly for India. The asymmetry of military and economic power and differences in size has not prevented domestic conflicts from spilling over across the border into India. These conflicts have endangered the Indian state, which is also vulnerable to separatist pulls and the demands of its own ethnic and peasant constituencies. Open borders, themselves a result of Nepal's landlocked situation, have linked Nepal's domestic politics to India's regional security. Ethnic separatism and peasant rebellion echo across the border. Informal ties and collaboration among protest movements endanger both India and Nepal. Oppressive governments in Kathmandu have sent the political opposition in search of safety and support to India. Indian attempts to secure a stable Nepal have unleashed a flood of nationalistic fervor in Nepal and, in turn, anti-Hindi and anti-Hindu slogans have angered Hindu nationalists in India. Last, but not least, ineffective management of rivers has devastated large parts of northern India, with floods leading to thousands of deaths and vast damage to the Indian economy.

The nature of Nepal's domestic instability would not have taken the form it did had Nepal not been an autocratic monarchy based on Hindu ideology and caste hierarchy. The Maoist rebellion would not have occurred had the mode of extraction not been based on exploitative patron-client relations constructed in a power pyramid culminating in an arbitrary kingship at the apex, where the king was regarded as the avatar of the god Vishnu. The limitations of this state fed the violent revolution that eventually destroyed the monarchy, weakened democratic parties, and plunged Nepal into a political deadlock. Nepal's domestic dilemmas are inextricably tied to India's security and stability.

India faces two possible scenarios with regard to Nepal's foreign policy. In the first, its special ties to Nepal will have to be modified if Nepal moves closer to China, although this may be an attempt on its part to furrow an independent international policy. In the second, a future Nepali government will retain neutrality, with closer cooperation on regional security concerns in South Asia. If a pro-China tilt were to occur, competition for influence in the Himalayan republic will intensify. The United States and India will exert greater efforts to prevent Nepal moving away from its traditional pro-India stance. Nepal's economic conditions will also constrain its desire for independence. The trade and transit treaty will continue to provide India with the leverage to balance Nepal's sovereign sensitivities against its own national security.

The domestic structure of present-day Nepal could move in two alternative directions. In one, a post-Dahal political consensus will emerge to provide a constitutional blueprint of a secular, federal, democratic Nepal with a mixed economy and a good neighborly foreign policy. The second and likely possibility is a progressively unstable Nepal led by series of experimental party coalitions and the resumption of violent activities by a new generation of revolutionaries. Although in a different way, each scenario can threaten India's security interests. The first is more manageable than the second.

Even if Nepal were to stabilize as a secular democratic state, it would remain highly sensitive to every real and imagined slight to its national pride and interests. This hyper-nationalism intensified by vast popular mobilization in recent years makes negotiations with "dominant' India difficult. Both Nepal and India can gain from cooperation on the management of river waters, deforestation, pollution and environmental protection, and energy generation. They can do away with trade barriers and establish a common market. But cooperation with India is fraught with risks for any government in Nepal. Nepal's leaders worry over being accused of succumbing to the dictates of a regional hegemon. But while cooperation is difficult, open hostility to India is equally difficult. India's post-1990 coalition governments have sought to ease Nepal's fears by making important trade concessions on a non-reciprocal basis to Nepal. Non-reciprocity requires India to expect no quid pro quo or return concessions from its smaller neighbor. But Nepal's domestic instability and violence have cast a dark shadow over prospects for institutionalizing a firm and mutually cooperative relationship between India and Nepal.

If Nepal Were to Be a Strong but Undemocratic State

Clearly, a weak Nepal is a security threat, but is the obverse true? Will a reasonably well-governed, strong, and unified Nepal enhance regional security? What if such a strong and well-governed Nepal was not a democracy? The answer would depend largely on the agenda of the government in Nepal and its domestic and foreign policy objectives. Given the current state of popular mobilization, it is doubtful whether the Nepalis can be persuaded to abandon the public square and accept an autocratic government, whatever its ideological complexion. The Maoists have understood this craving for popular control. A government without popular consent will not be a stable state. And an unstable state will endanger regional security. One might also argue that in the event that a strong autocratic state—perhaps a Maoist government reverting to revolutionary objectives—takes hold, it will seek to lessen India's influence in Nepal by towing an independent line. It could turn to Pakistan and China or to other states antipathic to India. However, Nepal's landlocked position, small size, and inferior position in conventional measures of power will make pursuit of anti-India policies dangerous. A strong non-democratic Nepal does not then enhance India's security. It will only do so provided cooperative norms take hold in the region. These are unlikely to be strengthened if Nepal pursues, or is perceived as pursuing, an anti-Indian policy and New Delhi suspects that regional states are ganging up against it.

If Nepal Were to Be a Strong Democratic State

What if Nepal were a strong democratic state? Would that enhance India's security and promote regional cooperation? Those who favor the "democratic peace" thesis argue that democracies do not go to war. Would a strong and democratic Nepal improve the prospects for regional peace? The answer to this question is a conditional one. Even if it is democratic, a strong Nepal must still contend with its geopolitical dilemmas and balance them against its desire for strategic autonomy. Relations with India will remain an issue in the competition for power and office no matter how strong a state Nepal might become. Neither a democratic Nepal nor an autocratic one can be depended upon to promote only pragmatic and restrained India policies or forego the temptation to use China as a counterweight against its other large neighbor. Nepal's location between India and China makes the balancing act even more difficult and the outcome uncertain. The only way to build regional security and cooperation is to then get India and China to agree not to compete for influence in Nepal, and to incorporate Nepal and other smaller Himalayan states into a web of broader regional cooperation that firmly adheres to respect for all states' sovereign independence and political integrity.

In fact, India and Nepal have three general options: to enter into a mutually attractive bilateral relationship; to make Indo-Nepal ties an integral part of South Asian cooperation; and, third, to go beyond South Asia and make Indo-Nepali ties a part of an understanding among the United States, India, and China. It is not enough to have a strong SAARC; peace and regional cooperation will require a broader geostrategic understanding between India and China.

The above suggests that while a weak state will jeopardize regional security, a strong state is no guarantee of peace and cooperation. Nepal cannot escape its geopolitical dilemma, whether it is an autocracy or a democracy, a strong or a weak state. It must also manage popular nationalism and the built-in fears and resentments of the larger India. Though powerful, India is vulnerable to cross-border movements of people and turmoil in Nepal. An unstable Nepal is a danger to India's security. Last but not least, regional cooperation is dependent on the worldview of Nepal's ruling classes. Nepal's room for maneuver is severely circumscribed no matter who assumes the reins of power in Kathmandu.

The course of Indo-Nepali relations suggests that geopolitics is not a static element of national or regional security when combined with ethnic nationalism and the intrinsic economic weakness of countries in South Asia. Whether regional cooperation norms are strong or weak will depend on how these three elements—geopolitics, ethnic nationalism, and underdevelopment—combine to shape the security environment in South Asia. These same elements will also determine the future of Indo-Nepal ties.

Notes to Chapter 12

1. Prime Minister Pushpa Kamal Dahal resigned on May 3 2009, when the president refused to let him fire the commander of Nepal's Royal army. The latter had refused to recruit the 'indoctrinated' Maoists cadres. The other parties in the ruling coalition also opposed the prime minister's decision. This led to Dahal's resignation although the Maoists continue to be a part of the government.

2. Central Intelligence Agency, "Nepal's economy," *World Factbook* (Langley, VA: Central Intelligence Agency, 2008), http://www.theodora.com/wfbcurrent/nepal/nepal_economy.html.

3. See Mahendra Lawoti, "Contentious Politics in Democratizing Nepal," in *Contentious Politics and Democratization in Nepal*, ed. Mahendra Lawoti (New Delhi: Sage, 2007), pp. 25–27.

4. A. F. K. Organski, *World Politics* (New York, Knopf, 1968). Also See Ronald Tammen, *Power Transitions: Strategies for the 21st Century* (New York, Seven Bridges Press, 2000).

5. For several other attempts to define weak states, see Commission on Weak States and US National Security, *On the Brink: Weak States and US National Security* (Washington, DC: Center for Global Development, 2004); the work of the Central Intelligence Agency-funded Political Instability Task Force in Robert H. Bates et al., *Political Instability Task Force Report: Phase IV Findings* (McLean, VA: Science Applications International Corporation); Robert Rotberg, ed., *When States Fail: Causes and Consequences* (Princeton: Princeton University Press, 2004); and, probably the best-known report, Foreign Policy and Fund for Peace, "Failed States Index 2008," *Foreign Policy,* July–August 2008.

6. Susan Rice and Stewart Patrick, *Index of State Weakness in the Developing World* (Washington, DC: Brookings Institution, 2008), p. 3.

7. T. Louise Brown, *The Challenge to Democracy in Nepal* (London: Routledge, 1996), pp. 1–15.

8. Joanna Pfaff-Czarnecka, "Debating the State of the Nation: Ethnicization of Politics in Nepal," in *Ethnic Futures: The State and Identity Politics in Asia*, ed. Joanna Pfaff-Czarnecka et al. (London: Sage, 1996), p. 50.

9. Sanjay Upadyaya, *The Raj Lives* (New Delhi: Vitasta Publishing, 2008).

10. Ali Riaz and Subho Basu, "The State-Society Relationship and Political Conflicts in Nepal (1768–2005)," *Journal of Asian and African Studies* 42, no. 2 (2007).

11. See M. M. Cameron, *On the Edge of the Auspicious: Gender and Caste in Nepal* (Urbana and Chicago, IL: University of Illinois Press, 1998).

12. A. Höfer, The *Caste Hierarchy and the State in Nepal: A Study of the Muluki Ain of 1854* (Innsbruck: Universitatsverlag Wagner, 1998), cited in Riaz and Basu, "State-Society Relationship," p. 136. Also see Pfaff-Czarnecka, "Debating," p. 52.

13. Brown, *Challenge*, pp. 7–8

14. Riaz and Basu, "State-Society Relationship," p. 133. See also Leo E. Rose and Margaret W. Fisher, *The Politics of Nepal: Persistence and Change in an Asian Monarchy* (Ithaca: Cornell University Press, 1970), pp. 122–123.

15. Madhav Joshi and T. David Mason, "Land Tenure, Democracy and Insurgency in Nepal," *Asian Survey* 47, no. 3 (2007), p. 400.

16. Ibid. Also see Riaz and Basu, "State-Society Relationship," p. 133.

17. Michael Bratton and Nicholas van de Walle, "Patrimonial Regimes and Political Transitions in Africa," *World Politics* 46, no. 4 (1994), p. 458.

18. Murlidhar Dharmadasani, *Indian Diplomacy in Nepal* (Jaipur: Aalek Publishers, 1976), p. 116.

19. Leo E. Rose, *Nepal: Strategy for Survival* (Berkeley: University of California Press, 1996), p. 23.

20. Ibid., p. 185.

21. Ibid., p. 194.

22. Narayan Khadka, "Crisis in Nepal's Partyless *Panchayat* System: The Case for More Democracy,"*Pacific Affairs* 59, no. 3 (1986), p. 430.

23. Joshi and Mason, "Land Tenure," p. 400.

24. Ibid., p. 403; also see M. A. Zaman, *Evaluation of Land Reform in Nepal* (Katmandu: Ministry of Land Reform, 1973), p. 33.

25. Pfaff-Czarnecka, "Debating," 51.

26. Mahendra Lawoti, "Democracy, Domination and Exclusionary Constitutional Engineering Process in Nepal, 1990," in Lawoti, *Contentious Politics*, p. 52.

27. See Susan Hangen, "Between Political Party and Social Movement: The Mongol National organization and Democratization in Rural East Nepal," in Lawoti, *Contentious Politics*, pp. 175–199.

28. Pfaff-Czarnecka, "Debating," pp. 60–61.

29. While almost all of Nepal's 75 districts were affected by the insurgency, the Maoists were in full control of at least five western districts—Rukum, Dolpa, Rolpa, Salyan and Pyuthun. Sudha Ramachandran, "Nepal Cashes in on Cannabis", *Asian Times Online*, April 21, 2004, http://www.atimes.com/atimes/South_Asia/FD21Df05 .html.

30. Shisir Khanal, "Committed Insurgents, a Divided state and the Maoist Insurgency in Nepal," in Lawoti, *Contentious Politics*, p. 80.

31. Li Onesto, "The Evolution of the Maoist Revolution in Nepal in an Adverse International Environment," in Lawoti, *Contentious Politics*, 121–142.

32. Jeff Goodwin and Theda Skocpol, "Explaining Revolutions in the Contemporary Third World," *Politics and Society* 17, no. 4 (December 1989), p. 495.

33. In July 2009, the four armed groups—Madhes Mukti Tigers (MMT), Madhesi Virus Killers (MVK), Tarai Samyukta Krantikari Party (TSKP) and Rajan-led Janatantrik Tarai Mukti Morcha (JTMM) presented a united platform to hold talks with the Maoist led government.

34. "When Maoists Take Over Nepal," *Time*, April 15, 2008.

35. International Crisis Group, "Nepal's Peace Agreement: Making it Work" (Asia Report no. 126, December 15, 2006.) Also see Prakash Bom, "Nepal Army Integration a Paradigm for Peace and Democracy," *American Chronicle*, October 18, 2008.

36. Jawaharlal Nehru, *India's Foreign Policy: Selected Speeches, September 1946– April 1961* (New Delhi: Government of India Publications, 1971), p. 436.

37. Manish Dabhade and Harsh Pant, "Coping with Challenges to Sovereignty: Sino-Indian Rivalry and Nepal's Foreign Policy", *Contemporary South Asia* 13, no. 2 (June 2004), p. 163.

38. B.C. Upreti, "India's Security Stakes in the Himalayas and Indo-Nepal Relations," in *Encyclopedia of SAARC Nations*, vol. 5, *Nepal*, ed. Virender Grover (New Delhi: Deep and Deep, 1997), p. 387.

39. Dabhade and Pant, "Coping," p. 163.

40. Ibid.

41. A Memorandum of Understanding was signed by New Delhi, the state government and Subhash Ghising, the leader of the Gorkhaland, in December 2005. New Delhi created an autonomous Council protected by the Sixth Schedule of the Constitution of India. But dissatisfied with the protection, a migrated population has formed the Gorkha Jana Mukti Morcha (GJMM), which is demanding a separate state

in the Darjeeling hills and has launched a movement against the granting of Sixth Schedule status to the region.

42. It is noteworthy that the Maoists have opposed the Mahakali treaty with India and want a revision of its agreements.

43. For details see South Asia Terrorism Portal, "Communist Party of Nepal-Maoist," (New Delhi: Institute for Conflict Management, n.d.), http://www.satp.org/satporgtp/countries/nepal/terroristoutfits/index.html.

44. Indo-Asian News Service, "Prachanda's Visit to Redefine India-Nepal Ties: Envoy," *Thaindian News*, September 13, 2008 http://www.thaindian.com/news portal/uncategorized/prachandas-visit-to-redefine-india-nepal-ties-envoy-inter view_10095467.html

45. On the details of the blockade and China's response, see John Garver, *Protracted Contest: Sino-Indian Rivalry in the Twentieth Century* (New Delhi: Oxford University Press, 2001), pp. 155–162.

46. Padmaja Murthy, "India and Nepal: Security and Economic Dimensions," *Strategic Analysis* 23, no. 9 (December 1999), http://www.ciaonet.org/olj/sa/sa_99mup01.html.

47. Dabhade and Pant, "Coping," p. 165.

PART IV
CONCLUSIONS

13 Transforming South Asia

Is a Pluralistic Security Community Feasible?

T. V. Paul and Theodore McLauchlin

This volume is intended to broaden the debate on security in South Asia, a pivotal region for global security, especially since September 11, 2001. South Asia—comprising eight states and about one-quarter of humanity—has not yet created a secure space in the interstate, intrastate, and human dimensions. Our aim has been to explore the core causes and contributing factors for the persistence of high levels of insecurity in this region. We begin with the assumption that the prevailing notions of regional security may not be sufficient to address the multifaceted challenges facing the region. Instead, we seek to explore two key drivers of insecurity: weak states and weak cooperative norms. These two features may have been caused by a number of other factors; hence, they are mainly intervening variables in producing the multiple insecurity dilemmas of the region.

In this chapter, we first recapitulate the definition of state capacity from the introduction. It combines two concepts: raw capabilities and legitimacy. We then discuss the common themes of the papers in this volume. Though they come from many different points of view and analyze a diverse array of countries, three key common themes emerge. The commonalities amount to dilemmas of state-building and security. These dilemmas operate at three different levels: within states, within the region, and in the region's interactions with global politics and economics. The first and most fundamental of these dilemmas is that states can gain security in the long term by extending their capabilities and legitimacy, but efforts at expansion can be repressive and can provoke violent resistance. A strong state may offer increased internal security, but a coercive state may not resolve all internal problems, even when it is able to provide a facade of order; hence, the need for legitimacy in understanding the capacity of a state and the resultant security it offers. The second dilemma is that at a regional level, weak states threaten their neighbors—but so can strong states. Thus, there may be two reasons for the spillover of internal conflict: sometimes states cannot prevent conflict from spilling over, and sometimes they have an interest in allowing spillover to undermine rival states from within. A strong state may not be a guarantor of peace at the inter-state level, and hence we emphasize the need for a strong state with legitimacy which abides by the norms of cooperation and nonintervention. These two major dilemmas are the focus of the volume. But we also place South Asia in a global context and suggest a third dilemma: the engagement of South Asia with global forces, including great power politics and globalization, can either improve security or leave populations vulnerable to externally driven pressures.

Concepts of State Strength: Raw Capability and Legitimacy

To begin with, it is important to explore what state strength means. To us, the concept of state strength welds two major concerns: capability and legitimacy. In the introduction, state capacity is defined as "the ability of a state to develop and implement policies in order to provide collective goods such as security, order, and welfare to its citizens in a legitimate and effective manner untrammeled by internal or external actors." This definition focuses on the provision of collective goods, and the capability to do so indeed receives the lion's share of attention under standard analyses of state strength.[1] But legitimacy is a crucial and complicated dimension of this formulation. We address capability and legitimacy in turn.

Capability
The various chapters make it clear that South Asian states face large challenges to their capability to provide many different public goods. It is tautological to suggest that there is insecurity because the state cannot provide the public good of security. But the contributors to this volume do not make this claim. Instead, we use state capability as a way of studying more interesting and insightful causal relationships.

In particular, the chapters analyze how states try to gain the capability to end their insecurity and the prospects for their success in doing so. The paradoxes and dilemmas on this front are sobering. In the introduction, Paul highlights what Kal Holsti calls the "state-strength dilemma": efforts to increase state capability for improved security provoke resistance and reduce security.[2] As Matthew Lange argues, summarizing the core arguments of the literature, the state's coercive force can both contain and instigate rebellion and insecurity. Accommodation with powerful challengers is a possible alternative but leaves the state center vulnerable to the wishes of peripheral elites. It is therefore unclear that accommodation improves security over the long run, either. If there is a peaceful path to state strength, it is apparently rare: historically, those states that emerged as strong most often have done so by centralizing, provoking rebellion, and defeating rebellion on the battlefield.[3]

The chapters demonstrate the relevance of this pattern to South Asia. Lange shows that it is a pattern stretching back to colonial India; the thinness of the British Raj required resort to local intermediaries in indirect rule. It seems no accident that one such intermediary, in aligning Kashmir with India, set the stage for the central source of interstate insecurity in South Asia and a continually relevant transnational security threat as well.

The historical relevance of this tension between accommodation and coercion is matched by its contemporary importance. Much of the recent research agenda on state weakness comes out of September 11, 2001; as Robert Rotberg argues, the attacks of that day indicated the dangers of ungoverned spaces for global security.[4] The chapters on Afghanistan and Pakistan specifically address how the Taliban and al-Qaeda threat emerged and where we stand with it. Rasul Bakhsh Rais details how both the Soviet puppet state and the Taliban regime in Afghanistan provoked local resistance as they attempted to impose central rule. And the Taliban's search for allies put it in league with al-Qaeda. It now appears necessary to try to respect the local authority of the multiple and fragmented centers of power in the country.

The swings between the garrison state and accommodation of Pashtun insurgencies and Islamist groups in Pakistan, chronicled by Lawrence Ziring, indicate that this acceptance of fragmentation is a dangerous game. If, as is currently proposed, the international coalition can somehow separate moderate from hard-line Taliban as it did in Iraq, steadily isolating and eliminating the latter, there might be some possibility for sustained gains in security while remaining realistic about the dim prospects of a centralized administration from Kabul. But for the central state, the problem with accommodation is its ambiguity: a client who is currently an ally may cease to be in the future; if so, the state will have facilitated the victory of its own rival.

Afghanistan and Pakistan are only the two most prominent cases. Other South Asian states evince somewhat similar patterns. For example, as Maya Chadda points out, the Nepali state's attempts to forward a centralized legal code to consolidate power in its own hands was not fully implemented, and instead the state pursued a strategy of co-optation and clientelism. Even then, patron-client relations isolated the peasantry and numerous ethnic communities, sowing the seeds for eventual Maoist insurgency.

Coercive capacity alone can only rarely bring security in the contemporary world. Therein lies the importance of legitimacy, a variable that needs further examination.

Legitimacy

Legitimacy, along with capability, carries a lot of freight. The definition implies, and the book's theoretical and empirical chapters elucidate, the idea that state strength is a kind of running dialog between state institutions and the citizenry. In that sense the volume carries on in the tradition of a productive research agenda focusing on the potential and actual synergies between state and society, rather than their opposition.[5] For Rotberg, "a nation-state fails when it loses legitimacy . . . when citizens realize that the state no longer cares about most of its inhabitants—then nearly everyone understands that the social contract binding rulers to the ruled and vice versa has been irreparably breached and allegiances are transferred to non-state actors." Ali Riaz, applying very different Gramscian concepts, places similar weight on legitimacy, suggesting that it is the failure of the Bangladeshi state to forward a hegemonic ideological project that keeps it weak. The public remains despairing of the corruption in Dhaka. People's loyalties have turned to civil society organizations and insurgent groups. Whether as a consequence of a failure of transaction or of a failure to impose a legitimacy project hegemonically, it is clear that the disconnect between people and state is a crucial dimension of South Asian state weakness and failures.

Mustapha Kamal Pasha analyzes a contrary claim. According to some, since states have lost their legitimacy, civil society can step in and provide security for citizens in resistance against the state's depredations. But Pasha levels several important critiques against this point of view. Civil society provides the ground for exclusionary organizations to emerge, as much as inclusive, empowering organizations; in South Asia these include Hindutva and religious fundamentalism in Pakistan. In any case, civil society is not actually autonomous from other social forces. Instead, the state can encourage some kinds of civil society organizations rather than others, as in Sri Lanka. Moreover, the prevailing conceptions of security inform civil society as much as they influence the state. Finally, cross-border currents impact the operation of civil society as well. All this is to suggest that civil society does not appear to be an autonomous solution to the legitimacy crisis of the state. The state appears to be indispensable, even if a positive symbiotic relationship with civil society is surely desirable. In the following section, we explore two different ways in which the state has sought to legitimate itself: through appeal to group identity and through the logic of democracy. Each of these approaches confronts significant dilemmas: in searching for legitimacy for the sake of state strength and security, state elites can often undermine security.

Much of the story of South Asian state weakness is the story of quests for state legitimacy. But, as the chapters describe, the search for legitimacy is actually the origin of a great deal of the insecurity in the subcontinent. Sankaran Krishna points out that in Sri Lanka, ethnicity "is one of the dominant means by which the nation makes sense to the people in a postcolonial setting and is inextricably intertwined with the tasks of development and modernization of society." The road to civil war had milestones at which the state allied itself with a hegemonic legitimacy project: making Sinhalese the official language and associating the state closely with Buddhism, along with effecting socioeconomic change in favor of the Sinhalese. A state may have a founding project, as in Pakistan, but as Lawrence Ziring notes, the notion of a Muslim homeland carried terrible legacies, including the murderous migrations of 1947 and the ongoing strife over Kashmir. The carnage prior to Bangladeshi independence in 1971 suggests that the bloodshed of partition and the Kashmir conflict was all for naught anyhow: Muslim identity was not enough to hold the country together, and the core institution—the army—could never provide unity, considering its composition.

David Malone and Rohan Mukherjee point out the very difficult problems India faces in regard to ethnicity. The acceptance of diversity, so laudable for outside observers, can confound Indian elites as it allows for local communal insurgencies. But these difficulties pale in comparison to India's experience with the large-scale identity project of Hindutva, with its consequences felt at Ayodhya and in Gujarat. The Indian experience of democracy, secularism, and federalism has merit in integrating a diverse nation, but the propensity of members of the political elite and some in the public to play the communal card creates insecurity within and without.

Though ethnicity is a crucial dimension of legitimating projects, others are relevant to the South Asian experience. As Maya Chadda argues, Nepal's combination of Hinduization and the patronage of local elites by the state systematically excluded ethnic communities and the peasant population. Thus exclusion had both class and ethnic dimensions. The rejection of Nepalese state formation by these excluded groups found its expression, finally, in Maoist rebellion and civil war. As the Indian state, in Malone and Mukherjee's estimation, moves to economic legitimization, the fate of its massive poor population may prove crucial to the success of this project.

It is worth highlighting that the damage from many of these legitimacy projects has much to do with how they make the state instrumental to other aims. These aims include the promotion of Islam in Pakistan and Bangladesh, Buddhist and Sinhalese identity in Sri Lanka, and occasionally Hindu as well as caste identity in India. What this does is to separate the people of the polity from the state: the point of the state is not to protect its citizens; the point of the state is to protect an abstract concept. This means that the goal or concept in question may sometimes need to be protected from a part of the populace—an out-group, such as the Sri Lankan Tamils. Moreover, it means that the state accepts a standard of legitimacy that it may not always be able to fulfill. For example, one of the ironies of Pakistan's politics, as Ziring's chronology makes clear, is that by accepting its role as a state for Muslims, the state set up its own latter-day challenges. If the state will not stand for legitimacy on its own terms, who will? Ultimately, fostering exclusive legitimacy projects is a way of gaining support for the state that carries very low initial costs. But it comes with inherent limits and longer term pitfalls.

Can legitimacy be achieved through democratic government? Some variants of social contract theory suggest that it might; and, through a neat kind of symmetry where the polity itself is the reason for the state's existence, democracy could remove the problem of an external standard of legitimacy that the public can be sacrificed to. Samuel Huntington, in contrast, famously declared that what separates the countries of the world is not the kind of government but the amount of government.[6] Recent research on regime type and its impact on civil war and polity duration suggests that inconsistent regimes—neither fully democratic nor fully autocratic—are most likely to end or experience rebellion.[7] A little democracy is a dangerous thing. But it is not fully clear whether inconsistency in regime type is a cause or a consequence of state weakness.

What does the South Asian experience, then, say about the appropriateness of including regime type in a concept of state strength? There is clearly some association between unstable democracy and state weakness: the fitful democratic experiences of Pakistan, Bangladesh, and Nepal, clearly outlined by Ziring, Riaz, and Chadda, contrast with India's long-standing experience. For Malone and Mukherjee, India's pattern of democracy allowed room for communal politics in the periphery, and its occasional spasms toward an illiberal polity occurred as elites attempted to centralize and eliminate the room for such conflicts. As Robert Rotberg suggests, democratic instability is a crucial indicator of state weakness. As is well established elsewhere, just declaring institutions to be democratic is no guarantee of their stability, which must be carefully cultivated and maintained. Here democracy appears to be a consequence of state strength. But if democracy is, indeed, nurtured and sustained, can it provide a bulwark of legitimacy against challenges to the state? That is, can it turn from a consequence to a cause of state strength, suggesting a stable equilibrium between the two? Here, the Indian experience is the crucial one: it is the only state in the region with long-standing democratic experience.

Michael Mann warns of the possibility that democratic government might put a patina of legitimacy on mass killing: democracy says that the people must rule, but might leave open the prospect that "the people" could be defined in an ethnically exclusive fashion.[8] This suggests that democracy must be accompanied by acceptance of universal citizenship and secularism. Democratic government does not solve the problem of the definition of the polity. Here, the suggestion that India is a state for the Hindus—that is, the abandonment of Indian secularism—is a way in which democracy can be turned to exclusion, repression, and state breakdown. In this vein, Paul Brass and Steven Wilkinson elsewhere suggest that Hindu-Muslim violence is very much put to electoral advantage, most directly at the local and regional level.[9]

The evidence Brass and Wilkinson present is compelling. But democracy and democratic institutions at the national level have provided some assistance for India. Malone and Mukherjee, analyzing the rise of the Bharatiya Janata Party (BJP) to power, declare that its behavior in office was "surprisingly pragmatic." The practice of democracy had much to do with this:

"Demographic and constitutional realities dictated that, in power, it could not exclude other religions, and it maintained India's traditional line on Kashmir. Moreover, the BJP, while playing on communal [and caste] issues (as do, all too often, other Indian parties) when these offered easy pickings, mostly contested elections not on religious grounds but on issues of democracy and governance." The democratic state appears to be a source of legitimacy itself, beyond Hindutva, at least at a national level. But in the face of Ayodhya and Gujarat, one can hardly be sanguine about the real existence of an exclusive Hindu project. Long democratic experience may check the project but does not obviate it.

Regional Dimensions and Problems of Cooperation

Insecurity and Regional Spillover

The second dilemma is that both weak and strong states may be threats to their neighbors. The first horn of this dilemma is that violence at the domestic level can spill over and threaten neighboring states in an interdependent geographical space like South Asia. There are powerful ethnic linkages that make such spillovers often bloody. The undemarcated borders between Pakistan and Afghanistan and the larger spread of the Pashtun population between the two states have generated opportunities for intense conflict, exploited by the Taliban, which operates from both sides. Divided Kashmir similarly opens up intense conflict between India and Pakistan as the majority Muslim population, spread between the two states, clamors for independence, which is opposed by the small minority of Hindus and Buddhists. The Tamils' autonomy struggle has generated conflict between Sri Lanka and India, although in recent years, this has subsided as India supports Sri Lanka's territorial integrity. However, the Tamil Nadu political elite's position in favor of the LTTE has made this relationship uneasy at times. The divided Bengali population in Bangladesh and India and the propensity of Bangladeshis, largely for economic reasons, to migrate to the border states of India, especially Assam and Tripura, create tensions in the India-Bangladesh relationships. Violence and political disorder in Nepal affect India, more recently through the Naxalites (ultraradical Maoists) who now operate unhindered in large chunks of tribal lands from Nepal to India's southern region.

Problems of legitimacy, as well, are clearly regional in scope. The legitimacy problems of one state have ramifications for its neighbors. Benjamin

Miller offers a broad view of these problems, suggesting that the state-nation imbalance—the incongruence between states and the political communities that serve as a basis of legitimacy—is a regional variable and not just a state-level one. Hence, as Rasul Bakhsh Rais and Lawrence Ziring both argue, the Soviet puppet state in Afghanistan provoked an Islamist reaction, and Pakistan's government saw an opportunity to address a legitimacy problem of its own. There is also a tendency among the Pakistani elite to harp on dated geopolitical views—that Afghanistan must be a vassal state of Pakistan so that it can reduce Indian power in the region. Pursuit of such a policy means keeping Afghanistan under Taliban-type dispensation and a very weak state in perpetuity.

Thus weak South Asian states may have an interest in weakening their neighbors as well. An important aspect of spillover, therefore, is that it is not always clear whether states *cannot* prevent spillover or *will not* do so. Both might be partly true: a state may not be willing to pay the high costs required to keep control of its borders and prevent transnational rebels from operating from its territory.[10] This also fits with the possibility that supporting a neighbor's rebels is not an ideal foreign policy tool; with rebel clients, the state does not have the central control that it does with its own military. This became clear as the Taliban got out of Pakistan's control. It might be, therefore, that weak states are not so much totally unable to clamp down on neighbors' rebels as unable to do so at any kind of reasonable cost, considering the foreign policy benefits that they may gain. In particular, the internal weakening of a neighbor can greatly hamper its ability to act as a coherent and powerful international player. For Miller, irredentism and revisionism are the province of strong states. With regard to its force projection capability, Pakistan has some elements of strength and has occasionally resorted to war with India over its territorial claims. However, its ability to engage in substantial revisionism is hindered by its own internal weaknesses. India, for example, gained a large advantage by exploiting the tensions between East and West Pakistan. As its own capabilities have weakened, Pakistan has itself resorted to less expensive options, promoting not only Kashmiri separatists but insurgent organizations of various kinds in India. Afghanistan's external incongruence led it to irredentism toward Pakistan in the 1940s and 1950s, but its internal weaknesses and collapse have squelched state-led revisionism. Indeed, Pakistan itself was heavily implicated in attempts to weaken Afghanistan internally so as to reduce the prospects of revisionism. Now, the push for a Pashtun homeland across the Durand Line comes from nonstate actors rather than states. They pose serious security threats, but threats of a different order.

The Pakistan-Afghanistan and India-Pakistan relationships thus suggest that classical international conflict has been replaced by the promotion of rebel groups in neighboring rivals, as a kind of substitute form of rivalry. This implies a new and different set of political problems. Hobbes argued that though sovereigns may fight each other, they at least can uphold order and security for their citizens *within* states. The chaotic international rivalry of promoting state weakness undercuts this logic. International insecurity has steadily been replaced by human insecurity. The difficulties are compounded by the problems of control over rebels: it is very, very difficult to ensure that conflict does not get out of hand when command and control are not as assured as they usually are with the armed forces of coherent states.

Maya Chadda provides a useful skepticism that strong states could lead automatically to reduced insecurity, drawing on Franco-German rivalry as a case of profound insecurity from the competition of strong states. We agree, but note that the internal coherence of the French and German states has at least allowed for a pluralistic security community to exist in the post-1945 era. State strength appears today to be a necessary condition for security, even if it is not sufficient.

Weak Norms of International Cooperation

The consequence of this regional dimension is a vicious cycle of state weakness: weakness in one state helps produce weakness in a neighbor. To a certain extent this vicious circle might occur even if states had genuine concern for international cooperation. But because states have often promoted each others' rebels, the absence of norms of international cooperation is brought to the foreground. As the introduction to the volume mentions, in South Asia, there is a paucity of such norms even though states are extremely sensitive to their sovereignty. They cling on to Westphalian sovereignty norms for themselves but are unwilling to abide by them in their behavior toward others. Moreover, just as it is difficult for analysts to disentangle whether states are *unable* or *unwilling* to prevent nonstate actors from cross-border action, it can be difficult for states to distinguish intentions from capabilities. An inability to control a rebel army may be misinterpreted as an unwillingness to do so. Mutual suspicion and weak norms of international cooperation are the consequence. But suspicion also primes states to interpret such events in the worst light possible. Even if Lashkar-e-Tayyaba merely got out of Pakistan's control when, in November 2008, it launched the brutal terrorist attacks in Mumbai, it can be difficult for India to believe it. Here is another manifestation of vicious cycles in action.

The weak norms also reflect and perpetuate the absence of strong regional institutions. The South Asian Association for Regional Cooperation (SAARC) has been in existence since 1985 but has yet to develop a strong foothold in the region. As weak as it is, it has serious difficulty managing international conflict. A more robust SAARC could more easily accomplish the international dialog that can keep security threats from spinning out of control. But SAARC itself appears weakened by the tensions among the states of the region. As classical cooperation theory suggests, a binding international institution is not necessary if states have harmonious interests and not possible if they have fully conflicting interests.[11] South Asia stands in the middle, but its states have such intense conflict that any kind of regional cooperation institution will be beset by serious difficulties. A South Asian security community built around SAARC is a faraway dream.

Global Entanglements

Great Power Involvement

Great power involvement in the region, though it could serve a stabilizing role, has come with major costs. The weak states of the region, especially Afghanistan and Pakistan, offer fertile ground for direct and indirect great power intervention, as the geostrategic importance of this region, stretching through the millennia, has only increased in modern times. The great powers have confronted strong nonstate actors, whose popular appeal and will to resist are strengthened with great-power manipulation.[12] The British experienced it in Afghanistan, but in the cold war era, it was an ill-fated intervention by the former Soviet Union that set in motion the fragmentation and decay of the Afghan state and in some sense the Pakistani state as well. The sudden departure of the Soviet Union followed by the United States opened up a space for Islamic fundamentalism, already generated through American, Pakistani, and Saudi support, and led to the Taliban's rise. With the Taliban's support for al-Qaeda and the latter's attacks on the United States, there occurred once again an intervention by external powers, with the divided Afghan population offering fertile ground for resistance. Pakistan's subsequent alignment with the United States and U-turn against the Taliban bought the regime external support, at the cost of internal resistance. In 2009, the central government in Afghanistan had very little control over large chunks of its territory, and the Taliban and its Islamic radicalism were gaining ground in Pakistan, weakening this fragile state even further. Great powers have limited capacity to change the situation on the ground as their commitment at best is limited largely to military suppression or reconstruction not sufficient to close the political space in which the Taliban operates.

But the great powers have a potentially positive role to play as well. The current U.S. administration has expressed the view that its engagement in Asia is integrated; developments in Iraq, for example, relate to those in Iran, and hence to Afghanistan, Pakistan, and India, and so on. One crucial current example of these relationships is the recent dramatic increase in tensions between India and Pakistan after the November 2008 Mumbai attacks and Pakistan's mobilization of forces on its south-eastern border. The United States could play an important role here in trying to manage the India-Pakistan diplomatic relationship, assuaging India's fears about potential Pakistani aggression and vice versa, and reducing the severity of the ongoing security dilemma between the two states. No other state than the United States appears capable of similar action. But if it does get involved in such a fashion, Washington must be cognizant of the difficulties that the great powers, itself included, have faced in confronting the politics of South Asia.

Globalization

Similar ambiguity surrounds another dimension of global engagement, the long-run process of globalization. Baldev Raj Nayar argues that chronic underdevelopment long kept the states of South Asia weak; and in any case, some strategies of state building (such as Pakistan's reliance on military spending) distorted and limited the gains from what economic growth did occur. With its prospects for improvement in the economies of South Asia, then, globalization has the potential to strengthen states, rather than weakening them as is often argued. But Nayar makes it clear that this rests in the realm of potential, and not certainty. Globalization also comes with increased social mobilization and the prospects of further demands on the state. Social groups of various kinds can be empowered by the development that occurs as part of the globalization process. And in any event, the management of globalization is contingent, in part, on existing institutions.

Of particular interest is India's turn toward global engagement, especially with its acceptance of economic globalization. Malone and Mukherjee argue that India's ambitions coexist, at times uneasily, with domestic and regional security concerns. But they argue that in fact the two are not as contradictory as it first appears: dealing with security threats has led India to a more pragmatic foreign policy, and thus to putting economic development and globalization at center stage. This suggests that Indian policymakers agree with Nayar: globalization can have positive security consequences. Whether that is actually achieved is a matter of careful management.

How Do We Build Peace in South Asia?

The volume projects the need for thinking seriously on capacity building and institution-based norm building in the region. Based on this initial analysis, what kind of changes are necessary for South Asia to emerge as a peaceful region? Can a peaceful security community emerge in South Asia? A pluralistic security community, according to Emanuel Adler and Michael Barnett, is a group of states that maintain "dependable expectations of peaceful change," relying on high levels of mutual trust and "shared identities, values and meanings."[13] South Asian states unfortunately do not yet show the signs of a pluralistic security community, as war is an ongoing possibility in some of the interstate relationships, and there is a profound deficit of trust and shared understandings of values and meanings.

What can be done to transform the region from its "vicious circles" of conflict to "virtuous circles" of cooperative relationships and, eventually, a pluralistic security community?[14] In order to achieve this, three solid pillars of the Kantian peace—institutions, democracies, and economic interdependence—are needed. These three pillars are mutually reinforcing and supporting of each other. There is strong evidence that mature democracies rarely fight each other. The emergence of strong democratic states (internally secure and legitimate) can change the dynamics of the region considerably. Similarly, military conflict is reduced among deeply interdependent economies. Faster economic development and integration of the economies in a common market, coupled with the creation of effective policies for sustainable and equitable development and the uplifting of marginalized groups in all of the region's states, would help ensure a clear common interest in peace. Countries bound by institutions and the norms they create help member states not to threaten or use force among themselves because these institutions serve as "agents of mediation and arbitration," helping to reduce "uncertainty," expand their "conception of interests at stake," and promote "norms and principles of appropriate behavior on a long-term basis."[15]

However, in addition to this Kantian tripod, improving state capacity is of vital importance, and is in fact interconnected with its three components. It is hard to ensure stable democracy, mutual prosperity, and solid international agreement among states that cannot effectively implement their agendas. What state weakness produces is not only insecurity and conflict but also a lack of control. Though the wars of strong states that command coherent militaries have been incredibly destructive because of the enormous forces they can bring to bear, they are easier to manage in one crucial respect: control means that it is possible to implement cooperation. The Kantian tripod helps to restrain strong states to ensure that they have no reason to choose to go to war with each other. The weak states of South Asia have security problems that are compounded by the presence of nonstate actors that are difficult to restrain. We cannot expect the Kantian tripod to succeed—or even to emerge in the first place—without addressing the problems of state weakness. On the other hand, the regional interconnectedness of security problems also means that state strength cannot be achieved without international cooperation. These two problems must thus be simultaneously addressed. This suggests that state capacity is a fourth crucial component of international peace, deeply embedded in the kinds of vicious and virtuous cycles that concern Russett and Oneal.

The primary lesson of this volume for policy, then, is the need to account for the weak-state environment. This implies attention to the core dilemmas that attend on state building. It is often the actions of state elites that generate state weakness, but these actions have origins. It is not enough to demand that state elites root out corruption or refrain from narrow ethnic appeals. State elites must be understood as operating under very difficult constraints. They must have some viable alternative to these security-undermining practices. Bilateral and regional level mechanisms must be created to deal with these sensitive issues.

A number of changes need to take place in order for planting the seeds for peaceful change in the region. First, elites in all countries must realize that their interventionist behavior (advertent or inadvertent) is threatening collective peace and order of the region. Short-term tactical gains have long-term negative consequences. But to ease this transition, we suggest a policy of reciprocity for foregoing short-run gains. Incremental gestures toward cooperative state-building can help. Second, they must also realize that regional interdependence exists in security matters: one cannot create security for oneself without taking into account the security of the other, and security of one helps the security of the other. Self-help taken to the extreme will not produce lasting security or peace in the region. Third, elites must also be willing to resolve existing territorial disputes through peaceful means. This would mean abandoning both the classical revisionism of aggression and irredentism and the more recent employment of client insurgencies in one's rivals and developing a strong regional approach to quell the reemergence of such movements. Respect for sovereignty involves respecting its cardinal principle—nonintervention in each other's internal affairs. Finally, minorities in each country must be integrated into the national mainstream with dignity and honor. This would help in terms of the increased congruence between nation and state and the prevention of secessionism and irredentism.

Rays of Hope?

All is not gloomy about South Asia, although the dominant theme of this volume is about the weak aspects of state capacity and perennial insecurities of the region. There are a number of limited but crucial aspects of South Asia that show signs of rudimentary peaceful change but that need strengthening in order to achieve a limited security community that at best eschews war at the interstate level. They are, first, the democratization of countries in the region. Bangladesh went to electoral mode in 2008, Nepal abolished its monarchy in 2008 and created a republican government, tiny Bhutan in 2008 initiated democratic elections for the first time, and Maldives replaced its thirty-year leader in a peaceful electoral process. In 2008 Pakistan held elections and got rid of military rule, only to form a very weak and fractious civilian government with its inability to control Taliban-led violence and facing the prospect of the military taking over power. India has been the most successful story as elections have taken place in May 2009 and a more stable coalition has taken power in New Delhi. Sri Lanka has the opportunity to emerge as a true democracy now that the civil war is over. But this can happen only provided the Sinhalese-led government creates a true inclusive democracy and a just society for minorities. However, democracy in South Asia is fragile and has yet to become deeply institutionalized. There still exists the prospect of misusing democratic rhetoric for fundamentally exclusionary purposes.

Second, economic growth rates of the region have been strong over the past decade or so. Regional economic interactions might also be increasing to some extent. The bilateral trade agreements of India and Sri Lanka have been successful. India has also embarked on preferential trading agreements with some of the smaller states of the region, as part of a broader program of engagement with these small states. The South Asian Free Trade Agreement (SAFTA) has some potential. More importantly, almost all economies of the region today are much more globalized than they were up until the 1990s. This integration in the global economy has pitfalls, especially when there is global economic meltdown, but the benefits are also there, as Baldev Nayar points out in his chapter.

Third, regional institution building through SAARC has been going on, though slowly. It has recently granted membership to Afghanistan and observer status to important extraregional players. SAARC managed at least to achieve the SAFTA treaty, and it has recently developed some centralized funds for development and poverty alleviation.

Fourth, civil society organizations that really do defend the public interest may be showing mettle. The clearest example is the Pakistan lawyers' movement, as Pasha discusses in his chapter. Though civil society has often allowed the promotion of exclusionary ideologies, this appears to be a case of civil society organizations defending constitutional government against threats from the state. The fact that it is attracting a high degree of attention and support suggests that it may serve as the basis of a more robust engagement between state and society. However, episodic victories of civil society are hardly equivalent to true and mature state-civil society engagement.

Fifth, a bilateral peace process began in 2004 between India and Pakistan, but it was severely disrupted by the November 2008 terrorist attacks in Mumbai. This process for the first time came out with out-of-the-box solutions to Kashmir, where both India and Pakistan expressed willingness to soften their borders and let Kashmiris have better interactions between them. Setbacks to the bilateral process are often caused by nonstate actors or state actors themselves who do not wish settlements that are not in their favor. This form of spoiler problem is indeed a great challenge for India and Pakistan in the future as well.

Sixth, some elements of stable deterrence seem to have taken place in the South Asia's nuclear relationship. The initial phase, with instability and limited wars at the tactical level coupled with stability at the strategic level, carried enormous risks of escalation and in any case created short-run security problems directly. It is possible that the nuclear standoff has begun to settle into more stable patterns.

Finally, at the global level, the United States has begun to treat India as a rising power, reducing incentives for Pakistan to engage in great power balancing for achieving parity and challenge to India's primacy in the region. Moreover, China and India have increased their trade manifold, despite a territorial conflict that still bedevils their relationships.[16] China and India's simultaneous rise could still generate balance of power politics in the region.

However, all these changes at best are rudimentary and can be easily upset by events like a victory of the Taliban in Afghanistan and Pakistan, or a resurgent military conflict between India and Pakistan. The small, fledgling democracies—Bangladesh, Nepal, and Sri Lanka—can once again go back to illiberal democratic models, military dictatorships, or exclusionary regimes. India can produce unsustainable coalitions, given its domestic political scenario. All these suggest that much work is needed to strengthen democracies, institutions, and economic integration in the region. The hope of a pluralistic security community in South Asia is farfetched, but achievable if only agents, that is, state elites, work toward mollifying the structural conditions that generate weak states and insecurity in this crucial region of the world. This they must do, so that the human sufferings of millions will not continue unabated and yet another generation become lost in maladies largely created by weak states and their uncaring or ineffective elites.

Notes to Chapter 13

1. James D. Fearon and David D. Laitin, "Ethnicity, Insurgency and Civil War," *American Political Science Review* 97, no. 2 (2003), pp. 75–90; Joel S. Migdal, *Strong Societies and Weak States* (Princeton: Princeton University Press, 1988); Theda Skocpol, "Bringing the State Back In: Strategies of Analysis in Current Research," in Peter B. Evans, Dietrich Rueschemeyer, and Theda Skocpol, eds., *Bringing the State Back In* (Cambridge: Cambridge University Press, 1985), pp. 3–43; Charles Tilly, *Coercion, Capital and European States, AD 990–1992* (Oxford: Blackwell, 1992).

2. Kalevi J. Holsti, *The State, War, and the State of War* (Cambridge: Cambridge University Press, 1996).

3. Youssef Cohen, Brian R. Brown, and A.F.K. Organski, "The Paradoxical Nature of State Making: The Violent Creation of Order," *American Political Science Review* 75, no. 4 (1981), pp. 901–910; Cameron Thies, "State Building, Interstate and Intra-

state Rivalry: A Study of Post-Colonial Developing Country Extractive Efforts, 1975–2000," *International Studies Quarterly* 48, no. 1 (2004), pp. 53–72; Tilly, *Coercion.*

4. For a countrary viewpoint, see John Mueller, "How Dangerous Are the Taliban? Why Afghanistan Is the Wrong War," *Foreign Affairs* online, April 15, 2009, http://www.foreignaffairs.com/articles/64932/john-mueller/how-dangerous-are-the-taliban

5. Joel S. Migdal, Atul Kohli, and Vivienne Shue, eds., *State Power and Social Forces: Domination and Transformation in the Third World* (Cambridge: Cambridge University Press, 1994); Peter B. Evans, *Embedded Autonomy: States and Industrial Transformation* (Princeton: Princeton University Press, 1995).

6. Samuel Huntington, *Political Order in Changing Societies* (New Haven: Yale University Press, 1968), p. 1.

7. Fearon and Laitin, "Ethnicity"; Håvard Hegre et al., "Toward a Democratic Civil Peace? Democracy, Political Change, and Civil War, 1816–1992," *American Political Science Review* 95, no. 1 (2001), pp. 33–48; Scott Gates et al., "Institutional Inconsistency and Political Instability: Polity Duration, 1800–2000," *American Journal of Political Science* 50, no. 4 (2006), pp. 893–908. For a critique of the first two works, see James Raymond Vreeland, "The Effect of Political Regime on Civil War: Unpacking Anocracy," *Journal of Conflict Resolution* 52, no. 3 (2008), pp. 401–425.

8. Michael Mann, *The Dark Side of Democracy: Explaining Ethnic Cleansing* (Cambridge: Cambridge University Press, 2005).

9. Paul R. Brass, *Theft of an Idol: Text and Context in the Representation of Collective Violence* (Princeton: Princeton University Press, 1997); Steven I. Wilkinson, *Votes and Violence: Electoral Competition and Ethnic Riots in India* (Cambridge: Cambridge University Press, 2006).

10. The phrase "Transnational Rebels" is Idean Salehyan's. Important research on these international connections includes Kristian Skrede Gleditsch, "Transnational Dimensions of Civil War," *Journal of Peace Research* 44, no. 3 (2007), pp. 293–309; Idean Salehyan, "Transnational Rebels: Neighboring States as Sanctuary for Rebel Groups," *World Politics* 59, no. 2 (2007), pp. 217–242; Salehyan and Gleditsch, "Refugees and the Spread of Civil War," *International Organization* 60, no. 2 (2006), pp. 335–366.

11. Arthur A. Stein, "Coordination and Collaboration: Regimes in an Anarchic World," *International Organization* 36, no. 2 (1982), pp. 299–324.

12. See David A. Kilcullen, *The Accidental Guerrilla* (Oxford: Oxford University Press, 2009).

13. Emanuel Adler and Michael Barnett, "A Framework for the Study of Security Communities," in *Security Communities*, ed. Adler and Barnett (Cambridge: Cambridge University Press, 1998), pp. 30–31.

14. These concepts are drawn from Bruce Russett and John R. Oneal, *Triangulating Peace: Democracy, Interdependence, and International Organizations* (New York: W.W. Norton, 2001).

15. Ibid., ch. 1.

16. For some of these changes, Amitabh Mattoo and Happymon Jacob, "Rays of Hope: The Not So Weak States of South Asia," paper presented at the Conference on Weak States and South Asia's Insecurity Predicament, McGill University, October 2008. See also Peter Jones, "South Asia: Is a Regional Security Community Possible?" *South Asian Survey* 15, no. 2 (2008), pp. 183–193.

Author Biographies

Editor

T. V. Paul is Director of the McGill University-Université de Montreal Centre for International Peace and Security Studies (CIPSS) and James McGill Professor of International Relations in the Department of Political Science at McGill University, Montreal, Canada, where he has been teaching since 1991. Paul is the author or editor of twelve books and more than forty scholarly articles and chapters. He is the author of the books *Globalization and the National Security State* (with Norrin Ripsman, Oxford, 2010); *The Tradition of Non-use of Nuclear Weapons* (Stanford, 2009); *India in the World Order: Searching for Major Power Status* (Cambridge, 2003, with Baldev Raj Nayar); *Power versus Prudence: Why Nations Forgo Nuclear Weapons* (McGill-Queen's, 2000); and *Asymmetric Conflicts: War Initiation by Weaker Powers* (Cambridge, 1994). Paul is the editor of *The India-Pakistan Conflict: An Enduring Rivalry* (Cambridge, 2005); and coeditor and contributor to four volumes, including *Balance of Power: Theory and Practice in the 21st Century* (with James Wirtz and Michel Fortmann, Stanford, 2004).

Contributors

Maya Chadda is a professor of political science at William Paterson University. She holds a Ph.D. from the New School of Social Research and is a research fellow at the Southern Asian Institute, Columbia University. Her publications include *Paradox of Power: The United States Policy in Southwest*

Asia (Clio, 1986); *Ethnicity, Security and Separatism in South Asia* (Columbia, 1996); and *Building Democracy in South Asia: Pakistan, Nepal and India* (Lynne Rienner, 2000).

Sankaran Krishna is a professor in the Department of Political Science at the University of Hawaii. His areas of work focus on ethnicity, nationalism, politics, political-economy, and international relations, especially as they pertain to South Asia. His books include *Postcolonial Insecurities: India, Sri Lanka and the Question of Nationhood* (Minnesota, 1999) and *Globalization and Postcolonialism: Hegemony and Resistance in the Twenty-first Century* (Rowman and Littlefield, 2008).

Matthew Lange has been an assistant professor of sociology at McGill University since 2004. His research explores the developmental legacies of British colonial rule and the causes of ethnic violence. His main works include *Lineages of Despotism and Development: British Colonialism and State Power* (Chicago, 2008) and *States and Development: Historical Antecedents of Stagnation and Advance*, edited with Dietrich Rueschemeyer (Palgrave/Macmillan, 2005).

David Malone is a Canadian diplomat and scholar. He is now the president of the International Development Center (IDRC) after being Canada's high commissioner in India. His books include *Decision Making in the UN Security Council: The Case of Haiti* (Oxford University Press, 1999); *Greed and Grievance: Economic Agendas in Civil Wars*, editor with Mats Berdal (Lynne Rienner, 2000); and *The Law and Practice of the United Nations*, with Simon Chesterman and Thomas M. Franck (Oxford, 2008).

Theodore McLauchlin is a doctoral candidate in political science at McGill University. His research interests include civil wars, ethnic conflict, intrastate security crises, civil-military relations, and regional security. His publications include an article in the journal *Comparative Politics*.

Benjamin Miller is a professor of international relations at the University of Haifa. Previously he taught at Duke University and the Hebrew University of Jerusalem. He is the author of *When Opponents Cooperate: Great Power Conflict and Collaboration in World Politics* (Michigan, 2002) and *States, Nations, and the Great Powers: The Sources of Regional War and Peace* (Cambridge, 2007).

Rohan Mukherjee is a senior research specialist at Innovations for Successful Societies, a research program at Princeton University. Previously, he worked as a research fellow at the Centre for Policy Research, New Delhi, and the National Knowledge Commission, an advisory body to the prime minister of India. His more recent work, on India-China relations, authored with David Malone of IDRC, appeared in Vol. 52 of *Survival* in February 2010.

Baldev Raj Nayar is a professor (emeritus) in the Department of Political Science at McGill University. His recent publications include *India in the World Order: Searching for Major-Power Status* (with T. V. Paul, Cambridge, 2003); *The Geopolitics of Globalization: The Consequences for Development* (Oxford. 2005); and *The Myth of the Shrinking State* (Oxford, 2009).

Mustapha Kamal Pasha is Sixth Century Chair and head of International Relations at the University of Aberdeen. He previously taught at the American University in Washington, D.C. His books include *Colonial Political Economy* (Oxford, 1998); *Out From Underdevelopment Revisited: Changing Global Structures and the Remaking of the Third World* (with James H. Mittelman; Macmillan, 1997); *Protecting Human Security in a Post-9.11 World* (co-editor, Palgrave, 2007); and *International Relations and the New Inequality* (co-editor, Blackwell, 2002).

Rasul Bakhsh Rais is a professor of political science, Department of Humanities and Social Sciences, at Lahore University of Management Sciences (LUMS). He is the author of *Recovering the Frontier State: War, Ethnicity, and State in Afghanistan* (Oxford, 2009); *War Without Winners: Afghanistan's Uncertain Transition after the Cold War* (Oxford, 1996); *Indian Ocean and the Superpowers: Economic, Political and Strategic Perspectives* (Croom Helm, 1986); and editor of *State, Society and Democratic Change in Pakistan* (Oxford, 1997).

Ali Riaz is professor and chair of the Department of Politics and Government at Illinois State University. His research interests include Islamist politics, South Asian politics, community development, and political economy of media. His publications include *Faithful Education: Madrassahs in South Asia* (Rutgers, 2008); *Islamist Militancy in Bangladesh: A Complex Web* (Routledge, 2008); and *God Willing: The Politics of Islamism in Bangladesh* (Rowman and Littlefield, 2004).

Robert I. Rotberg is the director of Program on Intrastate Conflict and Conflict Resolution, Belfer Center for Science and International Affairs at the Kennedy School of Government, Harvard University and president of the World Peace Foundation. He is the author and editor of numerous books and articles on U.S. foreign policy, Africa, Asia, and the Caribbean, most recently *Battling Terrorism in the Horn of Africa* (Brookings, 2005); *When States Fail: Causes and Consequences* (Brookings, 2004); and *Corruption, Global Security, and World Order* (Brookings, 2009).

Lawrence Ziring is a professor (emeritus) of political science at Western Michigan University. He was president of the American Institute of Pakistan Studies, and he has served on many occasions as a consultant for the U.S. Department of State on issues related to international security, and especially Pakistan. His works include *Pakistan in the Twentieth Century: A Political History* (Oxford, 2000); *Pakistan: At the Crosscurrent of History* (Oneworld, 2005); and *Pakistan: The Enigma of Political Development* (Dawson, 1980).

Index

Abernethy, David, 62
Adler, Emanuel, 305
adult literacy, *116*
Advani, Lal Krishna, 258
Afghanistan, 12, 195–219
    agricultural economy of, 204
    Bolshevik recognition of, 200
    British empire and, 199–200, 201
    civil society, underdevelopment of, 203
    cold war and, 202, 204–5, 303
    colonial legacy in, 199–200, 201
    ethno-nationalist identity in, 58, 77, 197–98, 211–12
    external actors in, 17, 18, 19
    as failed state, 6, 35, 36, 45, 49, 91, 114, 196
    frontier character of, 197–200
    geography of, 55
    on index of weakest states, 4, 196
    ISAF in, 196, 214, 215n4
    leadership in, 44
    Marxist revolution in, 205–6
    military action to contain violence, limitations of, 69n13
    as modern kingdom, 200–205
    Northern Alliance, 184, 190, 209
    as old Pashtun kingdom, 195–96, 198–99
    opium production in, 57
    Pakistan and. *See* Pakistan-Afghanistan conflicts
    Pashtuns. *See* Pashtuns
    reconstruction of, 211–15
    regional security issues, 77, 81, *84*, 86, 90–91
    as rentier state, 202, 205
    Russia / Soviet Union and. *See under* Russia / Soviet Union
    secessionism in, 81
    September 11, 2001 and U.S. invasion of, 69n13, 208, 211–13
    Soviet occupation of, 12, 17, 91, 162, 183–87, 206–9
    state capacity in, 295
    Taliban. *See* Taliban
    United States and. *See under* United States
Africa. *See also* specific countries
    Middle East and North Africa, 21, 79
    sub-Saharan Africa, 20, 53, 55, 81, 82
agriculture
    in Afghanistan, 204
    in Bangladesh, 257, 264n40
Ahmad, Moeen U., 41
Ahmad Shah (first king of the Afghans), 195

Barnett, Michael, 305
Barrington, Lowell W., 94n15
Basu, Subho, 273
Bengalis. *See* Bangladesh
Bertocci, Peter, 251
Bharatiya Janata Party (BJP), India, 16, 138,
    151, 152, 157, 162, 258, 299–300
Bhutan, 9, 10, 22, *84*, 155, 307
Bhutto, Benazir, 44, 187, 192
Bhutto, Zulfikar Ali, 44, 181–82, 192
bin Laden, Osama, 17, 91, 188–89, 191,
    194n21, 212
Birendra (king of Nepal), 271
BJP (Bharatiya Janata Party), India, 16, 138,
    151, 152, 157, 162, 258, 299–300
Bonn Process, 212
Botswana, 43, 68
Brass, Paul, 299
Brazil, 20, 66, 164, 169n43
Britain
    colonial legacy of. *See* colonialism
    ethno-nationalist identity in, 61
Buddhism
    Nepal, ethnic and religious identities in,
        267, 272, 276, 281
    in Sri Lanka, 222, 225
Burma / Myanmar
    Bangladesh and, 258
    colonial rule in, 63, 65
    Cyclone Nargis, 31, 32, 46
    domestic security, state affecting, 52
    external actors in, 17
    failed state status, on precipice of, 31–33,
        42
    Rohingyas, 254–55
Bush administration, 189, 235

Cambodia, 19, 35, 45, 46, 47
Canada, 60, 233
capacity or capability. *See* state capacity
Carroll, James, 62
caste system
    colonial legacy and, 64, 87
    in India, 16, 87, 137, 149, 151, 152, 270,
        298, 300
    in Nepal, 14, 270, 272–73, 274, 275, 283
    as regional problem, 11

CCOMPOSA (Coordination Committee
    of Maoist Parties and Organizations of
    South Asia), 281
CECA (Comprehensive Economic
    Cooperation Agreement), India and
    Singapore, 108
CENTO, 178
Chadda, Maya, 23–24n3, 265, 296, 298, 299,
    302, 313–14
Chandhoke, Neera, 143n44
Chatterjee, Partha, 137, 144n46
Chaudhry, Iftikhar Muhammad, 135–36
Chavez, Hugo, 20
Chechens and Chechnya, 78, 233
Chelvanayakam, S. J. V., 223
Chidambaram, P., 163, 231
China
    ASEAN states, border disputes between,
        19
    governance rankings in, *113*
    on HDI, *116*
    India and, 101, 102, 108, 155, 159–60,
        164, 309. *See also under* Nepal
    weak states in South Asia, as external
        actor in, 17–18
    Western intervention and downfall of
        Chinese empire, 60
civic nationalism, 76, 78, 94–95n16
civil society, 122–44
    blurring of social movement and
        government in Nepal, 271
    communalization in India, 124, 132,
        137–38, 139
    cross-border influences on, 132–33
    development partners' promotion in
        Bangladesh, 250–51
    different conceptions of, 128–30
    enhanced security provided by,
        questioning assumption of, 122–25,
        127–28, 138–40
    fracture and sectarianism in Pakistan,
        124, 131, 132, 133, 134–37, 139, 140
    growth of, in South Asia, 308
    Islamism and, 131, 132, 133, 134–35,
        136–37
    legitimacy and state strength, 296–97
    limitations of, 130–34